The Golf
Resort Guide
Western Edition

Jim & Barbara Nicol

HUNTER
PUBLISHING INC

Hunter Publishing, Inc.
300 Raritan Center Parkway
Edison NJ 08818
(908) 417 0482

ISBN 1-55650-569-8

Maps by Joyce Huber, PhotoGraphics

Cover photograph by Jeanine Henerby:
Chateau Whistler Resort, Hole #8

Contents

Introduction

With this edition we have added many new resorts, including those in Canada and Mexico. Please keep in mind: the rates we quote for the Canadian resorts are in Canadian dollars. Rates shown for locations in Mexico, however, are in U.S. dollars.

We have frequently been asked which resorts were our favorites. Clearly, some resorts and golf courses are a notch or two above the others. Listed below in alphabetical order are the top 35 large resorts followed by the top 15 smaller more intimate resorts. Our selection was based on the quality of lodgings, the amenities, the general ambience and the golf facilities.

The Top 35 Large Resorts

AMELIA ISLAND PLANTATION – Amelia Island, FL
BANFF SPRINGS HOTEL – Banff, Alberta, Canada
THE BROADMOOR – Colorado Springs, CO
CASA DE CAMPO RESORT – La Romana, Dominican Republic
THE CLOISTER – Sea Island, GA
COLONIAL WILLIAMSBURG INN – Williamsburg, VA
THE DORAL – Miami, FL
EAGLE RIDGE INN & RESORT – Galena, IL
THE GREENBRIER – White Sulphur Springs, WV
GROVE PARK INN & COUNTRY CLUB – Asheville, NC
THE HOMESTEAD – Hot Springs, VA
KIAWA ISLAND RESORT – Charleston, SC
KINGSMILL RESORT – Williamsburg, VA
THE KAPALUA BAY HOTEL – Maui, HI
LE CHATEAU MONTEBELLO – Montebello, Que, Canada
MARRIOTT at SAWGRASS RESORT – Ponte Vedra Beach, FL
MARRIOTT'S CAMELBACK INN – Scottsdale, AZ
MARRIOTT'S CASTLE HARBOUR – Tucker's Town, Bermuda
MARRIOTT'S DESERT SPRINGS – Palm Desert, CA
MARRIOTT'S GRAND HOTEL – Point Clear, AL

MAUNA LANI BAY HOTEL – Kohala Coast, HI
MAUNA KEA BEACH HOTEL – Kohala Coast, HI
PALM BEACH POLO & COUNTRY CLUB – West Palm Beach, FL
PINEHURST HOTEL & COUNTRY CLUB – Pinehurst, NC
THE PRINCEVILLE HOTEL – Princeville, Kauai, HI
THE RESORT at LONGBOAT KEY CLUB – Longboat Key, FL
SADDLEBROOK GOLF & TENNIS RESORT – Wesley Chapel, FL
THE SAGAMORE – Bolton Landing, NY
SCOTTSDALE PRINCESS – Scottsdale, AZ
THE WESTIN LA PALOMA – Tucson, AZ
THE WESTIN KAUAI – Lihue, Kauai, HI
THE WESTIN RESORT HILTON HEAD – Hilton Head, SC
THE WIGWAM RESORT & COUNTRY CLUB – Litchfield Park, AZ
WINTERGREEN – Wintergreen, VA
THE WOODLANDS RESORT – The Woodlands, TX

The Top 15 Smaller Resorts

THE BALSAMS GRAND RESORT HOTEL – Dixville Notch, NH
THE BOULDERS – Carefree, AZ
THE BRIARS INN & COUNTRY CLUB – Ont, Canada
CARMEL VALLEY RANCH RESORT – Carmel Valley, CA
DEERHURST RESORT – Huntsville, Ont, Canada
THE FOUR SEASONS RESORT – Nevis, West Indies
HOUND EARS CLUB – Blowing Rock, NC
LAS HADAS – Manzanillo, Colima, Mexico
THE LODGE at KOELE – Island of Lanai, HI
THE LODGE AT PEBBLE BEACH – Carmel, CA
MARRIOTT'S SEAVIEW GOLF RESORT – Absecon, NJ
OJAI VALLEY INN & COUNTRY CLUB – Ojai, CA
QUAIL LODGE – Carmel, CA
THE TIDES LODGE – Irvington, VA
SUN VALLEY LODGE – Sun Valley, ID

The top 50 resorts in italics are described in *The Golf Resort Guide (Eastern Edition)*, also available from Hunter Publishing. The others can be found in this, the Western Edition.

How To Get The Most From This Book

The following abbreviations are used throughout this book.

(EP): European Plan. No meals are included in the rates shown.

(BP): Bermuda Plan. Breakfast only is included in your rate.

(MAP): Modified American Plan. Two meals per person are included in rates. Usually these are breakfast and dinner.

(FAP): American Plan. All three meals per person are included.

GREEN FEES: Rates shown are per person. When two rates are indicated (for example: $35/$45), the first is for weekdays, the second for weekends or holidays. Rates shown are for guests of the resort – not walk-ons.

CART FEES: Rates are per cart for two players for 18 holes. Green and cart fees shown are rates reserved for guests of the facility. Rates are usually higher for "walk-ons."

LODGING RATES: All rates are based on double occupancy and are for two people unless otherwise noted. All rates are for resorts' peak golf season. In most cases, they are lower at other times of the year. Some resorts, however, do not have "seasonal" rates and remain the same throughout the year. All reserve the right to change rates without prior notice. Due to this fact, there may be a variation between the rates we indicate and those in effect at the time you make a reservation. The costs shown are designed as a guide only. None of the rates include taxes or gratuities unless so stated. Many resorts automatically attach a certain percentage to your bill which covers gratuities.

When making reservations, ask about such extras and what they cover. In some cases, you will find they cover check-in and baggage handling. This is, however, an exception.

CREDIT CARDS: While the great majority of hotels and resorts accept credit cards for payment, this is not always the case. Check the policy in advance.

TEE TIMES: When making reservations, be sure to request tee times, at least for the first day you wish to play.

GOLF PACKAGES: By and large, these represent a fair savings. But keep in mind that in many cases, due to travel time, on the days you arrive and depart no golf will be possible.

TRAVEL AGENCIES: We urge that you use a travel agency once you have made up your mind to book a reservation. In the great majority of cases there is no fee involved to you and you will find it can make your experience go more smoothly.

PETS: Few resorts will allow pets. In some instances you may find a kennel in a town near the resort. I suggest you ask the resort when making your reservations if such a facility is available.

Arizona

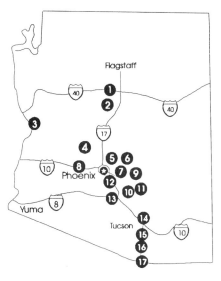

THE ARIZONA BILTMORE
24th Street and Missouri, Phoenix, AZ 85002; (602) 955-6600; (800) 528-3696

The word "tradition" sums up the Biltmore well. A lavishly landscaped resort completed in the extravagant late 1920s, it has not lost its stately atmosphere nor its quiet gentility.

With 500 rooms, including several wings and courts, 18 tennis courts (17 lighted) as well as professionals ready to assist you, enough dining areas to sustain a small city, three pools, a health center, sauna, and therapy pools, it is complete. The Biltmore Health Center, by the way, offers a highly personalized two-day medical evaluation and is located on the grounds of the resort.

With its new 39,000-square-foot conference center, this is

RATES (EP) Traditional room: $220. Classic: $275. Resort: $305. Green fees: $75, including cart. Golf package: 3 nights/3 day (includes lodging, golf, cart), $1050 per couple. MAP and FAP rates are available upon request. Rates quoted are for January-April.

ARRIVAL Air: Phoenix. Car: I-17 off Glendale exit, east to 24th, then south to Missouri.

one of only five hotels worldwide to win the McRand Conference Center Award for excellence in quality and service as a convention and meeting site. The hotel is also proud of the fact that for the past 30 years they have been the recipients of the Mobil Five Star Award.

While not owned by the hotel, there are two 18-hole golf courses adjacent to the property. The Links Course with a par of 71, playing at 6,300/5,726/4,912 yards, offers a typical resort layout. The Adobe Course reaches out a bit more with yardage of 6,767/6,455/6,094 and pars at 72/73. Although we have played both, and enjoyed each of them, we found the Adobe Course to be the better of the two.

THE ARIZONA GOLF RESORT
425 South Power Road, Mesa, AZ 85206; (602) 832-3202; (800) 528-8282

Accommodations consist of 150 rooms, some with kitchenettes, some with full kitchens as well as a few one- and two-bedroom suites. Each suite has a living room, dining area and a fully equipped kitchen. There are also fairway suites and casitas.

Dining facilities include Anabelle's Restaurant, plus a lounge, as well as the "19th Green" offering a coffee shop menu and cocktail service. Additional restaurants are within a short distance.

The resort has four tennis courts, an Olympic-size pool and access to a health club nearby (within 1/2 mile; additional fee required).

Golf is available on the resort's course. It has more than enough water hazards and bunkers to keep you honest. With a par of 71/71 it reaches out 6,574/6,195/5,782/5,124 yards.

RATES (EP) Rooms: $125. 1-bedroom fairway suites: $145. 2 bedrooms: (2 to 4 people) $270. Green fees: $45, including cart. Golf package: 3 nights/2 days (includes 3 nights lodging, daily breakfast or lunch, two rounds of golf, cart and tax), $658 per couple. The rates shown are for January 1-April 30.

ARRIVAL Air: Phoenix Airport (35 minutes). Car: Maricopa Freeway to Superstition Freeway. Exit on Power Road and continue north to resort.

THE BELL ROCK INN
6246 Highway 179, Sedona, AZ 86336; (602) 282-4161

This resort is in an area with an almost unique setting. The region's startling red rock cliffs are rapidly becoming world famous.

The Inn motel has 47 rooms including suites. There is a dining room, the Bell Rock Restaurant and lounge, and they are also capable of handling modest size meeting groups.

Amenities include a swimming pool and two tennis courts, with horseback riding available nearby. If you do not arrange time to sight-see this area you will have missed an outstanding experience. A must is a visit to the many shops and art galleries. Our first impression was that, while much more modest in size and number of shops, it is reminiscent of the Carmel/Monterey area.

Located about a mile away is a the Sedona Golf Resort Course. Designed by architect Gary Parks, it enjoys an outstanding visual setting. While the course is basically flat, Mr. Parks used every bit of the rolling terrain and multi-level topography available to create a masterpiece. Playing to a par of 71, it reaches out a substantial 6,642/6,126/5,637/5,030 yards. Obviously with four different tee setting you can bite off as much as you feel you want to handle. Water, by the way, comes into action on only three holes. The Director of Golf is John Benzel. For golf course information you can call (602) 284-9355.

The course acts as headquarters for Sports Enhancement and offers some interesting golf school classes. For detailed information on the golf school call (800) 345-4245.

RATES *(EP) Rooms weekdays: $76/$95. Weekends: $76/ $109. Suites $95/$1096. Golf package: 1 night 1/day (includes lodging, one round of golf with cart, one breakfast), $177/$201 per couple.*

ARRIVAL *Air: Flagstaff (45 miles) or Phoenix Sky Harbor Airport (90 miles). Private aircraft/charter flights: Sedona Airport (5,100 foot paved runway, lighted, radio equipped).*

THE BOULDERS
P.O. Box 2090, Carefree, AZ 85377; (602) 488-9009; (800) 553-1717

The Boulders has been judged one of the top 50 resorts. Having opened in December of 1984, it is set in the desert foothills northeast of Phoenix. The general area is one of saguaro cactus, Indian paintbrush, hollyhocks and giant boulders shaped by water, wind and thousands of years. Built to complement the terrain, the resort uses desert tones, textured natural surfaces with flagstone floors, hand-crafted Indian baskets, pottery and original art of the region. The net result is outstanding.

Within this majestic setting, the former owners, Rockresorts Inc., put together a complex which, following the normal pattern of their developments, has become one of the premier resorts. In addition to The Boulders, Rockresorts also created the magnificent Mauna Kea Beach Hotel, Caneel Bay and Little Dix Bay. In other words they know how to put the proper wheels on a resort development.

There are 120 individually sited casitas using natural wood, Mexican glazed tile, and adobe plaster surfaces. Each casita features a private patio and a full size wood burning fireplace. They represent some of the most unusual and, I might add, beautiful accommodations we have visited.

The main building is the site of the Discovery Lounge with its picture window views of the landscape and two of three dining rooms. The special Latilla is open for breakfast and dinner as well as a fabulous Sunday Brunch, while the Palo Verde dining room is available for all three meals. This part of the resort is also the location of the executive meeting facilities and has a 1,960-square-foot conference room.

The free-form swimming pool, backed by a beautiful waterfall, is a place to relax and enjoy a light meal or a libation. Not a bad way to go after a swim, a game of tennis or a round of golf. Horseback riding is nearby with picturesque trails to hike, ride or stroll.

Golf, under the direction of PGA professional Bob Irving, may now be played on the resort's 36-hole complex. The Boulders North Course reaches out a respectable 6,972/6,731/6,291,5348 and pars at 72. The South plays 6,926/6,543/6,073/4,984 with a par of 71.

We have not played the new configuration of two courses, only the older 18-hole layout. It was a golf course that could set your teeth on edge. While most certainly beautiful, it also could be deadly. There were many hidden problems that you discovered only after you had made your play. Looking at the yardage of the new

setup, I have to assume they didn't make it any friendlier.

There is a clubhouse and extremely well stocked pro shop. The Boulders Club House provides men's and women's locker rooms and a coffee shop. It's actually a great deal more than just a coffee shop and has recently undergone a complete renovation.

RATES (MAP) Casitas: $525 per couple. Green fees, including cart: $97. Golf package 3 nights/3 days (includes lodging, MAP, three rounds of golf with cart), $2,040. Rates are for January through mid-May.

ARRIVAL Air: Phoenix. Car: take I-17 north to Carefree Highway. Travel east to Scottsdale Road, then turn north for less than a mile.

DOBSON RANCH INN
1666 South Dobson Road, Mesa, AZ 85202; (602) 831-7000; (800) 528-1356

With 212 over-size guest rooms, accommodations consist of king and double queen bedroom arrangements. They also provide the use of their fitness center, swimming pool and the Other Place Restaurant. El Charro Lounge is available for evening entertainment. The Ranch has meeting facilities and can handle groups of from 10 to 300.

Located a short distance away (approximately one mile), is the Dobson Ranch Golf Course. Playing to a par of 72 this layout reaches out 6,587/6,196/5,065 yards. The course is supported by a lighted driving range, a putting green, restaurant and a well equipped pro shop. The head professional is Glen Harvey. For tee times call (602) 644-2291.

RATES   (EP)   Rooms: $101/106. 1-bedroom suites: $135. For poolside location add $15. Green fees: $50, including cart.

ARRIVAL Air: Phoenix Sky Harbor Airport (20 minutes). Car: south on I-10. Exit to Superstition Freeway east. Go to Dobson Road Exit (exit 6), You will see the resort signs after you exit.

FAIRFIELD FLAGSTAFF RESORT
1900 North Country Club Drive, Flagstaff, AZ 86001; (602) 526-3232

Flagstaff is one of the only areas within Arizona which experiences four distinct seasons. This is high country with skiing at nearby Fairfield Snow Bowl in the winter, rushing rivers and wild flowers in the spring, warm days and crisp nights in the summer. Fairfield Estates, located right in the middle of this ideal area, is surrounded by more than a million acres of national forest.

Accommodations are in fully equipped townhouse condominiums. If you prefer not to "condo it," there is a dining room available in the Clubhouse, or you might prefer to venture into nearby Flagstaff for meals.

Tennis can be played on 12 courts (eight lighted) with professionals available to assist. An Olympic-size pool and horseback riding are a few of the other features.

Golf is offered on 36 holes under the supervision of the Director of Golf, Jack Wright and staff. One course is closed for member play only. The Elden Hills course is, however, available for guest play. Parring at 72/73, it weighs in at 6,104/5,380 yards. It is well trapped and brings water into play on six holes.

RATES (EP) Townhouse: 1 bedroom and full-size kitchen (sleeps 4), $125. Sleeps up to 6, $165. Green fees: $35 / $40, carts $24.

ARRIVAL Air: Flagstaff. Car: Exit I-40 east of Flagstaff, to Country Club Drive.

FAIRFIELD GREEN VALLEY
P. O. Box 587, Green Valley, AZ 85622; (602) 625-6608

On approximately 5,000 acres with 15,000 permanent residents, this resort is actually a retirement community which welcomes visitors seeking a relaxing vacation and who may be interested in buying property. Should your primary interest be in buying property I suggest you call (602) 625-4441 or (800) 528-4930. The number listed above is for the rental office.

There are townhouse/casitas as well as private homes available for rental, all with living room, one bedroom and kitchen.

As a guest you have access to all of the recreational facilities normally reserved for residents, including six tennis courts and nine swimming

pools.

Golf is offered on four 18-hole championship courses. The Desert Hills layout is one of the more challenging courses in Arizona. Though not particularly long, playing at 6,476/6,183 yards, it pars at 72. It is well bunkered and brings water into play on six holes. There are also a number of other courses within the local area.

RATES (EP) Townhouse: $190 for two nights. Green fees: $25 / $30, carts $22. Golf packages are available. Rates are mid-December to April 1st.

ARRIVAL Air: Tucson. Car: south of Tucson (25 miles) on I-19.

FRANCISCO GRANDE RESORT
P.O. Box 326, Casa Grande, AZ 85222; (602) 836-6444; (800) 237-4238

The Francisco Grande, for a short period, lost touch with the passing years and suffered. Closed for almost two years, it now has been renovated and brought back to full life. It is amazing what an infusion of several million dollars can accomplish. The resort is a multi-level hotel with 112 guest rooms and suites. They are also able to handle meeting and conference groups of up to 350.

We understand the food service is as good or better than when we visited here. Dining is now offered in the Palo Verde Room or in a more informal setting on the outdoor veranda.

Activities include: use of a huge swimming pool, modern lighted Laykold tennis courts and, of course, golf.

The golf course has undergone extensive renovation with added trees and traps. Its length remains awesome as it reaches out 7,320/6,975/6,454/5,554 yards and pars at 72.

RATES (EP) Patio rooms: $56. Tower: $106. Suites $126/ $196. Green fees: $45/$505, including cart. Golf package: 2 nights/3 days (includes Tower room, green fees and cart, range balls, daily breakfast, taxes and gratuities), $432 per couple.

ARRIVAL Car: mid-way between Phoenix and Tucson turn west to Casa Grande. The resort is 4 miles west of Casa Grande on Highway 84.

THE GOLD CANYON RESORT
6100 South Kings Ranch Road, Apache Junction, AZ 85219; (602) 982-9090; (800) 624-6445

The natural beauty of this part of Arizona is legendary. About 40 miles (an hours drive) due east of Phoenix at an elevation of 1,715 feet, the 3,300-acre Gold Canyon Resort has much to offer.

Speaking of legends, Apache Junction is reputed to be the location of the fabled Lost Dutchman Mine. As the story goes, it is somewhere in the Superstition Mountains. Although many have sought and, in fact, are still seeking it, no one has been able to locate the Dutchman's gold.

Each of the resort's southwestern-style rooms and suites is positioned to offer a view of the mountains. The rooms are spacious, and each has a wet bar, fireplace and patio, with some featuring a private spa.

Their meeting facilities can handle groups of up to 130. The Clubhouse dining room features a varied and delightful menu. There is also an excellent 35-seat lounge.

Tennis, swimming and golf are

but a few of the activities available. Old western-style trail rides, with an experienced wrangler to assist, guided tours, overnight campouts and cookouts can also be arranged.

The golf course, under the supervision of the Director of Golf Phil Green is now an 18-hole layout. Parring at 71/72 it extends 6,398/6,004/5,686/4,876 yards and is one of the better courses in the area.

Adjacent to the resort is a development of interesting Casa Townhouses facing the golf course. They are now available to rent. Should you be interested you can call (602) 983-0670.

RATES *(EP) Rooms: $130/$180. Spa rooms: $210. Green fees: $70, including cart. Golf package: 1 night/1 day (includes lodging, breakfast, one round of golf with cart, bag storage), $310 per couple. Rates are January 1 to April 15.*

ARRIVAL *Air: Phoenix. Car: Highway 60 east to Apache Junction; continue 7 miles southeast on 60 to Kings Ranch Road. Turn left to the resort.*

HYATT REGENCY SCOTTSDALE
7500 East Doubletree Ranch Road, Scottsdale, AZ 85258; (602) 991-3388; (800) 233-1234

The Scottsdale Hyatt represents a slight change for Hyatt. The architectural design seems to reflect a definite Moroccan style. Although pleasing in appearance, it is unique.

While only four stories in height, the hotel appears more massive than it actually is. Perhaps this is due to the manner in which everything seems to unfold. With five different courtyards opening onto the lawn and tennis area, they stretch along the lakefront, overlooking the pools and the golf course. The view from the three-story atrium lobby is outstanding. All in all, the setting creates a quiet and relaxed atmosphere. An impressive art collection is showcased in and outside the hotel. The art includes sculpture, wall friezes, paintings and carvings. Some of the artifacts date back to 700 B.C.

There are 493 guest rooms within the main structure along with a special VIP wing (The Regency Club) located on the third and fourth levels. Each room has its own air-conditioning control, cable TV, private balcony and a fully stocked mini bar. There are six different categories of suites to choose from. Seven lakeside Casitas are also available.

The Golden Swan, overlooking the lagoon, functions as an indoor as well as an outdoor restaurant. The Squash Blossom, a 300-seat restaurant, provides a beautiful view of the cascading fountain area. Finally, there is Sandolo, for casual dining, with its view of the "water playground." While each of the aforementioned restaurants offers cocktail service the resort also has the poolside bar and snack bar. Should you go hungry or thirsty at this place, it is your own fault.

Including the 14,000-square-foot ballroom the hotel has 25 meeting rooms and can accommodate 1,500 theater-style and 1,200 in a banquet configuration.

Activities include: tennis on eight Laykold surfaced courts (four lighted) with a professional staff and supported by a tennis shop, a health and fitness center, saunas, massage rooms, therapeutic massage, croquet and a four-mile jogging and cycling trail laid out over the 640-acre Gainey Ranch property. Horseback riding is available nearby. There is a water playground consisting of a half-acre of pools with water falls, a three-story water slide, along with a sand beach.

Golf is served up on three distinctly different nine-hole layouts. Designed by Benz and Poellot, each nine pars at 36. The Arroyo nine features a meandering desert look, which makes sense as "arroyo" means a "desert wash."

The Lakes also lives up to its name. It is a "showcase nine." While a variety of water hazards come into play in the form of lakes, streams and ponds, it enjoys a garden-like setting. The Dunes is reminiscent of Scottish courses with its rolling moor-like terrain.

Using a crossover system the Arroyo/Lakes plays to a pretty substantial 6,818/6,252/5,790// 5,330 yards. The Dunes/Lakes combination reaches out 6,607/5,975/4,993 yards and the Arroyo/Dunes measures 6,662/6,113/5,681/5,151 yards. Available to assist is a professional staff under the supervision of the Director of Golf, Mike Frunko.

RATES   *(EP)*   *Rooms:*

*$250/$335. Suites: $350/
$800. Green fees: $105, including cart. Golf package: 1
night/1 day (includes lodging,
1 round of golf, with cart), $466
per couple. Rates are for January through May.*

***ARRIVAL** Air: Phoenix Sky
Harbor Airport (45 minutes).
Car: from the airport take 44th
street north to Camelback
Road. Turn right on Camel-
back and proceed east to
Scottsdale Road, where you
turn left and drive north to
Double Tree Ranch Road. Turn
right (east).*

LOEWS VENTANA CANYON RESORT

*7000 North Resort Drive, Tuc-
son, AZ 85715; (602) 299-2020;
(800) 234-5117*

The Ventana Canyon Resort is
in one of the prettiest parts of
Arizona, the Sonoran Desert.
Situated in the immediate
foothills of the Catalina Mountains, the resort structure
blends with the surrounding
area. It is a world of rock
spires, guarded by stately saguaro cacti.

While large (400 rooms), the
structure is not a high-rise.
The entire setting is park-like,
with all the amenities expected

of a first-rate resort, but with
an added dimension of peace
and quiet. All this, plus the
fact that you are only about 25
minutes from downtown Tucson.

Each of the rooms or suites has
a private balcony and is
equipped with a refrigerator
and mini-bar. The great majority provide views of either the
city of Tucson skyline or the
Coronado National Forest.
Loews meeting facilities are
quite large, with a capacity of
up to 1,300 people.

You will not want for food or
entertainment as there are
several restaurants, including
The Ventana offering French
cuisine, The Canyon Cafe with
a general menu, and The Flying V Bar and Night Club for
dining and entertainment.

Activities include: nature
trails, two swimming pools
with adjacent hot tubs, jogging, a beautiful tennis complex (10 lighted courts) with a
professional staff to assist,
Jacuzzis, saunas, a health club
and, of course, golf.

The golf course, a Tom Fazio
design, parring at 72 plays
6,969/6,380/5,753/4,780 yards.
This layout has now become a
private affair, available for

member usage only. Guests of the hotel, however, enjoy golfing privileges at The Canyon Course, also a Fazio design.

The Canyon Course measures some 6,818/6,282/5,756/4,919 yards and also pars at 72. While the front nine of the Canyon might well be considered conservative, the back side will offer you all the challenge you can handle. Water becomes a factor on only two holes.

RATES (EP) Rooms: $285 / $325. Suites: $425 / $700. Green fees: $90, including cart. Golf package: 2 nights / 2 days (includes lodging, 4 days green fees, cart, bag storage), $830 per couple. Rates are for January 15 to mid-May.

ARRIVAL Air: Tucson.

MARRIOTT'S CAMELBACK INN RESORT
5402 E. Lincoln Drive, Scottsdale, AZ 85253; (602) 948-1700; (800) 242-2635

The Camelback Inn has been judged one of the top 50 resorts. The history of the Inn goes back many years. In fact, it dates back to about 1936 and has been a favorite of a great many celebrities since that time. Although constantly updated and renovated, the Inn has not lost its grace nor its subdued splendor. It seems, in fact, to have gained stature over the intervening period. Having established a tradition for excellence, Marriott's Camelback Inn is one of only 21 hotels or resorts in the United States to have continually earned the Mobil Five Star Award. That's quite an accomplishment when you consider the fact that there are over of 20,000 hotels/resorts in this country.

Accommodations are in 423 rooms, including many adobe casitas decorated in a Southwestern motif. The rooms and suites are beautifully decorated and include all of the amenities one would expect of a resort of this caliber. The Inn has excellent meeting facilities and can handle both large as well as small groups functions.

Their dining rooms are among the finest in the Southwest. The Chaparral, while a bit formal, is superb (jackets are required, ties are optional). The Navajo Room, less formal but also outstanding, is available for all three meals. There is also the North Pool for casual dining, and available for breakfast, lunch, and Sunday brunch. Should you have an early tee time, consider breakfast at the Country Club. Again, both the service and the food are excellent.

Activities includes: three swimming pools (if you include the Spa pool), 10 tennis courts (6 lighted) with a professional on deck to assist, horseback riding (located nearby) and whirlpool baths. Certainly less strenuous but, nonetheless, interesting, are the resort shops on the grounds: a ladies' boutique, a men's "Gentry Shop," an Indian Art and Craft Shop and an outstanding Sport Shop featuring tennis, golf, and swim wear as well as casual shoes, etc. There are additional shops displaying a wide variety of items.

Golf, located at the Camelback Golf Club, may be played on two outstanding courses. The Indian Bend layout, a Jack Snyder design, lies in the shadow of Mummy Mountain. Parring at 72, this course reaches out a monstrous 7,014/6,486/5,917 yards. While there is little water coming into play the undulating fairways, trees and fast greens will more than keep your attention. The Padre Course was designed by Red Lawrence. It is a bit more in my league, with the mileage at 6,559/6,019/5,626 yards. The par is set at 71 for the men and 73 from the ladies tees. Although there is little water coming into play it is well trapped. The fact that the fairways are lined with beautiful eucalyptus trees also adds to the challenge.

The John Jacobs' Practical Golf School is available at this resort. Using personalized, proven teaching methods, and under the direction of PGA and LPGA teaching professionals, it is well worth looking into. For complete details call (800) 472-5007.

Both courses, as well as the fine golf shop, are under the

supervision of the Director of Golf, Joe Shershenovich.

RATES (EP) Lodging: $265. Suites: $475 and up. MAP or FAP plans and golf packages are offered. Rates are for January-May. Green fees: $70 / $80, including cart.

ARRIVAL Air: Sky Harbor International Airport. Car: north on Scottsdale Road, left on Lincoln Drive.

MARRIOTT'S MOUNTAIN SHADOWS
5641 E. Lincoln Drive, Scottsdale, AZ 85253; (602) 948-7111; (800) 782-2123

Literally in the shadow of Camelback Mountain the resort lies in a beautiful setting. The general surroundings and the overall atmosphere reflect the grace and enchantment of the southwest. Accommodations consist of 354 rooms, including six suites.

The Mountain Shadows has excellent meeting facilities. With its large ballroom and 12 separate breakout rooms, they are capable of handling groups of up to 1,200.

Shells Restaurant specializes

in seafood, and the Cactus Flower is a family-oriented dining room. The restaurant at the Country Club is also open to guests of Mountain Shadows. In the evening, a favorite gathering place is Maxfields Lounge, where you can dance to live music.

At your disposal are: eight lighted tennis courts, a steam room, sauna, masseur/masseuse, two swimming pools, and a fitness center. Horseback riding is available nearby.

Golf may be played on their 18-hole par-56 course which comes complete with a stream (in fact it has been referred to as a waterfall), highly unusual for this desert area. Tee times can also be arranged on the two fabulous Camelback golf courses. For details on the Padre and Indian Bend layouts see "Marriott's Camelback Inn."

The John Jacobs' Practical Golf School is available at this resort. Using personalized, proven teaching methods, and under the direction of PGA and LPGA teaching professionals, it is well worth looking into. For complete details (and lower scores), call (800) 472-5007.

RATES (EP) Rooms: $250. Suites: $245/$350. Golf packages are offered. Green fees: Mountain Shadows, $43, including cart. Camelback, $70/$80, including cart. Rates are for January through May.

ARRIVAL Air: Sky Harbor International Airport (approximately 20 minutes). Car: from Scottsdale Road turn west onto Lincoln Drive.

ORANGE TREE GOLF RESORT

10601 North 56th Street, Scottsdale, AZ 85254; (602) 948-6100; (800) 228-0386

Opened in January of 1989, this golf and conference center was developed on a beautiful 128-acre site. Being careful to blend the resort within the surrounding desert setting, the architects of Orange Tree have been quite successful in capturing the flavor of the southwest without resorting to the traditional and sometimes overwhelming cactus plants, Spanish tile and heavy stucco motif so common in this area. All in all, they have achieved a delightful change of pace.

Accommodations are 160 oversized and soundproof rooms along with two executive suites. You may select either a king size bed or a room with two double beds. Following a Southwestern architectural style, the rooms have been arranged in a series of two-story villas, with the majority enjoying a view of the golf course.

Amenities include: a 27-inch cable-equipped TV set in each room – plus a 9" TV located in the bathroom so you won't miss your soap opera while using the whirlpool spa built for two. Other equipment includes a VCR (they will arrange movie rentals) and an AM/FM stereo. These people are not savages – there is also a fully stocked wet bar in the rooms and ice makers. Each of the rooms has either a private patio or a deck.

With eight meeting rooms (14,000 square feet of meeting space), the Orange Tree can accommodate groups of from 10 to 500.

Dining is offered in Joe's American Grill & Bar. Located within the hotel, and overlooking the 18th fairway, the restaurant offers breakfast, lunch and dinner along with entertainment in the evening. There is, in addition, the Fairway Pavilion situated at the course, presenting a more casual setting. Light snacks and beverage service are also available in the pool area.

Now that you may well have eaten yourself into trouble, let's look at a few of the activities at your disposal. The Racquet & Fitness Club, a 25,000-square-foot facility, features 16 lighted, all-weather tennis and eight racquetball courts, an aerobics center, Nautilus work-out equipment, a heated swimming pool, therapy spas and a sauna.

While the resort is relatively new, the golf course has been in play for over 30 years and, obviously, is mature. Designed by Johnny Bulla, it features a complete practice area. The Orange Tree Golf Course stretches out 6,837/6,398/5,618 yards and pars at 72. While relatively flat, it is well trapped and has enough trees coming into play to create a definite series of challenges.

The new up-beat and extremely well-equipped pro shop is under the supervision of the Director of Golf, Mark Rose.

RATES *(EP)* *Rooms $180/$195. Green fees: $60/$70, including cart. Golf package: 2 nights/2 days (includes breakfast, lodging, 2 rounds of golf with cart, club storage, lockers, all taxes and gratuities), $576 per couple.*

ARRIVAL *Air: Phoenix Sky Harbor Airport (13 miles) or Scottsdale Municipal (4 miles). Car: from the Scottsdale Airport drive south to Shea Blvd. Turn west and drive to north 56th. Turn right (north), drive about a block and you have arrived.*

THE PHOENICIAN RESORT
6000 East Camelback Road, Phoenix, AZ 85251; (602) 941-8200; (800) 888-8234

The Phoenician is southeast of Camelback Mountain. While the exterior design is rather unusual, unfortunately it is not at all consistent with the ambiance of the area and is considered by many to be ostentatious or, as we have heard, "a bit on the tacky side." Others have called it "a monument to excess." Put together by Charles Keating (infamous for the savings and loan debacle), a great deal of money (not necessarily his) was obviously spent on lavish, garish amenities. questionable art work, a mother-of-pearl lined swimming pool, several Steinway pianos woth over a quarter million, $120,000 worth of Persian rugs – these are just a sample of what you will see. Ther are 580 guest rooms including 130 casitas. The hotel can handle meeting groups.

The various restaurants are the Main Dining Room, the Outdoor Terrace, as well as The Windows on the Green. Lighter fare is also available at poolside and at the Oasis. Be prepared: while the service is excellent, the prices are outrageous and you may well find yourself hungry after you have dined.

Activities include: use of a health spa, 11 tennis courts (including a stadium court) and six swimming pools. The Phoenician Golf Course, designed by Homer Flint, plays 6,487/6,033/5,058 yards and pars at 71/72.

RATES (EP) Rooms: $280/$395. Casitas suites: $740/$875. Green fees: $90, including cart. Rates are for peak season January through June.

ARRIVAL Air: Phoenix Sky Harbor Airport (nine miles).

THE POINTE HILTON ON SOUTH MOUNTAIN
7777 S. Pointe Parkway, Phoenix, AZ 85044; (602) 438-9000; (800) 876-4683

Built adjacent to South Mountain, this resort is just minutes from the airport and business center of the valley. Accommodations range from two-room suites to presidential and concierge-level suites (638 in total). Each suite features a refrigerator, honor bar, two phones, two TV sets as well as a private balcony.

The architectural style of the resort is Mediterranean. There are shaded walkways, fountains and seven outdoor swimming pools, as well as lagoons, on the impressive grounds. With 20,000 square feet of meeting space they are able to accommodate as many as 2,000 theater-style.

There are several dining areas. The Rustler's Roost, specializes in mesquite-grilled steaks and ribs (with a name like that what else could they specialize in), while Aunt Chilada's has Mexican cuisine. "Another Point in Tyme" is their signature dining facility. There is also the Sports Club for lighter fare.

Amenities include: 14 Plexi-pave tennis courts, indoor racquetball courts, weight machines, LifeCycles, Stair-Masters, rowers and treadmills. They also offer massage therapy, steam rooms and saunas. The resort has its own stable and the surrounding area presents excellent riding conditions.

Golf is played on the Pointe Golf Club. Reaching out a modest 6,003/5,400/4,700 yards, it pars at 70. In building this layout they were extremely careful to maintain the character of the Sonora landscape – including over 100 different species of wildflowerS, and every form of cactus known to exist in Arizona. These include 300-year-old saguaros, some ranging up to eight tons. The well stocked golf shop is under the supervision of Head Professional, Brett Greenwood.

RATES (EP) 2-room suite: $215. Presidential suite: $375. Concierge level: $230. Green fees: $105, including cart. Golf package: 2 nights/2 days (includes lodging, two rounds of golf with cart, club storage), $768 per couple. Rates shown are for January through April.

ARRIVAL Air: Sky Harbor Airport (Phoenix). Car: from *the airport take I-17 south. Get off on Baseline exit. Drive to 58th street and turn right. The resort is on your left.*

THE POINTE HILTON AT TAPATIO CLIFFS
11111 North 7th Street, Phoenix, AZ 85020; (602) 866-7500; (800) 876-4683

Laid out much like a small village the Tapatio Cliffs resort is in the northeast end of the valley. It is about 20 minutes from the business center of Phoenix. There are 584 suites to choose from. Offering different views, each unit is air-conditioned and features a private patio or balcony, two phones and two TV sets. The accommodations range from two-room and presidential suites, to concierge level suites. Each of the presidential lodgings features a wood-burning fireplace.

Their meeting capacity, with over 16,000 square feet of space, allows the resort to accommodate groups of up to 800 theater- and 400 classroom-style.

There are three different dining facilities. Some distance above the resort is Etienne's Different Pointe of View restaurant serving French cuisine. Transportation is provided. The Chuckwagon N' Saloon which specializes in steaks also serves up lively entertainment with a honkytonk piano player and singing hostesses. The clubhouse "Pointe In Tyme" restaurant with its turn-of-the-century decor presents a varied menu ranging from oysters Rockefeller to Cobb salad.

Amenities: 15 tennis courts, along with four racquetball courts, six swimming pools, including a lap-pool, horseback riding from their own stables, a fitness center with state-of-the-art equipment, steam, sauna and massage therapy.

The golf course at Tapatio Cliffs is called Lookout Mountain. Reaching out a respectable 6,617/5,834/4,552 yards, it pars at 72. A nice change of pace – there are only three holes with water coming into the picture. The head professional is Dale Williams.

RATES (EP) Two-room suites: $215. Concierge Level: $230. Presidential suites: $375. Green fees: $105, including cart. Golf package: 2 nights/2 days (includes lodging, 2 rounds of golf with cart, bag storage), $768 per couple. Rates are for January through April.

ARRIVAL Air: Sky Harbor Airport (Phoenix). Car: take I-10 to I-17 north. Get off on Thunderbird Road east. Drive to 7th street. Turn right – the resort is on your left.

RAMADA LONDON BRIDGE RESORT
1477 Queens Bay, Lake Havasu, AZ 86403; (602) 855-0888; (800) 624-7939

The London Bridge Resort enjoys a unique setting along with a most unusual architectural style. Covering some 110 acres the structure resembles an old English castle, complete with turrets and towers. The setting is further enhanced by the proximity of Lake Havasu as well as the "Old London Bridge." Dismantled stone by stone, it was transported from England and reconstructed at Lake Havasu in 1971.

Accommodations are in 170 rooms, including suites, spread over three floors. All suites feature an in-bedroom Jacuzzi, living room, wet bar and refrigerator. With a 6,500-square-foot convention hall, they can accommodate group functions of up to 500 banquet-, 900 theater- and 200 classroom-style.

The Kings Retreat Dining Room as well as the Knights Lounge are at your disposal. There are, in addition, many restaurants, boutiques, and specialty shops in the immediate area.

There is a lighted tennis court on property with 11 more less than half a mile distant, three outdoor heated swimming pools, and lake cruises on the resort's *Dixie Bell*, a 120-passenger sternwheeler. Lake Havasu is extremely large. Some 45 miles long, it provides room for all types of water activities including boating, sailing and fishing.

There are two regulation 18-hole courses located a bit over two miles away. The oldest, the London Bridge Golf Club, reaches out a respectable 6,618/6,298/5,756 yards and pars at 71/72. Working out of the same pro shop, the Stonebridge Course plays to a bit more modest 6,166/5,766/ 5,045 yards, with a par of 71. There is also the Queen's Bay Golf Course on premises. A nine-hole, par-three layout parring at 27, it measures 1,560 yards. The courses are supported by a pro shop and restaurant.

RATES (EP) Rooms: $75/$85 *weekdays, $150/$165 week-* *ends. Suites: $125/$200 week-* *days, $185/$250 weekends.* *Golf package: 2 nights/2 days* *(includes lodging, two rounds* *of golf with cart, two full break-* *fasts), $300 per couple.*

ARRIVAL Air: Lake Havasu *City (7 miles). Car: from I-40* *take the Lake Havasu/London* *Bridge exit. Travel 20 miles* *south. Resort will be on your* *left side (east side of Highway* *95).*

RANCHO DE LOS CABALLEROS
Wickenburg, AZ 85358
(602) 684-5484

The name is appropriate, as the resort is sited on 20,000 acres of rolling foothills and is a working ranch. The literal translation is "Rancho of the Horsemen." It is open only during the winter months of October through May each year. Accommodations consist of rooms in the Inn, plus some 14 one- to four-bedroom bungalows carefully decorated to bring memories of the Old West into each room. There are a total of 73 spacious rooms and suites. The Rancho is capable of handling meeting groups of up to 150.

Meals are served in the main dining room, offering a menu which is both varied and imaginative. And, I must hasten to add, the food is outstanding.

Children are welcome here, with indoor and outdoor playgrounds and trained counselors to supervise their activities. I know it will break your heart to be left alone to enjoy the resort's other amenities.

It can get quite cool in the evenings so warm clothing (sweater or jacket) is recommended.

They offer riding (60-horse stable), desert cookouts and perhaps a look at a cattle roundup. A few other activities available include complimentary tennis on four courts, skeet/trap shooting, scheduled square dances, swimming and, of course, golf.

Golf is now played on the new Los Caballeros 18-hole golf course. With a yardage of 6,965/6,577/5,896 it pars at 72/73. The course circles the entire resort and comes complete with lakes, traps and trees. There is a clubhouse, including a pro shop, locker rooms and a restaurant. Guest play may also be arranged for the Wickenburg Country Club, located approximately three miles away.

RATES (FAP) Lodgings: $256 per couple. Green fees: $55, including cart. Golf package: 3 nights/4 days (includes lodging in Sun Terrace Room, FAP, golf or riding each day – carts not included), $948 per couple. Rates quoted are for February-May.

ARRIVAL Air: Phoenix. Private aircraft: Wickenburg (4,200-foot paved) or the Rancho, 2,600 feet. Car: an hour's drive northwest of Phoenix on Highway 60/89, 2 miles west of Wickenburg on Highway 60.

REGAL McCORMICK RANCH
7401 North Scottsdale Road, Scottsdale, AZ 85253; 602) 948-5050; (800) 243-1332

This resort was originally internationally known for breeding and training Arabian horses. It has an unusual setting for the desert in that it is sited on the shores of a lake. There are 125 rooms and suites, plus 50 fully equipped two- to three-bedroom condominium villas. These villas, by the way, are quite large, with some ranging up to 2,200 square feet. They also have excellent meeting facilities. With the combined east and west Superstition Rooms they can handle groups of up to 300 theater- and 200 classroom-style. There are, in addition, eight smaller break out rooms.

Dining is provided in the Pinon Grille featuring southwestern cuisine. During the day a more casual setting is on the colorful terrace. Evening entertainment is served up in the Diamondback Lounge.

There is a heated swimming pool, a whirlpool and tennis on four lighted courts with a professional staff available to assist. With horseback riding (located nearby), biking, sailing and fishing on 40-acre Camelback Lake, there should be enough to keep you busy.

Golf can be played on The Palm Course, measuring 7,021/6,202/5,309 yards with a par of 72; or The Pine Course, stretching out 7,020/6,333/ 5,494 yards, also parring at 72. There is enough water coming into the action on the Palm layout to increase your sailing skills. The clubhouse facilities include a large pro shop, a dining room, as well as a lounge and locker rooms.

RATES (EP) Hotel rooms: $160/$220. Suites: $265/ $600. Condominiums: $245/ $340. Green fees: $70/$80, including cart. Golf packages: 3 nights/2 days (includes lodging, 2 rounds of golf and cart), $798 per couple. Rates are for January to mid-May.

ARRIVAL Air: Phoenix (25 minutes). Car: Scottsdale Road and McCormick Parkway (5 minutes north of downtown Scottsdale).

THE REGISTRY RESORT

7171 North Scottsdale Road, Scottsdale, AZ 85253; (602) 991-3800; (800) 247-9810

The Registry is a luxurious 76-acre resort and convention complex. Accommodations consist of 319 rooms, including suites. The meeting facilities are quite large, with modern audio/visual aids at your disposal.

Their restaurants include La Champagne, serving French cuisine, and Cafe Brioche for more casual dining. There is 24-hour room service provided as well. Live entertainment is a nightly feature.

Tennis certainly does not take

a back seat to golf at this establishment, with 21 courts, a professional staff and a separate tennis shop. Other amenities include horseback riding nearby, four swimming pools and a health spa.

Golf may be played on two 18-hole layouts. The Pines, with a par of 72, plays at 7,020/6,333/5,494 yards. This layout brings water into play on six or seven holes and has more than its share of trees. The Palms course reaches out a substantial 7,021/6,202/5,309, also parring at 72. With water in contention on nine holes and some of the toughest par-three's you would ever want to tangle with, you will find it more than enough of a challenge.

RATES   (EP)   Rooms: $165/$185. 1-bedroom suites: $225. Green fees, including cart: $70. Golf packages are available. Rates are for January-mid May.

ARRIVAL Air: Phoenix. Car: about 25 minutes from the Sky Harbor International Airport in Phoenix.

RIO RICO RESORT & COUNTRY CLUB
1069 Camino Caralampi, Rio Rico, AZ 85648; (602) 281-1901; (800) 288-4746

Rio Rico is nestled in the mountains at an altitude of 4,000 feet. While this altitude produces beautiful clear days it also tends to get a bit sharp in the evening. The magnificent scenery provided by the Santa Cruz Mountains is one of the more spectacular sights in Arizona.

The hotel dining room serves Mexican cuisine, seafood and steaks. Located only 12 miles from Nogales and the border of Mexico, you are on top of a bargainer's paradise for shopping, along with a wide selection of places to eat and be entertained. The Rio Rico Hotel has complete meeting facilities for groups up to 500 including eight breakout rooms.

In addition to tennis on four lighted courts, and an Olympic-size pool, the hotel offers riding and trap shooting.

Golf is available on a Robert Trent Jones, Jr. course. It stretches out an awesome 7,119/6,426/5,577 yards and pars at 72/71. This is an interesting layout with undulating terrain on the back side, a rather flat front nine and a liberal supply of water coming into play. The golf course is two miles from the hotel. Good news: shuttle service is available.

RATES (EP) Rooms: $70. Suites: $95. Apartments: $130. Green fees: $24, including cart. Golf package: 2 nights/3 days (includes lodging, MAP, unlimited golf with cart, bag storage) weekdays $360 per couple. Rates are for January-April.

ARRIVAL Car: 57 miles south of Tucson and 12 miles north of Nogales on I-19, Calabasas exit.

RIO VERDE RESORT & RANCH
18815 Four Peaks Boulevard, Rio Verde, AZ 85263; (602) 991-3350; (800) 233-7103

Rio Verde is an adult community consisting of approximately 600 homes and golf villas sited on 700 acres. Located 30 miles northeast of Phoenix, it has a quiet desert setting. The resort is situated in the awesome beauty of the Tonto National Forest. The backdrop of the beautiful McDowell, Superstition and Mazatzal mountains forms a spectacular setting for this area.

Accommodations are in private homes located either on or near one of the two 18-hole courses. They range in size from two to three bedrooms and are equipped with two baths, a kitchen (fully equipped for housekeeping), a barbecue unit and a washer/dryer.

The new 17,000-square-foot clubhouse features a cocktail lounge and restaurant. Durng the evening hours they offer dancing.

There are six tennis courts (two lighted) and two swimming pools. Facilities for horseback riding are provided at their 140-acre ranch. As a matter of fact a few of the homes have their own private swimming pools.

The Quail Run Course, reaching out 6,500/6,228/5,558 yards and parring at 72, is well bunkered, with water hazards in play on eight holes. The second 18, the White Wing Course, measures 6,456/6,053/5,465 yards, with a par of 71. Both courses operate from the new pro shop located in the clubhouse.

RATES (EP) Casa Bonita: $550/$850 weekly. Hacienda: $700/$900 weekly. Green fees:

$60, including cart. Rates are for mid-December to mid-April. There are now three night rentals available.

ARRIVAL Air: Phoenix. Car: take Scottsdale to Shea Blvd. Turn east (right), travel approximately 13 miles to Fountain Hill Blvd. Take a left, continue 12 miles to Forrest Road and you have arrived.

SCOTTSDALE PIMA SUITES
7330 North Pima Road, Scottsdale, AZ 85258; (602) 948-3800; (800) 344-0262

The location of the resort sets up a variety of activities. You are just minutes from outstanding shopping facilities – the Borgata, The Fifth Avenue Shops, historic Old Town Scottsdale and the famous Main Street art galleries. The Pima Resort offers accommodations in 93 rooms, including 53 two-room suites. Each is equipped with a guest service bar, is air-conditioned and has a private patio. The suites, which can be modified to a one- or two-bedroom configuration, have fully equipped kitchens and feature dining space and private covered patios.

Dining is available in The Patio Room, with cocktails served in The Sand Trap Lounge. The resort can handle meeting groups of from 15 to 300 people. Other amenities include a heated swimming pool and golf. Horseback riding and hay rides can also be arranged nearby.

Golf is played on a championship layout, located across the street and under the supervision of a professional staff. Playing 6,952/6,449/5,722, it pars at 72/73. This layout is fun to navigate. While it is appropriate for a beginner, it is also a challenge for an experienced golfer. The course is well bunkered and brings water into play on 10 holes.

RATES (EP) Rooms: $110. 1-bedroom suite: $145/$165. Pima two-bedroom suites: $215. Green fees: $45, including cart. Rates are for January through April.

ARRIVAL Air: Phoenix. Car: North Pima Road runs north and south and is due east of Scottsdale Road.

SCOTTSDALE PRINCESS
7575 East Princess Drive., Scottsdale, AZ 85255; (602) 585-4848; (800) 344-4758

The Scottsdale Princess has been judged one of the top 50 resorts . The Princess, from an architectural standpoint, is most impressive. Built on a slightly raised area, using the beautiful McDowell Mountains as a backdrop, it seems to loom up out of the desert somewhat like a huge Mexican estate. The general motif of "Old Mexico," complemented by earth tone colors, "old brick" courtyards, cottonwoods, even a bell tower, combine to produce a quiet, pastoral setting. Although the fabulous structure and layout play a part in our evaluation, it is also based on the overall ambience, the warmth of the hotel staff, and the level of service. But then they should be good at what they do. While this is the first of the Princess Resorts in the contiguous U.S., they have operated for several years with such world class properties as the Acapulco Princess and the Pierre Marques in Mexico, the Southampton Princess in Bermuda and the renowned Bahamas Princess Resort & Casino on Grand Bahama Island.

Accommodations consist of 400 rooms and suites in the main building, 125 casitas near the tennis complex and 75 golf villas. Each of the rooms has

three phones, a mini bar and either a private terrace or balcony. The casitas have a living room with a working fireplace (additional logs are just outside your door), a large bedroom, a walk-in closet and a bathroom in which you could hold the NBA play-offs.

The Grand Ballroom, one of the largest meeting facilities in the state and measuring some 22,500 square feet, can handle groups of 1,550 schoolroom- and 2,500 theater-style. A plus: there is a separate check-in and check-out section for meeting groups, keeping them out of the vacationer's way, or perhaps it's the other way around.

There are a total of four dining rooms along with six cocktail lounges – a perfect balance. The Marquesa is in a class by itself, featuring a most unusual cuisine (for this country). It is an intermingling of dishes taken from Catalonia, which includes northeastern Spain, the French region of Roussillon and from the Island of Sardinia. Among the ingredients used are olive oil, garlic, tomatoes, eggplant, seafood, beef, game, beans and even pasta – it is a delightful culinary experience. There is also La Hacienda for seafood and Mexican

fare; Las Ventanas, adjacent to the pool area; and the Grill at TPC. Entertainment and dancing is offered nightly in the Caballo Bayo Lounge.

Along with the two golf courses, there are 10 tennis courts, including a stadium court, a health and fitness center with racquetball and squash courts, aerobics, weight rooms, saunas, steambaths, loofas, herbal wraps, and three swimming pools. Adjacent to the resort is a 400-acre equestrian center with a four-mile cross country course and two polo fields.

The two golf courses, next to the hotel, are public facilities owned and operated by the city of Scottsdale, under the supervision of the Head Golf Professional, Jack Carter, and staff. The Stadium Course, home of the Phoenix Open, must be considered one of the better layouts in the country. Stretching out 6,992/6,508/ 6,049/5,567 yards, it pars at 71. A Tom Weiskopf and Jay Morrish design, it is a links type affair, with rolling terrain, multi-level greens, over 70 traps (a few six or seven feet deep) and water coming into play on seven holes. While fun to play, it is anything but a pushover.

The Desert Course is a more relaxing affair. Again, this is a Tom Weiskopf/Jay Morrish design. Measuring a bit more modest 6,525/5,877/5,314 yards, it also pars at 71. The courses are supported by an outstanding golf shop offering all the amenities.

RATES (EP) Rooms-Hotel: $230/$290. Cholla suites: $460. Casita: $600. Green fees: Stadium Course, $85, including cart; Desert Course, $49, including cart. Rates are for January through April.

ARRIVAL Air: Sky Harbor (approximately 1 hour). Private aircraft: (including private jets) Scottsdale Municipal Airport (10 minutes away). Car: the resort is about 1/4 mile north of the intersection of Bell Road and Scottsdale Blvd.

SHERATON SAN MARCUS

1 San Marcus Place, Chandler, AZ 85224; (602) 963-6655; (800) 325-3535

The original San Marcus Resort dates back many years – in fact the original structure was completed in 1912. Like many lovely old resorts, it fell on hard times and was virtually closed in 1979. Only the

lodge with its 44 rooms (built in 1961) and the golf course continued to function.

Starting in 1986 a dramatic $19 million rehabilitation and expansion of San Marcus, including the addition of three new wings, was begun. There are now a total of 295 rooms and suites – 45 overlooking the golf course and 250 in the new structures. There are also 11 executive suites. San Marcus has set aside some 30,000 square feet of function space for meeting and convention groups.

The three restaurants on the grounds include the 1912 Room, the Cafe, and Mulligan's Clubhouse Grill. During the evening you may want to visit the historic piano bar or perhaps dance a bit in the lounge.

Among the activities are tennis on lighted courts, swimming, a whirlpool, horseback riding, jogging, bicycling and use of an on-site fitness center.

The golf course, which recently underwent a complete renovation, measures 6,450/6,117/5,371 yards and pars at 72. While not heavily trapped, there is more than enough sand and, as usual, it seem to be in the wrong place. Water, coming into play in the form of three ponds and a canal on eight holes, is also a factor. All in all it is a fun layout to play.

RATES   (EP)   Rooms: $160/$200. Executive Suites: $260. Suites: $425. Green fees: $40/$55, including cart.

ARRIVAL Air: Sky Harbor International. Car: off I-10 onto Chandler Blvd. Travel east to intersection of Chandler Blvd. and Arizona Avenue.

SHERATON TUCSON EL CONQUISTADOR
10000 North Oracle Road, Tucson, AZ 85704; (602) 742-7000; (800) 325-3535

The El Conquistador architecture blends well into the locale. The 440 rooms, suites and casitas are done in a Western Spanish architectural motif, which is both impressive and beautiful. Their meeting facilities are also impressive, with rooms for groups from 10 to 1,200.

Dining is available in the White Dove, specializing in continental cuisine; the Last Territory, presenting Western fare; and the Sundance Cafe for breakfast, lunch or dinner.

They have not forgotten thirsty golfers either, as there are three cocktail lounges.

There are 16 lighted tennis courts with a pro shop and tennis professionals available to assist. In addition, there are four racquetball courts, a health club with a full spa program, a swimming pool and riding stables. With their 40 horse stables, the resort is able to set up trail rides, breakfast or dinner affairs, along with hayrides.

Golf can be played on 27 holes: the El Conquistador nine, a par three affair contiguous to the hotel, and the Canada Hills Country Club course, located nearby. The Club layout plays 6,698/6,215/5,316 yards and pars at 72. Bite off what you think you can handle. While relatively open, it is a fun course and a demanding one. The PGA professional is Carl Dalpiaz.

RATES   (EP)   Rooms: $250/$285. Casitas: $280 and up. Green fees: $75, including cart. Golf packages available. Rates are for January-May.

ARRIVAL Air: Tucson. Car: I-10 north, off at Miracle, then east to Oracle Road, then north.

TUBAC GOLF RESORT

P.O.Box 1297, Tubac, AZ 85646; (602) 398-2211; (800) 848-7893

The Inn is sited on the original Otero Spanish land grant in the lush Santa Cruz Valley. Just 25 miles from the Mexican border, it is surrounded by the Santa Rita range to the east and the Tumacacories to the west. Accommodations consist of Casitas (little houses), featuring a wood burning fireplace, a bedroom, and living room. Some have a full kitchen. The Villas have two bedrooms, two baths, living room, and kitchen. The full Villas, by the way, are handled by a local real-estate firm – (602) 398-2701.

The Otero and Santa Cruz Dining Rooms are well known throughout the area, for their food and service. The Founders Room is now primarily used for meeting groups.

There is a tennis court, a large swimming pool and horseback riding. Tours of the general area, as well as into "Old Mexico," can also be arranged.

The Santa Cruz River forms the main challenge of this golf course bringing water into the action on five holes. The trees and many traps also tend to keep your attention. Reaching out a strong 6,957/6,408/5,847/5,504 yards, it pars at 72/71. The LPGA professional is Joanne Lusk.

RATES (EP) Posadas: $98. Casitas: with kitchenettes $137. Weekly/monthly rates and golf packages are available. Green fees: $26, including carts. Rates are mid-December to April 30th.

ARRIVAL Air: Tucson or Nogales. Car: south from Tucson on Highway 19, off at exit 34.

THE TUCSON NATIONAL RESORT & SPA

2727 West Club Drive, Tucson, AZ 85741; (602) 297-2271; (800) 528-4856

Located on 650 acres of high chaparral desert, the Tucson National is architecturally distinctive. Its outward appearance is one of quiet formality.

Accommodations are 51 casita rooms, 116 villas and a townhouse – all with private patios or balconies, wet bars and refrigerators. 27 of the Executive Casitas have a living room, bedroom and a kitchen. Some of the accommodations are poolside while others are golf course oriented. Dining is provided in the casual setting of the Fiesta.

A few years back the Tucson National underwent a major renovation – with the addition of a second swimming pool, 79 poolside rooms, more villa suites, and a new 18,000-square-foot convention center allowing them to handle larger group affairs.

There are few spas in the world that can offer the variety of services available at the National, with deluxe massage, facials, herbal wraps, and special therapy.

Golf is played on 27 holes – the Gold, Orange and the Green nines. When inter-joined to form 18 holes, you have Orange/Gold at 7,108/6,549/5,764 yards with a par of 72/73. The Green/Orange combination weighs in at a yardage of 6,692/6,215/5,428, parring at 72. The Gold/Green nines play 6,860/6,388/5,502 and par at 72/73. Water hazards, bunkers and slightly undulating terrain make them all interesting as well as challenging affairs.

RATES *(EP) Lodging:*

$175 / $205. Green fees: $80, including carts. Rates are for January-May 15.

ARRIVAL *Air: Tucson (30 to 45 minutes). Car: route I-10 to Cortaro exit, travel 3.5 miles and you are there.*

VENTANA CANYON GOLF & RACQUET CLUB
6200 N. Clubhouse Lane, Tucson, AZ 85715; (602) 577-1400; (800) 828-5701

This 1,100-acre property north of Tucson is set high in the Sonoran Desert and uses the Santa Catalina Mountains as a spectacular backdrop. The resort offers 48 club suites within the clubhouse. Each of the one- or two-bedroom units – which, by the way, range from 800 to 1500 square feet – features a fully-equipped kitchen and a living/dining area.

The two restaurants in the clubhouse are the Terrace Lounge for casual dining and the Main Dining Room, serving continental cuisine. The resort can also handle small conference or management groups. They have a capacity for 45 classroom-, 75 theater- and 144 banquet-style.

There is tennis on 12 lighted all-weather courts, a 25-meter swimming pool, aerobic and exercise facilities, along with saunas, steam and whirlpool baths. Trained professionals are available to assist with each activity.

Two excellent golf courses await you. The Ventana Canyon Golf & Racquet Club course, a Tom Fazio design (referred to as the Mountain course), reaches out a substantial 6,959/6,356/5,671/4,825 yards and pars at 72. While water only comes into play on two holes, the desert terrain, complete with a tremendous number of cactus plants and trees, plus a profusion of traps, more than makes up for the water oversight. I would particularly like to warn you about hole number three. This is a par-three playing a short 104 yards, with the green at least 70 feet below your feet. It is easy to misjudge distance – and to do so can be lead to disaster .

The Canyon Course is also a Fazio design. A bit more modest in yardage it measures 6,818/6,282/5,756/4,919 yards and also pars at 72. Again water becomes a factor on only two holes but the cactus and traps can do a number on you.

Something that becomes a problem on both courses is the fact that there is really no rough. Should you stray off that beautiful green stuff you will come into contact with raw desert – rocks, sand, cactus, frustration.

RATES (EP) Club suites: 1-bedroom $265. Two-bedrooms: $369. Canyon suites: 1-bedroom $285. Ventana suites: two-bedrooms $390. Green fees: $89, including cart. Golf package: 2 nights / 3 days (includes lodging in club suite, 3 rounds of golf with cart, bag storage, unlimited practice balls), $935 per couple.

ARRIVAL Air: Tucson International Airport.

THE WESTIN LA PALOMA
3800 East Sunrise, Tucson, AZ 85718; (602) 742-6000; (800) 876-3683

The Westin La Paloma has been judged one of the top 50 resorts . It is part of a 792-acre development in Tucson's exclusive Catalina Foothills area.

The hotel, consisting of 487 guest rooms (including 40 suites) arranged in a village-style setting, has used South-

western-theme furnishings which complement the architecture and suggest a relaxing "oasis in the desert."

No one will want for food at this resort. You may choose from: The Desert Garden, the resort's main dining room with seating indoors or out; La Villa, specializing in seafood; "The Court Side Deli," for those who go the health food way; Sabinos, for poolside hamburgers; and the Cactus Club, La Paloma's high energy lounge for dancing. In the 35,000-square-foot golf clubhouse, you will find another restaurant and, of course, a lounge. If that is not enough there is also room service.

The meeting facilities are large enough to match the resort. Consisting of 42,000 square feet, separate breakout rooms and two large ballrooms, they are more than capable of handling groups of 20 to 2,000.

Recreational options include: 12 tennis courts (10 lighted), along with a tennis clubhouse, two racquetball courts, two swimming pools, one with a swim-up bar, spas, a fully equipped health club, jogging and cycling trails.

The Westin La Paloma Country Club's 27-hole golf course is a Jack Nicklaus Signature layout. While this is, to be sure, a resort course, it is also a championship caliber layout. As

Jack Nicklaus predicted during construction, it is "one heck-and-a-half" of a golf course. I can go along with that description. The 27 holes, when played in combination, are as follows. The Hill/Ridge nines reach out 7,017/6,464/5,984/4,878. The combination of the Ridge/Canyon nines plays an awesome7,088/6,635/6,011/5,125 yards. The final combination of the Canyon and Hill nines weighs in at 6,997/6,453/5,955/5,057 yards. Each pars at 72.

The various tee placements – on some holes there are as many as five different teeing areas – allow you to take on whatever you feel you can handle and, in some cases, offer a variation of from 80 to 100 yards per hole. For tee times call (800) 222-1249. The Director of Golf is Scott McGeachin.

Something different: they can provide a "Forecaddie" who stays with you throughout your round. He can save his weight in golf balls and you no small amount of frustration, by directing you away from many of the hazards, some of which are not readily visible.

RATES   (EP)   Rooms: $285/$340. Suites: $350 and up. Green fees: $85, including cart. *Golf package: 2 nights/2 days (includes lodging, 2 rounds of golf, cart, and a caddy), $620 per couple. There is also a 1 day/1 night package.*

ARRIVAL Air: Tucson. Car: 10 miles north of Tucson's business district and 17 miles from Tucson.

THE WIGWAM RESORT

300 Indian School Lane, Litchfield Park, AZ 85340; (602) 935-3811; (800) 327-0396

The Wigwam Resort has been judged one of the top 50 resorts. Since they seem to do everything right, it is difficult to describe this place without sounding like a paid advertisement. The fact that this magnificent destination resort has also earned the Mobil Five Star Award should come as no surprise. An indication of what you will find here: the property comprises 475 acres of manicured lawns and flower beds.

It is true that the Wigwam dates back to 1918-19 (coming into being as a resort in 1929). But, then, many resorts have operated for a lot longer. Any way you care to measure it, the Wigwam must be considered one of the best in the country. Lodgings now are in 331 rooms, suites or casitas located either near the pool, tennis, golf course, or gardens.

The centrally located Main Lodge houses the new and lovely Terrace Dining Room, lounge and private rooms available for all manner of social functions. A new addition is the Arizona Kitchen restaurant. While ties are required in the Terrace Room, the Kitchen restaurant is less formal. There is also the Grill on the Greens, located in the clubhouse. The resort's new meeting facilities arefirst rate. Now with 23,000 square feet of space they can handle groups of from 10 to 1,000.

Adjacent to the Lodge is a patio and large swimming pool – a delightful place for luncheon, a small libation or perhaps just to relax. While there are gift shops within the Lodge, the Village two blocks away has a number of interesting retail shops. There are 10 night tennis courts (six lighted), with a professional staff to assist, four practice alleys with ball machines and a separate tennis shop. Another new addition is the stadium court allowing spectator-attended tournaments. Other activities include: horseback riding and hayrides (from their own stables), a complete health club providing a massage facility and offering the use of exercise rooms, sauna, and whirlpool. You can also try your hand at skeet and trap shooting. Bicycles, ping pong tables, and shuffleboard are all available on a complimentary basis. A second swimming pool has been added adjacent to the newly constructed casitas.

There are three golf courses. The Gold Course stretches out 7,047/6,504/5,567 yards and pars at 72. The West Course, also with a par of 72, reaches out 6,865/6,307/5,808 yards. The Blue Course plays 5,960/5,178 yards and pars at 70. The Gold and Blue courses are Robert Trent Jones, Sr. designs, while the West course was designed by the late Robert Lawrence. Rated among the top 100 golf courses in the United States, the Gold layout is something else. Gleaming white sand traps, brilliant lakes (beautiful if you can avoid them), and huge greens add to the challenge.

The West Course brings into play a wandering stream and five lakes to keep your attention. The Blue layout offers well bunkered fairways and large greens, characteristic of Trent Jones, to spice up the action.

The Wigwam recently spent a considerable amount of money on the courses, putting in all new cart paths, cleaning out and redoing all the streams and water hazards and installing pumps to keep the water flowing. The Director of Golf is Keith Kalney and the Head Professional is Graig Allen.

The John Jacobs' Practical Golf School is available at this resort. Using personalized, proven teaching methods, and under the direction of PGA and LPGA teaching professionals, it is well worth looking into. For complete details, call (800) 472-5007.

RATES   (EP)   Rooms: $250/$280. 1-bedroom suite: $400 per couple. Green fees: Gold Course $85, including cart; the West and Blue courses $80, including cart. Golf package: 1 night/1 day (includes lodging, green fees, cart and club storage), $370/$395/$500 per couple. Rates shown are January to mid -May.

ARRIVAL Air: Phoenix Sky Harbor Airport (25 miles). Pick up can be arranged. Private aircraft: Phoenix/Litchfield Municipal Airport (3 miles away, an 8,600-foot paved runway). Car: 15 miles west of Phoenix on Glendale Boulevard, then south on Litchfield Road. Traveling on I-10 take Litchfield Road exit. Travel north to Indian School Road and turn east to resort.

Arkansas

1. Dawn Hill Golf & Raquet Club
2. Fairfield Bay Resort
3. The Red Apple Inn &
   Country Club
4. The Arlington Resort Hotel
   & Spa
   Hot Springs Village
   The Majestic Hotel
5. DeGray State Park

THE ARLINGTON RESORT HOTEL & SPA

Hot Springs National Park, AR 71901, (501) 623-7771; (800) 643-1502 Arlington Hotel; (800) 643-1504 Majestic Hotel

This is a resort complex consisting of two hotels – The Arlington and the Majestic. Although dating back to the 1870's, the present structure came into being in December of 1924. Over the years many changes have come about. The Board Room was added to accommodate television. For many years "Natural Ventilation" (open the window for Heaven's sakes) was the way it was done. Now of course the hotels are air-conditioned. The building of a six-story tower (completed in 1966), installation of three new elevators in 1969, and the new Conference Center, have all helped to bring the Arlington's two-hotel complex into the 20th century.

The Arlington has 488 guest rooms, including suites. The Majestic has 310 rooms. The dining facilities, located at the Arlington, consist of the Fountain Room, Venetian Room and the Captain's Tavern (the coffee shop). You can partake of evening entertainment or a libation in either the Lobby Bar or the Silk Saddle Lounge. The Majestic offers dining in the H. Grady Dining Room and, for a more casual experience, Grady's Grill.

Both the Majestic and the Arlington have excellent meeting rooms. The Arlington, with its 10,000-square-foot ballroom, can handle groups up to 900. The Majestic has approximately 4,900 feet of space set aside for group affairs and can handle up to 300.

The hotels have long been known for their thermal mineral baths and massages. You should not leave without trying a massage or the whirlpool baths (which, by the way, are maintained at body temperature).

Tennis is played on eight courts (four lighted) complete with tennis shop and resident professionals to offer assistance. Swimming pools, sun decks, jogging paths, exercise rooms, game rooms and racquetball are just a few of the activities available. emember, you are within a large National Park area with several lakes, including the Ouachita and Lake Hamilton, just begging to be fished.

The two courses are: the Arlington, reaching out 6,646/6,393/6,206 yards, parring at 72/74; and the Majestic, parring at 72, and playing 6,667/6,286/5,541 yards. There is also a 9-hole, par-three layout, measuring 2,929/2,717 yards.

RATES (EP) *Arlington Rooms: $68/$88. Mineral Water Rooms: $90/$125. Suites:* $250/$350. (EP) Majestic Rooms: $43/$70. Green fees: $24, carts $20. Golf package: 2 nights/2 days (includes lodging, 2 rounds of golf with cart), $218 per couple. Rates are mid-April through November.

ARRIVAL Air: Little Rock (53 miles). Private aircraft: Hot Springs Airport. Car: from Little Rock take I-30, connecting with State Highway 70 west. Turn north on Highway 7 and continue past Bath House Row to the resort.

DAWN HILL GOLF & RACQUET CLUB
P.O. Box 1289, Siloam Springs, AR 72761; (501) 524-5217; (800) 423-3786

Nestled among 715 acres of tall woods, rolling hills and lush meadows, this resort was planned and designed with relaxation in mind. Accommodations consist of two- to three-bedroom townhouse clusters, featuring natural stone fireplaces, loft bedrooms and fully equipped kitchens. There are also some private homes available. If you decide to dine out, there is a restaurant with a cocktail lounge for dancing.

Activities include: tennis on

four lighted courts, along with racquetball courts. Golf is played on the Dawn Hill Golf Course. Reaching out 6,768/6,434/5,307 yards, it pars at 72. It is an open layout with little water coming into play. There is a pro shop, lounge, restaurant and swimming pool to support the golf course.

RATES (EP) Townhouses: $110/$130. Green fees: $16/$18; carts $17. Golf packages are available for four people or more.

ARRIVAL Air: Siloam Springs (6 miles). Car: Route 68 near the Oklahoma border.

DeGRAY STATE PARK
Box 375, Arkadelphia, AR 71923; (501) 865-4591; (800) 633-3128

DeGray Lodge, and its convention center, is on Lake DeGray, within an hour's drive of Little Rock. It is also about 30 minutes from Hot Springs. The Lodge, a rustic 96-room wilderness structure fashioned from redwood and stone, rises magnificently from an island on beautiful DeGray Lake. While it may be "rustic," the amenities are quite modern. The re-

sort features an excellent restaurant, along with a 10,000-square-foot convention center for meeting and convention groups of up to 500 people.

The park has full camping facilities, along with tennis courts, a swimming pool and a 110-boat marina (boats and motors are available to rent). The lake, which covers some 13,500 acres, offers excellent fishing.

Golf is played on the DeGray State Park Golf Course. Weighing in at a pretty fair 6,930/6,417/5,731 yards, it carries a par of 72. Water comes into play on eight holes.

RATES (EP) Rooms: $55/$65. Green fees: $12, carts $15.

ARRIVAL Air: Hot Springs (21 miles). Private aircraft: Arkadelphia (11 miles). Car: I-30 exit to Highway 7, northwest 6 miles.

FAIRFIELD BAY RESORT
P.O. Box 3008
Fairfield Bay, AR 72088
(501) 884-3333

Fairfield Bay Resorts is in the foothills of the Ozarks. It was built north of Little Rock, and is set on the northwestern shore of Greers Ferry Lake.

Accommodations are in 350 bedrooms, suites, villas and condominiums. The villas and condos are equipped for house-keeping.

The heart of the resort is the conference center. This 14,000-square-foot meeting facility can handle groups of up to 400. It also happens to be the location of the indoor pool, health club, racquet club, lounges and restaurants. Less formal dining is available in the newly opened Village Cafe.

This is a large layout. In fact it is a year-round community, complete with a medical center, a fire station, several churches as well as riding stables with horses available for all levels of experience. There is also a youth recreation center, a marina (180 boat slips), a beach area, two swimming pools and two golf courses.

Tennis is available on 10 courts (four lighted), with a professional staff on deck. The tennis complex, by the way, has been rated one of the top 50 in the U.S.

The Mountain Ranch golf course plays 6,780/6,280/5,760/

5,325 yards and pars at 72. Showing tree-lined fairways, with water coming into play on only two holes, it is a nice change from the "Pacific Ocean" type. The Indian Hills Country Club layout, parring at 71, weighs in at 6,437/5,727/4,901 yards. On this course water is a bit more of a challenge with seven holes involved. We understand that the Indian Hills golf course is now restricted to member play only.

RATES (EP) Rooms: $75. Suites: 1-bedroom $155. 2-bedroom villas: $230. Green fees: $30, carts $20. Golf packages are available.

ARRIVAL Air: Little Rock. Car: 80 miles north of Little Rock. Entrance on Highway 16 west of Highway 65.

HOT SPRINGS VILLAGE
Box 5 DeSoto Center, Hot Springs Village, AR 71909; (501) 922-0303; (800) 643-1000

Hot Springs Village, 16 miles north of Hot Springs, is a large recreational community. Accommodations consist of town-houses or homes, fully equipped for housekeeping, which may be rented by the day, the week or month. Some have fireplaces and some are equipped with washer and dryer.

Within the village itself there are many activities: tennis on 11 courts, two recreational centers with swimming pools and game rooms, and a clubhouse. There is also a marina, with boat docking facilities, on Lake DeSoto. The Coronado Community Center also provides various social activities including square dancing.

I have only touched on the possible activities at your disposal. For example, within nine to 44 miles there are four lakes with over 2,200 miles of shoreline, providing all manner of water sports action.

There are several excellent restaurants on the property: the Village Bakery and Sandwich Shop, Mary Lee's Restaurant, the DeSoto Clubhouse and Lounge, the 19th Hole and the Wood-N-Iron Restaurant. There are many more in the general area. Also within the village are a grocery store, service station, gift shops, beauty shops, and a laundromat.

Golf is offered up on four 18-hole courses: the DeSoto, The Cortez, The Coronado and the newer Balboa. Three are full 18-hole championship courses, while the Coronado is an executive affair. Each has a pro shop and full facilities. Within a few miles are a total of eight other courses.

RATES (EP) Townhouses: $65/$115. Monthly: peak season $675 and up. Green fees: $25, carts $20. Excellent monthly golf rates are also available.

ARRIVAL Air: Hot Springs. Car: Highway 7, approximately 21 miles northeast of Hot Springs.

THE RED APPLE INN & COUNTRY CLUB
Eden Isle, Heber Springs, AR 72543; (501) 362-3111; (800) 255-8900

Nestled in the rolling hills of Arkansas and surrounded by 35,000-acre Greers Ferry Lake, the Red Apple Inn is one of the better resorts. Muted and handsome, sprinkled with works of art, fireplaces, patios, fountains and tapestries, it is a delightful place.

The rooms and suites, which offer views of the lake, are appointed with hand-carved furniture from Italy and Spain. There are also one- to three-bedroom condominium suites, each featuring a fireplace, living room and dining room, a fully equipped kitchen and a private deck or patio. The Red Apple is ideal for meeting groups and has an entire wing set aside for this purpose.

A Spanish gate, retrieved from an ancient castle, welcomes you to the "After Five Room" for cocktails. After dining here and experiencing this touch of French cuisine with a southern accent, you will understand why they have earned the Mobil Four Star Award. Now that they have installed a second dining room, served from the same kitchen, you can choose either the formal room (tie and jacket required) or the less formal area.

The Red Apple Inn has its own marina and offers water skiing, sailing (with professional sailing instructions available) as well as lake swimming. They also have Party Barges (24 feet with a capacity of 12). Tennis on five courts (three lighted), two swimming pools and fishing are a few of the other sporting activities available.

Golf is played on the Red Apple

Country Club's own course. Stretching out to 6,431/6,006/5,137 yards and parring at 71, it brings water into five holes on the front nine. Architect Gary Parks blended the rolling terrain and tree-lined fairways to create an interesting layout. The pro shop, under the direction of professional Mark Brugner, is well stocked.

RATES (EP) Inn rooms: $75/$95. Villa suites: 1 bedroom $105. 2 bedrooms: $125/$145. Green fees: $25, carts $18. Rates are for April-October.

ARRIVAL Air: Little Rock. Private aircraft: Herber Springs Airport (3 miles). Car: Highway 65 to intersection of Highway 25 – turn right on 25.

California

Northern California

1. Lake Shastina Golf Resort
2. Northstar at Tahoe
   Tahoe Donner Golf
   & Country Club
3. Resort at Squaw Creek
4. Rancho Murieta
5. Bodega Bay Lodge
   The Inn at the Tides
6. Double Tree Hotel
7. Sonoma Mission Inn
8. Clarion Inn Napa Valley
9. Half Moon Bay Lodge
10. Boulder Creek Lodge
11. Pasatiempo Inn
12. Ridgemark
13. Carmel Valley Ranch Resort
    Hyatt Regency Monterey
    The Inn & Links
    at Spanish Bay
    The Lodge at Pebble Beach
14. Furnace Creek Inn
    & Ranch Resort

BODEGA BAY - SONOMA COASTAL AREA

The history of this coastal area goes back a long way: claimed by Sir Frances Drake in 1579, by Juan Francisco de la Bodega in 1775, later by Russia, eventually becoming a U.S. Territory (1846), it is a world apart. A marsh seaside area, teeming with birds and wildflowers, it is one of the few peaceful, laid back places left in this extremely busy state.

Some 68 miles north of San Francisco on the spectacular Sonoma coast, Bodega Bay offers a variety of activities. There are many outstanding places to eat as well as a number of wineries to visit. Rather than golfing, one could spend days visiting the historic buildings and villages (most of which have been restored) and, of course, the art galleries and antique stores. Along with whale watching, one of the more delightful activities is to watch the many fishing boats unloading their catch.

The Bodega Harbour Golf Links was created by Robert Trent Jones, Jr. While there are virtually no trees coming into play, this oversight was more than remedied by the use of 58 pot bunkers on the first nine and 38 on the back side. By using undulating terrain, multi-level greens and the prevailing winds off the ocean, Mr. Jones introduced some unique challenges. All in all this course is one of the most fun layouts we have experienced in California. Parring at 70/71 it reaches out a modest 6,220/5,630/4,833 yards. For tee times call (707) 875-3538.

Accommodations are available in two hotels. Each is close by and each has golf packages. Details on the Bodega Bay Lodge and The Inn at the Tides are listed below.

BODEGA BAY LODGE
103 Coast Highway 1, Bodega Bay, CA 94923; (707) 875-3525; (800) 368-2468, Ext 5

Accommodations consist of 78 rooms, most with a fireplace, vaulted ceilings, wine cooler/refrigerators, a wet bar, and wicker and oak furnishings. Each room is also equipped with cable TV, including HBO, as well as a selection of in-room movies, and has a private balcony or patio offering a view of the bay.

Dining is available in the Ocean Club Restaurant. The Lodge can accommodate modest-sized meeting groups of up to 65 classroom- and 75 theater-style.

There is a glass-walled whirlpool spa, a swimming pool, sauna, and an exercise room. Located nearby are facilities for deep sea fishing, whale watching (in season). There are also bicycle trips, beachcombing and, of course, golf. For details on the nearby golf course refer to the foregoing text on the Bodega Bay - Sonoma Coastal Area.

RATES   (EP)   Rooms: $108/$158. Suites $188. Green fees: $35/$53; carts $24. Golf package: 1 night/1 day (includes lodging, one round of golf per person, continental breakfast), midweek $198. Weekend package also includes a five-course dinner for two at a cost of $338.

ARRIVAL Air: San Francisco International Airport (2 hours), or Santa Rosa Airport (35 minutes). Car: from San Francisco cross the Golden Gate Bridge (Highway 101) and drive to Petaluma. Drive west on East Washington/Bodega Avenue which turns into Highway 1. You can also pick up Highway 1 a few miles north of the Golden Gate Bridge and drive to Bodega Bay. While beautiful, we do not recommend this route. It is a most difficult winding road.

THE INN AT THE TIDES

800 Coast Highway 1, Bodega Bay, CA 94923; (707) 875-2751; (800) 541-7788

Situated on a hill overlooking Bodega Bay, the Inn has spectacular views of the harbor. In fact, one of the more intriguing activities is watching the fishing fleet moving about this busy harbor. Accommodations are in 86 rooms, each equipped with a small refrigerator, coffee maker and TV. Each unit features a woodburning fireplace. The resort suggests they are to be used on a mournful fog shrouded night or perhaps on a lazy afternoon curled up with a good book. The Tides welcomes modest-size meeting groups. While they prefer groups of from 20 to 30 they are capable of handling up to 65 classroom- and 75 theater-style.

The Bayview Restaurant offers a wide variety of dishes, but highlights fresh seafood. They also have an excellent wine list. Most of the food, particularly, fresh fruit, vegetables and eggs, comes from nearby local farms. There is, of course, a cocktail lounge. Room service is also an alternative. There is a complimentary continental breakfast served each morning at the Inn.

Directly across the highway from the entrance to the Inn is the Tides Wharf & Restaurant. Open for all three meals, the Wharf features all types of seafood specialties and is supported by a cocktail lounge.

There is an indoor/outdoor swimming pool, a sauna and whirlpool and, of course, beachcombing along this fabulous stretch of coast.

For details on the golf course refer to The Bodega Bay – Sonoma Coastal Area.

RATES   (EP)   Rooms: $105/$130.   Weekends: $130/$160.   Green fees: $35/$53, carts $24. Golf package: 1 night/1 day (includes lodging, 18 hole per person, continental breakfast), $140 per couple. Rates are for June through September.

ARRIVAL Air: San Francisco (2 hours) or Santa Rosa (40 minutes). Car: from San Francisco – cross the Golden Gate

Bridge (Highway 101). Continue to Petaluma. Take E. Washington Street/Bodega Avenue west. It turns into Highway 1. You can also pick up Highway 1 a bit north of the Golden Gate Bridge. While scenic, it is a narrow, winding road and a slow way to go.

THE MONTEREY PENINSULA AREA

Monterey played a significant role during the early days of Spanish influence. Today, Monterey, Pacific Grove, Carmel and Carmel Valley represent a virtual treasure box of intriguing shops, along with restaurants which can utterly destroy your will to remain slim. There are a seemingly infinite number of art galleries, photographic studios, antique shops and on and on. You could spend several months, perhaps even years, visiting each of these places and I doubt, even then, you could see all of them. Many of the items are made right there by the many talented local artists.

But then not everyone likes to shop. So how about a visit to Monterey's museums of history, literature (including the John Steinbeck Library) and

art. If that will not do it, then I would suggest a visit to the exciting Monterey Aquarium or to any of several wineries. If music is your thing why not visit The Carmel Bach Festival, the Monterey Symphony, the Chamber Music Society, the Monterey Jazz Festival or the Monterey Mozart Festival. And you should not miss the famous Carmel Mission.

If none of the above activities appeal to you – then consider sailing in the magnificent Monterey Bay, hot air ballooning over the area's vineyards, or a helicopter tour over Big Sur and the entire Peninsula. There is also, of course, Steinbeck's Cannery Row, Fisherman's Wharf, whale watching, and all manner of fishing, as well as the beaches of fabled Carmel-by-the-Sea.

I have saved the best for the last – a drive along the enchanting 17-Mile Drive, the beach area of Carmel, the white sand, the deer so sure of themselves they almost come to you – the quail, ducks, and the rabbits, and the overwhelming Pacific Ocean.

Within this area and adding to its magic are five fabulous resorts – the Carmel Valley Ranch, the Hyatt Regency

Monterey, the Inn & Links at Spanish Bay, the Lodge at Pebble Beach, and the Quail Lodge.

CARMEL VALLEY RANCH RESORT
One Old Ranch Road, Carmel, CA 93923; (408) 625-9500; (800) 422-7635

Carmel Valley Ranch has been judged one of the top 50 resorts. On 1,700 acres in the scenic Carmel Valley, the entire complex is nestled high above the clubhouse and the front nine of the golf course. The builders and architects should win an award for the manner in which the Lodge and the various buildings were sited. By careful planning they were able to take advantage of some of the most beautiful old oak trees we have seen.

Comprising 100 luxurious suites, as well as a beautiful main lodge, the resort has many amenities to offer its guests. The suites, built in clusters of four to five, range in size from 810 to a little over 1,200 square feet. They feature fully stocked wet bars (including refrigerators with ice makers). Each also provides a living room, a wood burning

fireplace, cathedral ceilings throughout, and private decks with views of the mountains, fairways and the valley. Many of the units also have a fireplace in the bedrooms. Eight of the one-bedroom suites include a private outdoor spa.

This is one of the few resorts on the Monterey Peninsula with a 24-hour guarded security entrance. Although I may have described some other resorts as having outstanding accommodations, the Carmel Valley Ranch lodgings are second to none.

A section of the lodge has been set aside to handle conference and/or social gatherings including a Grand Ballroom of 3,278 square feet.

The Dining Room, as well as the Lounge, are in contemporary ranch style architecture. Well worth seeing are the many artifacts and antiques on display around the lodge.

The Golf Clubhouse, with its view of the front nine, is available for breakfast, lunch and afternoon cocktails.

The tennis program (12 courts) is supported by a pro shop as well as a professional staff. A few of the other options include a free-form swimming pool, four spas and, of course, the golf course.

A Pete Dye design, the Carmel Valley Ranch course plays 6,515/6,055/5,582/5,088 yards with a par of 70. A typical Dye layout, it has small greens, some surrounded by sand traps with railroad ties forming a border. There are also three man-made lakes and the Carmel River which runs alongside four additional fairways.

While the front nine is fun, yet challenging, the back side can destroy you. The 10th hole, although tough, is fair. Holes 11 through 14 are something else. Some even call them "Mickey Mouse." I guarantee, you will never forget them. When you have finally passed these monsters and, provided you still want to play this game, you will find the back nine excellent. The course takes full advantage of the elevation changes as well as the rolling terrain of the area. The one adjective you won't use to describe the Ranch Course is "easy."

Located within the clubhouse is the pro shop, restaurant, a bar, and locker rooms. The golf facilities are under the direction of PGA Professional, Ted Goin.

RATES (EP) 1-Bedroom suites: $235/$255. Spa suites: $385. Master suites: $650/$675. Green fees: $80, including cart.

ARRIVAL Air: Monterey. Car: take U.S Highway 1 just past (south) the turn-off to Carmel and take a left (east) onto Carmel Valley Road. Continue approximately 7 miles. You must exit to the right onto Robinson Canyon Road. This turn-off is difficult to find. The road is just beyond the shopping center which will be on your right.

HYATT REGENCY MONTEREY
One Old Golf Course Road, Monterey, CA 93940; (408) 372-1234; (800) 233-1234

The setting of the hotel, surrounded by cypress, pine and gnarled oaks is one of the loveliest we have seen. Including suites, the Hyatt Regency Monterey offers 575 guest accommodations, some quite lavish. Although you are in "Steinbeck Country" where superb food is commonplace, the Peninsula Restaurant at the hotel more than holds its own. There are two swimming pools and six tennis courts to enjoy. The hotel is capable of handling meeting or convention groups of from 20 to 900.

As a guest of the Hyatt, you have preferred tee times and golf rates at Del Monte Golf Course or arrangements can be made at several other courses including Pebble Beach or Spyglass. The "Old Del Monte" layout has been around since 1897 and has hosted such famous players as Vardon, Hagen, Hogan and Bobby Jones. Playing 6,278/6,007/5,431 yards it pars at 72/74. It is heavily tree-lined and one of the most beautiful in the area.

RATES (EP) Rooms: $165/ $200. Suites: $275/$550. Green fees: $37, carts $24. The Hyatt does offer special room rates from time to time. Be sure to check.

ARRIVAL Air: Monterey. Car: from the north take Pacific Grove exit from Highway 1. Travel on Del Monte Road to Sloat Avenue, turn left, continue to entrance of the Hyatt Regency Monterey.

THE INN & LINKS AT SPANISH BAY
17 Mile Drive, Pebble Beach, CA 93953; (408) 647-7500;

(800) 654-9300

The architects of the Inn, which opened in early 1988 took full advantage of the outstanding vista offered by the rolling Pacific Ocean, the manicured golf course and the incomparable 17-Mile Drive.

Lodgings in this beautiful hotel consist of 270 rooms including 16 suites. Each has a gas burning fireplace as well as a mini-bar. All accommodations feature a deck or balcony providing views of the grounds, the forest or the ocean. In addition, there are 80 privately owned condominiums located a bit north of the clubhouse. With their meeting and conference facilities (14,000 square feet) they are capable of handling groups of up to 550 in a classroom configuration.

There are three dining rooms ranging from the rather formal Bay Club to the more casual Dunes Restaurant. The Clubhouse Bar & Grill is also available. As one might well expect the food as well as the service is excellent. Evening entertainment, accompanied by a libation, can be found in Traps or the Lobby Lounge.

The Inn has a spa, eight tennis courts (two lighted), supported by a tennis shop and a professional staff, a lap swimming pool, saunas and steam rooms.

Combining their talents, designers Robert Trent Jones, Jr., Tom Watson and Frank "Sandy" Tatum used the narrow, rolling fairways, large sand dunes and, with the help of restored coastal marshes, created a distinctly Scottish type golf course. The natural beauty of the area also added a dimension which could not be duplicated, providing sweeping views of the Pacific Ocean and the rolling terrain of white sand.

The Links is positioned directly along the ocean with a portion of the famous 17-Mile Drive passing through. It is not unusual to have cars stop to watch your tee shot. One point – if you enjoy strong breezes, and I mean constant wind, you will fall in love with this layout. The course plays 6,820/6,078/5,287 yards, parring at 72. The impressive new clubhouse accommodates the pro shop, locker rooms, a restaurant, bar and health club. The Head PGA Professional is Rich Cosand; the Vice President of Golf Operations is Paul Spengler.

If you are a guest of The Inn,

rounds of golf can be arranged at Pebble Beach, Spyglass Hill and Del Monte golf courses.

RATES (EP) Standard view: $230. Forest view: $275. Ocean view: $335. Suites: $500 and up. Green fees: $100 (includes cart). Guests of Spanish Bay Inn also have access to golf at Pebble Beach ($150) and Spyglass Hill ($100). Del Monte green fees are $37, plus cart at $24 (cart is optional at Del Monte). The green fees for The Links, Pebble and Spyglass include carts, which are mandatory.

ARRIVAL Air: Monterey. Car: enter the 17 Mile Drive at the Pacific Grove entrance.

THE LODGE AT PEBBLE BEACH
17 Mile Drive, Pebble Beach, CA 93953; (408) 624-3811; (800) 654-9300

The Lodge at Pebble Beach has been judged one of the top 50 resorts. Many things have contributed to the mystique of The Lodge: perhaps it is the location on the incomparable 17 Mile Drive, the view of the famous "Lone Cypress" reputed to be between 200 and 300 years old, the occasional mist and sound of a distant foghorn,

the murmur of the surf, the quiet solitude, the nostalgia of the "Crosby Tournament." Or it may be the extraordinary list of famous guests who have stayed here. Formerly called The Del Monte Lodge (until 1977), it is everything you may have heard. True, it is somewhat formal, but that too can be a refreshing change of pace. Actually in recent years it has relaxed its formal dress code. In operation since 1919, it has lost none of its charm, or elegance.

Lodgings are in 161 guest rooms, including six one-bedroom suites. Most are located in low rise buildings throughout the resort grounds. All provide a view of the lovely gardens, the seaside fairways, or overlook Carmel Bay. Many feature a brick hearth fireplace stocked with almond wood logs. The Lodge welcomes small conference groups and has 8,000 square feet of space to accommodate such activities.

You may choose to dine in The Cypress Room (jacket required), with its magnificent views of Carmel Bay, or try patio dining at Club XIX (jacket required). Should you prefer something more on the casual side, I recommend a

visit to The Tap Room, where entertainment and casual dining is provided nightly. You may have noticed, a bit of relaxation has crept in – ties are no longer required during the evening hours (thank God, at last). The Gallery overlooking the first tee is open for breakfast and a light lunch. Room service is available at all times throughout the day and night. You are, of course, in the Monterey Peninsula area with a plethora of restaurants and places to be entertained.

The Lodge is on the famous 17- Mile Drive. By all means set aside time to see it. The magnificent homes here may either inspire you or deflate you. The trip by cart around the course, even if only one of you plays, is well worth the time. You can see the exposed back of the houses without the interference of gates and trees. These homes, many built in the heyday of the flamboyant twenties (before income taxes), are truly something to behold.

Other activities include: swimming (an outdoor heated pool as well as the beach), tennis on 14 courts, including a stadium court, two paddle tennis courts, hiking, bicycling, exercise rooms, saunas, massage, steam rooms, aerobics classes, as well as sailing. The equestrian center is considered one of the best, with 34 miles of bridle paths, rings for dressage as well as a regulation polo field.

The fabled Pebble Beach Golf Links plays 6,799/6,357/5,197 yards, parring at 72. Designed by Jack Neville in 1919, it is one of the premier golf layouts in the world. Depending on how the wind changes, it can turn from tough to monstrous. Inasmuch as the Del Monte Forest abounds with deer, it is not at all unusual to have them cross in front of you on the course. Until a few years ago, Pebble Beach was the home of the Bing Crosby Tournament. It is now the location of the AT&T Pebble Beach National. Though it is sponsored by AT&T, and has been for several years, it will always remain the "Crosby." If you have watched any of the presentations on television, further description of this course is redundant. Pebble Beach was selected to host the U.S. Open in 1972, in 1982 and again in 1992. The Head PGA Professional is "R J" Harper; the Vice President of Golf operations is Paul Spengler.

If you are a guest of the Lodge,

Spyglass Hill (one of the most difficult courses around) is also at your disposal. Reaching out 6,810/6,277/5,556 yards, it pars at 72. Rounds can also be arranged at Del Monte (the oldest golf layout west of the Mississippi – circa 1897) and the Links at Spanish Bay. For details see The Hyatt Regency Monterey and The Inn & Links at Spanish Bay.

RATES (EP) Garden view: $280. Ocean view: $350 / $425. Suites: $855 / $1800. Green fees: (for registered guests) Pebble, $150, including cart; Spyglass, $100, including cart; The Links At Spanish Bay, $100, including cart; and Del Monte, $37, cart $24.

ARRIVAL Air: Monterey. Car: U.S. 101 to Carmel. San Francisco (130 miles). Los Angeles (330 miles).

QUAIL LODGE
8205 Valley Greens Drive, Carmel, CA 93923; (408) 624-1581; (800) 538-9516

Quail Lodge has been judged one of the top 50 resorts. It is one of only 21 resorts or hotels out of a total of approximately 20,000 in the United States to have repeatedly attained the Mobil Travel Guide's 5 Star

door hot tubs. Located at the Clubhouse and Lodge, the conference facilities are ideal for groups up to 200. Banquet-style, the maximum capacity is 350.

A definite plus is the location. Situated in the relative shelter of the Carmel Valley, the Lodge remains warm and sunny on many days when Carmel and Monterey are foggy and cold. The vista, spanning 850 acres of the beautiful Carmel Valley and golf club, is one of sparkling lakes, as well as the lush green valley itself.

Award. Once you have been a guest here you will understand why they have been so honored. Not content to remain as is, they have made several changes, including an impressive new entrance to the golf club.

Quail provides a unique choice of lodgings. There are a total of 100 guest accommodations, including 14 suites. The cottage units consist of five rooms, which can be "personalized" to your specific needs: one or two bedrooms plus sitting room, or all five as bedrooms. Each suite has a fireplace, fully stocked bar and refrigerator, a stereo unit with tape deck and, of course, a TV. The Executive Villas also feature private out-

The Covey Restaurant, with its superb selection and quality, plays no small part in the fact that Quail has received the Mobil Five Star Award year after year. Chives, mint, sage, thyme and curry are picked fresh from the chef's courtyard herb garden minutes before the meal is prepared. Or maybe it is the use of Carmel Valley's abundant selection of wild mushrooms and other fresh produce. Whatever it is, what they do with Seafood Paté, Rack of Lamb or Black-currant Duck (and many other entrees), can only be described as wonderful. While the dress code is informal, gentlemen are requested to wear jackets when dining in the Covey. A second restaurant, located in the clubhouse, is also available for breakfast and luncheon.

In addition to golf you may choose to walk these beautiful grounds, swim in either of the two pools, or enjoy a game of tennis with the professionals (four courts). Or forget the rest of the world, at least for a little while, and spend some time in the outdoor hot tub.

The Golf Club at Quail Lodge measures 6,141/5,453 yards with a par of 71. Some of its most delightful distractions are the many deer and birds on the course. At times they appear to be critiquing your swing. But then, perhaps I'm getting too sensitive about my game. The course is supported by an excellent clubhouse, complete with restaurant and lounge and a well-stocked pro shop.

The resident Teaching Professional, Ben Doyle (an outstanding instructor) and Head Professional, Dan Weiss, provide all the assistance you could require.

RATES (EP) Patio rooms: $225. Cottage suites: (sitting room, bedroom, wetbar, fireplace) $285. Executive villas: 1-2 bedroom suites (private hot tub,

wetbar/fireplace),$345/$515/ $860. Green fees: $75, including cart. Golf package: 2 nights/3 days, (includes lodging, 3 rounds of golf with cart), $619 per couple. Package plan rate is available Sunday through Thursday.

ARRIVAL South from Monterey, left on Carmel Valley Road, 3 1/2 miles to Valley Greens Drive. Turn right to the Lodge.

NAPA VALLEY AREA

Napa Valley happens to be the site of a great number of California's best vineyards. Many of these venerable old wineries crafted from hand-hewn stone are worth the time and effort to visit. I believe there are over 100 of them.

From Napa and Yountville with St. Helena on the north, many excellent and unusual eating experiences await you. Naming a few, there is Domaine Chandon, pricey but outstanding (707-944-2892), Mama Nino (944-2112) and, our favorite, Petri's at the intersection of Monticello and Vichy Street, Napa (253-1455). The food is superb and the prices are intelligent.

Two golf courses are also in this general area: the new Chardonnay Club and Silverado, an older resort. Both are covered in detail on the following pages. While there are various motels in the Napa Valley area, we recommend the Clarion Inn Napa Valley or the Vintage Inn in Yountville. Additional information on these places is listed in the following pages.

THE CHARDONNAY CLUB

2555 Jameson Canyon Road (St. Hwy 12), P.O. Box 3779 Napa, CA 94558; Golf Shop (707) 257-8950; Executive Offices (707) 257-1900

This represents a departure from our normal coverage, as the Chardonnay Golf Club is not a "resort" but rather a wonderful golf complex. Within an hours drive from San Francisco and about five miles south of the city of Napa, it offers a special golfing experience. The original 18 was built in 1987, the third nine in 1989 and the fourth nine in early 1993. The first 18 is called the Vineyards. Playing to a par of 71, it reaches out 6,811/6,410/ 5,983/5,571/5,200 yards. A

Scottish Links type layout, featuring rolling terrain, some tri-level greens and many traps, it will require your full attention. Although this is a public facility it is a great deal more than your average "public" course.

The Shakespeare Course came into the picture in early 1993. These layouts were so well received that two of the more prestigious California tournaments were scheduled here: The Stocker Cup, Northern California's largest amateur event, and the Northern California Open. Reaching out a substantial 6,981 yards, it pars at 72 and features three large lakes, rock outcroppings and, a 100-foot waterfall. The waterfall, by the way, starts on each side of the tee area and runs down toward the green. A most unusual hole. In the Scottish tradition the various holes have names: King Lear, The Tempest, A Lover's Complaint and, of course, the 18th is named All's Well That Ends Well.

The golf is supported by a new 28,000-square-foot clubhouse with restaurant and lounge, golf shop, and locker rooms.

The Club Shakespeare, unlike the Vineyards (which is open to the public), will be a semi-private course. Something to look into is a membership, which includes the opportunity to play Marriott's World of Golf. Open to members, with only a golf cart fee to be paid, are courses in Orlando, Florida, Camelback and Mountain Shadows in Arizona, the magnificent Grand Hotel in Alabama, Seaview, New Jersey, Griffin Gate in Kentucky, Wind Watch on Long Island, Las Palmas and Desert Springs in Palm Desert, Tan-Tar-A in Missouri and several others. Including the Napa property, that totals some 369 holes of golf.

RATES Green fees: $55 / $60, including cart. For details on places to stay refer to the sections on The Clarion Inn, Napa, and Vintage Inn, in Yountville.

ARRIVAL Air: San Francisco International (62 miles), Oakland Airport (50 miles). Private aircraft: Napa (5 miles). Car: from San Francisco / Oakland take I-80 north to Highway 37 west. Go one mile to Highway 29 north. Travel five miles to Highway 12 east. Go 1.3 miles to entrance.

CLARION INN NAPA VALLEY
3425 Solano Avenue, Napa, CA 94558; (707) 253-7433; (800) 333-7533

A few miles north of the Chardonnay golf complex (eight miles), the Clarion has an ideal location, offering several unexpected and delightful amenities. Accommodations are in 191 rooms, including four suites. A newspaper is delivered to your door each morning – a nice way to start the day.

The Inn has set aside 10,000 square feet to accommodate meeting groups. With 11 rooms they can handle 230 classroom- and up to 400 theater-style.

The 150-seat "Signature" Dining Room serves continental cuisine in a casual setting. While the food is good, the service is better. The Collections Lounge offers entertainment on Wednesday and Saturday evenings.

There are two lighted outdoor tennis courts, a heated outdoor swimming pool, and a spa. Various activities which can be arranged include ballooning, horseback riding, antiquing and wine tours.

For details on golfing refer to the "Napa Valley Area" and "The Chardonnay Club."

RATES (EP) Rooms: $99/$112/$130. Suites: $225/ $475. Green fees: $35/$53, carts $24. Golf package: (includes lodging and discount on green fees at Chardonnay Club Course).

ARRIVAL Air: San Francisco (65 miles). Private aircraft Napa (5 miles). Car; going north on Highway 29 turn left at Trancas Street. Cross rail tracks and immediately turn right. Resort is on your left less than a block away.

SILVERADO
1600 Atlas Peak Road, Napa Valley, CA 94558; (707) 257-0200; (800) 532-0500

The 270 accommodations at Silverado, range from studios to one- , two- , or three-bedroom condominiums. The condos have fully-equipped kitchens, living rooms with fireplace and either a patio or a balcony. Be advised: the "Studio rooms" are, in most instances, the second bedroom of a two-bedroom condo and are small.

While the two restaurants,

The Vintners Court and The Royal Oak, are good, they are extremely expensive (jackets required, ties optional). There are other good restaurants in nearby Napa, as well as a few miles north in Yountville and St. Helena. They serve excellent fare at a more intelligent and realistic price. An example is Petri's Restaurant: less than a half-mile from Silverado, the food and service are great and the prices are realistic. For reservations call 253-1455. For information on additional restaurants, refer to "Napa Valley Area" in the foregoing pages.

There are two 18-hole golf courses, several swimming pools, tennis on 23 plexi-paved courts (three lighted), as well as a practice putting green.

Other amenities are quite some distance from the resort. For boating you must travel 20 miles east of Napa. Horseback riding is available, about 25 minutes away. The mud baths, naturally heated mineral waters renowned throughout the area, are 39 miles north in Calistoga. The resort has no racquetball courts nor a health center on property. These activities are some five or six miles away.

Golf can be played on two courses. The North, stretching out 6,896/6,351/5,857 yards, pars at 72. The South layout, measuring 6,632/6,213/5,672 yards, also pars at 72. We have played both and found each of them all we could handle. There is a clubhouse, pro shop and restaurant. Golf carts are mandatory and, unfortunately, are always restricted to the cart paths. A rather unusual arrangement is in effect: while guests MUST use a golf cart restricted to the paths, members are allowed to walk.

RATES (EP) Rooms: $130. Studios: $175. Condominiums: 1-bedroom $235. 2 bedrooms: $340. Green fees: $85, including cart. Golf package: 2 nights/2 days (includes lodging, green fees with cart, free range balls and golf lesson), $590 per couple.
ARRIVAL Air: San Francisco (62 miles) or Oakland (50 miles). Private aircraft: Napa (5 miles). Car: north end of Napa, east on Trancas Boulevard – then left on Atlas Peak Road.

THE VINTAGE INN
6541 Washington Street, Yountville, CA 94599; (707) 944-1617; (800) 982-5539

Eight miles north of Napa this intimate 80 unit resort is most unusual. Each guest room has a vaulted ceiling, whirlpool spa bath and a wood burning fireplace.

In addition to the heated swimming pool and spa the Vintage also has two tennis courts. They are capable of handling modest-size conference groups.

Be sure to make reservations as far in advance as possible as this place has been discovered by the San Francisco crowd.

RATES (EP) Rooms: $134/$154. Deluxe: $154/$174. Suites: $164/$194. Highest rate is on weekends.

ARRIVAL Car: from Napa take Highway 29 north approximately XX miles. Take the Yountville exit turn left onto Washington Street and drive north. Resort will be on your left.

BOULDER CREEK LODGE
16901 Big Basin Highway, Boulder Creek, CA 95006; (408) 338-2111

Boulder Creek Lodge and Conference Center is located

among the towering redwoods in the Santa Cruz Mountains of north-central California. Accommodations are in condominiums with full kitchens, wood-burning fireplaces, spacious decks and cable television. The golf course runs throughout the complex. Their meeting rooms can handle groups of up to 50 people, or 125 banquet-style.

There are six swimming pools (at various locations within the resort complex), six tennis courts, The Redwood Dining Room, a cozy cocktail lounge and a golf course.

While short, playing 4,279/3,970 yards with a par of 65, the Boulder Creek Golf Course offers various challenges. The setting, with towering old trees, is one of great beauty. If you are not alert, you can easily get mixed up with a wandering creek and a lot of timber. For tee times call 338-2121.

RATES Condos: 1-bedroom $90. There are villas (kitchen, fireplace, 1-3 bedrooms), rates upon request. Green fees: $17/$26, carts $18. Golf package: 2 nights/3 days (includes lodging and golf), $236 per couple.

ARRIVAL Air: San Jose. Car: from Saratoga take Highway 9 over the mountain. Cross Highway 35 and continue into the town of Boulder Creek. Turn right onto Highway 236 at the service station. Travel 3 1/4 miles to the main building on left side of road. Allow 50 minutes from downtown Saratoga.

DOUBLE TREE HOTEL
3555 Round Barn Boulevard, Santa Rosa, CA 95401; (707) 523-7555; (800) 528-0444

Formerly the Sheraton Round Barn Inn, the Double Tree is in Sonoma County, the heart of the wine country of California, some 55 miles north of San Francisco. Sited on the historic Fountain Grove Ranch, the property overlooks Santa Rosa. The 247 guest rooms, which are larger than the average, have oversized desks, several phones, and cable TV.

The resort is well equipped to handle meeting and seminar groups. The two ballrooms, which can be divided into eight separate meeting areas, can accommodate groups of up to 250. There is also a restaurant and lounge

There is a swimming pool, a

whirlpool, and a jogging path. Located at the golf course are five tennis courts. Horseback riding is nearby. There are a great many wineries (nearly a 100) scattered throughout the greater Santa Rosa area. Tours can be arranged by the hotel.

The Fountain Grove Country Club course stretches out 6,797/6,380/5,644 yards and pars at 72. Winding up and down through these beautiful hills, it offers not only superb views but also all the challenge you could desire. While not easy, it is a fun layout to play. Should the course prove too much, there are always the wineries. I predict that in due time this layout will be considered one of the finest in northern California.

There is a unique and lovely clubhouse. Done in a Japanese architectural style it houses the small pro shop as well as an outstanding restaurant. The restaurant is not open in the early morning, however, so be sure to have breakfast prior to arrival. The phone number for the course is (707) 579-4653. The Head Golf Professional is J. Michael Jonas.

RATES   (EP)   Rooms: $79/$120. Suites: $180/$250.

Green fees: $35/$55 carts $24.

ARRIVAL Air: San Francisco. Private aircraft: Sonoma Country Airport. Car: from San Francisco travel north on Highway 101. Take the Old Redwood Highway/Mendocino Avenue exit. Stay right. At the first light swing left up the hill. Then take the first left again (up the hill). You are there.

FURNACE CREEK INN & RANCH RESORT
Death Valley, CA 92328, The INN (619) 786-2361; The RANCH (619) 786-2345

Furnace Creek Resort is quite different for a variety of reasons. Although its location in Death Valley is 200 feet below sea level, the lowest point in the contiguous 48 states, you can see the highest point from here as well – Mt. Whitney.

The resort is truly an oasis in the desert. Its beauty is highlighted by Death Valley, one of the bleakest, most inhospitable places on earth. How anything could survive the parched, burning heat of summer, and yet be so beautiful in the fall and winter, is difficult to comprehend.

We are really talking about two places: the Ranch, more of the Old West in flavor, with a casual dress code; and the Inn, on the "posh" side, with lighted tennis courts, the Oasis supper club and so on. Jackets are required but ties are optional in the evening.

There is much to do and see here, including the Borax Museum, the visitor's center and the opportunity to study the fascinating geology of this area. Due to the arid conditions, the landscape has remained virtually unchanged for thousands of years. There are, of course, swimming, riding and hiking available as well.

Golf is offered on an 18-hole layout playing 5,750/4,977 yards, with a par of 70/71. The many palm trees and the lush greenery provide a startling contrast to the desert. While the course is not long, it does pose its own special challenges.

RATES (MAP) The Inn: $250/$350 per couple. Suites: $325. The Ranch: (EP) $65/$94. Green fees: $25, carts $18. The season is January-May.

ARRIVAL Private aircraft: Furnace Creek (3,040-foot surfaced runway). Car: there are so many ways into Death Valley it is not possible to list them all.

HALF MOON BAY LODGE

2400 South Cabrillo Highway, Half Moon Bay, CA 94019; (415) 726-9000; (800) 368-2468 Ext 3

The Half Moon Bay Lodge is nestled on the fourth fairway of the Half Moon Bay Golf Links. There are 83 rooms, some with fireplaces and kitchenettes, all with either private balconies or patios. Room service is provided by a Swedish restaurant, the Last Whistle, adjacent to the Lodge. The Lodge also has three fully equipped conference rooms to accommodate business meetings.

There is an enclosed whirlpool spa and a swimming pool. In addition to the recreation offered by numerous nearby parks and beaches, there is riding, tennis and fishing.

About seven miles north you will find one of the best seafood restaurants anywhere – The Shore Bird. Drive north through Half Moon Bay and turn left at the first signal light (several miles). Though it's a bit removed from San Francisco, make reservations. The San Francisco crowd knows good food when they find it, and this place has been discov-

ered!

Golf on the Links is something else. Designed by Francis Duane and Arnold Palmer and using fully the picturesque setting of the area, the course brings water, barrancas (ravines) and bluffs into play. The course has been rated third in Northern California. Parring at 72, it plays 7,116/6,447/5,710 yards. It is one of the more beautiful, and challenging, golf layouts we have come across.

RATES   (EP)   Rooms: $108/$130. Suite: $150. Green fees: $68/$88, including cart.

ARRIVAL On Highway 1, 2 miles south of Half Moon Bay. From San Francisco Airport (30 minutes), take Highway 92 to Highway 1, then south.

LAKE SHASTINA GOLF RESORT

5925 Country Club Drive, Weed, CA 96094; (916) 938-3201; (800) 358-4653

The Shastina Golf Resort is about 75 miles north of Redding, California, and the same distance south of Medford, Oregon. Snow-capped Mt. Shasta provides the spectacular background for this resort and its 27 holes of golf. Accommodations are in condominiums located throughout the golf course, with some adjacent to the lake. Each includes a bedroom, living area and a fully equipped kitchen.

Other facilities include a clubhouse, site of the restaurant and lounge, two tennis courts, a swimming pool, and a spa. Accessible from the area are river rafting and water skiing. Fishing trips can also be arranged.

The Lake Shastina Golf Course, a relatively flat and open affair, reaches out 6,950/6,317/5,542 yards and pars at 72.

RATES (EP) $98/$148. Green fees: $38, carts $24, Golf package: 2 nights/3 days (includes lodging, unlimited golf and cart), $338/$358 per couple including tax.

ARRIVAL Air: Medford, Oregon or Redding, California. For private aircraft, a 3,800-foot runway (altitude 2,938 feet) is 5 miles from the golf course. Shuttle service to the resort is provided with prior request required. Car: I-5 from either direction approximately 1 1/2 hours.

NORTHSTAR AT TAHOE
P.O. Box 129, Truckee, CA 96160; (916) 587-0201; (800) 533-6787

Northstar is situated in one of the most scenic areas in the U.S. While basically a winter-oriented resort it offers a wide range of activities during the summer months. Accommodations consist of 230 units, divided between Village Lodge Rooms and one- to four-bedroom condominiums. The condos are fully equipped for housekeeping, with dishwasher and either gas log or woodburning fireplaces. There are also some private homes available to rent.

The resort is well set up to entertain meeting groups. With some 20,000 square feet of space, they can handle gatherings of from 10 to 150.

Starting in the spring, you can play tennis on 10 courts, enjoy horseback riding (barbecue dinner or breakfast rides can be arranged) or mountain biking through this beautiful forest area, or swim in the Olympic-size pool. The various streams and lakes provide a fisherman's paradise. There is also a "Minors Camp" for children of from two to 10.

Northstar offers super skiing during the winter. With 2,200 vertical feet of downhill, 65 kilometers of cross country trails, a 100-instructor ski school, they specialize in ski clinics.

But summer is the time to enjoy many other activities. You can attend a rodeo, an air show, a Shakespearian play or a music concert. The proximity of Lake Tahoe (six miles) also opens up all types of water sports. There is so much going on it is not possible to cover it all.

Summer is also the time to take on the challenging golf course, a Robert Muir Graves design. Reaching up to 6,000 feet above sea level, it provides some spectacular views. The yardage is 6,897/6,337/6,015/5,470, parring at 72. Surrounded by aspen and pines the course also has a creek, seemingly without a home, wandering throughout the area. Water, as a matter of fact, forms a good part of the challenge on 14 holes. Jim Anderson, PGA Professional, and his staff, are available to assist. There is a clubhouse, complete with pro shop and a restaurant open for breakfast and lunch.

Northstar is just seven miles from the California/Nevada border, offering gaming and big name entertainment as well as the awe-inspiring beauty of Lake Tahoe.

RATES (EP) Lodgette room: $89. Studio: $99. Village suites: (living room, loft, fireplace, kitchen, and bedroom), $123. There are also homes for rent. Green fees:, including cart $60. Golf packages are available. Rates are June-September (higher during the winter months).

ARRIVAL Air: Reno (40 minutes). Private aircraft: Truckee-Tahoe, 6,400-foot strip. Car: Highway 267 between Truckee and the north shore of Lake Tahoe (approximately 6 miles).

PASATIEMPO INN
555 Highway 17, Santa Cruz, CA 95060; (408) 423-5000

The Pasatiempo Inn is a beautiful "Spanish mood" building. With its 58 rooms, a restaurant, and cozy cocktail lounge, it is pretty complete. They can accommodate convention and seminar groups of up to 250.

The Pasatiempo Golf & Country Club, bordering the Inn, is one of the older and finer courses in the state. Little wonder, as it was designed by Dr. Alistair MacKenzie, the same man responsible for St. Andrews in Scotland, the Masters course in Augusta, and Cypress Point at Monterey. It has been judged by *Golf Digest* as one of the top 100 layouts in the United States. The course plays 6,607/6,281/5,626 yards, parring at 71.

In addition to the deep barrancas, sand traps and oak trees bordering the fairways, you can enjoy the breathtaking views of shimmering Monterey Bay or the Santa Cruz Mountains each time you approach the ball. All things considered you will find this a beautiful course and a true test of your game. At certain times it might test your vocabulary as well.

RATES (EP) Rooms: $75/$85. Weekends: $90/$100. Green fees: $55/$65, carts $25. Golf packages can be arranged when booking reservations.

ARRIVAL Car: from the north take Highway 17 (I-880) south to Pasatiempo Drive exit. The resort will be on your right.

RANCHO MURIETA
14813 Jackson Road, Rancho Murieta, CA 95683; (916) 985-7700

The Rancho Country Club is almost due east of Sacramento. There are 74 guest rooms, including 37 executive suites, along the golf course. Each suite has two bedrooms, two baths, living room, kitchenette (not equipped) and private patio. There are also some private homes, townhouses and villas available.

The Clubhouse is a massive structure of some 40,000 square feet and is the location of the Parasol Dining Room, a cocktail lounge, and meeting facilities. With the Marietta Room and several smaller breakout rooms, the resort can handle up to 225 in a theater-style and 175 in a banquet setting.

Outside the entrance to Rancho Murieta there is an excellent shopping complex, which includes restaurants, a bank, dental and medical offices and a grocery store.

There are six lighted tennis courts. In addition, there is swimming, saunas, hydra spas, volleyball, badminton, a jogging track, fishing and non-motorized boating. Located nearby is an equestrian center. There is definitely enough going on to keep you from becoming bored!

You will find two 18-hole golf courses here. The North Course, recently redesigned by Arnold Palmer, stretches out 6,839/6,335/5,608/5,507 yards, with a par of 72/73. The South Course measures 6,886/6,307/5,527 yards and pars at 72. Both are interesting in the manner in which they bring trees, water, bunkers, and undulating fairways into the action. The rather large, multi-level greens also tend to keep you awake. The Director of Golf is David Hall. For tee times call (916) 354-3440.

RATES (EP) Room B: $70. Room A: $115. Suite of A and B: $175. Green fees: $55, carts $20. Golf package: 2 nights/2 days (includes golf, cart), $392/$480 per couple.

ARRIVAL Air: Sacramento (35 miles). San Francisco (110 miles). Private aircraft: Rancho Murieta (3,800-foot paved landing strip). Car: east on Highway 50, south on Bradshaw Road, then left on Jackson Road. From Sacramento about 45 minutes.

RESORT AT SQUAW CREEK
1000 Squaw Creek Road, Olympic Village, CA 95730; (916) 583-6300; (800) 327-3353

The Resort at Squaw Creek is in the high country of the Sierra Nevada Mountains of Northern California. The floor of the valley, where the hotel and the golf course are located, is at 6,200 feet. The surrounding mountains top out at a bit over 9,000 feet. The entire area has a fascinating history involving the Indian culture, the early European explorers, and the settlers drawn to this magnificent country. Aside from the history, it offers some of the most breathtaking scenery to be found anywhere.

The resort itself is made up of two large connected complexes. The main group of buildings includes the lobby, with its vaulted ceilings, marble floors, and a massive granite fireplace. Most impressive of all is the fact that these huge, glass-fronted buildings blend so well into the surrounding valley setting.

Behind the main structure is the nine-story accommodations building. Referred to as the guest house, it contains 405 rooms and suites. All rooms have views of the beautiful valley and feature minibar, refrigerator and cable TV. The hotel is also well set up to handle business gatherings. With 33,000 square feet of space devoted to group affairs, including two large ballrooms and 24 breakout rooms, they can handle 570 classroom- and 860 theater-style.

There are three restaurants: Gussandi for intimate dining, the Cascades for a more casual setting, and Hardscramble Bar & Grill with a bistro atmosphere, open for lunch and dinner. Bullwhackers Pub serves cocktails. For your edification (should you not be aware), a bullwhacker was a mule or oxen driver – rough, tough and usually mean.

Although oriented to skiing and winter activities Squaw Creek is not a "rustic western" destination. In fact, it is quite modern and upbeat. This entire area (620 acres), was originally put together to handle the 1960 Winter Olympics and has grown since that period. Their winter activities are so extensive, with many lifts (the resort has its own lift directly outside the hotel lobby) and numerous ski trails, including slopes to accommodate beginners, I suggest you call for their ski season informational brochure.

The sports activity center is available to supply ski, golf, bicycle and tennis equipment. There is also a shopping arcade offering all manner of clothing, gift items, wines, spirits and various food items. The resort has two outdoor heated swimming pools (a lap pool and a water slide plunge pool), three outdoor spas, a health and fitness center, eight tennis courts (including the High Camp Tennis Club) an ice-skating pavilion and the golf shop. Guests can take advantage of one of the finest instructional programs to be found through the Peter Burnwash International (PBI program). An extra: fly fishing for trout in this area is outstanding. As a matter of fact, fly fishing clinics can also be arranged.

Last, but certainly not least, there is a Robert Trent Jones II designed golf course. The front nine of the golf course, running along the floor of the valley, is relatively flat. The second nine, however, begins to skirt the edge of the valley and will take you through some definite elevation changes. Modestly trapped, it brings water into contention on four holes. Playing 6,931/6,453/6,010/5,097 yards, the course pars at 71. The golf operations and excellent pro shop are under the supervision of the Director of Golf, Mancil Davis and Head Professional, Sam "Chip" McCraney.

RATES (EP) Rooms: $165/$210. 1-bedroom suite: $265/$845. Green fees: $79, including cart. Golf package are available. Rates are for summer season of mid-June through mid-September.

ARRIVAL Air: Reno, Nevada (42 miles). Car: from Reno travel Highway 395 north to I-80. West on I-80 to Highway 89. Take 89 south to the entrance to Squaw Valley. You are about 200 miles from San Francisco and 100 miles from Sacramento, California.

RIDGEMARK
3800 Airline Highway, Hollister, CA 95023; (408) 637-8151

Ridgemark Golf and Country Club has accommodations consisting of cottages, some equipped with Jacuzzi tubs. The dining room offers a diverse menu and, of course, has cocktail service.

The golf course, due to the mild climate, can be played year-round. It plays 6,834/6,204/5,564/5,724 yards, with a par of 72. Tennis courts are also available.

RATES (EP) Rooms: $70/$905. Green fees: $37/$52, including cart.

ARRIVAL Air: San Francisco (90 minutes). San Jose (45 minutes). Car: south of Hollister (2 miles).

SONOMA MISSION INN
P.O Box 1447, Sonoma, CA 95476; (707) 938-9000; (800) 358-9022

The history of the Sonoma Mission Inn stretches back to the mid-1800's. It was not, however, until 1927 that the present hotel came into being. Built along the soft beautiful lines of the old California missions, complete with a bell tower, it is most impressive. Although the resort has recently been brought into the present period, it was able to maintain the atmosphere of the gracious earlier time. The massive beams, potted palms, the huge two-story fireplace in the lobby, guest rooms featuring white plantation-type shutters and ceiling fans, all add to the general ambience.

There are 170 guest rooms, many with a fireplace and terraces. All rooms are air-conditioned. With their seven meeting rooms, the Inn is capable of handling meeting groups of up to 110 classroom- and 200 theater-style.

The Dinner Grille is the hotel's premiere dining room, although The Cafe, located directly across the parking area, offers Italian cuisine which is difficult to top. There is also a restaurant at the golf course.

In 1981 a state-of-the-art bathhouse including exercise equipment, a swimming pool, and beauty salon was completed. The Inn actually originated with the local Indians as a spa in the 1800's. The resort places great emphasis on the spa programs, offering a wide range of body treatments: hydrotherapy massage, herbal and seaweed wraps, facials, and body scrubs. The co-ed facilities include steam rooms, indoor and outdoor whirlpools, two lighted tennis courts and rowing machines.

The recently restored Sonoma Golf Club is less than a mile away. Originally designed by Sam Whiting and Willie Watson, architects of the well known Lake Course at the San Francisco Olympic Club, it was restored and redesigned by Robert Muir Graves. Playing 7,069/6,583/6,051/5,519 yards, it pars at 72. The entire layout is supported by a driving range, putting greens, a practice sand trap, along with a new clubhouse and pro shop. The SGA Head Professional is Ron Blum. For tee times call (707) 996-0300.

RATES *(EP)   Rooms: $185 / $325. Suites: $425 / $650. Green fees: $60 / $80, including cart. Golf package: 2 nights / 2 days (includes lodging at the Inn, 18 holes of golf, with cart, per night stay), $440 weekdays, $760 weekends per couple.*

ARRIVAL *Air: Santa Rosa Airport (25 miles). Private aircraft: Sonoma Country Airport,* paved runway (15 minutes). Car: from 101 turn east on Highway 37. Travel east to Highway 121. Then north on 121 to Highway 12. Left on 12 to three-way stop in town of Sonoma. Turn left and follow Highway 12 about 3 miles to resort.

TAHOE DONNER GOLF & COUNTRY CLUB
P.O. Box TDR #45, Truckee, CA 95734; (916) 587-6046

This four-season, family resort is in the Sierra Mountains near Donner, one of the most beautiful lakes in California. Its location, just 35 miles west of Reno and 15 miles north of Lake Tahoe, makes reaching the gambling tables an easy chore.

Accommodations are in one- to four-bedroom condominiums, fully-equipped, most with fireplaces. Rental arrangements must be made through the Truckee Realtors Group. For reservations you can call the following real estate firms handling home rentals in the area: Coldwell Banker (916) 587-5501 or NAT (800) 345-0102; Truckee-Tahoe Realty (916) 587-5990; McCormick Realty (916) 587-2897.

The marina on Donner Lake provides all types of boating activities including sailing and fishing. It is, however, a bit cold for swimming in this lake! Try the heated pool instead. There is an equestrian center with miles of riding trails. There are also six tennis courts.

Golf is played on the Tahoe Donner G & CC Course. This beautiful, tree-lined layout extends through the wooded rolling terrain 6,899/6,635/6,052 yards, parring at 72/74. It is an engaging course, complete with tree-lined fairways, ample traps, and water on eight holes. Golf season runs from late May to late September. Skiing takes over after that.

RATES Call for the latest rates and special packages.

ARRIVAL Air: Reno. Car: 2 miles from I-80 at Truckee.

SOUTHERN CALIFORNIA

1. Rio Bravo Resort
2. The Inn at Morro Bay
3. Sky Valley Resort
4. Black Lake Golf Resort
5. The Inn at Silver Lakes
6. The Alisal
7. The Four Seasons Biltmore
8. Ojai Valley Inn & Country Club
9. Radisson Suite Hotel at River Ridge
10. Sheraton at Industry Hills Resort

THE ALISAL
1054 Alisal Road, Solvang, CA 93464; (805) 688-6411

While The Alisal is a mere two miles from Solvang, it has a definite country setting enhanced by the presence of hundreds of wild deer, magpies, acorn woodpeckers, raccoons, bobcats and other wildlife. Although the resort's history dates back to the Spanish Land Grant period, it came into being as a guest ranch in 1943 and has been operated by the Jackson family since that time. As a matter of fact The Alisal is still a 10,000-acre working cattle ranch.

Lodgings are studios, two-room suites, two-room loft suites, or private bungalows. All 73 units are decorated in a delightful California ranch style and feature a wood burning fireplace. A word of warning – there are no phones or TV's in the rooms. Some people think this is a delightful change of pace, others feel cut off. Good news is that, while cleaning and laundry service are available, the resort also has a coin-operated laundry. There is a large color TV in the recreation room along with a TV set for adult viewing in the attractive library.

A visit to the nearby town of Solvang (two miles away) is a must. With its picturesque shops and Danish-style architecture, Solvang has great charm. There are some 22 wineries open to the public and, of course, the historic Mission Santa Ynez. Be sure to see this magnificent Mission.

The food and service here are excellent. Jackets are required in the evening and no smoking is allowed in the dining areas. The Oak Room offers live entertainment each evening, with dancing and cocktail service. There is also the Clubhouse snack bar and cocktail lounge located at the golf course. While the resort has a meeting capacity for groups of up to 175, such group functions are possible only during the fall and winter months.

Various activities include: horseback riding, including breakfast rides (riding instruction can also be arranged), a hot water spa, swimming pool, badminton, volleyball, croquet, and tennis on seven courts. In addition there is a 96-acre private lake providing many water related activities: sailing, windsurfing, pedal boats, and fishing (all tackle as well as boats are available – no license is needed). During the summer a children's program is in place. Under the supervision of an activities director, there is a full schedule of events to give you a bit of respite and, at the same time, allow the children some time off for good behavior.

The Alisal Golf Course, studded with oaks, is both beautiful and challenging. Parring at 72/73, it measures 6,286/5,919/

5,594 yards. While not monstrous in length, the many trees plus water in the form of a creek wandering throughout the entire layout will more than keep your attention. The golf course is supported by a new and enlarged pro shop, with locker rooms as well as a restaurant and lounge. The Director of Golf is John Hardy.

Now a new course has come into play. The River Course, situated along the Santa Ynez River, is just south of the town of Solvang. Reaching out 6,830/6,451/6,117/5,815, yards it carries a par of 72. There is also a golf shop, complete with snack bar, cocktail service, a driving range and a practice putting green.

RATES (MAP) Studio Room: $240. Executive studio: $255/$300. Two-room suite: $280 per couple. Green fees: $35, cart $20. Rates are for late-June through mid-September. Some package plans are available from late September through mid-June.

ARRIVAL Air: Santa Barbara (40 miles). Private aircraft: Santa Ynez. Car: U.S. 101 to Buellton, turn off to Solvang. In Solvang turn right on Alisal Road (2 miles).

BLACK LAKE GOLF RESORT

1490 Golf Course Lane, Nipoma, CA 93444; (805) 343-1718 CA; (800) 423-0981

For the newcomers to this part of California, Nipoma is just off Highway 101, with San Luis Obispo to the north and Santa Maria a few miles south. The resort is on 420 acres of slightly rolling terrain with accommodations consisting of condominiums. These two-bedroom units have fireplaces, a fully equipped kitchen, and private patios or decks. Some are adjacent to the golf course while others are tucked among the oaks.

There is a clubhouse complete with restaurant and lounge as well as a full service pro shop. It is also the location of a swimming pool and spa.

The Black Lake Golf Course, while not unique, is a bit unusual in that the first hole is a 127-yard par-three. Do not draw the wrong conclusion as this Ted Robinson-designed layout is a regulation championship course. Playing to a par of 72, the yardage is 6,412/6,068/5,614. Both nines bring trees into the picture, with the front side introducing you to water on seven holes.

Water only becomes a nuisance on two holes on the second nine.

RATES   (EP)   Deluxe: $109/$129. Executive $119/ $139. Weekends higher. Golf package: 2 nights/2 days weekdays only (includes lodging, two rounds of golf with cart, continental breakfast), $320 per couple.

ARRIVAL Air: Santa Maria. Car: turn off Highway 101 at Nipoma Drive, west to Pomeroy Road. Travel north to Willow Road (it is a few miles) and turn left. Proceed to resort.

FOUR SEASONS BILTMORE

1260 Channel Drive, Santa Barbara, CA 93108; (805) 969-2261; (800) 332-3442 Canada; (800) 268-6282

At the turn of the century this was known as the Santa Barbara Country Club. While the resort really dates back to 1908, the present configuration came into being in 1927, at which time it was host to many Hollywood stars. Then a succession of owners and management firms took over. Finally in 1987 the Four Seasons group purchased the Biltmore. Beginning in 1988, they proceeded to infuse over $16 million into the property during an 18-month restoration program. No rooms were added but renovation brought back the former genteel ambiance. Once again the Biltmore has flower-filled formal gardens, hand carved woodwork, wrought iron chandeliers, magnificent Spanish tile floors and much more.

The resort has 236 rooms including suites. Many have fireplaces, balconies or patios and vaulted ceilings. There are, in addition, 11 guest cottages ranging up to three bedrooms plus living room. With their many meeting rooms, and 14,000 square feet of space devoted to group affairs, the Biltmore is capable of handling gatherings of up to 350.

You may want to try the sophisticated La Marina Restaurant or the more casual Patio. Or 24-hour room service is an alternative. The beach-side Coral Casino Club has poolside dining in La Perla Restaurant & Lounge or The Raft for a light breakfast or lunch. Four Seasons also has a children's program in place. This complimentary service allows the children an opportunity to enjoy and the parents a chance to relax.

Amenities include: two swimming pools, three lighted tennis courts and a putting green. Bicycles may also be reserved. Additional activities include charter boat fishing, an ocean cruise through the Channel Islands, a visit to the polo matches and horseback riding. And a visit to one or more of the many wineries, or the almost endless number of shops and galleries in historic Santa Barbara might be in order.

There are three golf courses where play can be arranged. The Sandpiper, some 20 minutes north, La Cumbre Country Club, five miles distant, and the Montecito Country Club, a private course, about a mile away. Whatever you choose to do, budget time to visit and at least look around the historically rich city of Santa Barbara. Not doing so would be like going to Rome and never looking at a church building.

RATES (EP) Rooms: $270/$330. Suites: $450/$695.

ARRIVAL Air: Santa Barbara Airport. Car: from Highway 101 take the Olive Mill Road exit. Drive west to the end of the road and turn right. You are now on Channel Drive and the resort is on your right side.

THE INN AT MORRO BAY

State Park Road, Morro Bay, CA 93442; (805) 772-5651; (800) 321-9566

The seaside town of Morro Bay is a quaint fishing village. The clean fresh ocean air, the light wispy fog cover, the sound of the surf, the unhurried fishing boats coming and going from the marina, join to create a delightful setting. The Inn, located on the bay, has a direct view of this tranquil scene. There are 96 guest rooms, some with fireplaces and sweeping views of the bay, some with a pool or garden view. The Inn can handle modest-sized meeting or banquet groups

The Morrow Bay Dining Room is recognized throughout the area for its food and service and has, in fact, won several awards.

There is a heated outdoor swimming pool, miles of hiking trails, and the world-renowned Hearst Castle at San Simeon some 30 miles north. Or you can arrange a harbor cruise, or perhaps canoe around the bay. A fascinating pastime is simply to watch a band of sea otter cavort through the kelp. There are also many wineries to be visited. The Inn calls their life style "life in the slow lane."

The Morrow Bay Golf Course, located across the road from the Inn, plays to a modest yardage of 6,113/5,727 and pars at 71. Do not let the humble mileage lead you astray. This small, tight layout, situated on undulating terrain along with difficult greens, will more than keep your attention. Situated in Morrow Bay State Park, it offers the added distraction of fabulous views of the Pacific Ocean and Morro Bay. Tee times are difficult to set up. You can call (805) 772-4560 for the starter.

RATES   (EP)   Rooms: $55 / $105. Rooms with fireplace   and   Bay   View: $165 / $195.   Green   fees: $13 / $15, carts $18. The resort does not offer golf packages.

ARRIVAL Air: San Louis Obispo (12 miles). Car: from the north, exit Highway 101 onto Highway 46 at Paso Robles. Continue about 25 miles to Highway 1. From the south, exit Highway 101 onto Highway 1 and travel 15 miles to Morro Bay Boulevard.

THE INN AT SILVER LAKES

P.O. Box 26, Helendale, CA 92342; (619) 243-4800 CA; (800) 228-7209

The Inn has 40 guest rooms, each with either private patio or balcony. There is also a dining room and lounge. The two lakes mean that water sports are available. There is, in addition, a large swimming pool, a sauna, Jacuzzis, and four lighted tennis courts.

The Silver Lakes Country Club layout consists of 27 holes. When played in combination, they measure as follows: the North/East nines reach 6,689/6,328/5,465 yards; the South/North are 6,822/6,428/5,564 yards; the combination of the East/South plays 6,747/6,374/5,633 yards. No matter how you mix them, they come out to a par of 72. These are intriguing layouts, with water in play on several holes of each nine.

RATES (EP) Rooms: $56 / $70. Golf package: 2 nights / 2 days (includes lodging, continental breakfast, golf, and cart), weekends $310 per couple. Midweek: $240. Green fees: $25 / $35, carts $20.

***ARRIVAL** Off I-15 between* Victorville and Barstow, on the National Trails Highway about 95 miles from Los Angeles.

OJAI VALLEY INN & COUNTRY CLUB

Country Club Road, Ojai, CA 93023; (805) 646-5511; (800) 422-6524

The Ojai Valley Inn has been judged one of the top 50 resorts. It has also received many additional accolades. Ojai Valley's snow-capped mountains (specifically Topa/Topa Mountain, a part of the Sierra Madre Range), were the setting for the mythical paradise of Shangri-la in the movie *Lost Horizon* (circa 1937). If you saw this movie during its original showing, back up and ask for extra strokes.

The charming Inn, with its quiet and idyllic setting is 14 miles from the Pacific Ocean and approximately 90 minutes northwest of Los Angeles It is, however, at least a million miles from Los Angeles in gentility and culture. The name, "Ojai," by the way, is an Indian word meaning "the nest." As you might well suspect the resort has been a hide-away for people from Southern California for many years.

The mountains surrounding the valley not only add to its beauty but, because they hold down the wind, help to produce the gentle climate enjoyed here. The entire complex is surrounded by the golf course.

Recently renovated and completely restructured (it's extraordinary what $63 million can accomplish), the resort

now has 218 beautifully decorated guest rooms, each air-conditioned and equipped with a mini-bar. The 15 suites have parlors and most include fireplaces. All lodgings have either a terrace, patio or balconies. The general motif is one of warm Spanish/American design which blends into the surrounding area. Although the resort's roots and general design are from the 1920s, the architect responsible for the massive restoration did a masterful job of bringing everything into the present, while preserving the magnificent

qualities of an earlier time.

The Inn is well-equipped to handle meeting groups. With their new Conference Center, eight meeting rooms, a Board Room and the large ballroom, they can accommodate groups of 10 to 550. The meeting complex has its own kitchen facilities and can accommodate up to 400 for dinner.

Dining in the Vista Room, the more informal Oak Grill & Terrace, or The Club can be a delightful experience. People from the area travel many miles to enjoy the cuisine.

There are eight newly resurfaced tennis courts (four lighted), with the Director of Tennis, Tim Howell, and staff to assist. The new tennis complex includes a clubhouse, a well-stocked pro shop and a snack bar. Other amenities include: two swimming pools, a spa, exercise equipment and fitness classes, jogging trails, the use of bicycles on a complimentary basis, and lawn croquet. If you have biked or hiked into the village and have just plain run out of gas, you can catch the shuttle bus from Ojai's shopping arcade back to the Inn.

One final suggestion: take the

time to really "look" at the quaint village of Ojai. Its Spanish mission-style architecture, along with the boutiques, shops, galleries and the museum are more than worth the time.

The Country Club Golf Course originally designed by George C. Thomas, Jr. in 1923 and put together by Billy Bell, has long been regarded as one of the better layouts in California. In order, however, to bring it up to date yet continue its almost legendary reputation, Jay Morrish, a leading designer, was engaged. The restoration, including a modern irrigation system, is now complete. Playing 6,252/5,909/5,242 yards, the Ojai course pars at 70/71. With its lush fairways and rolling terrain, it is in a class by itself. While the front nine is fun, the back nine is something else. It must be considered one of the most unusual courses we have tried. Wandering through the foothills, the backside takes advantage of every tree (and there are more than enough of them), every ravine, gully and hill, to turn this nine into a shot-maker's course. There is a well-equipped pro shop, along with the assistance of an excellent professional staff, under the supervision of the Director of Golf, Scott

Flynn.

RATES *(EP) Lodgings: $190/$210/$230/$250 per couple. Deluxe suites: $335/$385/575. Green fees: $76, carts $28. Golf package: 2 nights/2 days (includes MAP, lodging, unlimited green fees, free range balls), weekdays $636, weekends $836 per couple.*

ARRIVAL *Air: Santa Barbara (30 miles). Car: take U.S. 101 south to Route 150. Turn east (left) onto 150 and travel into the town of Ojai. Turn right onto Country Club Drive and continue to resort.*

RADISSON SUITE HOTEL AT RIVER RIDGE
2101 West Vineyard, Oxnard, CA 93030; (805) 988-0130; (800) 333-3333

This resort has an interesting mix of amenities to offer its guests. While it calls itself a hotel, accommodations actually consist of 250 residential-style suites spread over a total of 32 buildings. Each suite has a full-size kitchen, cable TV, along with a cassette player, and all the equipment needed for housekeeping. There are also some two-story loft suites featuring wood burning fireplaces. A nice extra: you can start each day with a complimentary, cooked-to-order breakfast. There is a restaurant on premises called Mullarkey's Food & Spirits, should you choose not to do your own cooking.

In addition to golf, they have five lighted tennis courts, two swimming pools, three hot tubs, along with exercise and massage facilities. The hotel is equipped to handle group functions ranging from 20 to 300.

The course, adjacent to the hotel, reaches out 6,543/6,111/5,525 yards and carries a par of 72. It sports an island par three, number 14, playing 158 yards from the regular tees. Surrounded by water the green can be reached only by a small foot bridge. There are also several holes running directly along the Santa Clara River. The golf facilities and pro shop are under the supervision of PGA Golf Professional Marc Sipes.

RATES (EP) Studio suite: $95/$105. One bedroom with loft: $130. Golf package: 2 nights/2 days (includes lodging, green fees and cart for two rounds, full breakfast each morning, and all taxes), $258

per couple. Green fees: $15/$20, carts $16. Rates are for peak summer golf season.

ARRIVAL Air: Oxnard (5 minutes away). Car: resort is just a few blocks off U.S. Highway 101. Take the Vineyard exit and drive west 1 1/2 miles to the resort.

RIO BRAVO RESORT
11200 Lake Ming Road, Bakersfield, CA 93306; (805) 872-5000; (800) 282-5000

Rio Bravo is adjacent to a 110-acre lake. In this desert-like part of the San Joaquin Valley, water in any form is a rare commodity. Rooms each have a private balcony or patio. There are also some one- and two-bedroom units with sitting area, fireplace and wet bar. The dining room is considered one of the best in the valley. The resort is equipped to handle group affairs ranging in size from 10 to 170 banquet-style.

There are 18 tennis courts (14 lighted), along with a professional staff, two swimming pools, a fitness center, saunas, whirlpools, and sailing on Lake Ming. White-water rafting, kayaking or fishing on the Kern River can be arranged nearby.

The golf course, a Robert Muir Graves design, plays to a substantial 7,018/6,555/5,704 yards, with a par of 72. Although there is certainly enough water in the immediate area, the course has only two holes where it comes into play. There is a clubhouse, driving range, and practice putting surface.

RATES (EP) Rooms: $105. 1-bedroom suite: $210. 2-bedroom suite: $315. Green fees: $42, including cart. Golf package: 2 nights/1 day (includes two nights lodging, one round of golf with cart), $235 per couple.

ARRIVAL Air: Bakersfield Airport. Private aircraft: Rio Bravo (3000-foot runway 3 minutes away). Car: from Highway 99 north of Bakersfield take State Highway 178 east to Alfred Harrell Highway. Turn back in westerly direction to resort.

SHERATON AT INDUSTRY HILLS RESORT
One Industry Hills Parkway, City of Industry, CA 91744; (818) 965-0861; (800) 325-3535

On a hill overlooking the entire complex, the hotel comes packaged with indoor fountains, liberal use of marble, stained glass and a staff that can greet you in Spanish, French, German, Japanese and, even English. Meeting facilities are available with banquet seating for up to 1,500.

The resort provides 17 tennis courts, 15 miles of riding trails, three swimming pools, whirlpools, saunas and even billiards. A few years back they added an equestrian center, with a covered arena. The entire resort is referred to as a 650-acre "playground." The location is certainly convenient, just 40 minutes to Disneyland, and 50 minutes to Knott's Berry Farm or the Los Angeles Coliseum.

The 17 tennis courts (lighted for night play) are under the supervision of a professional staff. Teaching facilities include closed circuit video tape equipment to allow you to see yourself in slow motion replay. "Do I really look like that"?

Golf is offered on two 18-hole courses: the Dwight D. Eisenhower and the Babe Zaharias layouts. The Eisenhower 18, parring at 72/73, stretches 6,712/6,287/5,967/

5,637 yards. The Babe Zaharias Course, a bit shorter, plays 6,481/5,994/5,426 and pars at 71. You will enjoy the view provided by the St. Andrews station and the golf funicular, which operates on the Eisenhower course, lifting you from the ninth green up to the tenth tee. The entire complex is administered by a Director of Golf and a staff of five PGA and two LPGA professionals. The course is supported by an excellent pro shop.

RATES   (EP)   Rooms: $115/$150. Suites: $195 and up. Green fees: $40/$55, carts $22. Golf packages are available.

ARRIVAL Car: Highway 60 (Pomona Freeway) to the Azusa Avenue exit. North to Industry Hills Parkway.

SKY VALLEY RESORT
Star Route 1, Box 2931, Tehachapi, CA 93561; (805) 822-5581 CA; (800) 244-0864

This intimate lodge consisting of 84 guest rooms (including cottages fully-equipped for housekeeping) crowns a mountaintop in the rugged Tehachapi range. It is one of the most unusual settings we have seen. Guest rooms are studio

kings, loft suites and double bedrooms, all with a panoramic view of tall pines, greens and fairways. The conference rooms will accommodate up to 75 people. The attractive dining room has an outstanding view of the surrounding area spreading out below the hotel.

An equestrian center provides instruction and supervised trail rides. Boarding for privately-owned horses can be arranged on a space-available basis. There are five lighted tennis courts, a heated swimming pool, locker rooms with saunas, and a lounge offering food and beverage service.

Horse Thief Golf Course is a well-maintained, 18-hole layout. Parring at 72, it reaches out 6,650/6,317/5,723 yards.

RATES (EP) Rooms: $69/$79. Loft suites: $115/$125. Cottages $150/$180. Golf packages are available. Green fees: $22/$33, carts $22.

ARRIVAL Air: Tehachapi. Car: 56 miles from Bakersfield, 118 miles from Los Angeles. Located 16 miles west of Tehachapi on Route 202. It is not easy to get to this resort. Get local directions in Tehachapi and have patience.

SAN DIEGO AREA

CARLTON OAKS LODGE & COUNTRY CLUB

9200 Inwood Drive, Santee, CA 92071; 619) 448-4242; (800) 831-6757

You will find yourself in a quiet country setting at the Oaks Lodge. Bordered on one side by the 6,500-foot Laguna Mountains, and with rolling hills on the other side, the atmosphere here is one of relaxation. Accommodations consist of rooms in the Lodge. Air-conditioned, they offer a view of the golf course or tennis courts. A few are equipped with either a full kitchen or a kitchenette. The Oaks is set up to handle meeting or banquet groups of up to 300. Along with a casual dining room and lounge there is entertainment and dancing on the weekends.

The resort's location, in eastern San Diego County (20 miles from downtown San Diego), gives you access to the beach area and all of its water sport activities, Sea World, and the Mexican Border. In addition to the heated pool, there are four lighted tennis courts.

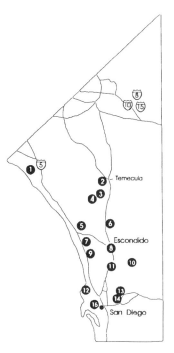

1. Ritz Carlton Laguna Niguel
2. Temecula Creek Inn
3. Pala Mesa Resort
4. San Luis Rey Downs
5. El Camino Inn & Country Club
6. Lake San Marcus Resort
7. Four Seasons Aviara La Costa
8. Castle Creek Inn & Spa
   Lawrence Welk Village
9. The Inn Rancho Santa Fe
   Whispering Palms Lodge & C.C.
10. San Vicente Resort
11. Rancho Bernardo Inn
12. Torrey Pines Inn
13. Carlton Oaks Lodge & C.C.
14. Singing Hills C.C. & Lodge
15. Carmel Highlands Double Tree Resort
    The Handlery Stardust

The golf course has just been renovated. A Pete Dye design, it now plays 7,109/6,613/6,084/5,772/4,817 yards and pars at 72. The challenging features of this course are found in a creek that meanders throughout the entire complex, aided and abetted by menacing ponds, rolling terrain and, of course, Mr. Dye's penchant for railroad ties.

RATES (EP) Rooms: $49 / $70. Suites: (1-bedroom with kitchenette, some with a full-size kitchen) $75. Green fees: $40 / $50, including cart. Golf packages are available.

ARRIVAL Air: San Diego. Car: from Highway 15 turn east on Highway 8, then north on Mission Gorge Road.

CASTLE CREEK INN & SPA
29850 Circle "R" Way, Escondido, CA 92026; (619) 751-8800; (800) 253-5341

Just 45 minutes north of San Diego this resort, while small, has a variety of amenities. Accommodations consist of 30 air-conditioned rooms. They are equipped to handle modest-sized meeting groups with a maximum capacity of 120.

There are two tennis courts, a swimming pool, a complete spa (massage, facials, herbal wraps) along with the Briarwood Dining Room and Sony's Tavern. A few attractions nearby include: the San Diego Wild Animal Park and Broadway Musicals featured at the Lawrence Welk Resort Theater.

Golf is offered at the Castle Creek Country Club. Parring at 72/73, it reaches out 6,254/5,899/5,476 yards.

RATES Rooms: $145. Green fees: $40, including cart. Golf package: 1 night / 1 day (includes lodging, green fees, and cart), weekdays $140; weekends $160 per couple.

ARRIVAL Air: San Diego Airport. Car: just north of Escondido off I-15. Turn east on Gopher Canyon / Old Castle Road. Then left on old 395. Go one half block, turn right to Circle "R" Way.

CARMEL HIGHLAND/ DOUBLE TREE RESORT
14455 Penasquitos Drive, San Diego, CA 92129; (619) 672-9100; (800) 528-0444

Approximately 30 minutes

north of San Diego the Highlands has an ideal location. You are within easy reach of Sea World, the acclaimed San Diego Zoo, Old Mexico, and of course the wonderful beaches of southern California. Other fun activities include tours and, in season, whale watching.

There are 172 guest rooms, including 16 suites overlooking or adjacent to the golf course. Carmel Highlands has 9,000 square feet of space set aside to handle modest-sized meeting groups. Trents is their primary evening dining room, with the less formal Terraces Cafe open for breakfast, lunch, and dinner. The Double Eagle Lounge offers nightly dancing, with live music on the weekends. There is also the Deli Bar, functioning as a 19th hole for the golfers as well as the swimming pool group.

They have six lighted tennis courts, with a professional to assist, along with two swimming pools. Also available is the 5,500-square-foot health and fitness center equipped with state-of-the-art weight systems and providing massage, saunas, and steam baths.

Known as Rancho Penasquitos Golf Course when it opened in 1960, it was substantially remodeled by Jack Daray. In addition to adding 20 bunkers, bringing the total to 75, many tees where lengthened and over 1,500 trees planted. In fact, the tree planting continues today, with about 200 added each year. As a result, the course has become a more challenging layout, and more fun to play. With all the improvements which were made, water comes into contention on only two holes. Reaching out a respectable 6,501/6,108/5,488 yards, it pars at 72/73

RATES   (EP)   Rooms: $129/$139. Suites: $180. Green fees: $40/$50, including cart. Golf packages are available.

ARRIVAL Air: San Diego International Airport. When making reservations you can arrange a pick up at the airport by Super Shuttle. Car: I-15 north to Carmel Mountain Road exit. Turn left. At third traffic light turn right onto Penasquitos Drive.

EL CAMINO INN & COUNTRY CLUB
3170 Vista Way, Oceanside, CA 92056; (619) 757-2200; (800) 458-6064

The Inn, adjacent to the El Camino Country Club, offers its guests all of the services of this private club. Overlooking the golf course, accommodations consist of 42 rooms. Some of these one- and two-bedroom units have living rooms and dining areas, while a few have either kitchens or kitchenettes. The dining room, located at the clubhouse, affords a commanding view of the course and the rolling hills beyond. Private banquets and receptions can be arranged.

In addition to two pools there are seven tennis courts (two lighted) with a professional tennis staff on hand.

The club's 18-hole course reaches out 6,774/6,439/5,831 yards, parring at 72. While water comes into play on only three holes, traps are intriguingly (or diabolically), placed around the greens.

RATES (EP) Rooms: $60 / $75. Green fees: $30, carts $20. Golf package: 2 nights/2 days (includes lodging, golf, cart, continental breakfast), $250 weekdays, $300 weekends per couple.

ARRIVAL Air: San Diego (35 minutes). Los Angeles (90 minutes). Car: I-5, off on 78 east, *then El Camino Real north to Frontage Road.*

FOUR SEASONS RESORT AVIARA
7100 Blue Heron Drive, Carlsbad CA 92009; (619) 929-0077; (800) 332-3442

The setting of this hotel is rather special. Opening in late 1993 it was built on rolling terrain offering spectacular views of the Pacific Ocean. The Spanish colonial architecture, along with fountains, intimate courtyards, vine-smothered trellises, and groves of eucalyptus trees create a sense of tranquility. Accommodations are in 443 rooms and suites, each featuring a private terrace, refrigerated private bar, and TV with a VCR. In addition the suites offer a bedroom and a living room. There is also a three-bedroom presidential suite and a four-bedroom villa. Also available: the Four Seasons "Club" accommodations, providing complimentary breakfast, afternoon tea, evening cocktails, and hors d'oeuvres (most resorts refer to this arrangement as "the concierge level").

The resort has set aside over 39,000 square feet of space for meeting and group activities.

With the many individual breakout rooms they can handle 1,275 theater- , 1,000 banquet- and 600 classroom-style. There is also over 20,000 square feet of outdoor space available.

A wide variety of dining choices await you: The California Cafe, the Mediterranean Dining Room, the Italian Trattoria, or the Pool Bar & Grille. There is, of course, 24 hour room service – how else could you arrange dinner on your own private terrace? There are also plenty of bars and lounges.

There are two swimming pools, plus a children's pool, 12 tennis courts, saunas, a fitness center, a European-style spa including steam rooms, massage facilities, and a whirlpool. There is a children's program available so you will have time to enjoy at least some of the amenities.

The golf course, designed by Arnold Palmer Associates, virtually surrounds the resort complex. Playing to a par of 72 this layout reaches a substantial 7,007/6,591/6,054/5,007 yards. Water comes into contention on only eight holes. You can play golf instead of going fishing all day. Unique to

the course are the stunning views of Batiquitos Lagoon. The Director of Golf is Jim Bellington; the Head Professional is Bill Crist.

RATES Contact the Resort for the latest rates and packages.

ARRIVAL Air: San Diego International Airport (25 miles). Car: from I-5 take the Poinsettia exit and travel east approximately 1 mile. Turn right at Alga Road and enter the Aviara residential development. Continue on Alga for 1/2 mile to Blue Heron Drive and turn right.

THE HANDLERY STARDUST HOTEL & CC
950 Hotel Circle, San Diego, CA 92108; (619) 298-0511; (800) 223-0888

The Stardust Hotel is done in an old and lovely Spanish style, but all else is contemporary. With air-conditioned rooms, lighted handball and racquetball courts, steam rooms, massage, beauty and barber shops, eight tennis courts (four lighted), golf and swimming, what more could you ask for?

Dining takes place in The

Crane Room, specializing in steak and seafood, and there is also a 24-hour coffee shop.

Golf is offered on 27 holes. Using a crossover system, you can play three 18-hole layouts: the Lake/River nines reach out 6,602/6,309/5,734 yards; the Valley/Lake combination plays 6,655/6,357/5,797 yards; and the River/Valley layout weighs in at 6,645/6,356/5,871 yards. All three combinations par at 72. There is also a par-three nine available.

RATES (EP) Rooms: $75 / $95. Suites: $145 / $185. Green fees: $45, including cart. Golf package: 2 nights / 3 days (includes lodging, MAP, 2 rounds golf), $295 per couple. Rates are June 16-September 15.

ARRIVAL Air: San Diego. Car: located in the Mission Valley Hotel Circle, near Highways I-5 and I-8.

THE INN RANCHO SANTA FE
Box 869, Ranch Santa Fe, CA 92067; (619) 756-1131; (800) 654-2928

Originally developed by the Santa Fe Railroad in the early 1920's, the Inn was sold to the Royce family in 1958 and has

been run by them since that time. There are rooms as well as cottages which can be set up as one-bedroom or multiple arrangements. Each is air-conditioned, many with fireplace, wet bars and either a kitchen or kitchenette.

The Inn has the capacity to handle small conference groups in separate meeting facilities, with all audio/visual aids available. Opening off the lobby are the Garden Room, serving breakfast, lunch, and dinner, and the Vintage Room, for lunch, cocktails, and dinner. (Jackets are required, ties are optional). During the summer months, the Patio Terrace features dancing under the stars on Friday and Saturday evenings.

There is a large heated pool, and the Inn also has a beach cottage at nearby Del Mar with showers and other facilities. Tennis can be played on three courts.

While Rancho Santa Fe has no golf course of its own, they can arrange golfing privileges at Rancho Santa Fe Country Club, a half-mile away, Whispering Palms Golf Course, two miles away, and Heritage Hills Country Club, four miles distant.

RATES (EP) Guest rooms: $80/$180. Large bedroom with fireplace and kitchen: $150. Cottages with full kitchen, living room, fireplace, private patio: $285/$475. Green fees – Rancho Santa Fe Course, $90, including cart; Whispering Palms, $40, including cart; Heritage Hills, $80/$90, including cart.

ARRIVAL Air: San Diego. Car: from I-5 turn off at Solana Beach. Now, on Lomas Santa Fe Drive (which changes its name to Linea del Cielo), keep straight on and you will run into the Rancho. Trust me. The parking lot is 4 miles from the I-5 turn-off.

LA COSTA
Costa Del Mar Road, Carlsbad, CA 92008; (619) 438-9111; (800) 854-5000

La Costa's location, 45 minutes from San Diego, gives access to many activities: the wonderful San Diego Zoo, Sea World and, of course, a trip to Old Mexico. Accommodations are in 300 rooms, some in the main hotel, others along the golf course or near the tennis complex. There are also 75 one- or two-bedroom suites.

Each of the five restaurants of-

fers a unique eating adventure. The food and service are excellent. Recently we tried Pisces, a short distance away, and specializing in seafood. This restaurant must be ranked among the best. After dinner you can visit the Tournament of Champions Lounge for nightly dancing and entertainment. If this is not your cup of tea, try some duplicate bridge, a movie in your room, or one in the hotel theater, which features first-run films each evening.

The new 50,000-square-foot Conference Center has added a new dimension to La Costa. They are now able to handle groups of up to 650 banquet-style. For details check with their sales and conference department.

La Costa's spa program is widely recognized as one of the best. Its private club-like complex for women, and a separate one for men, pampers you with facials, massages, whirlpools, loofah scrubs, pedicures, yoga classes, and exercise sessions. If you wish, you can really get into it with Swiss showers, Roman pools, and herbal wraps. The resort also offers a medical fitness evaluation program conducted by a permanent staff physician.

For the tennis player, there is a 25-court complex, under the direction of well known tennis professional Pancho Segura and staff. The program is supported by a full-line tennis shop and video instruction equipment. If you are not completely done in at this point, you might consider a swim in any of the four fresh water pools.

Golf is served up on two beautiful courses. The North measures 6,983/6,596/6,263/5,980 yards, with a par of 72/73; while the South layout shows a more modest yardage of 6,896/6,534/6,214/5,632, parring at 72/74. There are, of course, locker rooms, a snack bar, practice area and a pro shop.

While this is a lovely resort, they handle a great many convention and meeting groups; a twosome can get pushed aside when it comes time to play golf. If you are a twosome be sure your tee times are confirmed **in writing**.

A second warning: this is a busy place. At times the bellmen tend to get short-tempered and seem to forget who is the guest and who is the bellmen.

RATES   (EP)   Rooms: $215 / $250 / $325 / $400. Suites: $375/$730. There are many different packages: spa plans, golf, and tennis packages. Green fees: $75, cart $35.

ARRIVAL Air: San Diego. Private aircraft: Palomar (3 miles). Car: Los Angeles (2 hours). Take I-5 to La Costa Avenue exit, to El Camino Real, then left to the entrance.

LAKE SAN MARCUS RESORT

1025 La Bonita Drive, San Marcos, CA 92069; (619) 744-0120; (800) 447-6556

Guests of the Inn (Quails Inn) are really entering a private residential community, with the lodge fronting on Lake San Marcos. In addition to 142 rooms in the lodge, there are lakeshore cottages equipped with kitchens. There are also some private homes available. With their five separate meeting rooms, they can handle almost any group arrangement and have a capacity for 300 theater- or 160 classroom-style..

For dining you have a choice of either the Quails Inn Dinner House, the Country Club, or the Coffee Shop. There are also three cocktail lounges. The Quails Lounge provides dancing as well as entertainment nightly. Within a mile of the resort are a wide selection of restaurants and shops.

There are four tennis courts, three paddle tennis courts, and a total of four swimming pools. Kayot party boats, sailboats or canoes are available for rent.

Golf can be played on the championship Lake San Marcos Country Club course or on the Lakeview layout. The San Marcos reaches 6,484/6,260/5,959 yards and pars at 72/73. The Lakeside, an executive 18-hole affair, has a yardage of 2,700/2,226, with a par of 58.

RATES (EP) Rooms: $85/$95. Cottages: 1 bedroom $165; 2 bedrooms $220. Green fees: $45, including cart. There are weekly lodging rates. Golf package: 2 nights/2 days (includes lodging, breakfast and lunch each day, two rounds of golf with cart), $320/$355 per couple.

ARRIVAL Air: San Diego. Car: I-5, east on Palomar Airport Road. Right on Rancho Santa Fe Road (1,000 feet ahead).

LAWRENCE WELK RESORT
8860 Lawrence Welk Drive, Escondido, CA 92026; (619) 749-3000; (800) 932-9355

Within this 1,000-acre complex are gift and beauty shops, a fashion parlor, and even dental offices. There is also a market, Jonathan's Restaurant, and a pizza shop. There are 132 guest rooms at the Inn, plus 256 two-bedroom villas. The villas have living rooms, dining areas, and fully-equipped kitchens. Each has either a private patio or balcony. The new Greens Conference Center gives the resort a capability of handling meeting groups of up to 125.

The Lawrence Welk Dinner Theater, seating 300, features professional entertainment Tuesday, Thursday, Friday and Saturday evenings with matinees scheduled throughout most of the week. There is, of course, a cocktail lounge.

There are a total of five tennis courts, a spa and five swimming pools.

Golf can be played on The Meadow Lake Country Club course. Reaching a substantial 6,521/6,312/5,758 yards, it pars at 72/74. Also available is

The Fountains 18, an executive affair playing 4,002/3,581/3,099 yards, parring at 62. The resort also has a short par-three course of some 1,837 yards. In addition, there are at least 15 championship-caliber courses within a few miles of the village.

RATES Inn rooms: standard $95/$110. Villas: minimum 2 nights (up to 4 people) $220. Green fees: $30/$35, carts $20.

ARRIVAL Air: San Diego (33 miles). Car: 8 miles north of Escondido off I-15.

PALA MESA RESORT
2001 South Highway 395
Fallbrook, CA 92028
(619) 728-5881; (800) 722-4700

Pala Mesa has long been considered one of Southern California's better resorts. While modest in size, it has a beautiful setting and provides many amenities. Its location, in a beautiful valley between Los Angeles and San Diego, doesn't hurt either. Accommodations are in 133 rooms as well as several condominiums fully-equipped for housekeeping. Alexander's Restaurant presents a variety of outstanding fare and is supported by an excellent lounge. For group meet-

ings their eight separate conference rooms can handle 248 classroom- or 400 theater-style.

Tennis is a basic part of Pala Mesa's sports activities and they provide play on four courts with a professional staff to assist. There is also a swimming pool and a new fitness center.

The golf course is superb. Parring at 72, it plays 6,472/6,151/5,814 yards. While not particularly long, it can test your skill as well as your vocabulary. If your problem is a wild hook, I hope you have been a regular at church – as the first three holes might well destroy you. We took the time to come back and play this layout a second time, a luxury we rarely enjoy. The professional staff, under the direction of Chris Starkjohann, are first rate teachers and may be able to help your game.

RATES   (EP)   Rooms: $110/$125/$150.   Suites: $250. Condominium units (kitchens): 1 bedroom $150; 2 bedrooms $185. Green fees: $45/$60, including cart. Golf packages are available.

ARRIVAL Air: San Diego. Car: 55 miles north of San Di-

ego on I-15. Off at Highway 76, left, then first right west of I-15, about 2 miles.

RANCHO BERNARDO INN
17550 Bernardo Oaks Drive, San Diego, CA 92128; (619) 487-1611; (800) 854-1065

Rancho Bernardo is situated in a beautiful valley just 28 minutes from the San Diego Airport. The Inn has been recognized as a premiere resort for many years. Now after updating and refurbishing it has really matured, evolving into a lovely destination – formal where it should be formal and informal when informality is appropriate. The Inn's location adds another dimension to your visit and opens up the possibility of a trip to Tijuana, perhaps to see a bullfight or visit the Caliente Race Track. It is also close to Sea World, the San Diego Zoo and the beautiful beaches found in this area. The custom of serving "Afternoon Tea," with a background of piano music, offers a delightful pause to the day.

Accommodations, in 287 rooms and suites, provide for every convenience. They are close to the golf course, tennis courts, restaurants, lounges, the three warm spas and the swimming pool areas. Rancho Bernardo is also well prepared to handle meeting groups. For in-depth information contact their sales department.

You can dine in El Bizcocho, with its three-star gourmet cuisine (jackets required), or in the less formal Veranda Room. Both are supported by a large wine selection. Cocktails are available in two lounges. After dinner you can dance to your heart's content.

Tennis definitely does not take a back seat at this resort. As a matter of fact, the tennis facilities have been rated Five-Star by *World Tennis*. Playing on 12 courts (four lighted), the Inn offers a "Tennis College Program" under the direction of professional Paul Navratil. There are more than 35,000 graduates who will attest to the value of the instruction they have received. Also available: a complete fitness center with massage, steam, sauna and workout rooms.

Golf is played on one of California's most interesting courses. The West, a par-72 layout, plays 6,388/6,200/5,468 yards. An additional 27 holes are offered on the Oaks executive course, with each nine parring

at 30. The Director of Golf and his staff are available to help you with tee times and with your game. They also have a well stocked and merchandised golf shop.

RATES   (EP)   Rooms: $195/$250. Suites: $290/$465 up. Golf package: 2 nights/3 days (includes MAP, lodging, golf, cart, club storage, tennis time), $688 per couple. Green fees: $65, including cart. Rates are for January-April 15.

ARRIVAL Air: San Diego. Car: south from Los Angeles, drive I-5 to Oceanside, 78 to Escondido. Highway 15 south to Rancho Bernardo Road exit. From San Diego, travel north on 15.

THE RITZ CARLTON-LAGUNA NIGUEL
33533 Shoreline Drive, Laguna Niguel, CA 92677; (714) 240-2000; (800) 241-3333

Sited on a bluff overlooking the Pacific Ocean, the hotel reflects the architectural style of the Mediterranean. The location places you close to many attractions – fishing, shopping malls, the Mission at San Juan Capistrano, to name a few possibilities. The 393 rooms in the four-story hotel structure range from those with an ocean view, to an oceanfront court-yard location, or a poolside lanai. Their conference and meeting facilities allow them to accommodate groups of up to 700 banquet-style.

Should you go hungry or thirsty here, they are not to blame. At your disposal are The Dining Room, offering classic and contemporary French cuisine; The Cafe Terrace, an all-day restaurant and bar; The Club Bar, featuring live entertainment and dancing; The Library Cocktail Lounge, with its fireplace setting; and "The Bar," with piano entertainment in the evening. Recreational possibilities include: two miles of beach front, four tennis courts, two swimming pools, a fitness center with a steam room, sauna, whirlpool, men's and women's massage, and an exercise room.

The golf course, an 18-hole affair, was designed by Robert Trent Jones II. With a yardage of 6,224/5,655/4,984, it pars at 70. While obviously a short course, it brings into play 88 sand traps, four lakes and three ocean-side holes. It is not as easy as the short yardage might indicate.

RATES   (EP)   Rooms: $195 / $395. Suites: from $700 up. Green fees: $65 / $85, including cart.

ARRIVAL Air: Los Angeles or San Diego. Car: from San Diego on I-5 take Crown Valley Parkway west to Pacific Coast Highway, then south 1 mile to the hotel.

SAN LUIS REY DOWNS
31474 Golf Club Drive, Bonsall, CA 92003; (619) 758-3762

This golf and tennis resort nestled in the San Luis Rey Valley offers accommodations in 26 rooms, seven with kitchenettes. There is a dining room, snack bar, pool, lounge and a country club. For the horse lover they offer a thoroughbred training center, one of the largest in the country.

Tennis is on four lighted, all-weather courts. The resort provides an outstanding tennis shop and the services of teaching professionals.

The golf course is an interesting one with more than enough trees and water to keep you busy. Parring at 72, it plays 6,610/6,324/5,547 yards.

RATES (EP) Rooms: $65/$85. Green fees: $35/$45, including cart. Golf package: 2 nights/2 days (includes lodging, unlimited golf and cart), $250 per couple – weekends $298 per couple.

ARRIVAL Exit I-5 at Oceanside on Mission Avenue. Go east on Highway 76 for 13 miles, then follow signs.

SAN VICENTE RESORT
24157 San Vicente Road, Ramona, CA 92065; (619) 789-8290

Stretched over 3,200 acres of California's high desert, the resort has a lovely setting. Accommodations are rooms in the Lodge as well as condominiums (villas). Each villa has from one to three bedrooms, two baths, full kitchen (fully equipped for housekeeping) and a dining area. Specify if you wish to be near the tennis complex or golf course (about two miles apart).

San Vicente has a 6,700-square-foot conference center with accommodations for groups of 15 to 400. There is a dining room in the main lounge just off the first tee.

Tennis, located at the Ranch, is played on 24 courts with eight lighted. The tennis complex is supported by a clubhouse and pro shop. There is also the "Racquets" restaurant/lounge. The 23-acre Western Center offers rental horses and stables.

The golf course, parring at 72, measures 6,585/6,180/5,578 yards. This layout is equipped with more than its share of water. There are 12 holes in which water hazards come into play.

RATES (EP) Lodge: $65/$80. Condominiums: $100/$180. Green fees: $39/$49, including cart. Golf package: 2 nights/3 days (includes lodging, golf and cart), midweek $294 per couple; weekends $376 per couple. The phone number given above is for reservations at the Inn, but for condominium rentals call (619) 789-8678 or (619) 789-7070.

ARRIVAL Air: San Diego (38 miles). Car: Highway 67 to Ramona, right on San Vicente Road (7 miles). From Escondido take Highway 78 (19 miles) to Ramona, then straight ahead for 7 miles.

SHERATON GRANDE TORREY PINES

10950 North Torrey Pines Road, La Jolla, CA 92037; (619) 558-1500; (800) 325-3535

On a bit of high ground overlooking the fairways of the Torrey Pines golf complex and of the Pacific Ocean, the Sheraton Torrey Pines is in a position to offer its guests a wide variety of activities. Opening in early 1990, it is situated just a few miles from Sea World and the San Diego Zoo. If you have not visited either of these places they are a must. Accommodations here are 400 rooms, including 23 suites. Some have balconies or patios and some offer either a golf course or a view of the sea. With several rooms including a large 12,000-square-foot ballroom, the hotel can handle good-sized meeting groups.

While dining is most certainly available within the hotel (The Torreyana Grille or the Alfresco Terrace), there are a number of good restaurants in La Jolla. I suggest you try some of these well-known eateries.

On-site facilities include: three lighted tennis courts, an exercise room, saunas, a heated swimming pool, and a whirl-pool and spa. The sports concierge can arrange many other activities ranging from scuba diving and fishing to hang gliding or balloon rides. Guests also have privileges at the Shiley Sports & Health Center (Scripps Clinic) nearby.

Golf can be played on the two Torrey Pines championship layouts. Adjacent to the hotel, they are owned and operated by the city. For complete details refer to "Torrey Pines Inn."

RATES   (EP)   Rooms $165 / $250. Suites: $400 / $450. Green fees: $45, carts $25.

ARRIVAL Air: San Diego International Airport (18 miles). Car: take I-5 north to Genesee Street. Turn north and drive to Torrey Pines Road.

SINGING HILLS COUNTRY CLUB & LODGE

3007 Dehesa Road, El Cajon, CA 92021; (619) 442-3425; (800) 457-5568

The 102-unit lodge, nestled in an ancient olive grove, provides immediate access to the course, two swimming pools, the dining area, and the tennis courts. Lodgings consist of rooms and suites. The rooms are exceptionally large and well-appointed. Comprising a bedroom with a large sitting area, a walk-in dressing area, and an oversized bathroom, they would be considered suites in most resorts.

Adjacent to the pro shop is a breakfast/lunch dining area and, on the other side, the dining room. Facilities are available to accommodate small business groups with banquet seating for up to 300. The location of the resort is ideal. You are 20 minutes from the San Diego Zoo, 25 minutes to Sea World, and 40 minutes from Tijuana in Mexico.

The Willow Glen Golf Course reaches 6,605/6,207/5,585 yards and pars at 72. The Oak Glenn plays 6,132/5,749/5,308 yards, with a par of 71. They have used raised tees, six lakes, strategically placed bunkers, natural rock outcroppings and the aged oaks and sycamore trees to enhance the beauty and character of this course. There is also a par-54 executive layout available.

The friendly professional staff, led by the Director of Golf Operations, Tom Addis, is justifiably proud of these golf

facilities and their 4,000-square-foot pro shop. The golf shop is well stocked and the merchandise sensibly priced. This entire layout is one of the best in Southern California.

RATES (EP) Rooms: $79/$85. Jr. suites: $94/$99. Executive suites: $110/$1250. Green fees: $25/$305, cart $18. There are golf packages during summer and fall – weekdays only.

ARRIVAL Air: San Diego (30 minutes). Car: off Highway 8 to El Cajon Boulevard, then to Washington Avenue (turns into Dehesa Road), and travel 2 miles.

TEMECULA CREEK INN
Box 129, Temecula, CA 92390; (619) 728-9100; (800) 962-7335

Temecula Creek Inn is situated in the foothills of the beautiful Santa Rosa Mountains. The resort has recently undergone extensive renovations and now has a distinct Southwestern motif. They can accommodate meeting groups of up to 200.

Their dining room, while small, offers a fine menu. As a guest you can enjoy the convenience of an excellent club, well-appointed rooms with private balconies, and the use of their two tennis courts.

The golf course is a bit unusual, with a front nine that seems open, offering little challenge. It may even tend to lull you a bit, although it really is not all that tame. But the back nine, which can do everything but turn you loose, will open your eyes wide. Parring at 72, the course stretches some 6,784/6,375/5,747 yards. Serving up 56 silica sand traps it also brings hills and ravines into the act. While difficult to handle, it is one of the more picturesque golf courses in the area. There is a small full-line pro shop providing all the amenities.

RATES (EP) Rooms: $105 / $115. Suites: $135 / $150. Green fees: $33 / $45, carts $22. Golf package: 2 nights / 3 days available midweek only (includes lodging, MAP, unlimited green fees, no cart), $480 per couple.

ARRIVAL Air: San Diego. Car: from Escondido, I-15 north to Indio / Highway 79, then east.

TORREY PINES INN
11480 North Torrey Pines Road, La Jolla, CA 92037; (619) 453-4420

Torrey Pines Inn has a unique location. It is on top of two 18-hole public golf courses (the home of the Andy Williams Open Tournament). Their dining room offers an outstanding view of the rolling golf layouts with the Pacific Ocean forming the backdrop. The Inn has three private meeting rooms and can handle modest-size seminar groups.

The head professional and staff have their work cut out for them overseeing this extremely busy 36-hole layout. The South course plays 6,649/6,345 yards, with a par of 72/76; the North layout measures 6,317/6,047, with a par of 72/74. Both courses show extremely long yardage for the ladies.

RATES (EP) Rooms: $72 / $82. Green fees: $40 / $46, carts $22. Golf package: 1 day / 1 night (includes lodging, 1 round of golf with cart), $198 / $224 per couple.

ARRIVAL Air: San Diego (25 minutes). Car: I-5 to Genesee, then north on Torrey Pines Road.

WHISPERING PALMS LODGE & COUNTRY CLUB

P.O. Box 3209, Rancho Santa Fe, CA 92067; (619) 756-2471

The lodge, located close to San Diego, provides access to a wide range of activities: a day trip to Tijuana, a visit to the beautiful beaches, an afternoon at Sea World or the San Diego Zoo are some of the possibilities. Of course the resort itself offers a variety of activities such as golf, tennis, swimming, or riding. There are 102 rooms, including suites. The Lodge can also accommodate from 10 to 250 for meetings with both MAP or FAP plans available.

Andy Volkert, tennis professional, heads up the action on the 11 all-weather tennis courts (two lighted). The 27-hole golf course plays as follows: the North/South, measuring 6,346/6,051/5,684 yards, pars at 72; the North/East nines combine to 6,141/5,860/5,564 yards with a par of 71; the South/East 18, weighing in at 6,443/6,131/5,776 yards, also has a par of 71. The golf operation, along with a well-stocked pro shop, is under the direction of PGA professional John Combs.

RATES (EP) Rooms: $82. Suites: $138. Green fees: $23/$28, carts $23. Golf package: 2 nights (includes lodging, 2 rounds of golf per person with cart, 2 breakfasts), $280; weekends $295 per couple.

ARRIVAL Car: Between Oceanside and San Diego. East off I-5, on Via DeValle (2 1/2 miles).

THE COACHELLA VALLEY – DESERT AREA

The area known as the Coachella Valley comprises Palm Springs, forming the northwestern boundary, and Coachella on the southeast. There are now several other rapidly growing communities in between: Cathedral City, Palm Desert, Desert Hot Springs, Rancho Mirage, La Quinta, Indian Wells and Indio.

Discovered in the early '20s by Hollywood's elite, it is no longer a group of sleepy little villages. While the area has changed over the years, the one thing which has not been altered is the magnificent clear blue sky, the mild climate, soaking your body in a warm

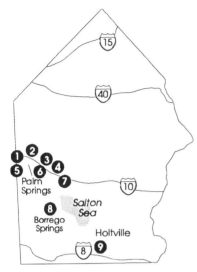

La Quinta Hotel Resort
PGA West
7. Indio
   Indian Palms Country
   Club Inn
8. Borrego Springs
   La Casa del Zorro
   Rams Hill
9. Holtville
   Barbara Worth Country Club

---

outdoor pool or playing a round of golf on a manicured course, while the rest of the country is slipping and sliding behind a snow plow. There are enough shopping centers to keep even the most ardent shopper busy. Gift and antique shops as well as photography and artist studios are surpassed in number only by those in the Carmel/Monterey area.

One could make a career out of eating here, with cuisine ranging from hamburgers to sumptuous Mexican meals or gourmet cuisine from every part of the world.

While the various Chambers of Commerce advise you to bring warmer apparel for evening, "summer months – June through mid-September – are warmer." There is one of the most masterful understatements of all time. I have seen the temperature climb well over 125 degrees. I don't

1. Palm Springs
   Doubletree Resort
   Lawrence Welk's Oasis
   Resort
2. Cathedral City
   Cathedral Canyon Rentals
3. Rancho Mirage
   Marriott's Rancho Las Palmas
   The Westin Mission Hills
   Resort
4. Palm Desert
   Avondale Country Club
   The Lakes Country Club
   Marriott's Desert Springs
   Resort
   Marriott's Villa Rentals
   Monterey Country Club
   Palm Desert Resort & C.C.
   Palm Valley Country Club
5. Indial Wells
   Hyatt Grand Champions Resort
   Indian Wells Racquet Club
   Stouffer's Esmeralda Resort
6. La Quinta

care how low the humidity is, when it gets that hot it becomes no place for a human being to linger, much less a golfer.

Within this area there are over 60 golf courses, 20 or more world-class destination golf resorts, plus a few more located a bit further south in the Borrega Springs region. While not as large, the Coachella Valley is rapidly becoming the West Coast version of "The Myrtle Beach" golf scene.

AVONDALE COUNTRY CLUB
75-800 Avondale Drive
Palm Desert, CA 92260
(619) 345-2727

Avondale is basically a private country club rather than a resort hotel. However, for several reasons, we wanted to list it. The course is super, the people are warm and friendly, and they do rent beautiful homes around the course. For home rentals call (619) 346-9690. Some, by the way, are equipped with a private pools.

The clubhouse is one of the most impressive we have seen. Its basic design, with an expanse of glass in the dining area, opens up a panoramic view of the desert and the mountains.

The Avondale Golf Course is one of the best layouts in the area. A challenging, course, it is well-manicured and fun to play. Measuring 6,771/6,386/ 5,766 yards, it pars at 72. To reach the pro shop, call (619) 345-3712. The extremely well-stocked and managed golf shop is under the direction of head professional Fred Scherzer.

RATES 2 bedrooms off-fairway, without heated pool $1,100, with pool $1,450, weekly. Green fees: $55/$65, carts $20.

ARRIVAL Avondale Drive is off Country Club Drive between Bob Hope Drive and Washington Street.

BARBARA WORTH COUNTRY CLUB
2050 Country Club Drive
Holtville, CA 92250
(619) 356-2806; (800) 356-3806

This 103-room motel overlooks the golf course and offers a heated swimming pool, a lap pool, a whirlpool, driving range, and a dining room and lounge. The country club now has meeting facilities and can host groups of 25 to 500.

The golf course plays at 6,239/5,902 yards, parring at 71/73, and has a pro shop and locker rooms.

RATES (EP) Rooms: $57; weekly $371. Golf package: 2 days/2 nights (includes lodging, 2 days golf with cart, all taxes), weekdays $209 – weekends $225 per couple. Green fees: $18/$20, carts $18. Rates are for November-May.

ARRIVAL Air: El Centro-Imperial. Car: 8 miles east of El Centro, 2 miles from Holtville.

CATHEDRAL CANYON RENTALS
68-733 Perez Road, Cathedral City, CA 92234; (619) 324-3463

The phone number above is to a real estate group rental office. The 450-acre country club community is surrounded by privacy walls and security gates. Available activities include a 27-hole golf course, 10 tennis courts (7 lighted), and a spacious clubhouse with restaurant and lounge. Within this area are numerous swimming pools, therapy pools and over 800 homes. Although the golf course has been acquired by the Lawrence Welk group, all of the activities are still available to guests of Cathed-

eral Canyon. Accommodations are one- and two-bedroom homes (equipped for housekeeping), many with a convertible den. Maid service can be arranged at additional cost.

The Lawrence Welk Country Club Course is now a 27-hole layout. For details on the course refer to Lawrence Welk's Desert Oasis on the following pages.

RATES Homes: $150/$200. Weekly: $750/$1,000. Monthly $2,000/$2,600. Green fees: $59, carts $28. Rates are for mid-December through May.

ARRIVAL Air: Palm Springs. Car: via I-10, 110 miles from Los Angeles and 5 miles from the Palm Springs Airport.

DOUBLE TREE RESORT
Vista Chino & Landau Boulevard, Palm Springs, CA 92263 (619) 322-7000; (800) 637-0577

The Double Tree is on 347 acres less than five miles from the center of Palm Springs. Accommodations are 300 rooms in the four-story hotel plus 200 fully-equipped one- and two-bedroom condominiums. The resort is well set up to handle meeting groups with its 12 meeting rooms, and two ball-rooms. The Promenade Cafe is available for casual dining. The Oasis Lounge offers entertainment and dancing nightly and there is the Vista Bar for a quiet libation.

Recreational amenities include: an outdoor heated pool, a lap pool, two hydrotherapy pools, men's and women's exercise rooms, a massage center, 10 tennis courts (five lighted), two handball courts, and two handball/racquetball courts.

The Desert Princess Golf Course, under the direction of professional Dave McKeating, plays 6,636/6,164/5,719/5,326 yards, parring at 72. While basically flat, it brings water into play on 11 holes. There are now 27 holes to be played.

RATES *(EP)   Rooms: $200/$230. Suites: $300/$750 and up. Condo: 1-bedroom $225/$300. Green fees:$60/ $75, including cart. Rates are January through May.*

ARRIVAL *Air: Palm Springs International. Car: off 1-10 at the Date Palm exit, turn right on Vista Chino. Travel approximately 1 mile and you have arrived.*

HOTEL INDIAN WELLS
76-661 Highway 111, Indian Wells, CA 92210; (619) 345-6466; (800) 248-3220

The Inn has 152 rooms, each with a patio or balcony. Each unit offers either a mountain view, country club or poolside location. The Loren Room is available for dining and there is Jake's lounge for evening entertainment. The resort has a meeting capacity of up to 150.

There is a swimming pool, with tennis located nearby. Golf is played just across Highway 111 at the Indian Wells public golf courses, For full details on these two championship layouts refer to Hyatt Grand Champions Resort below. Guests now have playing privileges on the Indian Wells Country Club's 27 holes – home of the Bob Hope classic.

RATES *(EP) Rooms $165. Suites: $265. Golf package: 1 night/1 day (includes lodging with mountain view, green fees and cart), $199 per couple.*

ARRIVAL *Air: Palm Springs Airport (14 miles). Car: from I-10 take Washington to Highway 111. Then drive west to Club Drive.*

HYATT GRAND CHAMPIONS RESORT

44-600 Indian Wells Lane, Indian Wells, CA 92210; (619) 341-1000; (800) 233-1234

There are 340 rooms and suites, along with the Reqency Club Level (concierge floor). The various penthouses occupy the top floor of the hotel and also have private (European-trained) concierge service provided. I am almost reluctant to mention the one- and two-bedroom Garden Villas for fear you will think I am putting you on. These sumptuous villa suites which are sited around private spas have a butler assigned to each villa court. The meeting facilities are excellent, with a capacity of 500 classroom- or 660 banquet-style.

The three restaurants range from a steak house (Austin's), to less formal fare (The Trattoria California Restaurant). In addition there is Charlie's Restaurant overlooking the clubhouse court, offering outside dining, as well as the poolside Bar and Grill for snacks and sandwiches. The Pianissimo Lounge provides a library-fireplace atmosphere during the cocktail hour.

Tennis can be played on grass, clay or hard surface courts, with a 10,500-seat stadium court available so your friends can watch your spectacular performance. Additional amenities include: a health and fitness center, four swimming pools, 24 whirlpool spas located throughout the hotel property, walking, hiking and bicycle paths.

The resort is adjacent to two 18-hole public golf courses designed by Ted Robinson. The East layout, with a par of 72, reaches out 6,686/6,259/5,521 yards. The West 18, also parring at 72, measures a fair 6,478/6,115/5,387 yards. The West Course, while shorter, offers undulating terrain as well as multi-level greens to keep you honest. At first view it looks easy and open. It is neither. Along with waterfalls, the East course has a par-three island hole, while the West offers a par-four island green to shoot for. Each of these layouts comes equipped with a tough dogleg finishing hole.

RATES (EP) Split-level parlor suite: $285 and up. Penthouse suite: $375. Villas: 1 bedroom $725 / $925. Green fees: 960 / $100, including cart.

ARRIVAL Air: Palm Springs.

Car: from the airport, travel south on Highway 111 (approximately 20 minutes). Resort entrance will be on your left.

INDIAN PALMS COUNTRY CLUB & INN

48-630 Monroe, Indio, CA 92201; (619) 347-0688

Accommodations include rooms at the Inn or two- to three-bedroom condominiums. Along with nine tennis courts (five lighted), there are several swimming pools. There is a small pro shop, tennis shop, lounges and dining in the historic clubhouse overlooking the 18th green.

Golf is available on three nine-hole courses making possible (by mixing) three different 18-hole layouts. The yardage from the back tees of each 18 is 6,403/6,284/6,279, and each has a par of 72. Water comes into play on 15 of the 27 holes.

RATES *(EP) Inn: $74. 2-bedroom condominiums: weekly $550. Guests of Inn are offered complimentary green fees and tennis Monday through Thursday. Carts: $20/$25. Weekend green fees: $45, including cart.*

ARRIVAL   *From   Palm*

Springs: east on Highway 111 through Indian Wells. In Indio, turn right on Monroe Street.

INDIAN WELLS RACQUET CLUB RESORT

46-765 Racquet Club Drive, Indian Wells, CA 92260; (619) 360-5068

Vacation homes at Indian Wells are nestled in a cove in the shadow of the majestic Santa Rosa Mountains, 20 minutes from Palm Springs and its shops and restaurants. Accommodations are in studios or one- , two- and three-bedroom townhouses, which are fully-equipped for housekeeping. The resort is also set up to handle meeting groups of up to 100.

Indian Wells Racquet Club Resort clubhouse offers casual dining as well as a cocktail lounge. There is a great view of the Indian Wells Country Club golf course and clubhouse from here. The entire area abounds in excellent restaurants.

There are 10 tennis courts, and a group of trained teachers to assist you. For those who prefer a leisurely pace, there are four private pools close to your studio or townhouse.

While there are many golf courses in this area, the Indian Wells Country Club, adjacent to the racquet club and the home of the Bob Hope Classic, offers 27 holes of outstanding golf. It is a fun layout and one you will long remember. You most certainly will remember it if you should be so unfortunate as to tangle with any of the rock canyon walls. And you can definitely get "involved" should you spray a few shots.

Directly across the road is the Indian Wells 36-hole public golf complex. For details refer to Hyatt Grand Champions Resort.

RATES (EP) Studio: $140; weekly $840. Studio suite: $150; weekly $900. Deluxe 1-bedroom: $185; weekly $1080. Rates are for December 26-April 30. Green fees: $75/$100, including cart.

ARRIVAL Air: Palm Springs. Car: south on Highway 111 to Indian Wells.

IRONWOOD COUNTRY CLUB
49-200 Mariposa Drive, Palm Desert, CA 92260; (619) 568-1259

Ironwood Country Club is pri-

vate, with security gates, impeccably manicured grounds, two fine golf courses, a large and beautiful clubhouse and dining room, swimming pools, 14 lighted tennis courts, and a bit more. Although a private club, rental of privately-owned homes and villas can be arranged through their rental office, with a minimum of one week's stay. There is a damage deposit of $250 required, which will be returned after your unit has been vacated and inspected. Maid service is provided once each week. Additional service can be arranged at the prevailing rate.

Golf can be played on either: the North Course, 6,238/5,563 yards, parring at 70; or the South, parring at 72. The South layout stretches 7,286 yards from the masochist tees, or can be played at 6,808/6,518/5,909 yards.

One real plus: the people and the staff are friendly at Ironwood – something you don't always find. Please remember that Ironwood is a private club; thus certain tee times are reserved for members and club events.

RATES (EP) Villas: 1 bedroom $975 per week. Monthly $2,750. 2 bedrooms $1,250 per *week. Monthly $4,550. Rates are for mid-December through April. Green fees: $85, including cart.*

***ARRIVAL** Air: Palm Springs. From Highway 111 take Portola Drive north. Resort entrance will be on your left.*

LA CASA DEL ZORRO
Borrego Springs, CA 92004; (619) 767-5323; (800) 824-1884

Borrego Valley is nestled against the 8,000-foot-high Santa Rosa mountains. Within this setting is La Casa del Zorro. While the resort has been in operation for several years, it has recently undergone a complete renovation. The rooms have been remodeled with new rugs, new furniture, wall coverings and new bathroom fixtures. Accommodations consist of single rooms, suites, deluxe suites, and casitas ranging from one to four bedrooms and bath. Some have a fireplace and all have small refrigerators. Since our first visit here they have added three new buildings (44 guest units), bringing their total to 77. They now also offer meeting facilities and are capable of handling groups up to 300 people.

The dining and lounge areas have also been expanded to keep up with the rest of the resort. The food (continental cuisine) is good – as is the service. Jackets are required for dinner except during the summer.

La Casa now offers swimming in three pools as well as the use of six lighted tennis courts. They also have a beauty salon and a gift shop.

The Rams Hill 18-hole championship course is one of the most beautiful we have played. For complete details refer to "Rams Hill" listed in this book.

***RATES** (EP) Studio: $98. Suites: $110/$145. Deluxe suites: $135/$180. Casitas: (1-4 bedrooms), $180/$450. Green fees: Rams Hill CC $75, including cart.*

***ARRIVAL** Air: Borrego Springs for commercial and private aircraft (5,000 feet of paved and lighted runway). Phone ahead for courtesy car pick-up. Car: from Temecula, take Highway 71, which becomes 79, continue to Montezuma Road, turn southeast.*

THE LAKES COUNTRY CLUB

75-375 Country Club Drive, Palm Desert, CA 92260; (619) 568-4321 Reservations (619) 345-5695

While the impressive Santa Rosa Mountains provide a beautiful background for the entire resort, they really set off the magnificent 40,000-square-foot clubhouse. With its massive stone fireplaces, ranch-style atmosphere, large planters and views of the surrounding area, the clubhouse has become the focal point of The Lakes resort. The golf shop is on the main level, along with a fine dining room, and several shops featuring the latest in high fashion. On the lower (ground level) can be found the locker rooms and the Santa Fe Grill.

The resort's name is appropriate. There are a total of 21 lakes covering 25 acres spread throughout the resort complex. The grounds are further enhanced by the presence of over a thousand towering palm trees. Guests stay in one- to three-bedroom condominiums, each fully-equipped for housekeeping. In fact, so well-equipped that you may not want to return home. Just to cover a few of the amenities,

each condominium has a microwave oven, range, refrigerator (with ice dispenser), washer, dryer, disposal, dishwasher, gas barbecue, and a furnished patio.

In addition to golf, there are 15 tennis courts (eight lighted), a well-equipped tennis shop and clubhouse, overlooking the center stadium court. There is, of course, a professional staff available. They also have a sophisticated video tape system allowing you to review your game. There are swimming pools throughout the grounds, convenient to each condominium grouping.

Golf is an experience on this layout. True to its name, water comes into play on at least nine of the 18 holes. Measuring a modest 6,502/6,130/5,504 yards, the course pars at 72. Architect Ted Robinson did an outstanding job of blending water, trees, Scottish-style grass bunkers, mixed with rolling terrain, to produce a fun course which will give you all you can handle. In charge of this layout and the superb pro shop is PGA professional Mike Clifford. For the clubhouse call (619) 568-4321.

RATES (EP) 2 bedrooms $350. Green fees: $90, including cart.

There are packages, also discounts for length of stay. Rates are for mid-December through April.

ARRIVAL *Air: Palm Springs. Car: I-10 to Palm Desert exit.*

LA QUINTA RESORT
49-499 Eisenhower Dr., La Quinta, CA 92253; (619) 564-4111; (800) 854-1271

During Hollywood's heyday, La Quinta was the gathering place for many celebrities: Garbo, Davis, Swanson, Chaplin, Gable, Hepburn and many other top names in the movie industry. Unfortunately many years have intervened and, while much money has been spent on this resort, it still seems to linger in the past. Sited on 900 acres, lodgings range from rooms and cottage suites to a number of privately-owned villas. Tennis can be played on 30 courts. There is a clubhouse complete with dining room and bar, a pro shop, several pools, and a spa.

There are now three 18-hole golf courses, of which two are available to all guests. The Mountain course is restricted to member play. The Citrus course was reserved for select guests, but we understand it is now available a bit more often for guest play. This Pete Dye design reaches out a substantial 7,135/6,477/5,932/5,106, parring at 72. While in general I do not like Dye courses, this one is an exception. It is not only beautiful, but it's fair as well. Available to all resort guests, The Dunes plays 6,874/6,307/5,775/5,005 yards, also with a par of 72. Though quite long, it is open and appropriately named – it spreads all over the desert.

Private homes on the grounds can be rented. Should you be interested call (619) 564-6098.

RATES *(EP)   Rooms: $195/$290. Cottage suites: $325/$2,000 per night. Green fees: $85, including cart. Rates are December-April.*

ARRIVAL *Air: Palm Springs. Private aircraft: Thermal (10 minutes). Car: from Palm Springs (19 miles southeast).*

LAWRENCE WELK'S DESERT OASIS
34567 Cathedral Canyon Drive, Palm Springs, CA 92264; (619) 321-9000 CA; (800) 824-8224

Formerly known as the Cathedral Canyon Resort Hotel, it

has been taken over by the Lawrence Welk group. Accommodations are 162 suites. Each unit includes a sitting room, dining area, full kitchen, and either a balcony or patio. I know the accommodations sound a bit like a condominium complex. I assure you, however, it is a hotel.

In the Oasis Dining Room & Lounge there is live entertainment five evenings a week. The resort has a giant, uniquely-shaped swimming pool, a spa and an activity center with a weight room, billiards, ping pong, etc.

The Lawrence Welk Country Club, next to the hotel, offers tennis on 10 courts (seven lighted), including a stadium court. A resident tennis professional is available for clinics and to arrange matches. There is also a clubhouse with a restaurant, lounge and pro shop.

The golf course has grown to 27 holes. Using a crossover arrangement, you can play the Lake View/Mountain View nines at 6,505/6,172/5,346 yards; the Mountain View/Resort Course, reaching 6,477/6,067/5,452 yards; and the Lake View/Resort Course combination, with a yardage of 6,366/6,021/5,376. No matter

how you combine them, the par remains at 72. With water coming into play on 16 of the 27 holes, plus many hungry bunkers, it will offer you plenty of challenge. Supported by an excellent pro shop, the entire golf operation is under the supervision of Head LPGA Professional, Joe Beth "JB" Kemp. For tee times call the pro shop at 328-6571.

RATES   (EP)   Suites: $219/$239/$269. Green fees: $75/$85, including cart. Rates shown are for mid-December through May 30th.

ARRIVAL Air: Palm Springs. Car: from State Highway 111 turn onto Cathedral Canyon Drive. From I-10 drive west on Ramon Road, then left on Cathedral Canyon Road.

MARRIOTT'S DESERT SPRINGS RESORT & SPA
74855 Country Club Drive, Palm Desert, CA 92260; (619) 341-2211; (800) 228-9290

Marriott's Desert Springs has been judged one of the top 50 resorts. In the spectacular setting of Palm Desert, Marriott has built one of the most magnificent hotels to be found anywhere. The eight-story atrium entrance with water cascading down to a lower level pool, gondolas, along with several species of white swan (and all of this is indoors), is so spectacular that on weekends the hotel is crowded with local people wandering around, not really believing what they see – much like folks at a county fair. Currently rated as a Mobil Four Star resort, we predict it will not be long before it is rated as a Five Star. Opened in late 1987, Marriott claims this as one of the largest desert resorts in the nation. Sited on 400 acres, sporting a 30-acre fresh water lake, 892 guest rooms, a 51,000-square-foot separate wing set aside for meetings, 10 restaurants and lounges, it seems their claim may be justified. There are also enough shops of various types to make you feel as if you were living in a department store complex.

The 65 suites range in size from 900 to 3,100 square feet, while the regular guest rooms, featuring mini-bars and refrigerators, run 450 square feet.

There are two swimming pools, 16 tennis courts (eight lighted), a 27,000-square-foot health spa which includes jogging paths, a lap pool, therapy pools, sauna and whirlpools,

Swiss showers, a luxurious array of salon and beauty treatments.

Golf is available on two Ted Robinson golf courses. The Palms plays 6,761/6,381/6,143/5,492 yards, parring at 72. Sited on gently rolling terrain, well-trapped, with water coming into play on 10 holes, this course will keep your attention. The newest layout, the Valley Course stretches 6,713/6,366/6,084/5,348 yards and also pars at 72. In addition to the tennis pro shop there is a full-line golf shop and a professional staff under the supervision of the Director of Golf, Tim Skogen.

The John Jacobs' Practical Golf School is available at this resort. Using personalized, proven teaching methods, and under the direction of PGA and LPGA teaching professionals, it is well worth looking into. For complete details, call (800) 472-5007.

RATES (EP) Standard: $265 / $325. Suites: $375 and up. Green fees: $80, including cart.

ARRIVAL Air: Palm Springs (13 miles). Car: I-10 from Los Angeles (120 miles).

MARRIOTT'S RANCHO LAS PALMAS RESORT

41000 Bob Hope Drive, Rancho Mirage, CA 92270; (619) 568-2727; (800) 228-9290

The structure of Rancho Las Palmas is impressive, reflecting early California-style architecture with graceful arches, rough textured stucco, exposed wooden beams, and red tile roofs. The rich Spanish-style furnishings as well as the paintings, tapestries and authentic Mexican tile add to its gentle southwestern ambiance. Lodgings are 456 hacienda-style rooms and suites, each with patio or balcony, and all near the golf course or the various small lakes. There are also a great many condominiums. For condo rental call (619) 345-5695. This resort, like all Marriott operations, is well set up to accommodate meeting and conference groups.

Dining options include The Cabrillo Room, serving French cuisine, The Fountain Court (a bit less formal), and The Sunrise Terrace, which offers patio dining. Each has good service and a wide menu selection. The Rancho Las Palmas has earned several awards including The Golden Key, The Pinnacle, The AAA Four Diamond and the Mobil Four Star Award.

Tennis can be played on 25 courts (eight lighted), with a pro shop and video analysis equipment available. Some of the other amenities include: two swimming pools with companion hydrotherapy pools, a fitness center, and once-a-week aerobic classes.

There are 27 holes of golf to test you. The North/South nines measure 6,019/5,716/5,421 yards, parring at 71. The West/North combination reaches 5,558/5,295/4,985 yards and pars at 70. The West/South combination weighs in at 5,569/5,219/4,886, again with a par of 70. Winding among six small lakes, 80 sand traps, over 1,500 tall palm trees, and the condominium structures themselves, these are entertaining courses to play.

The John Jacobs' Practical Golf School is available at this resort. Using personalized teaching methods, and under the direction of PGA and LPGA teaching professionals, it is well worth looking into. For complete details, call: (800) 472-5007.

RATES (EP) Rooms: $215/$280. Suites: $450/ $750. Green fees: $80, including cart. Rates are for December 26-May 30.

ARRIVAL Air: Palm Springs. Car: I-10 off at Bob Hope Drive.

MARRIOTT VILLA RENTALS
1091 Pinehurst Lane, Palm Desert, CA 92260; (619) 779-1208; (800) 526-3597

While a basic part of the Marriott Desert Springs Hotel, the villas function as a separate operation and are situated immediately adjacent to the resort and spa. The villas are two-bedroom, two-bath suites ranging in size up to 1,650 square feet and featuring a whirlpool spa, formal dining area, fully-equipped kitchen with microwave, self-cleaning oven, dishwasher and disposal. They also have a gas-log fireplace as well as a washer/dryer unit.

As a guest of the villas you have access to all of the amenities of Marriott's Desert Springs Resort. For detail on the golf and other facilities, refer to Marriott's Desert Springs Resort & Spa.

RATES (EP) Guest Suite: $120/$145. 1-bedroom villa: $275. 2-bedroom villa: $395. Weekly and monthly rates are also available.

MONTEREY COUNTRY CLUB
41-500 Monterey Avenue, Palm Desert, CA 92260; (619) 568-9311; reservations (619) 345-5695

The accommodations at Monterey are condominiums and homes, most with fireplaces and wet bars, fully-equipped for housekeeping. Within this 360-acre resort complex you will find 19 tennis courts (10 lighted) including a sunken championship court with built-in stadium seating and a 3,000-square-foot tennis clubhouse. There are also several swimming pools scattered throughout the area. The main clubhouse overlooks the largest on-property lake as well as the 9th and 18th holes. The upper level is the location of the dining room, while the lower level contains the pro shop, locker rooms, and snack shop.

Golf can be played on 27 holes. Using a crossover arrangement, you wind up with: the East/West combination, reaching out 6,096/5,798/5,250 yards and parring at 71; the East/South nines at 6,041/5,780/5,242 yards, also parring at 71; and finally the West/South combination of nines, which runs 6,133/5,838/5,346 yards, parring at 72. With water on 15 holes, plus some interesting uphill and downhill fairways, it becomes an intriguing combination of golf holes. For tee times call (619) 340-3885.

RATES (EP) 1-bedroom condo with den: $270. 2-bedroom condo: $325. Green fees: $75/$85, including cart. There are discounts for weekly or longer stays. Rates are for mid-December through April.

ARRIVAL Air: Palm Springs.

PALM DESERT RESORT & COUNTRY CLUB
77-333 Country Club Drive, Palm Desert, CA 92260; (619) 345-2781; reservations (619) 345-8426

The center of the resort is their impressive clubhouse. It also happens to be the location of the Papagayo Dining Room as well as the golf shop and check-in area. Accommodations are villas, each with living room, fully-equipped kitchen, bedroom, dinette, and private patio. The two-bedroom units have two baths. The Palm Desert Resort can provide a full spectrum of conference and meeting facilities accommodating up to 200 per meeting group.

Tennis, under the supervision of a professional staff, is offered on 17 lighted courts with a 1,000-seat amphitheater as the center court. There are also two indoor racquetball courts and 20 swimming pools scattered throughout the property.

The golf course, parring at 72, plays 6,506/6,202/6,026/5,434 yards. With sand, water and rolling terrain, it is one of the most enjoyable desert courses I have played. That is, until I reached the 9th hole. I was not speechless, but I was unprintable. Suffice to say, it is different. The pro shop, under the direction of professional Tom Bienek, offers one of the finest selections of equipment and clothing we have seen anywhere in the U.S. In fact it could be called a small department store. The selection not only includes golfing and casual wear but also a choice of bathing attire.

RATES (EP) Villas: 1 bedroom

$169. 1 bedroom plus den: $175. 2 bedrooms: $195. Green fees: $70/$75, including cart. Rates are for January-April.

***ARRIVAL** Air: Palm Springs. Car: from Los Angeles, I-10 to Washington Street exit, right on Country Club Drive.*

PALM VALLEY COUNTRY CLUB
976-200 Country Club Drive, Palm Desert, CA 62260; (619) 345-2737; reservations (619) 345-5695

Accommodations are well-equipped homes and condominiums either near to or on the golf course. The 83,000-square-foot clubhouse, the center of the resort's activities, is a magnificent setting for dining. This is also where you will find the golf and tennis pro shops, both quite large and offering a wide selection of clothing. On the lower level are the spa, racquetball courts, a coed weight room, an aerobics room, saunas, massage and steam rooms, whirlpools, tanning rooms, and more.

Next to the clubhouse is a 25-meter swimming pool and an outdoor jogging trail. When you add that to the 19 tennis courts (10 lighted) and include

a stadium court, I think you will agree there are more than enough activities to keep you occupied.

The South golf course stretches 6,545/6,105/5,429 yards, parring at 72. With water on 12 holes, palm trees all over the place, as well as half the Sahara Desert used as sand traps, this layout will keep your attention. Or perhaps I should say it had better keep your attention. The North course is an executive layout playing 4,245 yards, with a par of 63. Both courses, as well as the pro shop, are under the direction of Head Professional Scott Walter. For tee times call (619) 345-2742.

***RATES** (EP) 1 bedroom: $305. 1 bedroom and den: $325. Green fees: $80/$85, including cart. There are discounts for stays of a week or longer. Rates quoted are for mid-December through April.*

***ARRIVAL** Air: Palm Springs.*

PGA WEST
55-900 PGA Boulevard, La Quinta, CA 92253; Reservations (619) 345-5695

The PGA West is, in fact, a resort community. It is on

2,200 acres surrounded by four (eventually to be five) championship golf courses and with a spectacular 63,000-square-foot clubhouse. Accommodations are in condominiums and homes, with future plans for the construction of a world-class hotel. Each condo is fully-equipped for housekeeping, including washer/dryer, a barbecue, patio furniture, and an enclosed garage. Daily maid service can be arranged

Supported by its own tennis club, providing all of the expected amenities, are 19 tennis courts with an exhibition center court offering a seating capacity for 3,000 spectators. You can choose to play on clay, grass or hard surface. Plans call for a substantial expansion of the tennis complex.

There are now four courses. The TPC "Stadium Resort Course," a par-72 Pete Dye design, reaches out 7,271 yards from the psychopathic tees. Anyone playing from these tees is either a masochist or in dire need of a session with a good psychiatrist. The remaining tee settings measure 6,821/6,313/5,228. Mr. Dye used the natural undulation of the desert to create a Scottish links type of layout. He also introduced water on nine

holes. The 17th, a par three, is aptly named "Alcatraz." While only 128 yards from the regular tees, you will find yourself shooting at a green measuring some 28 by 31 yards. The location of the widely telecast Skins Game, it is as rough as the pictures indicated. While playable from the white tees, for the average weekend golfer I would suggest staying away from the championship and blue tees.

The Jack Nicklaus Course, available for guest play, measures 7,264/6,671/6,064/5,175 yards, also parring at 72. Bringing water into play on seven holes, this is an entertaining layout. Something of interest – the 9th and 18th holes share a green, which is reminiscent of many Scottish courses. The other two courses are the Arnold Palmer Private Course and the Jack Nicklaus Private Course. These two are restricted to member play and are not available for guests of the resort. Both of the resort courses are under the supervision of PGA Professional Jeff Walser. For tee times call the Pro Shop at (619) 564-7170 or (619) 564-7429.

RATES (EP) Condo: (1 bedroom / with den) $305 / $325. There are discounts for stays of

5 nights or longer ranging from 15 to 60%. Green fees: $75/$150.

ARRIVAL Air: Palm Springs or Thermal Airports. Car: from Highway 111 travel west on Jefferson Street (about 5 miles).

RAMS HILL
P.O. Box 664, Borrego Springs, CA 92004; (619) 767-5028 CA; (800) 524-2800 NAT; (800) 732-9200

Few places in the world can match the beauty and grandeur of the Anza-Borrego desert. The surrounding peaks (sometimes snowcapped) reflecting brilliant blues and greens, the desert with an ever-changing palette of colors, and the stark silence, all combine to produce a state of profound peace. The only possible drawback to this area is its remoteness – it is a long way from major shopping and dining areas. Many regard this is a definite plus; others feel cut off. Within this setting and located on 3,200 acres, Rams Hill is in the process of building a resort residential community. At the present time there are many homes completed, with an impressive clubhouse and golf course in

place. The rental units are, by the way, fully-equipped for housekeeping. The mix will eventually encompass custom homes, patio homes, and casitas.

The restaurant in the clubhouse is first rate. Specializing in French cuisine, they boast the services of a world-renowned chef.

The Rams Hill Golf Course stretches 6,866/6,328/5,694 yards and pars at 72. A few of the hazards include: water on six holes, 56 white sand bunkers and the magnificent views from most of the tees. It really does make it difficult to keep your mind on the game. Ted Robinson, architect of Rams Hill, took advantage of the natural terrain, creating rises and falls of more than 100 feet on several holes. We found it a fascinating layout to play. The course is supported by an excellent golf shop. For tee times call (619) 767-5124.

RATES (EP) 1-bedroom unit $145/$190. One bedroom and den: $165/$190. 2-bedroom home: $190/$250. For weekly rates deduct 10%. Green fees: $55, including cart. Rates are January through April.

ARRIVAL Air: Borrego

Springs. Car: from Palm Springs area travel south on Highway 86, then west on State Road 22.

STOUFFER'S ESMERALDA RESORT
44-400 Indian Wells Lane, Indian Wells, CA; (619) 773-4444; (800) 468-3571

A great deal of attention and planning went into this resort. It consists of eight multi-storied buildings, an eight-story glass-enclosed atrium entrance, a massive dual grand staircase, with several 40-foot palm trees, and a stream running through the lobby area. Situated on 21 acres this massive chateau-like structure offers accommodations in 560 guest rooms including suites. Rooms have French provincial furnishings and louvered windows rather than curtains. Each has a sitting area, television sets in the bedroom and bathroom, and a small balcony.

With 33,000 square feet of space devoted to meeting activities, including ballrooms and many smaller breakout rooms, they are well qualified to handle large group functions. Along with a series of lounges there are two restaurants serving Mediterranean and Continental cuisine.

There are three swimming pools (one featuring a poolside gazebo bar), seven tennis courts (three lighted), two whirlpools and a health and fitness center.

Golf can be played on two layouts near the hotel. Owned and operated by the city of Indian Wells, the East and the West golf courses have some unusual features. For details on this golf complex refer to "Hyatt Grand Champions Resort."

The Esmeralda and Hyatt Grand Champions hotels are 1/8 of a mile apart and both are located on top of the courses.

RATES   (EP)   Rooms: $260 / $350. Suites: $300 / $2000. Green fees: $90 / $100, including cart. Golf packages are available.

ARRIVAL Air: Palm Springs. Car: the resort is on Highway 111 just a few miles south of Palm Desert.

THE WESTIN MISSION HILLS RESORT

Dinah Shore & Bob Hope Drive, Rancho Mirage, CA 92270; (619) 328-5955; (800) 228-3000

A 360-acre resort development, Mission Hills adapted a Moroccan design using classic stucco, arches, colonnades and formal courtyards. Sixteen two-story buildings house the 512 guest rooms, including 40 suites. All accommodations have private patios, separate dressing rooms; many have cathedral ceilings as well as golf course views. The suites have a living room and wet bar, some with fireplace, whirlpools, even grand pianos in a few. The 34 suites in the Royal Oasis Club, offer guests a variety of special services. Mission Hills is also well set up to handle meeting and convention groups with its 39,000-square-foot conference center. They can accommodate 1,100 banquet-, 1,600 classroom- and over 2,500 theater-style. You can have cocktails and dine either in Bella Vista, serving California cuisine, or La Concha, specializing in fresh seafood and pasta. There are several lounges located within the hotel as well as by the three swimming pools: Las

Brisas and the Caliente Bar, Las Hadas, at the west pool, and the La Paloma, at the east pool.

Amenities include: a seven-court tennis center (with a sunken stadium court), along with a complete health and fitness center. While each of the three swimming pools has a hydrotherapy spa, the main pool also features a 60-foot waterslide.

The Mission Hills Course, owned and operated by Westin, plays 6,706/6,196/5,629/4,841 yards, with a par of 70. Unlike many desert courses you won't have to swim, as water is a factor on only five holes. Inasmuch as it is a Pete Dye design, you know you are going to be looking at a

few railroad ties, as well as small hard greens and deep pot bunkers. The course and golf shop are under the supervision of Golf Professional John Herndon. The second course is Gary Player's first undertaking in the Palm Springs area. With 18 acres of lakes and streams, water comes into the picture on six holes. It is lushly landscaped with over 50,000 shrubs and 2,500 trees in place. Reaching out 7,038/6,524/6,010/5,431 yards, it also pars at 72.

RATES   (EP)   Rooms: $250/$300. Suites: $425 and up. Green fees: $105, including cart. Golf packages are available.

ARRIVAL Air: Palm Springs. Car: I-10, take Ramon Road exit, drive to resort (2 miles).

Colorado

BEST WESTERN INN AT PUEBLO WEST
201 S. McCulloch Boulevard, Pueblo West, CO 81007; (719) 547-2111; (800) 448-1972

The Inn is eight miles west of I-25 and about five miles from Lake Pueblo. Accommodations consist of 80 oversized rooms, some with patios, all with complimentary CNN, ESPN and HBO Television. A nice extra: you can make local phone calls without an additional charge. There is a restaurant and lounge and they offer an outstanding Sunday champagne brunch. The Inn can accommodate modest-size meeting groups of up to 100 theater- and 56 classroom-style.

Amenities include: two lighted tennis courts, an outdoor heated swimming pool, a volleyball court, jogging, and bicycling trails.

The golf course, next to the resort, reaches out 7,305/6,725/5,793 yards and pars at 72. Interesting is the fact that water becomes a challenge on only four holes. The golf course is supported by a pro shop, snack bar, and lounge. The Head Professional is Dave Lewis. Pueblo West is also host to the Craft-Zavichas golf school. While the school welcomes male students, it is particularly attractive to lady golfers.

RATES (EP) Rooms: $62 / $74. Green fees: $12 / $15, carts $14. Golf package: 2 nights / 2 days *(includes lodging, green fees for 2 rounds, breakfast), $195 per couple. Rates listed are for the period of June through September.*

ARRIVAL Air: Pueblo Airport (15 miles). Car: on I-25 take Highway 50 west about 10 miles. You will see Best Western signs to guide you.

THE BROADMOOR
P.O. Box 1439, Colorado Springs, CO 80901; (719) 634-7711; (800) 634-7711

The Broadmoor has been judged one of the top 50 resorts. Steeped in tradition since its opening in 1918, the Broadmoor has preserved its glowing past while more than keeping pace with the present. The original hotel, known as Broadmoor Main, is a unique blend of old world grace and modern convenience. It stands today with its magnificent Italian Renaissance decor largely intact. The Broadmoor has won the Mobil Five Star Award each year since 1960. Keep in mind that only 20 hotel/resorts in the United States out of approximately 20,000 earn this award. The fifth and final phase of a five-year, $15-million renovation is almost complete. Perhaps this constant

drive to become better is the reason they truly are better. Many changes were made, such as the renovation of all 550 guest rooms, the addition of Espresso's continental cafe, or the transformation of the 18,000-square-foot Colorado Hall into a modern and elegant meeting facility.

There are, in total, eight restaurants and five lounges, not including the Winter House. Jackets and ties are required in most of the dining areas after 5 pm. The exception is The Tavern, the Golf Club, and now Espresso's. Three fine restaurants are located in the "Main": the Tavern, with its original Toulouse-Lautrec lithographs; the Garden Room, and the stately Main Dining Room.

The nine-story Broadmoor South adjacent to the Main, with its Penrose Dining Room and Lounge, offers a spectacular view of the mountains. Broadmoor West, on the west side of the lake, is a hotel (resort) complete unto itself. With dining, dancing and entertainment, it also showcases Oriental art dating back to the Ming and T'sing dynasties.

The Broadmoor is one of the more popular meeting and convention centers in the country, with over 100,000 square feet of meeting and display space.

The younger set has not been forgotten. During the July-August period and in effect Monday through Saturday, the hotel provides a supervised program for children ranging in age from 6 to 12.

While well known for winter sports , it has much to offer in the summer: tennis on 16 plexipave all-weather courts, under the watchful eye of professional Bob Scott and staff, swimming, squash, skeet and trap shooting, bicycle rentals, and boating. Horseback riding is available and tours of this scenic area can also be arranged. During the winter months ice skating becomes king. As a matter of fact, the Broadmoor is world-renowned for its ice skating facilities and has hosted the World Figure Skating championships as well as international hockey competitions.

Golf, under the supervision of well-known professional and Director of Golf, Dow Finsterwald and staff, can be played on three courses. The East Course, designed by Donald Ross in 1918, presents a significant yardage of 7,218/6,555/5,920, with par set at

72/73. The West, a Robert Trent Jones 1965 design, stretches out 6,937/6,109/5,505 yards, parring at 72/73. Both courses start from the same pro shop (very well-stocked) adjacent to the hotel and are under the direction of Head Professional Mike Tayler.

And now we come to the South Course, reaching what appears to be a modest 6,781/6,108/5,609/4,834 yards, with the par set at 72/70. Sounds easy, but this layout is one which can wring your soul and, as a matter of fact, your tail. On the first nine there is one hole where you are allowed a view of the green from the tee box (the eighth). In fact from the third tee it is difficult to determine where the fairway is.

Ed Seay, of the Arnold Palmer organization, designer of the South Course (1976), found a new way to keep everyone completely alert. On the front nine there are "barrancas" (ravines usually filled with brush) making an appearance on eight holes. On the second nine there are only two barrancas coming into play. I will not describe the 18th hole, as it should remain a surprise – something to be long remembered by each golfer. Suffice to say it is a tough closing hole.

The South Course is some distance above the hotel, with a view of the surrounding countryside that is something else. As a matter of fact the elevation of this layout averages around 6,000 feet. Should you get excited about how far you are hitting the ball, remember it's not really you. The South Golf Course is supported by its own golf shop, under the supervision of professional Hal Douglass. There is transportation provided to and from the course.

The John Jacobs' Practical Golf School is available at this resort. Using personalized teaching methods, and under the direction of PGA and LPGA teaching professionals, it is well worth looking into. For complete details call: (800) 472-5007.

RATES   (EP)   Main: *$215/$260. South: $215/$260. West: $280. Suites: $330/$450. Green fees: $65, carts $28.*

ARRIVAL *Air: Colorado Springs.*

COPPER MOUNTAIN RESORTS

P.O. Box 3001, Copper Mountain, CO 80443; (303) 968-2882; (800) 458-8386

The Mountain Resorts are actually a group of five management companies, operating a total of 21 different condominium buildings in one resort area. Included in the list of condominiums are the Copper Mountain Inn, Copper Junction, Copper Valley, Foxpine Inn, Village Point, Anaconda, Bridge End and Snowflake, the latter with its own restaurant.

Mountain Plaza and Village Square, also with their own restaurants, are in the heart of the village, with shops and restaurants readily available. Two new condominiums, the Greens and the Woods, are at the golf course.

The telephone number shown above will give you the reservation department for accommodations. They can arrange lodgings from a studio to a one-bedroom condominium to a penthouse suite with five bedrooms sleeping 24. They now have a meeting and conference center as well.

There are many activities: horseback riding, swimming,

boating on Lake Dillon, tennis, fishing, Jeep tours, windsurfing, rafting, and bicycling. During winter skiing becomes king. With over 1,500 feet of vertical drop, 96 trails, many lifts and areas for both advanced skiers and beginners – the facilities are outstanding.

Golf can now be played on the Pete Dye-designed Copper Creek Golf Club. Measuring 6,129/5,742/5,159/4,358 yards with a par of 70, it is an exciting layout. The facilities are complete with clubhouse and pro shop.

RATES (EP) Lodge rooms: $99. Condominiums: 1 bedroom $115/$1450. Green fees: $60, including cart. Rates are for June-September.

ARRIVAL Air: Denver. Car: I-70 west, exit at 195, approximately 75 miles.

FAIRFIELD PAGOSA
P.O. Box 4400, Pagosa, CO 81157; (303) 731-4141; (800) 523-7704

In the early days of Pagosa, accommodations meant a teepee or lean-to amid towering spruce and ponderosa pine. Today the resort has an Inn as well as condominiums – but they are still surrounded by the same spruce and ponderosa pines. The 101-room inn offers not only lodgings but also a view of the lakes and craggy peaks of the magnificent San Juan Mountains. Dining is provided in the Great Divide or the Rendezvous Cocktail Lounge. By the way, should you be interested in a condo rather than hotel accommodations call: (800) 365-3149.

This family-oriented complex serves up every type of activity you could wish for: bicycle, boat and ice skate rentals, a health spa, indoor swimming, saunas, hydrotherapy pools, and game rooms. There is a stable offering horseback riding, chuckwagon cookouts, winter sleigh rides, and a racquet club (six courts) along with its own pro shop. Baby sitting service is also available.

As you may well have guessed by now, Fairfield Pagosa is quite large. The project itself is 18,000 acres with six lakes and five miles of the San Juan River on site. An additional 2 1/2 million acres of national forest and 226 thousand acres of primitive area border Pagosa.

The Pagosa Pines Club course is now a 27-hole layout. Pine

1/Pine 2 nines weigh in at 6,748/6,282/5,392 yards, parring at 71. Pine 1/Meadows, parring at 72, plays an awesome 7,256/6,524/5,380 yards. Finally, the Pine 2/Meadows combination completes the picture, reaching out 6,956/6,154/5,126 yards, also with a par of 72.

The clubhouse provides a full line pro shop and snack bar and is under the direction of PGA Professional Arne Fremstad and staff. During the winter months the golf shop functions as a snowmobile and ski rental center.

RATES (EP) Inn: $59/$69. Suites: $100/$120. Condos: $120/$150. Green fees: $45, including cart. Golf packages are available.

ARRIVAL Air: Durango. Private aircraft: Pagosa Springs (6,500-foot paved runway). Car: U.S. 160, 3 1/2 miles west of Pagosa Springs.

IRON HORSE RESORT RETREAT
P.O. Box 1286, Winter Park, CO 80482; (303) 726-8851; (800) 621-8190

Accommodations here are condominiums of one, two or three bedrooms. Each is equipped for housekeeping, with balcony, fireplace, living and dining areas, microwave and dishwasher. Some also provide a private Jacuzzi tub, a wet bar, and a washer/dryer. The resort can handle smaller meeting groups and is well set up to do so. The facilities allow groups of from 10 to 120.

If you decide not to coook for yourself, there is the Rails Bar & Restaurant.

Amenities include: indoor and outdoor swimming pools, four outdoor hot tubs, weight and exercise rooms, and a steam room. Of course winter is the time of the premier action in this area. The resort offers 18 lifts, manicured ski runs, sleigh rides, snowmobiling, and virtually every other winter activity.

Golf can be played on the Pole Creek Golf Club course. Parring at 72, it weighs in at a fair 6,882/6,230/4,956 yards. They did not name this Pole Creek just for kicks. The creek meanders throughout the course, forming four lakes. The course includes some elevated tees and greens, is well trapped, and has a setting of great beauty.

RATES (EP) 1 bedroom: $100; 2 bedrooms, 2 baths $130. Premium: $125 / $155. Green fees: $50, carts $22. There are several different packages including golf.

ARRIVAL Air: Denver (90 minutes). Car: from Denver I-70, exit #232 onto I-40, north to the resort.

KEYSTONE RESORT
P.O. Box 38, Keystone, CO 80435; (303) 468-2316; (800) 541-0346

The Keystone Resort, 75 miles west of Denver is in the 9,300-foot-high Snake River Valley. The 152-room lodge, along with 900 condominiums and homes, make up this four-season resort complex. All condominiums provide fully-equipped kitchens and fireplaces. Old Western ambience pervades the spacious 50-year-old Ranch House, with its bar, golf shop, and locker rooms. A recent addition, the 58,000-square-foot Keystone Resort Conference Center, now has a capacity of up to 1,800 people. The resort also offers a child care and an all-day activities program.

As for dining, Keystone offers something for everyone: the Bighorn Steak House, the Gar-

den Room for continental dining, and the Edgewater Cafe for casual family meals.

There are four winter ski areas here: Keystone, Outback, North Peak and Arapahoe Basin, in total offering superb skiing on 1,600 acres with 20 lifts and a high-speed gondola.

There are 14 tennis courts (two indoor) with a complete pro shop and lounge available. Other activities include: backpacking, bicycling, kayaking, sailing, fishing, raft trips, horseback riding, and swimming in several different pools.

Golf is played on a Robert Trent Jones, Jr. course three miles south of the village. Rimmed by towering peaks, it plays 7,090/6,521/5,720 yards and pars at 72. It is an interesting and beautiful layout as it traverses the woods and meadows, bringing a nine-acre lake and various ponds into play. It is said to be the highest course in the United States, with portions lying above 9,300 feet.

RATES (EP) Lodge: $170. Condominiums: 1 bedroom $130 / $175. Green fees: $80, including carts.

ARRIVAL Air: Denver. Car: I-

70 west to exit 205. East on U.S. 6 for 6 miles.

SCANTICON-DENVER RESORT

200 Inverness Drive West, Englewood, CO 80112; (303) 740-8300; (800) 346-4891

A multi-storied hotel, this resort seems to be primarily geared to meeting groups. Accommodations are in 302 guest rooms. There are several alternatives for dining: the Black Swan (jackets required, ties optional) or, less formal, the Garden Terrace and the Copenhagen Restaurant.

Amenities include: indoor and outdoor swimming pools, tennis courts, saunas, whirlpools, an exercise room, and jogging trails nearby.

Golf is available on the Inverness Golf Club course. Designed by Preston Maxwell, it reaches out 6,948/6,407/5,681 yards with a par of 70/71. The clubhouse contains a pro shop, locker rooms, the clubhouse grill, and a snack bar.

RATES (EP) Rooms: $130; 1-bedroom suite: $179. Club floor room: $149; Executive suite: $209. Green fees: $60, carts $22. Golf packages - available weekends only: 1 night/1 day (include lodging, breakfast, green fees ,and cart), $209 per couple.

ARRIVAL Air: Stapleton International. Private aircraft: Centennial Airport (1 1/2 miles). Car: I-25 to County Line exit – turn left (east). 2nd stoplight is Inverness Road. Turn left to resort.

SHERATON STEAMBOAT RESORT

P.O. Box 774808, Steamboat Springs, CO 80477; (303) 879-2220; (800) 848-8878

The nucleus of this resort complex is the Sheraton Village Hotel with 276 guest rooms and the conference center. A few steps away are the 58 luxurious rooms and 75 condominium units of the Thunderhead Lodge. For reservations at the Thunderhead you can call: (800) 525-5502.

There are three restaurants: Cipriani's, specializing in Italian cuisine; the Soda Creek Cafe for lighter dining; or Remington's Restaurant. There are also two lounges.

If you are a ski enthusiast, you know about this famous winter resort. Over 300 inches of powder and all the amenities associated with world-class skiing make this one of the best.

Four lighted tennis courts are close to the hotel. Other activities include: whitewater rafting down the Green, Yanpa, or Colorado Rivers; sailing and waterskiing on Steamboat Lake; and excellent fishing in the 900 miles of rivers, streams, or 109 lakes. Four-legged critters are a big part of Steamboat Springs life, with trail rides, western dinner rides, or hayrack rides available.

This Robert Trent Jones, Jr. resort course measures 6,906/6,276/5,647 yards and pars at 72. While you do get some help in the form of the 7,000-foot altitude, the 77 sand traps and seven water holes will bring you quickly back to reality.

RATES (EP) Rooms: Village $69/$99; Suites: $149/$199. Condos: $69/$139. Green fees: $48, carts $24. Golf packages are available. Rates are for late May-September 30.

ARRIVAL Air: Denver (153 miles) with shuttle flights or private aircraft to Hayden (23 miles from Steamboat Springs). Car: I-70 off at Sil- *verthorne exit. Travel north to Kermmling. Then west on U.S. 40 to resort.*

THE SILVERTREE RESORT HOTEL
Box 5009, Snowmass Village, CO 81615; (303) 923-3520; (800) 525-9402

Something new has been added to the Snowmass complex: The Silvertree Hotel – with a three-story atrium lobby, 248 guest rooms along with 12 suites. Situated on the slopes of the rugged Rocky Mountain Range, accommodations offer views that must be seen to be believed.

In addition to the hotel there are a number of one- , two- , and three-bedroom condominiums and homes equipped for housekeeping. These units have fireplaces and swimming pools. This entire area was set up to accommodate skiing and related winter activities, so things are arranged in a village-like setting. These accommodations are, to say the least, luxurious. Some of the names are Terracehouse, Litchenhearth, Woodridge, Interlude, and Snowmass Mountain Condominiums. The toll free number listed above can arrange reservations at the hotel or the various condos.

Within the hotel are three restaurants and a lounge. The resort also has excellent meeting facilities. With 10,000 square feet of space set aside for group activities, they can accommodate groups of up to 400.

Activities include: two swimming pools, two whirlpools, and a state-of-the-art health club with steam room and sauna. There are many additional activities which can be arranged within the village or are located nearby: tennis courts, white water rafting, hot air-ballooning, western trail rides, cycling, hiking, and fly fishing. A variety of outstanding shops and boutiques are close by as well.

Golf can be played on the Snowmass Golf Club links. For details refer to The Snowmass Club.

RATES (EP) Hotel rooms: $115/$175. Suites: $325/ $650. 1-bedroom condominiums: $98/$120. Homes: $155.

ARRIVAL Air: Aspen. Car: from Aspen take Highway 82 northwest 4 miles – enter Snowmass Village and drive approximately 3 miles.

SKYLAND RESORT & COUNTRY CLUB
P.O. Box 879, Crested Butte, CO 81224; (303) 349-7541; (800) 428-3770

Skyland Resort is in the heart of the majestic Colorado Rocky Mountains. Sited in the beautiful Slate River Valley at the base of the towering Crested Butte Mountain, it offers excellent skiing in the winter and golf during the summer. Guest rooms are set up for light housekeeping (kitchenettes). They are equipped with small refrigerators and microwave ovens. Some units have an additional loft bedroom. There are restaurants, tennis and racquetball courts, a Jacuzzi, and a swimming pool.

Golf is played at the Skyland Country Club. Parring at 72, it measures an impressive 7,208/6,635/5,747 yards. One of the major challenges is the overwhelming stark beauty of this area, making it particularly difficult to keep your mind on the game.

During the summer the John Jacobs Practical Golf School operates at this resort. Using personalized teaching methods, and under the direction of PGA and LPGA teaching professionals, it is well worth looking into. For details call: (800) 472-5007.

RATES *(EP) Rooms: $79 / $85. Green fees: $70, including cart. Golf package: 1 nights / 1 days (includes lodging, golf and cart, club storage), $150 / $175 per couple. Rates are for July-August.*

ARRIVAL *Air: Gunnison. Car: north of Gunnison on State Route 135.*

THE SNOWMASS LODGE & CLUB
P.O. Box G 2, Snowmass Village, CO 81615; (303) 923-5600; (800) 525-6200

Snowmass, in the Snowmass/Aspen valley, is nestled high in the Colorado Rockies. Obviously a mecca for ski enthusiasts, it is now becoming known for its summer activities.

Each spacious guest room here has a private balcony offering a view of the mountains. Adjacent to the lodge, accommodations are available in villas, as well as condominiums with fireplaces and fully-equipped kitchens. Snowmass can also handle meeting groups in the new Fairway Conference Center with a capacity of 225 thea-

ter-style.

While open for all meals, the Four Corners Grill is particularly charming for candlelight dining. Then perhaps you might have a nightcap in the Bar Lounge.

Physical fitness buffs will have a field day here. The tennis professionals "hold court" on 11 courts (two indoor). They are on different levels surrounding the Summerhouse Restaurant. On the other side of the lodge, swimmers will find the heated lap pool, coed whirlpool and recreation pool with a diving area. There are three racquetball and squash courts, steam rooms, saunas, whirlpools, weight and massage rooms, lockers and showers. During the summer months guided hiking, horseback riding, and fishing expeditions can also be arranged.

Snowmass recently spent over a million dollars in renovating the Golf Links. Now playing 6,900/6,055/5,008 yards, it pars at 71. While an open layout, it is exceptionally well trapped. In playing golf here keep in mind that you are at almost 9,000 feet. If you were not aware of this, you will be after your first tee shot.

RATES (EP) Lodge rooms: $165/$230. Club Villas: 1 bedroom $230. Green fees: $59, including carts. Golf packages are available. Rates are June-August.

ARRIVAL Air: Aspen. Car: from Aspen, Highway 82 northwest 2 miles to enter Snowmass Village. Now on Brush Creek Road go 3 miles, turn left onto Highline Road. Club limousine available from airport.

TAMARRON
P.O. Drawer 3131, Durango, CO 81302; (303) 259-2000; (800) 678-1000

In the south-western corner of Colorado, Tamarron is on 750 acres in the high mountain valley of the San Juan Mountain Range. The great hewn timber inn offers a wide variety of accommodations: rooms featuring two queen-size beds, suites with living room/kitchen facilities, Loft Inn suites, townhouses with one to three bedrooms, and condominiums. These units, by the way, are exceptionally well-equipped and beautifully furnished. There is a small general and liquor store for basic needs. Another nice feature – there are washer/dryer combinations on each floor of the main lodge and in each of the condominium clusters. Tamarron also has meeting facilities that can handle groups up to 500.

For candlelight dining there is Le Canyon or the San Juan Club for a more informal setting. Even if you choose accommodations in one of the townhouses or condominiums, room service is available.

In the winter this is a ski buff's delight. The slopes of Purgatory average over 200 inches of snow, providing skiing, sleigh rides, tobogganing, ice skating and snowmobile tours.

During the warmer months a few of the activities include: fishing in Tamarron's private lake (tackle and bait provided – no license required) or fly fishing the beautiful Animas River with a professional guide (all equipment included), white-water rafting, horseback riding, or a hayride and steak cookout. Swimming the indoor/outdoor pools, tennis on indoor and outdoor courts with a professional staff on deck, are other possibilities. There is a complete health club and a supervised children's program.

Tamarron warms into a high country golf resort of unusual beauty during the summer months. Fairways wind amid tall stands of ponderosa pine, age-old oaks, and aspen. This is some of the most intriguing scenery you will find on any golf course. In fact, one of the most difficult parts of playing here is keeping your mind on the game and not on the scenery or the wildlife. The Tamarron Golf Course, an Arthur Hill design, plays 6,885/6,340/5,380 yards with a par of 72. It offers some of the most interesting golf holes (maybe terrifying would be more appropriate) we have seen. Some of the elevation changes from one part of the fairway to another are spectacular. At this altitude (8,000-plus feet) your golf ball does some rather unexpected things. The course is supported by a driving range as well as a full pro shop. The Head Professional is Steve Nichols.

RATES (EP) Deluxe Room or 1-bedroom townhouse: $149; suites: $216/$365. Green fees: $80, including cart. Golf package: 3 nights/3 days (includes lodging, 3 days golf, cart, club storage, a golf clinic), $1,014 per couple. Rates are for May-October.

ARRIVAL Air: Durango. Car: 18 miles north of Durango on U.S. 550.

VAIL-BEAVER CREEK AREA

For many years Vail and Beaver Creek have been known for their superb skiing. The area is also known for its magnificent mountain and forest settings which are virtually unmatched in this country. But, alas, winter does come to an end. The beauty is still there and so are the many restaurants, bars, shops, hotels, condominiums, all representing a huge dollar investment and earning virtually nothing.

The resorts of Colorado have discovered golf. They did not ease into the field but went in under a full head of steam, employing such august names as Jack Nicklaus, Arnold Palmer, Pete Dye, Robert Trent Jones, Jr. and Gary Player to produce some of the finest golf courses found anywhere.

Two such areas are Vail Village Resorts and the Beaver Creek Resort complex, located approximately 10 miles apart. Due to their proximity, most of the amenities are available to guests of either resort.

Within a 20-mile radius there are four first-class championship golf courses. Each course has full pro shop, locker rooms and restaurants. The golf season in this area is late June to mid-September.

Both resort areas provide ample meeting and convention facilities.

Due to the great number and diversity of accommodations, it is not possible to list their rates. The majority are posh, expensive winter lodgings at vastly reduced summer rates. There are also golf packages available allowing play on several courses. When making reservations request this information. Oh, yes, there is also tennis, with over 50 courts in the area.

THE BEAVER CREEK GOLF CLUB

Now semi-private, this was designed by Robert Trent Jones, Jr. Playing to a par of 70, the course measures 6,464/6,026/ 5,202 yards. This layout stretches along Beaver Creek and into the valley with native spruce and aspen lining the fairways and presenting some well bunkered greens. For tee times call (303) 949-7123.

EAGLE-VAIL GOLF CLUB

This lies between Vail Village and Beaver Creek in the residential community of Eagle Vail. The course plays 6,819/6,142/4,856 yards and pars at 72. Considered one of the most challenging in the valley, its 10th hole, a par three, plays from 208 to 124 yards. The tee sits 250 feet above the green. Your ball spends so much time in the air you may have to get a permit from NASA. For tee times call (303) 949-5267.

SINGLETREE GOLF LINKS

Now semi-private, this lies west of Beaver Creek at the Berry Creek Ranch. Designed by Jack Nicklaus' company, GOLFORCE, Singletree resembles a Scottish links with its hilly fairways, deep bunkers, and natural grass roughs. Parring at 71, this layout stretches 7,024/6,435/ 5,907/5,293 yards. It has co-hosted the Gerry Ford invitational. For tee times call (303) 949-4240.

VAIL GOLF CLUB

This was Vail's first. Just east of Vail Village, it reaches out 7,048/6,282/5,934/5,303 yards, with a par of 71/72. Gore Creek winds throughout this 18-hole layout. For tee times call (303) 476-1330.

THE VAIL/BEAVER CREEK RESORT ASSOCIATION
241 East Meadow Drive, Vail, CO 81657; (303) 476-5677; (800) 525-3875

The above number will put you in touch with reservations in Vail as well as the Beaver Creek area. In fact, it gives access to accommodations such as lodge rooms, condominiums, townhouses, and private residences. Including the many hotels, there are well over 20,000 guest lodgings available.

These full-service communities have over 100 restaurants, nightclubs, and bars, more than 300 shops, many heated lodge swimming pools, saunas, whirlpools, drug stores, banks, and other services.

VAIL ASSOCIATES INC.
P.O. Box 7, Vail, CO 81658; (303) 949-5750; (800) 525-2257

The above numbers will also put you in contact with a wide variety of accommodations within the Vail/Beaver Creek area.

Hawaii

THE ISLAND OF OAHU

Although one of the smaller islands in the chain, Oahu is the population center, the hub of commercial activities and still the location of the largest number of restaurants and nightspots. You will also find many wonderful hotels and a few golf resorts. While crowded with people and heavily congested with traffic, it remains beautiful.

SHERATON MAKAHA RESORT & COUNTRY CLUB
84-626 Makaha Valley Road, Makaha, HI 96792; (808) 695-9511; (800) 325-3535

The Sheraton Makaha is high in the Makaha Valley overlooking the famous Makaha surfing beaches. Accommodations are in several clusters of two-story cottages with a total of 200 guest rooms, surrounded by beautiful gardens. The resort has set aside 10,000 square feet for meetings and receptions. They are well-equipped to handle groups of up to 240 banquet- or 300-theater style.

The dining facilities, while informal, are excellent and range from the coffee shop, the Pikaki Cafe, to the elegant Kaala Room. There is also the Lobby Lounge with its view of the golf course and the ocean beyond – a great place to view a spectacular Hawaiian sunset.

If, on certain days, you tire of loafing on the beach or soaking in the pool, there are many activities open to you: horseback riding along the beach, tennis, surfing, scuba diving, deep sea fishing or perhaps a Hawaiian outrigger canoe ride.

Golf is played on the resort's West Course reaching out 7,090/6,398/6,041 yards, with a par of 72. It is a beautiful layout with more than its share of traps and the most difficult putting greens we have seen. Since our visit they have added a collection of "pot hole bunkers." In fact the course has undergone a complete multi-million dollar renovation including a new irrigation system as well as changes on several of the holes.

RATES   (EP)   Rooms: $95/$170. Suites: $260/$340

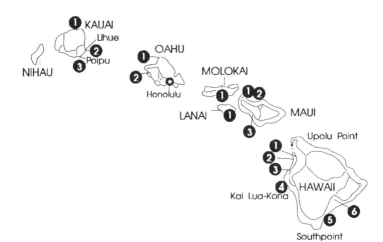

MAUI

1. Kapalua Bay Hotel
2. Hyatt Regency Maui
   Kaanapali Beach Hotel
   Maui Marriott Resort
   Royal Lahaina Resort
   Sheraton Maui Hotel
   The Westin Maui
   Condos
   Kaanapali Alii
   Kaanapali Plantation
   Kaanapali Royal
   Maui Eldorado
   The Whaler at Kaanapali Beach
3. The Wailea Area
   Four Seasons Resort
   Grand Hyatt Wailea
   Kea Lani Hotel
   The Maui Inter-Continental Wailea
   Stouffer's Wailea Beach Resort
   Maui Prince Hotel at Mekena

HAWAII

1. Mauna Kea Beach Hotel
2. Mauna Lani Bay Hotel
   Mauna Lani Point Condos
3. Hyatt Regency Waikoloa
   Royal Waikoloan
   The Shores at Waikoloa
   Waikoloa Villas
4. Keauhou Beach Hotel
   Keauhou Resort Condos
   Kona Surf Resort
5. Sea Mountain At Punalu's
6. The Volcano House Inn & CC

OAHU

1. Turtle Bay Hilton
2. Sheraton Makaha Resort & CC

LANAI

1. The Lodge at Koele
   Manele Bay Hotel

MOLOKAI

1. Kalua Koi Hotel & Golf Club

KAUAI

1. Princeville
   Hanalei Bay Resort
   Princeville Hotel
   The Cliffs
   The Hawaiian Island Resorts Inc.
   Princeville Travel Service
2. The Westin Kauai
3. Poipu Beach Area
   Hyatt Regency Kauai
   Kiahuna Plantation
   Sheraton Kauai Hotel
   Stouffer Waiohai Beach Resort

and up. Green fees: $85, includ-
ing cart.

TURTLE BAY HILTON
Kahuku, Oahu, HI 96731;
(808) 293-8811; (800) 445-8667

Located on the northern part of
Oahu, this hotel is on a point of
land with water on three sides.
Due to the way the resort is
oriented you cannot see another structure. The secluded
beaches serve up the usual
tropical tranquility one comes
to expect out here.

Tennis can be played on 10
courts (four lighted) with ball
machines. They offer horseback riding and rent equipment for dune cycling along a
five-mile stretch of beach.

The golf course, a George Fazio
design, is beautiful, but has a
few problems. Perhaps I
should reword that. In playing
it, *I had a few problems.* The
course has small greens, lots of
sand, and what they refer to as
an "ocean breeze." I refer to it
as WIND. It measures a substantial 7,036/6,366/5,701
yards with par set at 72/74.

RATES *(EP) Rooms:*
$160/$350. Suites: $460 up.
Green fees: $75, including cart.
ARRIVAL *Air: Honolulu (1*

hour). Car: Kamehameha
Highway north

THE ISLAND OF HAWAII

The "Big Island" is one of sharp
contrasts, with Hilo on the
eastern "wet side" and the
warm and dryer Kona and Kohala coast areas on the other.
There are about 96 road miles
between the two, separated by
the volcanic mountains of
Mauna Loa, at 13,680 feet,
Mauna Kea, at 13,796, and Mt.
Hualalai, at 8,271 feet. Although the volcanoes are an
obvious attraction, the island
is also rich in history, for this
was once the home of the kings
of Hawaii.

KAILUA – KONA RESORT AREA

At the heart of the "Big Island's" famed Kona Coast, the
Keauho-Kona area is an open
door to Hawaii's history, heritage, and hospitality. There
are a multitude of things to do
and see: visiting century-old
churches and tiny villages
along the coast, tennis, golf,
marlin fishing or just day-
dreaming and relaxing.

Although the various resorts offer good food, if you are visiting for any period of time or are staying in a condominium you may want a change of pace. As a possible alternative I suggest Jamison's By The Sea. Formerly named Dorians, its name may have changed but the food is still magnificent. The address is 77-6452 Alii Drive, Kona. Phone for reservations (808) 329-3195.

As a guest of several resorts in this area, you can also use the Kona Country Club Course. This Bell-designed layout plays 6,589/6,165/5,499 and pars at 72/73. Lava-bordered fairways, a profusion of sand traps and flowering shrubs, along with the wind, make this a tester. The Head Professional is Rob Wohlgemuth. The Alii course, the newest addition, is on the hillside above the pro shop area. Measuring 6,451/5,823/4,886 yards and parring at 72, it offers some of the most spectacular views we have seen.

KEAUHOU BEACH HOTEL
78-6740 Alii Drive, Kailua-Kona, HI 96740; (808) 322-3441; (800) 367-6025

When you walk the grounds of this hotel and stroll past ancient rock carvings or the summer home of Hawaiian kings, you feel as if you have stepped back 1,000 years in history. Although it has undergone extensive remodeling, the "old flavor" has been retained and the hotel remains the same lovely place it has always been.

The rooms have recently been renovated, with each overlooking the tropical gardens and the coast. Each room is equipped with a refrigerator. The Kuakini Terrace is available for casual dining, with the Makai Bar offering nightly Hawaiian entertainment. Room service is also provided.

They offer tennis on six courts and have, in addition to a pool, a small sand beach. (There are not many sand beaches on this side of the island).

Guests can play the Kona Country Club golf courses described in the "Keauhou-Kona Beach Resort Area."

RATES (EP) Rooms: $95 / $1,605. Suites: $230 / $310. Green fees: $75, including cart. They offer package arrangements including golf, cart rentals, tennis, etc. Check when making reservations.

THE KEAUHOU RESORT CONDOMINIUMS

78-7039 Kam II Road, Kailua-Kona, Island of Hawaii, HI 96740; (808) 322-9122; (800) 367-5286

This represents a definite change. This 48-unit cluster of one- and two-level townhouses is set in a five-acre tropical garden setting. Each unit has a fully-equipped all-electric kitchen with an ice maker, a dishwasher, washer/dryer, and color TV. Most units have an ocean view and all have either one or two lanais. You might want to compare the rates indicated with those of some of the other resorts.

There is a swimming pool on property. You are a short distance from the waters of the Kona Coast and world-class fishing, snorkeling, and scuba diving.

The property is right alongside the Kona Country Club Course. For details on golf refer to "Keahou-Kona Beach Resort Area."

RATES (EP) Five-night minimum, 1-bedroom unit $75/$85, weekly $525/$595. There is a 10% discount on stays of over four weeks. The management of the resort has access to tee times at special rates.

KONA SURF RESORT

Keauhou Bay, Island of Hawaii, HI 96740; (808) 322-3411; (800) 367-8011

The Kona Surf Hotel is sited along the fabled Kona Coast. Rising some six stories, it sits like a castle at the entrance to Keauhou Bay. With the bay on one side, the ocean and golf course on the other, it is a spectacular setting. Accommodations are in 535 rooms including suites, with the majority of the rooms offering a view of the Pacific Ocean. All rooms are air-conditioned and each has a private lanai. They are also equipped with cable TV, refrigerators, and individual coffee makers. The Kona Surf is well set up to handle meeting and conference groups with a capacity of 800 schoolroom- and 1,000 banquet-style.

Restaurants include the elegant S.S. James Makee or the more casual Pele's Court. For entertainment, there is dancing in the Puka Bar or Hawaiian music on the Nalu Terrace.

The resort offers a choice of fresh or saltwater pools, deep sea fishing, snorkeling, tennis on three lighted courts with a resident professional to assist and, of course, golf.

Guests can play golf on the Kona Country Club course, which overlooks the hotel. For details and a description of the courses refer to "Keauhou-Kona Beach Resort Area."

RATES   (EP)   Rooms: $99/$175. Suites: $375/$550. Green fees: $65, including cart.

THE KOHALA COAST AREA

The Kohala Coast area, stretching north of Kona, is experiencing rapid growth. With little rainfall, a number of wonderful golf courses and magnificent hotels, this area has a great deal to offer.

No matter how good a resort's food, if you stay for more than a day or two, you will probably want to try other places to eat as well. In the small town of Kamuela, a few miles from The Mauna Kea Beach Resort, is the Edelweiss Restaurant. I promise you won't be disappointed.

HYATT REGENCY WAIKOLOA
Kohala Coast, Waikoloa, HI 96743; (808) 885-1234; (800) 233-1234

Opened in early 1989, the Hyatt Regency Waikoloa is not a small resort. Located on 62 ocean-front acres of Waiulua Bay this $360 million hotel presents another alternative for a Hawaiian vacation.

The 1,240 guest rooms are in three low-rise structures: the Ocean, the Palace, and the Lagoon Towers. There are extensive tropical gardens, as well as flagstone walkways throughout the grounds and extending along the shoreline. There is also a magnificent lobby with a huge grand stairway leading to the lower lagoon. With 19 meeting rooms and two auxiliary ballrooms, the Regency can handle large meeting groups. Remember, you are in Hawaii – large areas of outdoor space are also usable for meetings.

Recreational possibilities include: eight tennis courts with an exhibition court (seating 750), a racquetball court, a 25,000-square-foot health spa complete with Jacuzzis, weight and aerobics rooms, saunas, steam baths, facials, herbal wraps, loofah scrubs and, of course, massage rooms. There are two swimming pools, with the main one some 22,000 square feet, sporting waterfalls, slides, and a grotto bar. Nearby can be found horseback riding, deep sea fishing charters, sailing, and windsurfing.

There are two golf courses readily available: The Beach Golf Club designed by Robert Trent Jones, Jr. and the newer $16 million Morrish/Weiskopf-designed championship course called The Kings Golf Club. For details on these two refer to The Royal Waikoloan Resort. There is also a golf course in the Waikoloa Village. For details refer to the Waikoloa Villas.

RATES   (EP)   Rooms: $250/$390. 1-bedroom suite: $575/$875. Green fees: $80, including cart.

MAUNA KEA BEACH HOTEL
Kohala Coast, HI 96743; (808) 882-7222; (800) 882-6060

The Mauna Kea Beach Hotel has been judged one of the top 50 resorts. Surrounded by lush green fairways, tropical gardens, and beautiful crescent white sand beaches, this hotel is something special. I have always believed that Hawaii was more a state of mind than a place, and the Mauna Kea, with its air of solitude, grace, and feeling of complete relaxation, enhances this belief.

The open-air architecture allows gentle trade winds to enter the courtyards which are graced with a priceless collection of over 1,600 works of Asian and Pacific art. We have walked the various levels of the hotel to see the art on display and, it was well worth the time.

I will not attempt to describe the decor of the 310 rooms, including 10 suites, as this should remain a stunning, but pleasant, surprise. They can handle medium-sized meeting groups and can accommodate (in the Lloyd Sextan Gallery and three breakout rooms) up to 200 theater- and 125 classroom-style.

Dining here is an experience you will remember. You may wish to start with breakfast at either the Pavilion, the Garden, The Terrace, or perhaps the "19th Hole" (coffee and rolls only), next to the pro shop. For an elegant evening (jackets required) there is the

Batik Dining Room. Surprisingly, with all these dining options, the resort is perhaps best known for its bountiful luncheon buffets. Presented daily on The Terrace these have gained wide recognition. There is always the choice of candlelight dining on your own private lanai (and believe me they handle this just right). Of course, no visit to Hawaii would be complete without a luau. This gastronomical treat is presented each Tuesday evening. *Gourmet Magazine* reports that "Mauna Kea has the reputation of setting the best table in the Islands," a statement with which we fully agree. As a matter of fact if you don't get out of the dining areas, start exercising and stop eating, your doctor may well forbid you to ever come here again.

While there are many evening activities – dancing at the Pavilion, movies each evening in the Sextan Gallery – our favorite entertainment was watching the giant Pacific manta ray. From a lighted viewing area overlooking the ocean you can watch the huge devilfish as they swirl, almost seeming to dance. It is a spectacular sight.

Even though there is a beautiful pool, ocean swimming from one of the finest beaches on the island is at its best. Scuba diving from the 32-foot power boat, *The Island Voyager,* horseback riding, along with jogging on the two-mile cinder trail, are a few of the activities. Tennis is played on 13 plexi-pave courts. The tennis complex, under the direction of professional Jay Paulson, has been designated a "Five Star Tennis Facility." Something new has been added in the form of a complete fitness center equipped with state-of-the-art equipment. There is now a complimentary children's program in place. Featuring a fully trained staff it is available during typical "family vacation periods."

The golf course, a Robert Trent Jones Sr. design and acclaimed as one of the best in the nation, is perched on top of a lava flow. Much of the top soil had to be brought in. What an undertaking that must have been.

The course stretches out 7,114 yards (masochist tees), 6,737 yards (championship), 6,365 (regular tees), with a par of 72. From the ladies' tees the par remains at 72, and the yardage is set at 5,277. With a great many traps (120), lava-bound fairways and occasional gusting wind, you may well find par 72 elusive. Several changes have been made to the Mauna Kea course. The greens, which were among the slowest in the country, are now being cut lower. Although they are still not extremely fast, it is a vast improvement. The rough has been cut a bit lower, speeding up play, and they have installed additional tee areas allowing variations on the yardage.

While a great deal has been said about the third hole, a par three playing 180 yards from the men's tees and reaching across the Pacific Ocean, our favorite is the magnificent view from the 11th green, looking back at the hotel.

I don't want to overdo the superlatives, but the pro shop, under the supervision of Director of Golf John "J D" Ebersberger, offers a selection of golf and casual attire which surpasses that found in many of the better department stores.

Now a new course is on the scene: located a bit south of the hotel and designed by Arnold Palmer & Associates, it is something else. Coming into play in late 1992, the Hapuna Golf Course has some of the most scenic holes to be found on the islands. That's saying a lot when you consider you are in an area where spectacular scenery is all around you. The first and 18th as well as the driving range are on the west side (ocean side) of the highway. The remaining holes stretch along the mountainside. Attaining an elevation of some 700 feet, the views are startling. As with the original Robert Trent Jones course the ocean side features mature coconut trees, but the upper level has been left more in a desertlike state with native grass and shrubs. Reaching out 6,875/6,534/6,001/5,550 yards, it pars at 72. It is supported by its own clubhouse and pro shop.

RATES (EP) Mountain View: $260/$325. Beachfront: $400. Ocean view: $410/$475. For MAP plan add $70 per person per night. Green fees: $60, carts $40. Golf packages are not available during the peak season. Rates are for January through December.

THE MAUNA LANI BAY HOTEL

One Mauna Lani Drive, Kohala Coast, Island of Hawaii, HI 96743; (808) 885-6622; (800) 367-2323

We have selected Mauna Lani Bay Hotel as one of the top 50 resorts. Situated on the edge of the Kohala Coast, the resort is a modern 350-room structure, with its unique design providing virtually every room an ocean view. Rooms are equipped with refrigerators and tropical ceiling fans (they are also air-conditioned). While the rooms are larger than normal their nine-foot ceilings make them appear even more spacious.

Something new has been added – five "magnificent" (there is no other way to describe them) Bungalows. Each of these free-standing units, with 4,000 square feet of space (including swimming pool), includes two master bedrooms, two and one half bathrooms, a fully-equipped serving kitchen, a private swimming pool, its own steam bath, whirlpool and spa. Each has a butler assigned along with a private chef to prepare whatever the guest has requested for lunch or dinner. These units can be reserved through the hotel number shown above.

Mauna Lani is well prepared to handle conference groups. With their 4,800-square-foot main ballroom and three 600-square-foot breakout rooms they can accommodate over 300 classroom-style. You are in Hawaii, so the outdoor area adds another significant dimension.

Dining is offered in the Bay Terrace, the award-winning Le Soleil Restaurant, the golf club restaurant, and the poolside Ocean Grill. There are also several lounges throughout the resort. Jackets are required at Le Soleil during the evening hours. While all of the restaurants are good we particularly liked the relaxed atmosphere and food served up by the golf club restaurant, now called Knickers. Reservations are advised as this is one difficult place to get into, but definitely worth the effort.

The Tennis Garden features 10 variable-speed courts. There is also a completely supervised health, sports, aerobic, and physical fitness center. Other activities include: deep sea fishing trips, glass-bottom-boat cruises, helicopter sightseeing trips, horseback riding, sailing, bicycling, jogging, scuba diving, snorkeling, windsurfing and, of course, swimming. Plus my favorite sport – sitting in the sun doing absolutely nothing.

Many tours are available from the hotel to see the historically rich countryside.

Country Club Golfer magazine referred to Mauna Lani Bay's 18-hole course as "an outstand-

ing golfing experience." We would have to agree with that evaluation.

There is now, however, a new kid on the block. Opening in late 1991 and called the South Course, it encompasses a new nine, joined with the front nine of the older layout. Weighing in at a strong 7,015/6,370/5,331 yards, it pars at 72. The North Course, which was formed by a combination of the original back nine and a newly constructed nine, reaches out 6,968/6,335/5,398 yards and also pars at 72. They are not only fun to play but offer astonishing views. The South Course also sports a par five of 601 yards with water along the entire side – stretching from tee to green. The North layout has a couple of interesting challenges: number six with an "island tee box" and the ninth hole, a 459-yard par four.

Virtually sculpted from lava with some "over the ocean" holes you will not soon forget, these courses will test not only your skill but your nerve as well. They can also test your vocabulary should you tangle with the many lava outcroppings sprinkled around. The resort has provided an excellent pro shop and a professional staff headed up by the

Director of Golf, Jerry Johnston.

RATES *(EP) Rooms: $275 / $325 / $375. Suites: $725. Ocean villas $350 / $425. Bungalows: $2,500 / $3,000. Green fees: $80, including cart. Golf packages are not available during peak season mid-December through mid-April. There are, however, several different golf packages at other times of the year.*

MAUNA LANI POINT CONDOMINIUMS
Kohala Coast, Island of Hawaii, HI 96743; (808) 885-5022; (800) 642-6284

The Point has approximately 116 condominiums, ranging from one to two bedrooms (1 1/2 to 2 1/2 baths), and they rank among the best we have seen. Beautifully appointed, they are equipped with the latest in appliances including microwave ovens and washer/dryers. Daily maid service is also provided. You have a choice of either an ocean or golf course view.

The location, on the same property as the Mauna Lani Hotel, also has several advantages. The dining facilities, as well as the tennis courts and the golf

course are available. You will, however, incur a fee for the use of the Mauna Lani Hotel facilities. For details on the dining rooms and the golf courses refer to Mauna Lani Bay Hotel above.

RATES *(EP) 1-bedroom unit: $240 / $310 2 bedrooms: $325 / $410. Green fees: $80, including cart.*

ROYAL WAIKOLOAN RESORT
HC02 Box 5300 Kohala Coast, Waikoloa, HI 96743; (808) 885-6789; (800) 537-9800

Sited on a half-mile crescent of Anaeho'omalu Bay overlooking a serene lagoon, the Royal Waikoloan is an outstanding destination. The subdued elegance, priceless artifacts, warm old-style Hawaiian atmosphere and welcome extended to guests are all part of the charm. The location provides a large and beautiful white beach, something hard to find on the "Big Island" and permitting a wide variety of water activities. Each of the 546 rooms, including 18 lagoon cabanas, has its own private lanai overlooking the bay or the ocean. The cabanas are under a concierge arrangement and include a continental breakfast and cocktails with hors d'oeuvres each evening. The resort has excellent meeting facilities with some 20,000 square feet of space plus several breakout rooms set aside to handle group functions.

There are three restaurants: the open air coffee shop, the intimate Tiare Room with rich Koa Wood and crystal, specializing in continental cuisine, and the Royal Terrace, overlooking the ocean and offering both Hawaiian and international entertainment. Then there is the Garden Cafe for outdoor, casual dining. To even things out there are three bars.

Activities include: tennis on six courts with professional guidance, freshwater swimming pools, horseback riding at nearby Waikoloa stables, a fitness center, and all types of ocean action from fishing, catamaran sailing, scuba, and snorkeling to kayaking and canoeing.

Designed by Robert Trent Jones, Jr., the Waikoloa Beach Golf Course opened in 1981. Parring at 70 and reaching out 6,566/5,958/5,094 yards, it spreads over 150 acres. Lush with palm trees, bougainvillea, oleander and plumeria, it visually denies the solid lava flow over which it was built. The clubhouse offers food service, a bar, and locker rooms.

The newest course is The Kings Golf Club layout designed by Weiskopf-Morrish. While the Beach Course is a fun affair and not all that demanding, with the Kings layout they took off the gloves. Reaching out 7,074/6,594/6,010/5,459 yards, it pars at 72. A Scottish type, featuring six lakes (a total of nine acres of water) and 83 traps, it is no pussycat. Some of the traps are as much as 70 feet deep!

The John Jacobs' Practical Golf School is available at this resort. Using personalized teaching methods, and under the direction of PGA and LPGA teaching professionals, it is worth looking into. For details (and *lower scores), call: (800) 472-5007.*

RATES *(EP) Rooms: $99 / $135 / $175 / $195. Cabana: $250. Green fees: Kings Course $85; Beach Course $75, including cart.*

THE SHORES AT WAIKOLOA
Star Route 5200, Waikoloa Village, HI 96743; (808) 885-5001; (800) 922-7866

The name of this resort can be misleading as it sounds as if you are in a beach area. These suites are sitting on top of a Robert Trent Jones, Jr. course, approximately six miles from the water. But, even though you are not on the beach, the location is excellent, as you are close to some of the finest hotels to be found anywhere. Among them are the Mauna Kea Beach Hotel, the Mauna Lani Bay Hotel, the massive Hyatt Regency Waikoloa, and the Royal Waikoloa. Their restaurants and golf courses are all available to you. Lodgings here consist of well-furnished one- or two-bedroom suites. Each unit has a fully-equipped kitchen and a private lanai. The resort provides daily housekeeping service.

For details on the Waikoloa Village Golf Course refer to the text on the Waikoloa Villas.

RATES (EP) One-bedroom unit: $195/$315. Two bedrooms: $240/$255. The resort offers some packages including car rental.

WAIKOLOA VILLAS
Box 3066 Waikoloa Village Station, Kamuela, Hawaii 96743; (808) 883-9588; (800) 767-4474

The Waikoloa Village is 15 miles north of the Kona Airport on Highway 19 and then six miles east. The Villas (104 units) are well-furnished condominiums ranging from one to three bedrooms with fully-equipped kitchens, washer/dryers in each unit, and weekly linen service. The Villas are near the golf course.

Amenities include: two swimming pools, whirlpools, cabanas and a unique gazebo area, tennis courts and horseback riding. The ocean beaches are about seven miles away.

The Club at Waikoloa Village golf course, a Robert Trent Jones, Jr. layout, plays 6,687/6,142/5,558 yards, with a par of 72. The course is supported by a pro shop and a professional staff under the direction of Head Professional, Randall Carney.

RATES (EP) 1-bedroom condo: $115. 2-bedroom condo: $125. Green fees: $60, carts $25. They offer a monthly green fee schedule. Golf packages are available.

THE KA'U COAST

While still on the Big Island we now have shifted to the east side, where the startling black sand beaches are found. It is the home of one of the most active volcanoes in the world, Kilauea Crater, and of "Madame Pele," the Hawaiian goddess of volcanoes. It is also where you will find two resorts, SeaMountain at Panulu'u and the Volcano House Inn.

SEAMOUNTAIN AT PUNALU'U
P.O. BOX 70, Pahala, HI 96777; (808) 928-8301; (800) 488-8301

Half the accommodations here are represented by one company, the remainder by another. You can call either the above numbers or the following for information: (808) 928-6200; (800) 344-7675.

This resort captures the essence of the word "Hawaii" and all it represents. On the southeastern side of the Big Island a few miles north of the southern tip, the setting is most unusual – with lush green sugarcane fields behind it, the Pacific Ocean fronting the entire property, and black lava rock and palm-fringed lagoons all about. This is not a hustle-bustle place, but rather one for reflective moments, serene beauty, and barefoot quiet. It is more a colony than a resort. If you seek night life, this is not the place. Accommodations are studios and one- to two-bedroom cottage apartments fully-equipped for housekeeping, including washer/dryers.

Aside from swimming at the black sand beaches, there is a pool, tennis courts nearby and the Panalu'u Black Sands Restaurant, open seven days a week. Something relatively new is the Broiler Restaurant at the pro shop.

The golf course, parring at 72, reaches out 6,492/6,106/5,663 yards. A Jack Snyder design, with water hazards, traps, pine trees, lava outcroppings, black sand beaches and wind, this can be a tough and challenging layout. The day we played we were blessed with little wind but still found it all we could handle. This course, by the way, is the southernmost golf layout in the United States.

RATES (EP) Studio: $86 / $96. 1 bedroom: $112 / $123. 2 bedrooms: $142 / $157. Green fees: $35, including cart. Rates are

for *mid-December through
April. Minimum stay is 2
nights.*

THE VOLCANO
HOUSE INN &
COUNTRY CLUB
*Kilauea Crater, Big Island of
Hawaii, HI 96718; (808) 967-
7321*

The Volcano House Inn is one
of the few tropical hotels in the
world where you will enjoy sitting in front of the lounge's
roaring fire. Its old-time Hawaiian charm has delighted
visitors for over a century. The
setting is extraordinary, with
misty ohia and giant fern forests in the midst of volcanic
landscapes, active craters,
lava tube caverns, and steam
vents.
The walls of the lounge are
lined with the works of world
famous artists, drawn here to
have their go at painting the
enchanting view of the volcano
or their vision of Madam Pele,
the Hawaiian goddess of volcanoes. The Volcano House was
originally a country home built
of lava and perched on the edge
of Kilauea Crater. Keep in
mind this is an old inn and
rather small (41 guest rooms).
While the rooms are comfortable, elaborate they are not.

The emerald-green fairways of
the Volcano Golf Course are
bordered by dark forests of
pine and scarlet-blossomed
ohia trees, while in the background rise the towering
slopes of 13,680-foot Mauna
Loa. The course plays 6,119
yards and pars at 72. At 4,000
feet, watch that you do not
overshoot the 15th green or
your ball will surely come to
rest in the crater.

RATES *(EP) Rooms: $69 / $79.
Green fees: $33, carts $23.*

ARRIVAL *Air: Hilo (29 miles).
You are on the opposite side of
the island from Kona.*

There are several other places
to stay in the immediate area.
Primarily intimate bed &
breakfast inns and chalets
along with several vacation
homes (some directly along the
fairways), they are a great way
to pamper yourself. They are
indeed delightful places to enjoy Hawaii. Call (808) 967-
7244, (800) 736-7140, or (800)
937-7786 for information.
These numbers put you in
touch with Volcano Reservations, representing some 80
properties scattered throughout the island.

THE ISLAND OF KAUAI

Justifiably referred to as the Garden Island, Kauai presents a mixture of scenery: ferns and grottoes to the north, deserts to the west, flowers everywhere and, in the middle, towering mountains, with a spectacular "Grand Canyon" some 4,000 feet deep – certainly one of the least accessible places in the world.

Kauai, the northern-most island in the Hawaiian chain, is also the oldest. It is generally accepted that this island was populated between 200 and 300 A.D., some 500 years prior to any of the others. Kauai is rich in history and legends – something for you to dig into on your visit should you be interested.

On the east side of the island is the Westin Kauai; at the northern end is Princeville, the location of Hanalei Bay Resort and The Princeville Hotel. On the south side, in the Poipu Beach area, is the Kiahuna Plantation, the Sheraton Kauai Hotel, the Hyatt Regency Kauai, and the Stouffer Waiohai Beach Resort.

THE PRINCEVILLE RESORT AREA

Within the 9,000-acre resort community of Princeville can be found golf, the new and huge 60,000-square-foot Prince Golf clubhouse, a shopping center, approximately 400 homes, a wide range of condominiums, and 10 restaurants. Various types of accommodations are available: the lovely Princeville Hotel, the Hanalei Bay Resort, as well as the many condominiums and rental homes.

Also within this resort property are 20 outdoor tennis courts and two fully-equipped pro shops, along with professionals to assist, a health club, helicopter tours, boat tours, scuba diving, snorkeling, kayaking and horseback riding.

Princeville now offers 45 holes of golf, 27 of which have been rated among the nation's top 100. They are also the home of the LPGA World Match Play Championship. The Ocean/ Woods combination stretches 6,912/6,365/5,631 yards; the Woods/Lake combination plays 6,878/6,357/5,543 yards; while the Lake/Ocean nines weigh in at 6,900/6,306/5,516.

All three combinations par at 72. Each of the nines lives up to its name, bringing into play a bit of ocean, a bit of the woods and more than a bit of lake. An ongoing improvement and expansion program taking place over the next few years may take one nine at a time out of play. Involving replanting of fairways, a new irrigation system and additional tee settings, the renovation is designed to lift the caliber of golf here to even greater heights.

Now a new layout has been added – the "Prince Course," also a Robert Trent Jones, Jr. design. While quite new it has been judged one of the finest in the islands (it has also been deemed the most difficult).

Originally they named each of the holes, in the traditional Scottish fashion. While they no longer do so, we thought you might like to know about some of the original names, such as Burma Road, Hazard, Waterfall, and Dunkirk. Dunkirk is not all that difficult if you can clear the two ravines, stay right of the O.B. stakes, avoid the six deep bunkers, and land on the postage-stamp size green. If you can, this hole is a "piece of cake." I will not attempt to describe the par-five,

597-yard Burma Road or the Eagles Nest, a par-four featuring a 150-foot drop from tee to fairway. From its five tee settings the course plays to an awesome 7,309/6,960/6,521/6,005/5,338 yards with a par of 72. Play from the back tees is limited to handicaps of nine or less. Thank God, they would not let me play from those masochistic tee settings. The course is now supported by the new clubhouse, featuring a restaurant and lounge as well as locker rooms and a 4,000-square-foot pro shop. The Director of Golf Operations is Bob Higgins.

The Airport, two miles from the Princeville complex, is served by Aloha Island Airways. Both Hertz and Avis cars can be rented at the airport.

HANALEI BAY RESORT
P.O. Box 220 Hanalei, Kauai, HI 96714; (808) 826-6522; (800) 827-4427

All accommodations consist of condominiums, each with one or two bedrooms, fully-equipped kitchens including washer/dryer, cable TV, and daily maid service. Dining and cocktails are available in several restaurants: the Princeville Lanai, the Snack Bar (Makai Golf Course clubhouse), and Bali Hai (Hanalei Resort).

Activities here include: tennis on eight courts, sailing a catamaran beyond the reefs, looking for porpoise, flying fish, or trolling for game fish, and horseback riding over the Princeville ranchland.

A word of warning: winter brings dangerous swimming conditions to the north shores of the islands. So think before you venture too far out.

Golf can be played on the Princeville complex surrounding this resort. For a more detailed description of the golf facilities refer to "The Princeville Resort Area."

RATES (EP) Condominiums: 1 bedroom $240; 2 bedrooms $350. Green fees: $70, including cart.

PRINCEVILLE HOTEL
Princeville, Kauai, HI 96714; (808) 826-9644; (800) 826-4400

Princeville Hotel has been judged one of the top 50 resorts. The film "South Pacific"

was shot on these magnificent white beaches. That will give you an idea of the area's beauty. The Princeville Hotel originally opened here as a Sheraton in late 1985.

I never will understand why a decision was made to virtually gut this lovely place – but in 1989 a complete redo got underway and the hotel was closed. The public area as well as the guest rooms, meeting facilities and restaurants underwent complete restructuring and renovation. The hotel reopened in May of 1991.

Now there are 252 rooms, including suites, with many offering a view of beautiful Hanalei Bay. Complimentary 24-hour butler service is also at your disposal. The 6,600-square-foot Grand Ballroom, which can also be divided into four separate meeting rooms, can handle as many as 700 reception- and 540-banquet style. Of course, more intimate groups can also be comfortably accommodated.

A real plus, at least to me, is the fact that they have not lost sight of "Hawaii." The decor is muted and quiet, matching the soft Hawaiian ambiance which makes this area so alluring. They do not overwhelm you with it, but from time to time you can hear the soft strains of classical Hawaiian music in the background.

There are three restaurants: the Cafe Hanalei with its open-air setting overlooking beautiful Hanalei Bay; the Mediterranean restaurant La Cascata serving authentic southern Italian cuisine; the Beach Restaurant & Bar for lighter fare served poolside. There are, of course, lounges along with evening entertainment and 24-hour room service as well.

Activities include: swimming in both pool and the ocean (there is an excellent beach), deep sea fishing, horseback riding, and tennis. Something extra: Papillon Helicopters offers a variety of sightseeing flights presenting views of the rugged canyon area. It is probably the most spectacular flight you will ever make and well worth the time and money.

Guests of the resort hotel have playing privileges on the 45 holes of the Princeville courses. For details on these courses refer to "The Princeville Resort Area."

RATES   (EP)   Rooms:

$295/$410. Prince room: $450, Suites: $825 and up. Green fees: Makai Course $75, Prince Course $95, including cart. Golf packages are available.

ARRIVAL *Air: Lihue Airport. Commuter flights also run to and from the Princeville Airport.*

CONDOMINIUM LODGINGS – PRINCEVILLE AREA

For condominium-type lodgings and reservations in the Princeville Resort complex, as well as the Hanalei Bay Resort (which is listed in this book), contact the following:

THE CLIFFS
P.O. Box 1005 Hanalei, HI 96714; (808) 826-6219; (800) 367-6046

HAWAIIAN ISLANDS RESORTS INC.
P.O. Box 212 Honolulu, HI 96810, (808) 531-7595; (800) 367-7042

PRINCEVILLE TRAVEL SERVICE
P.O. Box 990 Hanalei Kauai, HI 96714; (808) 826-9661; (800) 445-6253

THE EAST SIDE OF KAUAI

This part of Kauai, the location of the Westin Kauai, is less than two miles from the major airport of Kauai and the town of Lihue.

THE WESTIN KAUAI
Kalapaki Beach, Kauai, HI 96754; (808) 245-5050; (800) 228-3000

The Westin Kauai has been judged one of the top 50 resorts. Guests are transported to the hotel via a stretch Cadillac limousine. This drive is taken along the resort's "private road" from the airport. Enroute you will see a portion of the 200-plus acres of botanical gardens and lawns. Upon arrival you board an escalator to the lower level. There you are greeted by the sight of a huge two-acre reflecting pool complete with various species of swans and ducks. Finally (if you are lucky) you can find the main lobby. On the way to your accommodations you will see the main swimming area. You may have noticed I said "area" rather than pool. Amounting to 26,000 square feet of water, it is huge.

Guests stay in the Beach Tower, fronting Kalapaki Beach, and Surf Tower, a 10-story structure. Additional accommodations are available in the four-story Bay Tower, the 10-story Ocean Tower (286 rooms) and other buildings, for a total of 847 guest rooms.

For meetings and conferences the resort has set aside 41,000 square feet of space including a 17,200-square-foot ballroom.

There are many restaurants and lounges (some 15 or more) scattered throughout the complex – ranging from informal (swim wear acceptable) to one where jackets are required (in Hawaii that is formal). By all means attempt to dine at the Inn on the Cliffs Restaurant. Not only is the food outstanding but getting there is an adventure. You can elect to arrive via a magnificent motor launch and return in a carriage drawn by massive Clydesdales. A great way to wind up a Hawaiian evening. One of the newer additions, Pura Follia Ristorante Italiana, is also a dining experience to savor and remember. There is nightly entertainment, and much more available. Yes, the place is large!

Other amenities include: eight

tennis courts, supported by a separate tennis shop and a professional staff. They also have a central stadium court seating 1,000. The tennis complex is also the location of two additional restaurants. The Terrace (what they do to a tuna sandwich I will leave for you to discover and enjoy) and The Masters, a world-class dining room open for dinner six nights a week.

Within the Lagoons Golf & Racquet Club there is a complete European health spa, including Jacuzzi, massage, body buffs, herbal wraps, facials, saunas, and steam baths. There is also a regulation-size swimming pool along with over 1,400 feet of beach along Kalapaki inlet. We are not done yet. There are 35 carriages to transport guests along an eight-mile carriage road with over 100 horses (Clydesdales, Belgians, and Percherons). There is also an inland waterway system with 90 outrigger canoes and 40 "taxi boats." There are a total of 70 shops with some located in the hotel and others in the two shopping villages on the lagoon. They really do seem to have thought of everything. There is even a 1,000-square-foot chapel by the sea. I understand it is kept busy performing marriages.

Although both golf courses are Jack Nicklaus-designed layouts, the Kauai Lagoons, spreading over 190 acres, is principally intended for the recreational golfer. It shows a yardage of 6,942/6,545/6,108/5,607 with a par of 72. The 262-acre Kiele Lagoons layout is a tournament-class affair, complete with substantial gallery areas. This course weighs in at 7,070/6,637/6,164/5,417 yards and also pars at 72. The golf shop is under the supervision of Mark Spandoni and the Director of Golf, Kim Worrel.

RATES   (EP)   Rooms $195 / $500. Suites: $500 / $1,800. Green fees: Kauai Lagoons Course, $80, including cart; the Kiele Championship Course, $115, including cart.

THE SOUTHEAST "POIPU BEACH" AREA

Stay with us as. We are still on Kauai. This area of the island is conceded to be the "dry" side. There are four topresorts, the Hyatt Regency Kauai, Kiahuna Plantation, the Sheraton Kauai Hotel, and the Stouffer Waiohai Beach Resort. The Hyatt, Sheraton, and Stouffer offer hotel rooms, while lodgings at the Kiahuna Plantation consist of fully-equipped condominiums.

A short distance away from each of these resorts is the Kiahuna Golf Club. A Robert Trent Jones, Jr. design, it is a beautiful layout. Parring at 70, it stretches out 6,380/5,669/4,901 yards. While only a modest amount of water comes into play (on six holes) it seems to be just where it should not be. The course is supported by a well-stocked pro shop and is under the direction of PGA Golf Professional Charlie Ortega. Carts are mandatory and must keep on the cart paths at all times.

Also a part of the clubhouse is the Waiohai Terrace Restaurant, home of Kauai's famous Sunday Champagne Brunch.

HYATT REGENCY KAUAI
1571 Poipu Drive, Poipu Beach, Kauai, HI; (808) 742-1234; (800) 233-1234

Opened in early 1991, the Hyatt Kauai is on 50 acres at Keoneloa Bay. Rather than the normal massive Hyatt structures, they have used a more traditional Hawaiian architectural style. Extensive gardens, open-air courtyards, and the fact that none of the structures are higher than a coconut tree lend a relaxing Hawaiian atmosphere. Accommodations (605 guest rooms) include 41 suites along with 38 Regency Club rooms, offering concierge service and amenities.There are 19 meeting rooms including several breakout rooms as well as five smaller conference suites. The capacity is 1,500 theater- and 650 classroom-style.

The resort has three restaurants, ranging from Italian or seafood to continental cuisine. One of the lounges overlooks the lagoon area and offers open-air dancing, while the second, the more intimate Library Lounge, has a view of the ocean.

There is a 500-yard sand beach, two swimming pools –

one a small 12-person affair, and the other an action pool with waterfalls and slides. They also have a salt water lagoon system complete with islands. There are four tennis courts. Nearby activities include horseback riding, sailing, scuba diving, and deep sea fishing. Along with a 25,000-square-foot fitness center there are massage rooms, hydro, facial and luffa rooms, sauna, steam rooms, whirlpools, and a lap pool.

While the resort opened in early 1991, the golf course did not open until 1992. A Robert Trent Jones Jr. layout, it plays to a yardage of 6,845/6,210/5,555 with a par of 72.

RATES   (EP)   Rooms: $230/$300/$345.   Suites: $425/$700. Regency Club: $345. Green fees: $85, including cart.

ARRIVAL Air: Lihue Airport (25 minutes). Car: follow signs to the Poipu Beach area.

KIAHUNA PLANTATION
RR #1 Box 73, Koloa, Kauai, HI 96756; (808) 742-6411; (800) 367-7052

At one time this 35-acre site was part of the oldest sugar cane plantation in Hawaii. The resort offers a blend of the "old legendary Hawaii" (quiet and peaceful) and an almost endless list of activities. The grounds are filled with fruit trees, tropical flower gardens, and lily ponds – truly a beautiful setting. Accommodations here are in 253 well-equipped condominiums. Ranging from one- to two-bedroom units, they feature a separate living and dining area, lanais, and fully-equipped kitchens. They come with ceiling fans, rattan furniture, and cable TV. Although there are no washer/dryers in the units, coin-operated machines are available. The resort provides daily maid service, 24-hour front desk telephone, a baby sitting service, plus rental car arrangements.

Even though you have the equipment to prepare your own meals, you might well find the restaurants here irresistible. They range from casual lagoon-side barbecue pits and picnic tables to the Courtside Bar & Grill and the Clubhouse Restaurant. There is also one of the island's award-winning restaurants, The Plantation Gardens.

Diversions include: swimming

from one of the best beaches in the islands or pool swimming, snorkeling, surfing, sailing, tennis on 10 courts with a professional to assist, deep sea fishing, helicopter tours and trips to the Waimea Canyon (some 4,000 feet deep), historic Hanalei and, of course, golf.

You won't have to be concerned with the children keeping busy. They will be pretty well tied up with arts & crafts, shell collecting, lagoon fishing, lei-making, basket weaving and hula lessons, to say nothing of swimming.

The Kiahuna Golf Club, less than 1/2 mile away, is a beautiful layout. For complete details refer to "The Southeast Poipu Beach Area."

RATES (EP) 1-bedroom condo (1-4 people): $150 / $170 / $210/$280. Rates are for high season mid-December to mid-April. Lower at other times. Green fees: $55, including cart. Golf packages are available.

ARRIVAL Air: Liuhie Airport (15 miles). Car: from the airport take Highway 50 west (signs will say Poipu Beach). Turn off onto Highway 520 and follow signs to Poipu Beach.

SHERATON KAUAI HOTEL
RR #1 Box 303, Koloa Kauai, HI 96756; (808) 742-1661; (800) 325-3535

The Sheraton Kauai, with its 456 guest rooms and suites, fronts along one of the better beach areas in Hawaii. The hotel itself consists of the garden, the lawn, and the ocean vista wings. All rooms are air-conditioned and have private lanais.

Recently refurbished, the Drum Lounge is a favorite spot for viewing the spectacular Hawaiian sunsets. For dining the hotel offers the Outrigger Room or the Lanai Terrace Restaurant. In addition there is the Breakers, specializing in steak and seafood, and the Naniwa, with Japanese selections and a Polynesian revue offered every Wednesday and Sunday evening. For lighter fare there are the Poolside Cafe and the Makihana Snackshop & Bar. The hotel has set aside 6,717 square feet for meeting groups. This space is supplemented by an additional 17,230 square feet of outdoor area. Depending on the weather they can handle up to 1,200.

There are three tennis courts, swimming at either the ocean

front or garden swimming pools, a whirlpool spa, snorkeling, sailing, or perhaps just soaking up the sun with an occasional dip in the calm blue waters of the ocean.

For details on the golf course, refer to "The Southeast Poipu Beach Area."

RATES   (EP)   Rooms: $115/$185/$350. Suites: $400 and up. Green fees: $65, including cart.

ARRIVAL Air: Liuhie Airport (15 miles). Car: from Liuhie take Highway 50 west (signs will say Poipu Beach). Turn off onto Highway 520 and follow signs to Poipu Beach.

STOUFFER WAIOHAI BEACH RESORT
2249 Poipu Road, Box 174, Koloa, Kauai, HI 96756; (808) 742-9511; (800) 426-4122

The Waiohai Resort is on the southern tip of Kauai's Poipu Beach. There are 430 guest rooms, including 21 suites all featuring wet bars, refrigerators, and private lanais. The suites have separate living rooms. Their meeting rooms can accommodate up to 900 banquet-style.

For dining you can select from the Waiohai Terrace (breakfast and dinner), or the Tamarind Restaurant for contemporary cuisine. There is also the Beach Bar & Grill located poolside for lighter fare. They also have several lounges.

The magnificent sand beaches in this area make possible all manner of water sports, such as surfing, catamaran sailing, windsurfing, or snorkeling. There are, in addition, three fresh-water swimming pools, six tennis courts, a fitness center and massage facilities.

For details on the golf course refer to "The Southeast Poipu Beach Area."

RATES   (EP)   Rooms: $150/175/$360. Suites: $465. Green fees: $75, including cart.

THE ISLAND OF MAUI

Many years ago, when the only method of reaching the Hawaiian Islands was by ship, Oahu was the ultimate destination. Then along came aircraft and some of the heartier souls ventured to the outer islands. Not too many however. After droning along for 2,600 miles from the West Coast in a piston driven aircraft, with the knowledge that you would have to grind your way back, most people settled for the beauty and relaxation of Waikiki. But the advent of the jet turned the islands into a reachable destination. And, with the sudden flood of new *Haoles,* the islanders felt they had been overrun. Seeking to rediscover the "Old Hawaii," they began a retreat to the out-lying areas.

The rest is history. The development of Maui has been rapid and, although not nearly as congested as Oahu, it is gaining. It is a place of beautiful beaches, magnificent hotels, condominiums, and golf courses by the ton. It is also the location of Lahaina, the first capital of the islands, and of Mt. Haleakala, a dormant volcano rising to almost 10,000 feet.

THE WAILEA AREA OF MAUI

Wailea is on the southwest coast of the island, only a 35-minute drive (via a new limited-access highway) from Kahului Airport. Dominating the area from the southeast is Haleakala (House of the Sun), the world's largest dormant volcanic crater. Its slopes embrace 500 square miles of tropical rain forest, arid deserts, lush cattle ranches and some of the most spectacular scenery anywhere on this planet.

Golf is available to guests of the various hotels or condominiums of Wailea on two 18-hole layouts. Each of these two courses will provide not only a real test of your skill but views which make it difficult to keep your mind on the game.

The Wailea Blue Course, reaching out 6,743/6,152/5,686 yards, pars at 72. While this layout brings water into contention on four holes it is more open – perhaps more forgiving than the Orange. The Orange Course, also with a par of 72, measures a healthy 6,810/6,304/5,644 yards. Both are beautiful, but once again the Orange must be considered the more difficult of the two. It is tighter and more demanding from a placement standpoint. Both operate from the same pro shop. The Director of Golf is Terry Young and the Head Professional is Rick Castillo. Good news – a third course will join the group. The Gold

Course is expected to come into play in either late 1994 or early in 1995.

Now to get back to Wailea: in addition to golf, there is a picturesque hillside tennis complex offering 14 courts (11 hard and three grass), a pro shop, and an exhibition stadium seating 1,200.

Hotel accommodations are at the 550-room Maui Inter-Continental Wailea and the 347-room Stouffer Wailea. Three recent additions include the 787-room Grand Hyatt Wailea, the 380-room Four Seasons Resort Wailea, and the 450-unit Wailea Suite Hotel.

Although the restaurants at the various resorts are excellent, should you want a change we suggest The Wailea Steakhouse Restaurant, adjacent to the Blue Course at Wailea on 100 Wailea Ike Drive. You will find it very good indeed. For reservations call (808) 879-2875.

FOUR SEASONS RESORT WAILEA
3900 Wailea Alanui, Wailea, Maui, HI 96753; (808) 874-8000; (800) 334-6284

The resort is on 15 acres on the southwest coast of Maui, a bit over 35 minutes from the airport. It happens to have one of the best beaches in the islands. Guest accommodations are 372 rooms and suites, with many offering an ocean view. Each unit has a built-in refrigerator-bar, color TV and a VCR. The Club Floor rooms on the seventh and eighth floors give you access to the private club level (concierge floor). Among the special amenities offered with these rooms are daily continental breakfast, afternoon tea, and sunset cocktails. The Four Seasons has set aside 24,000 square feet of space to handle meeting groups and can accommodate from 10 to 600.

The Seasons (the main dining room), opening directly onto the ocean, specializes in Polynesian, fresh island fish, and American dishes. There is also the Pacific Grill, a casual restaurant, the Cabana Cafe, the Sunset Bar, and the Lobby Lounge.

Available on premises are two lighted tennis courts, a 40 x 80-foot swimming pool, whirlpools and, of course, the magnificent beach. As a guest you also have access to all of the offerings described under the section titled "The Wailea Area of Maui." This includes tennis as well as the two golf courses.

RATES   (EP)   Rooms: *$275 / $550.   Club   Floor;* *$450 / $630. Suites: $550 /* *$775. Golf package: 3 nights / 3 days (includes ocean-view room, 3 rounds of golf, including cart, 3 days use of full-size car (automatic and air), $1,470 per couple.*

GRAND HYATT WAILEA

3850 Wailea Alanui Drive, Wialea, Maui, HI 96753; (808) 875-1234; (800) 233-1234

The Grand Hyatt seems determined to live up to its name "Grand." A massive eight-story resort (787 rooms, including 53 suites), it is perched along the south Maui shore. The target was to create a spectacular destination resort and spectacular it is. The meeting and conference facilities are also large with 55,000 square feet of space devoted to group activities. A 2,000-foot-long river pool, 15,000 square feet of pool and deck area, a huge lobby bar, Japanese gardens throughout the property, hot tubs, swim-in caves, a bubbling spring, and a swim-up bar are some of the spectacular features of the Hyatt Wailea.

There are several dining possibilities, including the main dining room, a coffee shop, a lobby bar and the various restaurants located in the general area. Hyatt has included a "Camp Hyatt" facility designed for children. The 20,000-square-foot installation offers a computer learning center, video game room, a 60-seat children's theater, an outdoor playground and, to top it off, the "Hyatt Riot" soda fountain.

Guests of the Hyatt can play golf on the Wailea golf courses as well as use the 14 tennis courts. For details refer to "The Wailea Area of Maui."

RATES   (EP)   Rooms: *$350 / $475. Suites: $500 and up. Green fees: $65 / $75, including cart.*

KEA LANI HOTEL

4100 Wailea Alanui Drive, Wailea, Maui, HI 96753; (808) 875-4100; (800) 659-4100

Located across from the two Wailea golf courses and tennis facilities, this is an all-suite hotel. There are 413 one-bedroom, 24 two-bedroom, and 13 three-bedroom suites. Each of the one-bedroom units has a living room, separate bedroom, mini-kitchen (refrigerator, microwave, wet bar, dinnerware, coffee maker) along with ceiling fans, and a private lanai with breakfast table. Each also has two TV sets (one in the bathroom so you won't miss even a small part of your favorite soap opera), a VCR, and stereo system. The ocean-front villas have a private swimming pool, two baths, a full-service kitchen, along with washer/dryer units. The hotel is well set up for group functions and can handle 450 classroom- and 500 banquet-style.

Beyond the many restaurants in the immediate area, the hotel itself has the Kea Lani Restaurant, Cafe Ciao, and the Polo Beach Grille. In addition to golf and tennis, there is a 22,000-square-foot lagoon-style swimming pool, beautiful Polo Beach, and a health spa complete with an exercise fitness room.

One final point: they offer a Keike Lani (kids program). Operating seven days a week it can turn your Hawaii vacation into a delight and let the kids enjoy their trip.

RATES (EP) 1-bedroom suite: $225/$375. Villas: $795/$995.

THE MAUI INTER-CONTINENTAL WAILEA

P.O. Box 779 Wailea, Maui, HI 96753; (808) 879-1922; (800) 367-2960

Prior to actual construction, two years of research went into siting the structure. This was done in order to take maximum advantage of the incredible location. As a result, 80% of the 550 rooms offer an ocean view.

Six restaurants provide a wide selection of cuisine, running the gamut from the coffee shop, the Wet Spot (the pool area), the Lanai Terrace, with a magnificent view of the Pacific Ocean, and the Kiawe Broiler to the Holiday-award-winning La Perouse Restaurant (open for dinner only), serving seafood. Then perhaps try a visit to the Inu Inu Piano Bar & Lounge to watch the sun go down as it can only be seen in Hawaii. Inu Inu means "Drink Drink."

The Inter-Continental is well-equipped to handle meeting groups, with its 13 breakout rooms in addition to the ballroom, and can accommodate 300 classroom- and 500 banquet-style.

There are, in addition to golf, many other activities: snorkeling, sailing, surfing, catamaran sailing, deep sea fishing, swimming (two swimming pools), as well as ocean swimming. They offer tennis on 11 courts (three lighted) backed up by a professional staff. You can also elect to put the body down on the beach and just unwind. During the winter months whale watching can be added to the list of activities.

The resort is situated almost on top of two of the better courses on this island. For details refer to "The Wailea Area of Maui." Golf can also be played at the Makena course three miles south of the hotel. For details on this course refer to the "Maui Prince Hotel at Makena."

RATES   (EP)   Rooms: $169 / $209 / $279.   Suites: $395 / $695. Golf packages are not available during peak season. Green fees: $65 / $75, including cart.

MAUI PRINCE HOTEL at MAKENA
5400 Makena Alanui, Kihei, Maui, HI 96753; (808) 874-1111; (800) 321-6284

Just three miles south of Wailea, this attractive 310-room six-story resort, situated on 1,800 acres, offers almost every Hawaiian amenity and recreation facility you could wish for. All rooms and suites are air-conditioned and are equipped with remote-controlled TV and refrigerators. The Prince resort can handle modest-size meeting groups. With their four meeting rooms they can accommodate 50 classroom- and 300 banquet-style. A thoughtful extra: upon check-in you will find a fruit basket as well as a small flower arrangement in your room.

There are three restaurants: the Prince Court, for American Cuisine; the Cafe Kiowai, with a garden setting; and the Hakone, an authentic Japanese restaurant. All are backed up by 24-hour room service. There is also the Molokini Lounge with a variety of nightly entertainment.

A sample of available activities includes: tennis (six courts, two lighted) with a professional staff on deck, swimming (two pools and the beautiful beach), sailing, or perhaps just loafing and sunning. During the winter months a favorite pastime is watching the humpback whales as they cavort along the coast of Maui.

The Haleakala (mountain

side) Golf Course was designed by Robert Trent Jones, Jr. Parring at 72, it measures 6,739/6,210/5,441 yards. While water is brought into play on only three holes, there are 64 traps to avoid. Be sure to bring a camera, as the golf course and ocean views, particularly on the back nine, are such that you will be angry with yourself if you can't get a few pictures. Now in play is the Molokini (ocean side) course. Opening in 1993, it is even more spectacular than the original layout. The Head Professional is Howard Kihune. The golf club provides a large (4,000-square-foot) clubhouse and pro shop. Hidden from view, behind the pro shop, is an excellent restaurant and lounge.

RATES   (EP)   Rooms: $210/$330. Suites: $400/ $800. Green fees: $65, including cart. Golf package: 2 nights/2 days (includes room with partial ocean view, 2 rounds of golf with cart), $595 per couple.

ARRIVAL Air: Maui's Kahului Airport. Car: from Kahului Airport drive south to Wailea. Continue on for 3 more miles.

STOUFFER WAILEA BEACH RESORT
Wailea, Maui, HI 96753; (808) 879-4900; (800) 992-4532

A multi-story structure, the Stouffer Wailea is 35 minutes from the Kahului airport. With the landscaped gardens and many waterfalls, the setting is serene. In addition to 347 rooms in the main buildings, there are lodgings in the Makapu Beach Club, offering seclusion and luxury. All rooms are equipped with TV, VCR, HBO, and individual air conditioning controls. A nice extra that we wish all hotels offered: there are laundry facilities in each wing. Stouffer Wailea is well set up to handle meeting groups and has a capacity for 280 indoors and as many as 700 outdoors banquet-style.

The dining options include the Raffles Restaurant (*Travel/ Holiday* award), the Palm Court for less formal dining, or the Maui Onion for cocktails and/or a light repast by the pool. They claim their "Raffles" outdoes its namesake in Singapore. Unfortunately we did not get the opportunity to test this claim. But the Stouffer Resort has been awarded the AAA Five Diamond Award.

In addition to its many other amenities the resort has two large swimming pools. All of the usual beach activities are available including: windsurfing, scuba and snorkel charters, sunset sails, horseback riding (located nearby), tennis at the Wailea complex, as well as golf. For details on golf and tennis refer to "The Wailea Area of Maui."

RATES (EP) Rooms: $215/$400. Suites: $585/ $890. Green fees: $65/$75, including cart. Golf packages are available at $849 per couple. Rates are for December-April.

WAILEA ELUA VILLAGE
3600 Alanui Drive, Wailea, Maui, HI 96753; (808) 879-4055; (800) 367-5246

If you are tired of eating out every meal and want to relax and just soak your body in the sun and ocean, I have an excellent alternative. There are many individually owned condominiums which can be rented (approximately 150). Located at the above address these furnished condos range in size from one to three bedrooms. Each unit has a private lanai, living room, and kitchen. They are well-equipped (micro-

wave, disposal, dishwasher, washer/dryer, ice maker) and are across from the Wailea Blue Course, fronting directly on the ocean.

Within the complex there are two swimming pools as well as one of the better beaches on the island. There is also a paddle tennis court. A couple of extras: they have a 24-hour security gate entrance, a small library at the manager's office, mail service, and a barbecue adjacent to each of the swimming pools. Maid service is provided once a week. However, arrangements can be made (at additional cost) for daily service.

RATES One bedroom, garden view $195; ocean view $230; ocean front $300. Two bedrooms: $275/$315/$405. Special tennis and golf privileges are available. Rates are for peak season December 15 to March 31.

THE LAHAINA-KAANAPALI-KAPALUA AREAS

This large stretch of beach on the northwest side of Maui offers many world-class hotels, several luxury condominium complexes, over 150 shops, 60 restaurants, and an outdoor whaling museum. In addition there are a dozen dinner and lounge shows, 28 tennis courts, 36 holes of golf (if you include Kapalua, there are 90 holes), and all the beach activities you expect in the islands: snorkeling, surfing, outriggers, deep sea fishing, etc. Each of the hotels is well-equipped to handle meeting groups.

The Royal Kaanapali courses are available for guests of the various hotels and condominiums. The South plays 6,555/6,067/5,485 yards and pars at 71. The North, reaching out 6,994/6,136/5,417 yards, pars at 71/72. The older of the two, the North, a Robert Trent Jones design developed in 1961, starts at the ocean and winds its way up the lower reaches of the mountain. It provides some beautiful views enroute. The South, originally an executive layout and redesigned by A. J. Snyder, although flat, brings into play palms, monkey pod trees, banyans, and brilliant bougainvillea. Both courses operate out of the same pro shop. There are a few places on the back nine of the South course where, if you were to hook just right, you could easily find yourself in the

lobby of one of the hotels. Green fees: $70, including cart.

For information on the Kapalua courses refer to the Kapalua Bay Hotel & Villas.

HYATT REGENCY MAUI
200 Nohea Kai Drive, Lahaina, Maui, HI 96761; (808) 661-1234; (800) 233-1234

The Regency is on 18-plus acres of tropical forest complete with lagoons, waterfalls, and grottoes. The 815 rooms offer views of either the ocean, mountains, or the Royal Kaanapali golf course. Meeting and convention groups are accommodated in the Lahaina Wing of the hotel, with 25,000 square feet of banquet and meeting space.

For dining, there is the elegant Swan Court, Spats, specializing in Italian cuisine, the Lahaina Provision Company for steak lovers and, for dinner shows, the Sunset Terrace. Whatever your favorite libation may be, you will find it at any of the three lounges – the Atrium Lobby, the secluded Grotto Bar, or the Weeping Banyan. One of the island's favorite drinks is a "Fog Cutter." Should you dive too deeply into a "Fog Cutter" you may well wind up emulating a "Weeping Banyan."

All of the amenities indicated under "The Lahaina-Kaana-pali-Kapalua Area" are available to guests of this resort.

RATES   (EP)   Rooms: $230/$410.

KAANAPALI BEACH HOTEL
2525 Kaanapali Parkway, Lahaina, Maui, HI 96761; (808) 661-0011; (800) 262-8450

This hotel's spacious rooms are arranged in a semicircle, creating an enclosed courtyard that opens onto the beach and those famous Maui sunsets. The gentle, tropical air allows dining and cocktails to be served in the open court, with dancing under the stars.

All amenities described under "The Lahaina-Kaanapali-Kapalua Area" are available to guests of this resort.

RATES   (EP)   Rooms: $145/$195. Suites: $525.

KAPALUA BAY HOTEL & VILLAS
One Bay Drive, Maui, HI

96761; (808) 669-5656; (800) 367-8000

Kapalua Bay Hotel has been selected as one of the top 50 resorts. A bit north of the Kaanapali complex of resorts, this hotel is situated within the 23,000-acre Kapalua Plantation property on its own 1,500 acres. The resort is nestled between the coastline and the rolling hills of a lush pineapple plantation. There are 194 guest rooms in the hotel plus 130 villas, some offering bay exposure, others a golf course view. Each room is equipped with a refrigerator along with cable TV and has a separate sitting area and a private terrace. The villas include fully-equipped kitchens, washer/dryers, and daily maid service.

The resort is well set up to accommodate meeting groups and can handle gatherings up to 200 classroom- and 350 theater-style. The younger set has not been forgotten as there is now a year-round supervised children's program. Intended to entertain as well as educate, it is run by trained counselors.

There are a number of dining places to choose from: the Pool Terrace for casual dining and cocktails; the Garden Restau-

rant and Lounge; or for gourmet dining, the Bay Club (jackets suggested). There is also a
restaurant adjacent to the
main pro shop of the Bay
Course called The Grill & Bar.
Not only are the food and the
service good here, but it is a
wonderful place for people
watching. Make reservations
early as it is one busy place.

Activities include: swimming
in several fresh water pools
(between the hotel and the villas there are about 10), tennis
on 10 private courts (four
lighted), with a professional
and staff available. Recently
added is an exercise facility;
with a stair climber, treadmill,
multicisor and two ergome-
ters, there is more than

enough diabolical equipment
for you to destroy yourself. It is
a few minutes by shuttle to
three sand beaches offering up
snorkeling, scuba, surfing,
sailing, or deep-sea fishing.
Conversely, the secluded
coves, coral reefs and clear
water bays make doing nothing a welcome option. Another
alternative: shopping in the six
clothing, three jewelry, two
art, at least three gift shops,
and The Market Restaurant,
all on the premises.

Two of the three golf courses
are Arnold Palmer designs.
The Bay, parring at 72,
stretches 6,600/6,051/5,124
yards. The Village Links
reaches out 6,632/6,001/5,134
yards with a par of 71. Both

courses take full advantage of the natural terrain, rolling hills, lava outcroppings and the spectacular views offered from elevations up to 750 feet above the sea. Water only comes into play on four holes of Village layout and on six of the Bay Course.

The newest addition, the Plantation Course, is high on slopes of the old pineapple plantation, affording panoramic views of the ocean. Designed by the team of Bill Coore and Ben Crenshaw, it opened in mid-1991. Parring at 73 (that's right the men's par is 73), this course reaches out a monstrous 7,263 yards. The opening hole will more than get your attention. A par four, this gem measures 473 yards. The 18th is a 663-yard par 5. The Plantation has already been selected as the site of the Kapalua International Tournament.

While the pro shop for the Village course is quite modest, the golf shop at The Bay layout is outstanding. The new Plantation golf facility is supported by a 33,000-square-foot clubhouse. With two dining areas, it has a grill room as well as locker rooms and a pro shop. All three golf shops are under the supervision of the Director

of Golf, Gary Planos.

RATES (EP) Hotel: garden view $215/$260; ocean view $300/$350; ocean front $415. Suites: $750/$1,250. 1-bedroom villas: $275/$375. 2-bedroom units: $375/$475. Green fees: $70, including cart. Golf package: 3 nights/4 days (includes lodging, green fees, cart, club storage), $945/$1,050 per couple. Rates are for the peak season mid-December to mid-April. MAP rates are also available.

MAUI MARRIOTT RESORT
100 Nohea Kai Drive, Lahaina, Maui, HI 96761; (808) 667-1200; (800) 228-9290

The Maui Marriott is directly across from the Royal Kaanapali golf course. It has 720 rooms in two nine-story towers, with a four-story lobby between. They have a variety of dining areas, ranging from a Japanese steak house to the rustic atmosphere of old Lahaina Town.

The resort offers the use of five lighted tennis courts, a pro shop and a special electronics game room for the younger set. All of the amenities and activities indicated under "The Lahaina-Kaanapali-Kapalua Area" are available to guests of this resort.

RATES *(EP) Rooms: $179/$255. Suites: $375 and up.*

ROYAL LAHAINA RESORT
2780 Kekass Drive, Lahaina, Maui, HI 96761; (808) 661-3611; (800) 447-6925

The Royal Lahaina is built on 27 acres. Accommodations range from luxurious private cottages to guest rooms. Each of the 514 lodgings includes air-conditioning and refrigerators. Some units have kitchenettes.

Among the amenities: three swimming pools, three restaurants, and a nightly luau. There are also three cocktail lounges. This resort happens to be the location of the Royal Lahaina Tennis Ranch with its 11 courts.

Guests can take advantage of all the other attractions described under "The Lahaina-Kaanapali-Kapalua Area."

RATES *(EP) Rooms: $130/$235. Cottage studio suites: $225/$290.*

SHERATON-MAUI HOTEL
2605 Kaanapali Parkway, Lahaina, Maui, HI 96761; (808) 661-0031; (800) 325-3535
Wrapped around a splendid black rock promontory, this is the hotel that started it all at Kaanapali. Occupying the broadest expanse of Kaanapali Beach, the Sheraton-Maui provides some of the finest snorkeling, sailing, and surfing to be found. You have a wide choice of accommodations: rooms, suites and deluxe ocean-front cottages.

There are enough restaurants to satisfy any gourmet, ranging from breakfast to candlelight dining.

Two freshwater pools and three lighted tennis courts are also at your disposal.

Guests can use all the amenities listed under "The Lahaina-Kaanapali-Kapalua Area."

RATES *Rooms: $129/$300. Suites $300/$600.*

THE WESTIN MAUI
2365 Kaanapali Parkway, Lahaina, Maui, HI 96761; (808) 667-2525; (800) 228-3000

Originally it was the Maui

Surf, and I once described this beautiful resort as bright, comfortable and casually elegant. Acquired by Westin Hotel in 1986 and reopened in late 1987, they have spent $155 million to produce a world-class destination. The changes have been massive. The multi-million dollar art collection displayed throughout the hotel includes items gathered from China, Hong Kong, Bangkok, and Indonesia.

Immediately upon entering the hotel you are confronted by a lagoon and waterfalls in the front entrance and the lobby area. The inhabitants of this lagoon are an international group, ranging from graceful Siberian mute white swans to North American wood ducks, mandarin ducks, and South American whistling tree ducks. I do believe there might even have been a couple of just plain ducks in there somewhere.

Accommodations are in the 11-story Ocean Tower and the 11-story Beach Tower. All rooms are air-conditioned and equipped with remote control TV, mini-bar and a small private balcony. Each room or suite has a view of either the ocean or the Royal Kaanapali golf course. There are also 37 posh rooms available at the Royal Beach Club (concierge level), bringing the total of guest rooms to 854.

The Westin Maui has set aside 31,000 square feet of space to accommodate meeting and conference groups. With their 8,820-square-foot Valley Isle ballroom and many breakout rooms, they can handle groups from 11 to 1,100.

There are eight restaurants and lounges, so if you hunger or thirst here you have a problem of choice only. Live entertainment and music are offered in several of the restaurants and lounges.

The Westin has what is recognized as possibly the best stretch of Kaanapali Beach for swimming, snorkeling, surfing and sunning. The resort virtually revolves around 55,000 square feet of pools, waterfalls, and meandering streams. There are five free-form swimming pools on various levels. Three of the pools are joined by two waterslides ranging in length from 20 to 150 feet. It looked like fun (we didn't test out the waterslide). There is also a coed health club.

Guests have playing privileges on the nearby 18-hole Royal

Kaanapali golf course as well as The Royal Lahaina Tennis Ranch with its 11 courts. The hotel provides complimentary shuttle service to each location.

For detailed information on the golf courses refer to "The Lahaina-Kaanapali-Kapalua Area."

RATES (EP) Courtyard views: $195. Ocean views: $300. Royal Beach Club: $375 / $395. Suites range from $600 to $2,000. Green fees: $90, including cart.

LAHAINA-KAANAPALI AREA CONDOMINIUMS

KAANAPALI ALII
50 Nohea Kai Drive, Lahaina, Maui, HI 96761; (808) 667-1400; (800) 642-6284

This 11-story resort is on the beach across from the Royal Kaanapali golf complex. Accommodations are one- to three-bedroom condominiums. Each unit has a full kitchen, with two baths, a living room, and a washer/dryer. The one-bedroom units are 1,500, and two-bedrooms are 1,800

square feet. Additional amenities include VCR and twice-daily maid service. Through their concierge service such extras as baby sitting can be arranged.

While the resort does not have a restaurant of its own, specialized room service menus are available from several nearby restaurants.

There are three tennis courts as well as a swimming pool, in addition to the beach.

RATES 1-bedroom condo: $225 / $250 / $295. 2-bedroom unit: $280 / $450. Rates are for January 5th through March.

KAANAPALI PLANTATION
150 Puukolii Road, Lahaina, Maui, HI 96761; (808) 661-4446

These are modern condominium apartments (one to three bedrooms) equipped for family-style living with full electric kitchens, washer/dryers, and daily maid service. Each unit has a private entrance.

While not right on the beach, they are within easy walking distance. They offer a pool, tennis courts, and access to all the amenities listed under "The

Lahaina-Kaanapali-Kapalua Area."

RATES (EP) 1 bedroom: $125. 2 bedrooms (up to 4 people): $210.

KAANAPALI ROYAL

2560 Kekaa Drive, Lahaina, Maui, HI 96761; (808) 667-7200; (800) 367-7040

These condominiums, bordering right on the golf course, are two-bedroom, two-bath units with fully-equipped kitchens and washer/dryers. They are unusually spacious with sunken living rooms and nine-foot ceilings.

There are two tennis courts, swimming pool, sauna, and Jacuzzis. Guests have access to all the amenities listed under "The Lahaina-Kaanapali-Kapalua Area."

RATES (EP) 1 bedroom: $175/$195.

MAUI ELDORADO

Kaanapali Beach, Maui, HI 96761; (808) 661-0021; (800) 367-2967

A luxury low-rise hideaway in a lush garden setting, the Maui Eldorado is surrounded by mountains, the golf course, and the Pacific Ocean. Each of the two-story apartments has living room, dining area, fully-equipped kitchen, including dishwashers and icemakers.

Units are one and two bedrooms (750 to 1,800 square feet) and offer the use of three swimming pools. They also have their own private beach cabana.

Guests have access to all the amenities described under "The Lahaina-Kaanapali-Kapalua Area."

RATES (EP) Studio: $135/$150. 1 bedroom: $160/$180. 2 bedrooms: (up to 6 people) $210/$240.

THE WHALER AT KAANAPALI BEACH

2481 Kaanapali Parkway, Lahaina, Maui, HI 96761; (808) 661-4861; (800) 367-7052

The Whaler consists of two large condominium complexes with 360 suites fronting right on the beach. Accommodations are one- to two-bedroom suites equipped for housekeeping.

Large lanais, a mini-market, and underground parking are a few of the basics. An oceanside pool, paddle tennis, four tennis courts, saunas, and exercise rooms complete the facilities.

Guests have access to all of the amenities described under "The Lahaina-Kaanapali-Kapalua Area."

RATES *Studio: $175/$190. 1 bedroom: $215/$250. Rates are for mid-December through April.*

THE ISLAND OF LANAI

Lanai is the sixth largest of the major Islands in the Hawaiian group. Located between Maui and Molokai it is about 30 minutes by air from Honolulu. Triangular in shape (18 miles long and up to 13 miles wide), it has remained generally unspoiled. In 1924 the Hawaiian Pineapple Company (later to become Dole) established Lanai City. It is a culture based on farming, ranching, and fishing, and little has changed here since that time. Even now the population is a modest 2,400. Now, however, two Rockresort properties have opened here – The Lodge at Koele (1990) and the Manele Bay Hotel (1992). Lanai City, looking over the

pineapple fields, is 1,650 feet above sea level. It is just below the 3,375-foot Lanaihale Mountain, the dominant peak on the island. The area enjoys a rather temperate climate. While the elevation, along with the stands of Norfolk pines shading the town, produce cool nights, the days are pleasant and warm.

Shopping on the island is extremely limited. There are only a handful of stores including three old-time general stores. There are, however, gift shops at the two resorts, along with the golf shops. As a possible alternative, the bustling seaport of Lahaina (on the island of Maui), with its profusion of shops and boutiques, is only a nine-mile ferry ride away.

THE LODGE AT KOELE
P.O. Box 774 Lanai City, Island of Lanai, HI 96763
(808) 565-7300; (800) 321-4666

The Lodge at Koele has been judged one of the top 50 resorts. The developers of the Mauna Kea Beach Hotel, The Boulders in Arizona, and Caneel Bay on St. John's Island, have done it again. They were able to join the elegance of an English manor and the rustic warmth and peaceful setting of this island. Blending high beamed ceilings, natural stone fireplaces, artifacts gathered from throughout the world, the tropical setting of huge banyan trees, and the overwhelming garden fragrance, this beautiful and unusual lodge has been described as reminiscent of a worldly plantation owner's residence. Some of this feeling may stem from the effect of the wide porch surrounding the hotel.

There are 102 guest rooms and suites. A few of the more unusual features in the rooms include four poster beds, ceiling fans, and beautiful oil paintings. You can choose from Garden, Koele, or Plantation rooms. The suites range from Terrace mini-suites to full suite arrangements. All suites have butler service provided.

The dining room serves a mixture of Hawaiian cuisine and traditional continental dishes (jackets are required in the evening). Most of the food comes from the island farms, ranches, or surrounding waters.

Activities that await you include all types of water sports at the Hulopoe Beach Park. Adjacent to the Manele Bay Hotel you can swim, sun, surf, snorkel, scuba dive, deep sea fish, and find some of the best whale viewing locations in Hawaii. Other activities are tennis, horseback riding from the Lanai Ranch stables (affiliated with the hotel), and swimming in the hotel pool. One activity I recommend: a dawn ride followed by a hearty ranch-style breakfast. Hunting on the island is a big thing, as the island is virtually overrun by deer, quail, wild turkey, partridge, pheasant, and mulon sheep. Guided tours can be arranged by the hotel, and include the opportunity to see the Garden of the Gods, Petroglyphs, and the ruins of King Kamehameha's summer home.

The new Greg Norman/Ted Robinson-designed championship golf course was opened for play in 1991. It takes full advantage of the natural terrain with its stands of Norfolk and Scotch pine trees. They placed the first nine on a high plateau, providing a spectacular view of the Pacific Ocean (a few miles distant), while the second nine was built in the valley surrounded by those towering pines. Reaching out 7,014/6,628/6,217/5,425 yards, it pars at 72. The Director of Golf is Charlie Ortega. Guests of the lodge also have golfing

privileges at the new Nicklaus course at the Manele Bay Hotel.

RATES   *(EP)   Rooms: $295 / $350. Jr. suites: $475. Suites: $675 / $975. Green fees: $95, including carts.*

ARRIVAL *Air: Lanai Airport (now undergoing a $50 million dollar renovation). When making reservations advise the resort of your flight number and time of arrival. They will meet and transport you to the lodge.*

THE MANELE BAY HOTEL

P.O. Box 774 Lanai City, The Island of Lanai, HI 96763; (808) 565-7300; (800) 321-4666

This is a change of pace from the Lodge at Koele. Overlooking the sand beaches and water of Hulopoe Bay, it is comprised of villas and suites, many offering sweeping views of the ocean. Rooms, each with a private lanai, range from garden, ocean view, and ocean front to deluxe ocean front. It is larger than the Lodge, with a total of 250 suites and villas and it can accommodate meeting groups of up to 300. Opening in 1991, it follows the Rock-resort tradition of attention to detail. There are three dining areas, ranging from the Main Dining Room, to the Specialty Gourmet Room, or the Pool Grille for lighter fare.

There is a swimming pool, tennis courts, a full-service spa, a massage treatment program, and many water sports. For more details covering horseback riding, hunting, and water sports, refer to The Lodge at Koele. All of the activities and amenities of the lodge are at your disposal, including golf.

The golf course scheduled to open in late 1994 is a Jack Nicklaus design. With several over-the-water holes and the added distraction of the magnificent views of the Pacific Ocean, this layout will give you all you can handle.

RATES (EP) Rooms: $295 / $350 / $395 / $475. Suites: $595 and up.

ARRIVAL Air: Lanai Airport. There are 90 or more flights each week to this island. When making your reservations be sure to advise them as to the flight number and time of arrival. Arrangements will be made to pick you up and trans-port you to the resort.

THE ISLAND OF MOLOKAI

Ah! Molokai. Long the favorite of the Hawaiians, an island unspoiled, innocent, secluded, and beautiful.

KALUA KOI HOTEL & GOLF CLUB
P.O. Box 1977, Maunaloa, HI 96770; (808) 552-2555; (800) 777-1700

For many years this resort operated as the "Sheraton Molokai." Now the Kalua Koi, there have really been few changes. The original builders were wise enough to blend the hotel structure into the general fabric of the island. Consisting of 33 buildings, the tallest being two stories, the hotel has been constructed in a rambling rustic Polynesian style. All 290 rooms and suites have high beamed ceilings, tropical fans, and rattan furnishings. Meander down the garden walkway to the Ohia Lodge, a restaurant where cocktails and Molokai music create the special atmosphere so unique to the islands.

You can swim in the pool or in the sparkling Pacific, or take a picnic lunch from the hotel and tour the island, or perhaps play a set of tennis, with a professional available to assist. Tennis is complimentary for guests. Golf is offered on the hotel's Kalua Koi course – playing 6,618/6,211/5,437 yards and parring at 72. Designed by Ted Robinson, it features some water, along with ingeniously placed trees and traps.

RATES (EP) Rooms: $120/ $135. Suites: $175. Cottages: $240. Green fees: $70, including cart.

ARRIVAL Shuttle service is available from the airport to the hotel.

Idaho

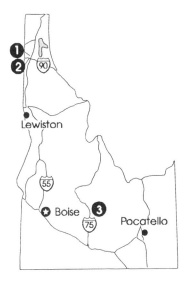

1. Twin Lakes Village
2. Coeur d'Alene Resort
3. Ketchum-sun Valley Area
   Radison Elkhorn Resort
   Sun Valley Lodge & Inn

KETCHUM-SUN VALLEY AREA

Since so many articles have been written and so many photographs released about this area, perhaps a little history is in order. In 1935, Averell Harriman, then Chairman of the Board of Union Pacific Railroad and a long-time avid ski buff, sought means to increase traffic from the east to the west via his railroad (and in the process create a ski facility he would enjoy). After much searching he happened on Ketchum. In December of 1935 "Sun Valley," the first complete ski resort in the United States, came into being.

The idea was that a visit to this resort area was to be a "roughing it" outing. That is, roughing it Hollywood style – glass-enclosed swimming pools, exquisite food, impeccable service, and orchestras performing nightly. At a later date, the Sun Valley Center for Arts and Humanities and many other amenities were added, thus transforming it into an all-season operation rather than just a winter ski resort.

It is, in reality, a large, self-contained village, with an opera house (movies), its own lake (rowing and paddleboat rentals), swimming pools, horseback riding, skeet and trap shooting, whitewater raft trips on the Salmon River, and fishing. Within the valley itself there are a total of 85 tennis courts and in Hailey (13 miles away) there are several indoor lighted courts. Of course, you can also choose to just relax. Additional services include: a drug store, barber and beauty shop, post office, several clothing stores, a florist, bank, hospital, taxi service, excellent meeting and convention facilities and so many restaurants I could not name them all. During the summer months there is a jazz festival, motorcycle and bicycle races, flower and musical festivals, a backcountry run, a Mexican Fiesta Grande, ballet performances, parades, a rodeo, and much more.

Today there are two major golf resorts in Sun Valley – The Radisson Elkhorn Lodge & Condominiums and The Sun Valley Lodge, Inn & Condominiums. Each has its own championship golf course and provides excellent winter skiing.

For a wide selection of possible accommodations in addition to the two aforementioned resorts, call the Sun Valley-Ketchum Chamber of Commerce's new toll-free reservations number: (800) 634-3347.

RADISSON ELKHORN RESORT
P.O. Box 6009, Sun Valley, ID 83354; (208) 622-4511; (800) 632-4101
Accommodations at Elkhorn

are 132 guest rooms in the Lodge and 80 condominiums fully-equipped for housekeeping. In fact you can request the condo be stocked prior to your arrival, a nice touch which beats last-minute shopping after a tough day of travel.

Should you prefer to dine out, there are several good restaurants: Tequila Joe's featuring Mexican food; Jesse's for fish and beef; and for breakfast and lunch, the Clubhouse Cafe.

Elkhorn's meeting and conference facilities can handle groups of up to 350.

A great many activities await you: tennis on 16 Laykold courts, seven spas, five swimming pools (two Olympic size), hiking in one of the most spectacular areas in the United States – Sawtooth National Recreation Area – with elk, deer, moose and bighorn sheep. Additional attractions include: horseback riding, hayrides, folk art and music festivals, water skiing, windsurfing, biking, balloon and glider flights, or even bar hopping in nearby Ketchum.

The Elkhorn layout, like the Sun Valley course, is a Robert Trent Jones, Jr. design. Stretching out 7,160/6,610/

5,701 yards, the course pars at 72. With elevation changes from 6,150 feet to 5,750 feet on the front nine, and Willow Creek becoming a nuisance on the back side, it is a tester. There is a full-line pro shop under the direction of PGA Professional, Jeff Steury, and staff.

One caution: you are playing golf at 6,000 feet above sea level. If you play from the blue tees you will feel as if you are playing about 6,400 yards not 7,100. Your ball gets that much extra carry. Don't, however, try to make the same shots when you return to the beach area or you are going to be embarrassed.

During the winter months when the snow starts coating the ground the ski season moves into high gear. With transportation provided every 30 minutes to Mount Baldy and lifts for Dollar Mountain virtually at your door, you have 16 lifts and 64 runs ranging from gentle to hair-raising. There are also cross-country trails and helicopter lifts available, not to mention sleigh rides and ice skating.

RATES *(EP) Lodge rooms: $88/$158. Suites: $268/$368. Studio condo: (kitchenette)*

$78/$98. Fully-equipped 1-bedroom condo: $188. Green fees: $52, including cart. Rates quoted are for the summer season.

ARRIVAL *Air: Salt Lake City or Boise, Idaho with flight connections to Sun Valley. Car: State Highway 75, approximately 80 miles from Twin Falls, Idaho.*

SUN VALLEY LODGE & INN
Sun Valley, ID 83353, (208) 622-4111; (800) 786-8259

Sun Valley Lodge has been judged one of the top 50 resorts. Accommodations are provided in the original and beautiful Lodge (recently updated) and at the Inn. In addition there are eight large groupings of condominiums which are equipped for housekeeping.

While there are a number of fine restaurants (as well as intriguing shops) in the Sun Valley Village, you need go no further than the Lodge itself. The Lodge Dining Room (for many years called The Duchin Room) serves excellent food and the entertainment (dance music) is in a class by itself. On the main level and available for all three meals is Gretchen's. Again the selection, preparation and manner of presentation is memorable. The Duchin Lounge, with dancing to music from a few years back, has become a favorite gathering place in the evening. Jackets are required, ties are optional.

Sun Valley Lodge offers a play school program, designed to offer the children six and under a fun vacation while you do "whatever." They also provide a "Young Summer" program for the 7-to-11 age group and a Teen Summer program for ages 12 to 18. All the programs are under the supervision of trained professionals and include activities such as tennis, fishing, skin diving, horseback riding, archery, indoor and outdoor ice skating (available year-round) golfing, shooting, sailing, kayaking, hayrides, and hiking. Adult activities include: bowling, game rooms, horseback riding, tennis on 18 courts, and the use of three swimming pools.

During the winter months Sun Valley Lodge becomes a skier's paradise. Known as "the grand dame of American ski resorts," it offers downhill and cross-country courses (vertical rises of up to 3,144 feet), as well as the assistance of 160 certified instructors. With the new high-speed lifts in place (installed in 1989), they are now capable of lifting some 1,500 skiers per hour to the top of Mt. Baldy within 10 minutes. Baldy has 12 lifts, 57 runs, 3,400 vertical feet of drop, with a summit at 9,140 feet. Dollar Mountain has four lifts, 13 runs, 628 feet of vertical drop, and a summit elevation of 6,638 feet.

Other winter activities include sleigh rides and ice skating. As a matter of fact the traditional Sun Valley Lodge Terrace hosts elaborate ice shows with world-class skaters. Starting in mid-June and terminating in September, these performances take place each Saturday evening, on one of two Olympic-size rinks.

Golf can be played on the Robert Trent Jones, Jr.-designed Sun Valley Resort course. Reaching out 6,565/6,057/5,241 yards, the men's par is set at 72 and the ladies' at 73. Trail Creek, which wanders all over the place, plus tight fairways, and trees make this no run-of-the-mill resort course. While a manicured layout, the Sun Valley course will present you with some extremely interesting and challenging shots. There are, for example, a couple of par-threes which may well produce a hard swallow. Not only is the course well bunkered but its beauty has been further enhanced by the use of brilliant "Petersburg White" sand.

The small pro shop is under the direction of PGA professional Bill Butterfield and has a luncheon terrace.

RATES   (EP)   Lodge: $97/$153. Inn: $97/$128. Condo: 1 bedroom $125; 2 bedroom, $145. Green fees: $55, carts $26. Golf packages are available. Rates are for June-September.

ARRIVAL Air: Salt Lake City or Boise with flight connections to Hailey Airport (14 miles). Car: State Highway 75 (Twin Falls is 81 miles).

THE COEUR D'ALENE RESORT
Second & Front Streets, Coeur d' Alene, ID 83814; (208) 765-4000; (800) 688-5253

Accommodations in this 18-story hotel consist of 338 guest rooms ranging from the Parks Wing to the Lake Tower, which includes a penthouse suite. There are also 20 condomini-

ums fully-equipped for house-keeping. In addition to laundry and cleaning service through the   hotel,   there   are washer/dryer facilities within each of the condo units. With 17 meeting rooms (a total of 20,000 square feet), they can hande group affairs of up to 850 theater-style.

Dining is available in Beverly's. Located on the seventh floor, it offers a beautiful view of the lake. Less formal is the Dockside, a family restaurant on the boardwalk. Entertainment is presented in either Beverly's Lounge or the Shore Lounge on the lobby level.

The resort has an indoor and an outdoor swimming pool, a racquetball court, a complete fitness center, and four tennis courts at the golf club. Huge Lake Coeur d'Alene (10 miles wide at its mid-point and 25 miles long) opens up a host of activities, including excellent fishing. Guests can rent several different types and sizes of power boats. Provided you are a guest of the resort, you can moor your own craft at the dock. Horseback riding (20 miles of trails) and white water rafting (75 miles of rivers) are available. During the winter months this area turns to skiing. Although the hotel provides excellent transportation, the ski areas are between 45 and 75 miles away.

While the course is on slightly rolling terrain, there are four holes reaching up into the hills, with elevation changes of 300 to 400 hundred feet. Designed by golf architect Scott Miller, The Coeur d'Alene Resort Golf Course plays to a modest 6,309/5,899/5,490/4,446 yards and pars at 71. They are quite proud of the 14th hole, a "floating green." It is, at least so far, unique. Inasmuch as the green can be floated to a new location, changing the yardage from 100 to 175 yards, the question is not only where is the pin, but where in heck is the green? The golf course is supported by a 15,000-square-foot clubhouse with a large pro shop, locker rooms, and a snack bar. A fun extra: you drive to the course (about 2 miles), or travel by boat – out and around the point (10 minutes). The Director of Golf is Mike DeLong.

RATES (EP) Park Wing: $120/$150. Lake Tower: $225/$255. Suites: $450 and up. 1-bedroom condos: $185. 2 bedrooms: $250. Green fees: $90, including cart. Golf package: 1 night/1 day (includes lodging, one round of golf with

cart, and caddy), $280/$360 per couple. Rates are for June through September.

ARRIVAL Air: Spokane Washington International Airport (40 miles). Car: take I-90 east. Take exit number 11 of the interstate. Resort is at the intersection of Sherman Avenue and Northwest Boulevard.

TWIN LAKES VILLAGE
Route 4, Box P-551, Rathdrum, ID 83858 ; (208) 687-1311

Twin Lakes, an intimate village-type complex, is situated on 160 acres. Accommodations are offered in well furnished condominiums (one to three bedrooms). They have completely equipped kitchens, living rooms, and fireplaces. The hub of activity is the clubhouse, site of the dining room, lounge, Jacuzzi, meeting rooms and, on the lower level, the pro shop.

The proximity of the lake provides immediate access to fishing, boating, and sandy beaches, with several swimming pools and tennis courts at various locations within the grounds.

Golf is now played on a full-size, 18-hole course. Measuring 6,158/5,836/5,362 yards, it pars at 71/72. It is a beautiful layout, taking advantage of the lush terrain and magnificent trees which surround the entire area. There is a small, but well-equipped golf shop with PGA professional Randy Buckenberger on deck to lend assistance.

RATES (EP) Suites: 1 bedroom $95 per night, $465 per week; 2 bedrooms $115/$125 per night, $545/$600 per week. Rates are for June-August; during July/August a minimum stay of one week is required. Green fees: $20, carts $20.

ARRIVAL Air: Spokane (30 miles) or Coeur d'Alene (20 miles). Car: from Rathdrum, 5 miles north on 41.

Illinois

1. Eagle Ridge Inn & Resort
2. Marriott's Lincolnshire Resort
3. Nordic Hills Resort
4. Pheasant Run Resort
5. Indian Lakes Resort
6. Oak Brook Hills Resort
7. The Inn at Eagle Creek

EAGLE RIDGE INN & RESORT

Box 777 Highway 20 West, Galena, IL 61036; (815) 777-2444; (800) 892-2269

Eagle Ridge Inn has been judged one of the top 50 resorts. The Inn has to be considered one of the best kept secrets in the United States. Upon arrival, we expected to find a modest little resort. What we encountered was a world-class destination. Here in the northwest corner of Illinois, perched on a ridge overlooking Lake Galena, the Eagle Ridge Inn takes a back seat to few other resorts. It is quite large, covering 6,800 acres, supported by impressive restaurants and with two of the most beautiful golf courses we have seen. *Golf Digest* listed them in 1988 among the top 75 resort courses in America. Accommodations are 80 rooms in the charming Inn or you can choose from over 260 one- to four-bedroom resort homes, condominiums, or townhouses, some on the fairway, others by the lake. These lodgings are first rate, with the quality of equipment (including washer/dryers) and furnishings excellent. With the new lodge and increased space they are well-equipped to handle meeting groups of 10 to 550 theater-style. Eagle Ridge also offers a supervised children's recreational program during the summer season – Monday through Saturday.

Additional attractions include: an indoor swimming pool, a sauna, whirlpool, four tennis

courts, sailing, and fishing. There is also a fitness center offering many types of exercise equipment. The Shenandoah Riding Center is one of the Midwest's finest and can handle both experienced riders and novices. During the winter months the South Course golf shop turns into an indoor golf school. At the same time cross country skiing, ice skating, sleigh rides, tobogganing, and snowshoeing become king. Snowshoeing is, by the way, the greatest way to disable yourself that has ever been devised.

By all means take the time to visit the quaint town of Galena. Just six miles from Eagle Ridge, the place is enchanting. It will transport you back in time for a glimpse of what life was like in the 19th century.

Golf can be played on the Eagle Ridge North course, reaching out a hefty 6,836/6,386/5,578 yards and parring at 72. The terrain is hilly with small creeks running throughout and is well trapped. While bringing water into contention on only one hole on the front side, it makes up for that with the second nine showing water on seven holes.

The second 18, the South course, plays 6,762/6,361/5,609 yards, also with a par of 72. Again, with undulating terrain and water in play on 10 holes, you will find it all you can handle. Each course is supported by a large clubhouse with a restaurant and a golf shop. A recent addition is an executive nine-hole layout, a great way to sharpen your iron play. Parring at 34 it plays to a yardage of 2,648/2,641/2,255. All golf operations are under the supervision of the Director of Golf, John Schlaman.

The resort offers a three- or five-day golf school. Included are accommodations, meals, carts and green fees, five hours of instruction daily, videotape playback and on-course instructions. It's certainly worth a try.

RATES (EP) Inn: $155/$225. Homes or Townhouses: 1 bedroom $150/$225. Green fees: $80, including cart. There are many different package plans available, including golf packages.

ARRIVAL Air: Dubuque (25 miles) or Chicago a bit over 150 miles. Car: Route 20, 6 miles east of Galena, Illinois.

INDIAN LAKES RESORT
250 West Schick Road, Bloomingdale, IL 60108;(708) 529-0200; (800) 334-3417

The six-story atrium lobby, with sunlight filtering through the many hexagonal skylights, touching the profusion of tropical trees and plants, is a most unusual and pleasing sight. They recently underwent a multi-million dollar renovation. The 308 guest rooms, 23 suites, and 28 meeting and banquet rooms (not to mention its proximity to O'Hare Airport), make it an excellent choice for meetings and conventions. They have a meeting capacity of 12 to 1,200. The resort is actually a little over 30 minutes from O'Hare International and about an hour from downtown Chicago.

Three restaurants, four lounges, a health club, indoor and outdoor swimming pools, six tennis courts and two 18-hole golf courses complete the list.

Golf can be played on the Iroquois Trail 18, 6,580/6,239 yards, parring at 72, or the Sioux Trail layout, playing 6,564/6,225 yards and also with a par 72. With only two tee settings that yardage gets a little much for the ladies. The Director of Golf is Brian Ihnat.

RATES   (EP)   Rooms: $135/$145. Suites: $245/ $395. Green fees: $46, including cart.

ARRIVAL Air: O'Hare Airport. Car: between Bloomingdale Road and Gary Avenue on Schick Road.

THE INN at EAGLE CREEK
Eagle Creek State Park, Findlay, IL 62534; (217) 756-3456; (800) 876-3245

The Clarion Inn, on 11,000-acre Lake Shelbyville, is within Eagle Creek State Park. While the park offers backpacking or organized camping, a marina and boat launch, a beach, picnic areas and, during the winter, cross country ski trails, the Inn adds a bit of luxury and relaxation. Accommodations are in 138 rooms, each with a patio or balcony. There are also 10 suites with fireplaces. The Inn can handle meeting and small convention groups. The meeting rooms include a small theater, closed circuit TV and state-of-the-art audio/video aids. There is also a detached conference retreat with separate sleeping accommodations. Something of general interest – the majority of the paintings, furnishings, and quilts on display are the work of the local Amish community.

There are two dining rooms, the Wildflowers Room and, on the lower level, Fox's Lounge & Grill. Depending on the weather, dining can be on the patio.

The resort also has four tennis courts, an indoor swimming pool, a sauna, whirlpool, and an exercise room. Archery, hunting, fishing, hiking, and bicycling are at your disposal as well.

Golf can be played on a Ken Killian-design course. Reaching out a respectable 6,923/6,563/5,923/4,977 yards, the course pars at 72. While water comes into play on only four holes (and only then if you are having a dismal day), the undulating terrain laced with ravines more than makes up for the lack of water. It is a challenging and entertaining golf course. The Head Professional is Jerry Groark.

RATES (EP) Rooms: $112/ $125. Suites: $145. Green fees: $45, including cart. Golf package: 2 nights (includes lodgings, 54 holes of golf with shared cart, two continental breakfasts), $422 per couple. Rates shown are for April through October.

ARRIVAL Air: Mattoon or Decatur. Private aircraft: (seaplane Lake Shelbyville), or Shelby Country Airport. Car: from state 51, I-57, or I-70 to Findlay. Resort is on the west side of Lake Shelbyville just east of Findlay. You can arrange pick up by the resort from the airport or from Amtrak in Mattoon.

MARRIOTT'S LINCOLNSHIRE RESORT

Marriott Lane, Lincolnshire, IL 60015; (708) 634-0100; (800) 228-9290

The Lincolnshire offers 393 rooms, plus two restaurants

and two lounges. There are, in addition, a total of 21 meeting rooms with a capacity of 870 theater- and 1,000 banquet-style. They also offer legitimate theater presentations, game rooms, the use of canoes or paddleboats on the private resort lake, tennis on five indoor courts, four racquetball courts, and a health spa.

You can tee up on the resort's own course. Parring at 71, it measures 6,600/6,6315/5,795 yards. A Fazio design, you know you are going to look at raised, and often small, greens. While the general terrain is flat, the course is made interesting by water on five or six holes.

RATES (EP) Rooms: $149. Suites: $325. Green fees: $60, including cart. Golf package: 2 nights/3 days (includes lodging, breakfast, green fees, cart, bag storage), $325 per couple.

ARRIVAL Air: Chicago. Car: on Route 21.

NORDIC HILLS RESORT
Nordic Road, Itasca, IL 60143; (708) 773-2750; (800) 334-3417 Approximately 30 minutes from O'Hare Airport, this resort makes an excellent meet-

ing place. In addition to the 22 meeting rooms, there are 220 guest rooms and six luxurious penthouse suites.

Dining is offered in the Scandinavian Room or the less formal Vulcan's Forge, with cocktails and entertainment available in the Skoal Lounge or the Playroom Bar. Activities include: eight indoor racquetball courts, six bowling lanes, five outdoor tennis courts (three lighted), indoor and outdoor swimming pools, and a full health club with exercise equipment.

The resort has its own 18-hole, 5,897-yard, par-71/73 course. Playing privileges are also extended at the nearby Indian Lakes Resort and its two championship layouts.

RATES (EP) Rooms: $125/ $135. Suites: $160/$400. Green fees: $42/$46, including cart.

ARRIVAL Air: Chicago. Car: the resort is on Old 53 Rohlwing Road and Nordic Road, off Highway 20.

OAK BROOK HILLS HOTEL & RESORT
3500 Midwest Road, Oak Brook, IL 60522; (708) 850-

5555; (800) 445-3315

With a setting 25 minutes from either O'Hare or Midway International Airports, the resort is a natural for meeting groups. An 11-story structure, it is a bit over four years old. The proximity to downtown Chicago as well the nearby five star Oak Brook Center, with Neiman-Marcus, Saks Fifth Avenue, Marshall Fields, and Nordstrom's, means the non-golfers in the group can really live it up. Accommodations are in 385 rooms, including suites. For special attention there is also a concierge level. With 27 meeting rooms (35,000 square feet of space), including the 140-seat amphitheater, Oak Brook is capable of handling group affairs of up to 950 classroom- or 1,500 theater-style.

Ascots, the main dining room, with its golf course view, offers a wide range of cuisine. For more intimate dining there is Waterford. For lighter fare it's Hogans – where else but at the golf course. During the evening hours you might visit The Lobby Bar or the nightclub, Chukkers Lounge.

There is a large swimming pool surrounded by a sun-deck, five lighted tennis courts, an exercise/weight room, a lap pool, a sauna, whirlpool, and massage facilities.

The Oak Brook Hills golf course is a Dick Nugent design. Parring at 70, it plays 6,409/6,019/5,339 yards. Featuring some beach-type bunkers along with water on 12 holes, plus a few oak, pine, and spruce trees, it is set on gently rolling terrain. Golf is under the supervision of Head Professional Randy Bolstad.

RATES (EP) Rooms: $159/$169. Concierge level: $179. Green fees: $45/$55, including cart. Golf package 2 nights/2 days (includes lodging, two rounds of golf with cart, $40 per couple, dinner coupon which can be used at any of the restaurants, bag storage), $375 per couple.

ARRIVAL Air: O'Hare or Midway Airports. Car: from O'Hare take 1-294 south to 1-88 west. Exit at Route 83 south. Go 1 mile to 31st street. Turn left onto 31st and travel to Midwest (1 mile). At this point turn left and travel to resort.

PHEASANT RUN RESORT
P.O. Box 64, St. Charles, IL 60174; (708) 584-6300; (800) 426-8700

Pheasant Run resort, on 200 acres in the Fox River Valley, is about 45 minutes from Chicago. Consisting of 550 rooms and a new convention center with 12,320 square feet of meeting space (a capacity of from 20 to 1,250), this is certainly no roadside motel.

A choice of dining rooms includes: the Smuggler's Cove, the Baker's Wife Steak House, and the dinner-theater, showing Broadway hits. For musical entertainment and dancing there is the Baker's Wife Lounge or Bourbon Street, jumping with New Orleans Dixieland music.

After you have destroyed yourself weight-wise with the above, you might try the complete health spa, tennis on the nine outdoor courts, a swim in the indoor or outdoor pools, or perhaps a round of golf. Pheasant Run offers not only a super pro shop but an interesting golf course as well. The Challenge has five lakes, sloping greens and too many traps. It plays at 6,315/5,955/5,472 yards and pars at 71/73.

RATES (EP) Rooms: $102. Tower rooms: $123. Green fees: $38, carts $23. Golf package: 2 nights/2 days (includes lodging, MAP, with 1 night a din-

ner show, green fees), $366 per couple.

ARRIVAL Air: Chicago. Private aircraft: DuPage County, paralleling the golf course. Car: on Route 64, 3 miles east of St. Charles.

Indiana

1. Fourwinds: A Clarion Resort
2. French Lick Springs

FRENCH LICK SPRINGS

French Lick, IN 47432; (812) 935-9381; (800) 457-4042

French Lick Springs Golf & Tennis Resort is in a quiet corner of southern Indiana. The first hotel, built in 1837, was destroyed by fire in 1897 and rebuilt to its present format. In order to entice guests, they even constructed a railroad line running from Chicago to their front door. It was a popular place during the '20s and '30s. Gambling was a large part of the attraction. On 2,600 acres with densely wooded hillsides (butternut and oak trees), footpaths and lovely gardens, the resort has a beautiful setting. While large (480 rooms, including suites), the resort still retains its original charm. Recently added are villas and condominiums. Numbering close to 100, these two-bedroom units are fully-equipped for housekeeping. If you are interested in a condo call (812) 936-5000. There is dining at Normans, Le Bistro (for a quick breakfast), and the Hoosier Rib Room. There is also an entire wing set aside to handle group meetings.

The tennis complex consists of 12 indoor and 13 lighted outdoor courts, with USPTA professional Mike O'Connell on hand. Other facilities include: an outdoor and an indoor swimming pool, four bowling lanes, skeet and trap shooting, two golf courses, a health spa, and horseback riding from the resort's own stables.

The golf course adjacent to the hotel is called the Valley Course. A par-70/71, it plays 6,003/5,687 yards. The Country Club course, three miles away, is under the direction of

PGA Professional Dave Harner. Reaching out 6,629/6,291/5,781 yards, it pars at 71/73. Designed by architect Donald Ross, it uses hilly terrain, with trees along holes six, seven, and eight, a little water on three holes, and traps to keep you alert. I will not describe the 18th green other than to say one look at it will hold your full attention. This will most definitely be true if your ball is on the upper level and the pin is on the lower.

RATES (MAP) Rooms: $124/$159 per couple. Condominiums: (EP) $250. Green fees: Valley course $26; Country Club course $45, including cart. Golf package: 1 night/2 days (includes MAP, lodging, green fees and cart), $198 per couple. Rates are April-October.

ARRIVAL Air: Louisville (75 minutes). Car: Highway 150 to 145.

FOURWINDS: A CLARION RESORT

Lake Monroe, P.O. Box 160, Bloomington, IN 47402; (812) 824-9904; (800) 252-7466

The resort is on the shores of Indiana's Lake Monroe. Accommodations consist of 126 rooms, all equipped with private steam baths, a nice way to wind up the day. Their nine-room meeting and conference center has a capacity of 250.

Classic French and American dishes are served in the Tradewinds or, for a small libation, try the Windjammer Lounge.

They claim their marina is the largest one of its type in the United States. This could be true. It is huge. You can bring your own craft or, if you prefer, rent a pontoon boat for a tour of the lake or a little fishing. There are also tennis courts, an indoor/outdoor pool, Jacuzzi and saunas. Golf is played on The Pointe championship course. Ranked among the best in the country, it measures 6,639/6,131/5,252 yards, parring at 71.

RATES (EP) Rooms: $75/$98. Suites: 1 bedroom $135 and up. Green fees: $45, including cart. Golf packages are available.

ARRIVAL Air: Bloomington (10 miles). Car: from Bloomington, take Highway 37 south, Harrodsburg exit, east to Fairfax Road, then south to the resort.

Kansas

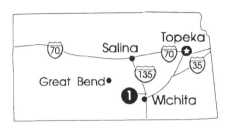

1. Terradyne Resort

TERRADYNE RESORT HOTEL & COUNTRY CLUB

1400 Terradyne, Andover, KS 67002; (316) 733-2582; (800) 892-4613

We were particularly pleased to be able to include Terradyne in this edition as they represent the first and, as far as we know, the only golf resort in the state of Kansas. While the resort is basically a private community country club development with a limited number of building lots (101), the construction of the hotel has made it possible for them to host meeting groups and travelers. To highlight the hotel entrance the architect used Italian marble throughout. To say the least, it is impressive. There are a total of 42 guest rooms

(including suites). The suites, by the way, have a sitting and dining area, a wet-bar, and a refrigerator. They also offer the "Club Room Suite" arrangement. With its common sitting room, an extremely large bathroom area with several showers, and 11 separate sleeping rooms (accommodations for 14), it is ideal for groups.

Dining is provided in the Greens Dining Room (capacity 120) as well as the Blairemore Room, seating 60 people. There is also the Men's Grill, offering a selection ranging from steaks to sandwiches, or the Pool House, serving a more casual menu ranging from salads to sandwiches. The resort can accommodate meeting and conference groups of up to 225 theater-style and also has three breakout rooms.

Additional amenities include two indoor racquetball courts, a fully-equipped weight and exercise room, a sauna and whirlpool, three lighted tennis courts with a tennis professional on hand, an outdoor swimming pool and, of course, golf.

Designed by Donald R. Sechrest, Terradyne Golf Club was named in October of 1989

by *Golf Digest* as one of the top
five golf courses in Kansas. Introducing characteristic Scottish-style peaks, rolling
fairways, bunkers and high
rough, this layout is a welcome
change from many found in
this area. Depending on the
season of year, water can become a factor on as many as 11
holes. The course plays
6,704/6,215/5048 yards, with a
par of 71. For tee times call
733-5851

RATES *(EP) Rooms: $79 / $85;
suites $125 / $165 per couple.
Green fees: $20, carts $16. Golf
packages are available.*

ARRIVAL *Air: Wichita International Airport (40 minutes).
Private aircraft: Andover (10
minutes). Car: from Wichita
take Highway 54 east to Green-
wich. Take a left (north) to Central Street. Go right (east) to
159th. Turn left and drive 1/4
mile.*

Louisiana

1. Toro Hills Resort

TORO HILLS RESORT
P.O. Box 369, Florien LA 71429; (318) 586-4661; (800) 533-5031

This large resort hotel was built around two swimming pools, a children's pool, and lighted tennis courts. In addition to the hotel accommodations they now can offer lodgings in over 23 fully-equipped condominiums. Toro Hills has meeting facilities, separated from the hotel, with rooms that can be divided to accommodate groups up to 200 banquet- or 300 theater-style.

There is a now a new restaurant, lounge, and office.

Golf is played on the Toro Hills course, virtually surrounding the property. With its lush, tree-lined fairways, and water coming into play on five holes, it is an entertaining layout. Playing 6,548/6,307/5,329 yards, it pars at 72. The resort provides a pro shop and a clubhouse, with the 19th hole for a quick libation.

RATES (EP) Rooms: $45/$55. Condominiums: 2 bedrooms, kitchen, 2 baths $125. Green Fees: $16/$18. Carts: $18. Golf package: 2 nights/3 days (includes lodging, green fees, cart, taxes), $183 per couple; weekends $194 per couple. Lodging in a condo: $224/$264 per couple. Rates are March-September.

ARRIVAL Air: Shreveport (2 1/2 hours). Private aircraft: Hodges Garden, 2,200-foot strip. Car: U.S. 171 between Many and Leesville.

Michigan

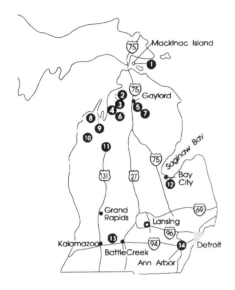

1. The Grand Hotel
2. Boyne Highlands
3. Boyne Mountain
4. Shanty Creek/
   Schuss Mountain Resort
5. Hidden Valley Club Resort
   Treetop Sylvan Resort
6. Schuss Mountain Resort
7. Garland Resort
8. Sugar Loaf Resort
9. Grand Traverse Resort
   Waterfront Park Inn
10. Crystal Mountain
11. McGuire's Motor Lodge
    & Resort
12. Bay Valley Inn
13. Gull Lake View Golf Club
14. Radisson on the Lake

BAY VALLEY INN
2470 Old Bridge Road, Bay City, MI 48706; (517) 686-3500; (800) 292-5028

Bay Valley, with its 150 guest rooms, offers a comfortable country-inn atmosphere. Dining is provided in the Heatherfield Restaurant overlooking the golf course, or in the intimate English Room. The Players Lounge is available for dancing. The resort is a natural for meetings, with a capacity of 310 theater- and 210 banquet-style.

A resident tennis director supervises activities on the six indoor and six outdoor tennis courts. Other amenities include: swimming pools, a sauna, and a Jacuzzi/whirlpool bath.

Designed by Desmond Muirhead/Jack Nicklaus, the resort's championship course is reminiscent of many of the Scottish layouts. Parring at 71, this beautiful and challenging course plays 6,610/6,113/5,587/5,151 yards. Apparently the Scots liked water, as the course has over 60 acres of the stuff – unfortunately not in just one place, but seemingly wherever you look. When you add the well-placed traps and trees, it becomes a challenge.

RATES (EP) Inn: $99. Green fees: $45, including cart. Golf packages are available. Rates are for June to mid-October.

ARRIVAL Air: Tri-City Airport. Car: I-75, take M-84 Saginaw Road exit. Turn right, go 1 block, then at Standard Station right again.

BOYNE HIGHLANDS
Harbor Springs, MI 49740; (616) 526-2171; (800) 462-6963

Situated in northern Michigan, Boyne Highlands is just four miles from Lake Michigan. Long recognized as a winter resort, it has also moved into prominence as a summer destination. Lodgings are provided at the Highland Inn (165 rooms) as well as the new Heather Highlands Inn Condo Hotel (72 units). Including the many privately-owned condominiums, the resort can handle over 800 guests. Each unit features a fireplace, fully-equipped kitchen, and balcony. The Highlands, with its remodeled conference center, is well set up to handle meeting groups.

Swimming in two pools, saunas, fishing, tennis on four courts, with horseback riding nearby, are a few of the activities available. There is also a children's program as well as a baby sitting service.

There are now three regulation courses, plus a nine-hole par-three affair on the premises. The Moor Course, parring at 72, plays a monstrous 7,179/6,521/6,032/5,459 yards. The Heather links weigh in at an even more generous 7,218/6,554/6,090/5,263 yards, also parring at 72. Due to the general terrain of heavily wooded hills and lots of water, these layouts provide a wide variety of possible shots and a great deal of challenge. There is a well-stocked pro shop, a putting green, and driving range.

In mid-1990 the Donald Ross Memorial Course came into play. They have selected 18 of the most memorable holes designed by Mr. Ross, one of the world's finest golf architects, and have duplicated them. Examples include: Pinehurst Course #2, Scioto, Oakland Hills, Royal Dornoch, Seminole, and many others. To say the least it has produced a unique and intriguing golf adventure. With a par of 72, it plays 6,840/6,308/4,977 yards. This new facility is supported by a 17,000-square-foot clubhouse featuring two restaurants, lounges, tennis, as well as a golf shop, locker rooms, a driving range, and a practice putting green.

You can also play the two courses at Boyne Mountain, some 26 miles away. For details on those, see Boyne Mountain Resort.

RATES (EP) Hotel room: $95/$130. Condos: $140/$180. Green fees: $65/$80, including cart. Golf package: 2 nights/2 days (includes dinner each night, lodging, green fees, cart), $520 per couple.

ARRIVAL Air: Emmett County Airport (11 miles from Boyne Highlands).

BOYNE MOUNTAIN
Boyne Falls, MI 49713; (616) 549-2441; (800) 462-6963

Boyne Mountain, bounded by Deer Lake and U.S. 131, has long been recognized as a winter sports complex. Recently, it has gained acceptance as a summer destination as well. Accommodations are over 400 rooms, including the Deer Lake Beach Villas, each with private suites and full kitchens; the Mountain Villa condominium complex; Edelweiss Lodge; Boynehof Lodge; the Cliff Dweller; and the Main

Lodges. Boyne Mountain Resort is an ideal place for meeting groups. There are a variety of dining rooms and lounges.

There are three swimming pools, saunas, fishing, sailing, the Beach Club, and a tennis complex with a total of 14 courts.

The Alpine Links, plays 7,017/6,546/6,014/4,986 yards and pars at 72. The Boyne Monument Championship Course, opened in early 1986, stretches out 7,086/6,377/5,744/4,904 yards, also parring at 72. The resort offers two driving ranges, a pro shop, and golf on a par-three executive course.

RATES (EP) Rooms: $95. Villas: 1 bedroom $125. Green fees: $65/$80, including cart. Golf package: 2 nights/2 days (includes lodging, MAP, green fees, and cart), $620 per couple.

ARRIVAL Air: Traverse City. Private aircraft: Boyne Mountain, 4,200-foot lighted runway. Car: off U.S. 131, 1 mile south of Boyne Falls.

CRYSTAL MOUNTAIN
12500 Crystal Mountain Drive, Thompsonville, MI 49683; (616) 378-2000; (800) 968-7686

The resort, while small enough to allow individual attention, has all the amenities of a larger facility. Accommodations are varied and include: one- or two-bedroom condominiums, some overlooking the 18th green; the Hamlet's 38 poolside rooms, each including a whirlpool (built for two); and The Colony rooms, with private Jacuzzi/whirlpool baths. Some also have a fully-equipped kitchen as well as a fireplace. Within easy walking distance of the Lodge and pool are found the Village Chalets and Resort Homes – each fully-equipped for housekeeping. Crystal can also accommodate group functions of up to 200 banquet-style.

If you do not care to cook for yourself, you can visit the main dining room, also offering dancing and entertainment.

There are indoor and outdoor swimming pools, tennis on two courts, a fitness center, jogging, biking trails, with boating, charter fishing, and canoeing available on the Betsie and the Platte Rivers nearby. During the summer months a Camp Crystal kids program is put in place to give the parents a break. During the winter their slopes, are set up for nighttime skiing.

Golf is offered on a course selected by *Travel Weekly* as one of the "Par Excellence" resort layouts. Now consisting of 27 holes, they play as follows: Mountain Meadows/Ridge nines combine to play 6,732/5,955/4,983 yards, parring at 72; Creek/Meadows is 6,320/5,657/4,859 yards, with a par of 71; the Ridge/Creek plays 6,450/5,698/4,784 yards, also parring at 71. With water coming into play, undulating terrain, trees and well trapped greens, they will give all you want.

RATES (EP) Motel room: weekdays $69/$95; weekend $135/$145. Pinehurst 1 bedroom: $185/$199. Green fees: $32, carts $24. Golf packages are available.

ARRIVAL Air: Traverse City or Cadillac (36 miles). Car: north on U.S. 31, turn east on County Road 602, 6 miles north of Bearlake.

GARLAND RESORT
Country Road 489, Lewiston, MI 49756; (517) 786-2211; (800) 968-0042

The fact that Garland is a family-owned and operated resort probably has a great deal to do with the tranquility guests experience here. The setting, which contributes to the relaxed atmosphere, is not unlike a small village.

Rather unusual is the fact that they used peeled logs for the construction of the buildings. The combination of the log structure blended with the modern interior is extremely effective. The lobby tends to set the tone with imported Italian marble floors, highlighted by stained glass windows and a huge, cut stone fireplace.

There are 25 guest rooms in the Inn and 32, including four suites, in the south wing. Most have either a balcony or patio. There are also 28 one-bedroom and 16 two-bedroom, two-bath villas. Some of the lodgings feature a shower/spa, some a Jacuzzi. The villas have a fireplace, wet-bar, and small refrigerator. The resort's new conference center allows them to handle up to 120 people banquet- and 160 theater-style.

Herman's Restaurant has a wide selection ranging from casual snacks to fine dining. There is also patio or poolside cafe-style dining as well as room service.

Amenities include: a practice putting green and driving range, lighted tennis courts, bicycle trails (along with rentals), an outdoor swimming pool, an indoor lap pool, a Jacuzzi, sauna, whirlpool, and exercise and weight rooms. The stream fishing in the immediate vicinity is outstanding. Some distance away (about 25 miles), there is canoeing, sailing, charter fishing, and horseback riding.

During winter they offer 50 kilometers of cross country skiing, and a lighted ice skating rink. Or perhaps you will elect (as I did), to snuggle up to a warm fire and watch the others enjoy the outdoor winter activities.

There are now a total of 63 holes of golf plus a practice range. The Swampfire course weighs in with a yardage of 6,868/6,419/5,937/4,812 and a par of 72. If you care to, you can bring along your paddle boat, as water comes in on 15 of the 18 holes. The Reflections course, the newest addition, measures a more modest 6,464/5,966/4,767 yards, also parring at 72. Don't let the yardage fool you. While this gem does not have much water (in play on only seven holes), it has sand traps sprinkled all over the place (I think there were over 50). It also has tree-lined and tight fairways to keep you honest. Most unusual is the fact that the Reflection layout has six par fives, six par fours and six par threes. I can not recall another course with this configuration.

Then we come to the Monarch. It is relatively open, with water a factor on 13 holes. No extra problems are needed, as its length gives you all you can handle. The yardage is an outrageous 7,101/6,585/6,056/4,861, with a par of 72.

Last, but by no means least, is Hermans's Nine, parring at 36. Sporting only ten traps and no water, this layout reaches out a respectable (when played twice) 6,756/6,448/5,168 yards. All of the courses operate out of the same pro shop and are under the supervision of the Director of Golf, Lee Woodruff.

RATES (EP) Inn rooms: $140/$240 per couple. Suites: $260/$300. 1-bedroom villas: $300. Green fees: $60, including cart. Golf package: 2 nights/3 days (includes lodging, MAP, 3 rounds of golf with cart, club storage, gratuities, and tax), $990 per couple. Rates are for the peak summer season.

ARRIVAL Air: Detroit. Private

aircraft: Garland (on property 5,000-foot paved runway). Arrangements can be made for you to be picked up by their private jet and flown directly to the resort. Car: from I-75 north to exit 254. After exit turn right at the first light and take M-72 east to Luzerne (16 miles). Turn left (north) at blinking light on Country Road 489 – travel 14 miles to resort.

GRAND HOTEL
Mackinac Island, MI 49757; (906) 847-3331; (800) 334-7263

While the golf course is, to say the least, modest, the resort itself is so extraordinary that we could not bring ourselves to leave it out of the book. After all there are other things in life than championship golf. Your adventure starts when you leave the ferry or air taxi and step into the gleaming hotel carriage. Attended by an immaculately clad coachman, resplendent in his hunting pinks and complete with top hat, you will travel to the Grand. On the ride to the hotel you will glimpse the quiet wilderness of the island, with a view of both passing ships and departing guests. Your first sight of the Grand is breathtaking: pristine white, it sits on a high bluff overlooking the Straits of

Mackinac, where Lakes Huron and Michigan touch. A dowager Queen, over 110 years of age, the Grand Hotel is beautifully preserved and vibrantly alive. The spell does not break when you arrive and step into the Grand Hotel parlor, entering a world where the tradition of demitasse and after dinner cordials, evening concerts and dressing for dinner still applies. Jackets and ties are required after 6 PM. Indulge in the proud tradition of high tea, complete with sandwiches, freshly baked cakes and tortes, or request a picnic basket prepared for bikers, strollers, golfers, or horseback riders.

The accommodations do nothing to dispel the setting with their excellent furnishings. The meeting rooms can handle groups up to 600.

There are many activities: bicycling through the hills, swimming in the great Serpentine pool, tennis and shuffleboard, or enjoying the 500 acres of gardens. The fact that automobiles are not allowed on the island adds to the atmosphere of tranquility.

Golf is available on a nine-hole executive course. Playing it twice, the yardage is 4,670/4,488/4,106.

RATES (MAP) 1 bedroom: $290/$470 per couple. Green fees: (18 holes) $24, carts $20. The resort is open May through November.

ARRIVAL Air: Pellston Airport. Car: park at Mackinac City or St. Ignace. It is a 30-minute ferry ride across the Straits to the Island.

GRAND TRAVERSE RESORT
6300 North U.S. 31, Grand Traverse, MI 49610; (616) 938-2100; (800) 748-0303

Much of Michigan's lower peninsula is covered by thick pine and hardwood forests, lush cherry orchards, deep lakes and fish-filled streams. Traverse Bay washes ashore here at the gateway to the Great Lakes. This resort has undergone a giant transformation in recent years. The grounds now encompass 920 acres, including a half-mile of shoreline along East Bay. There are over 345 condominiums and 244 hotel rooms. The new 15-story, 186-room Tower, really the centerpiece of the resort, has two floors with over 20,000 square feet of shopping space. Also within the Tower is the 16th-floor cabaret-style Trillium Restaurant and lounge.

The Beach Club, on East Grand Traverse Bay, provides additional accommodations in the form of 150 studio and one-bedroom villas. Many of the rooms are equipped with two-person whirlpools.Your evenings can vary from pizza with the children, to candlelight dining over Italian cuisine, to lounges with entertainment and dancing. There are four restaurants and five lounges. With the various meeting rooms and ballrooms, they can accommodate groups of up to 2,000.

The year-round sports complex includes: weight rooms, aerobic classes, tennis on indoor and outdoor courts with a resident professional staff, racquetball, indoor and outdoor pools, saunas, and whirlpools. There is also deep-water charter fishing, canoeing, sailing, hunting, and waterskiing.

The original golf course, home of the 1983 Michigan Open, is a par-72/73, reaching out 6,741/6,049/5,139 yards. It brings water into play on 11 holes and is well trapped. The Bear Course, first used in 1990 for the Open, reaches out 7,065/6,176/5,281 yards. A Jack Nicklaus-designed layout, it pars at 72. Anyone who wants to play from the blue tee

setting on this layout needs the assistance of a psychiatrist. The Bear presents several different challenges including multi-level fairways, many extremely deep bunkers, four lakes, and water hazards on 10 holes. All in all it is one tough golf course. The score card says, "Attention golfers, beware of deep bunkers and terraced fairways." I suggest you pay attention to those words. The Head Golf Professional is Ken Hornyak.

The John Jacobs' Practical Golf School is available at this resort. Using personalized, proven teaching methods, and under the direction of PGA and LPGA teaching professionals, it is well worth looking into. For complete details, call: (800) 472-5007.

RATES (EP) Hotel: $170. Tower: $210/$235. Condo studio: $125/$160. 1-bedroom condos: $190/$225. Green fees: Bear Course $125, including cart; Resort Course $70. Golf package: 2 nights/2 days (includes lodging, two rounds of golf with cart), $470/$630 per couple. There is an additional charge of $45 per person to play the Bear Course. Rates are for June through August.

ARRIVAL Air: Traverse City.

Car: U.S. 31, 6 miles north of Traverse City.

GULL LAKE VIEW GOLF CLUB
7417 M-89, Richland, MI 49083; (616) 731-4148

The resort, on Gull Lake, now offers the new Fairway Villas: 24 two-bedroom, two-bath units with kitchen and living room they can be rented as described, or as one-bedroom, one-bath units. The recently remodeled clubhouse has banquet facilities for 200 and provides the 19th hole lounge for cocktails and sandwiches.

There are now four golf courses. The West measures 6,300/6,058/5,216 yards and pars at 71/72. The first nine is fairly open while the back side brings water into play on six holes and has many trees. The newer East course, while shorter, plays 6,002/5,546/4,918 yards and pars at 70. It provides its own stimulation with water on 10 holes, tree-lined fairways, and small greens. The Bedford course, parring at 72, gets a little exciting with its rather long yardage of 6,890/6,554/6,076/5,106. The newest of the group is the Stonehenge course. On rolling, wooded terrain, it

reaches out 6,656/6,234/5,775/5,191 yards and again pars at 72.

RATES (EP) Villas: $125. Green fees: $22/$26, carts $22. Golf package: 2 nights/3 days (includes lodging in a villa, green fees), $299 per couple.

ARRIVAL Air: Kalamazoo. Car: I-94, exit 85.

HIDDEN VALLEY CLUB & RESORT
P.O. Box 556, Gaylord, MI 49735; (517) 732-5181; (800) 752-5510

Gaylord is in the northern region of the Michigan peninsula. Each of the nine lodges has its own unique charm and European alpine decor. Both dining rooms in the Main Lodge offer outstanding views and a menu selection ranging from light fare to fine dining. There are also two lounges. While ties are not required, after 6 PM jackets are requested. They are able to handle meetings, conferences, and banquet groups.

Hiking trails, a private lake, swimming in a heated pool, canoeing, fishing, four tennis courts, even a private wooded picnic area, are a few of the amenities.

Golf is played on the Hidden Valley Club course. A William H. Diddel design, it plays 6,386/6,123/5,591 yards, with a par of 71/73. There is a clubhouse and a small golf shop under the supervision of Head Professional Mark Hogan.

RATES (MAP) Rooms: weekdays $98/$140 per couple; weekends $110/$150. Green fees: $35/$45, including cart. Golf package: 2 nights/2 days (includes lodging, MAP, 2 rounds of golf, cart, taxes and gratuities), weekdays $422; weekends $500 per couple.

ARRIVAL Air: Detroit. Private aircraft: Otsego Airport. Car: 1 mile east of Gaylord on M-32.

McGUIRE'S MOTOR LODGE & RESORT
Mackinaw Trail, Cadillac, MI 49601; (616) 775-9947; (800) 632-7302

On 320 acres overlooking Lake Cadillac, McGuire's has 123 well appointed guest rooms. The resort is well set up to handle modest-size meeting groups and can supply the audio/visual aids required. Dining in the Terrace Room with both a menu selection

and, on Saturday evening, a smorgasbord can be followed by dancing in the Irish Pub. Added attractions include: a heated indoor pool, a sauna, whirlpool spa and two game rooms. Tennis is available on two outdoor courts with additional courts available in Cadillac. Across the street are a total of 14 racquetball courts, along with a complete athletic club, including weight rooms.

As for golf there are 27 holes: the Norway, a 9-hole affair playing 2,792 yards, parring at 36; and the Spruce course, stretching out 6,601/6,202/5,217 yards, with a par of 71. Professional Bill Snider and staff are on deck to assist.

RATES (EP) Rooms: $60/$95. Suites $170. Green fees: $34, including cart. Golf package: 2 nights/3 days (includes lodging, 2 breakfasts, 1 dinner per person, unlimited green fees), $364 per couple.

ARRIVAL Air: Cadillac. Car: 1 mile south of Cadillac on Highway 131.

RADISSON ON THE LAKE
1275 Huron Street, Ypsilanti, MI 48197; (313) 487-2000; (800) 333-3333

The location of the Radisson (15 minutes from the airport), makes it an attractive place for meetings. Accommodations are 236 rooms along with seven executive board room suites. All rooms have a spacious desk, two phones (one with a computer hook-up), and most offer a view of the golf course or lake. The resort also offers a Plaza Club room level (concierge level), which includes a complimentary continental breakfast each morning and cocktails in the evening. There are 27,000 square feet of space set aside to accommodate group functions. Dining is in the Fairways, with evening entertainment in Players sports lounge.

There is a health club with an indoor swimming pool, whirlpool, steam room, weight room, and sauna bath. There are also jogging and bicycling trails, tennis courts, and boating facilities. In the winter they offer ice skating and cross-country skiing as well.

Inasmuch as the terrain is generally flat, to introduce a bit of spice the architect of the Huron Golf Club (Karl Litten), discovered water. In fact he must have loved the stuff. Bad enough that the front nine is virtually surrounded by Ford

Lake but there are six or seven ponds involving nine holes getting into the act. Parring at 72, this layout measures 6,755/ 6,470/6,150/5,185 yards. The course is supported by a driving range, practice green, and an excellent pro shop, under the supervision of the Director of Golf, Tom Pendlebury.

RATES   (EP)   Rooms: $99/$135. Suites: $145 and up. Green fees: $20/$27, carts $20. Golf package 2 nights/2 days (includes lodging, a buffet breakfast and buffet lunch each day, two rounds of golf with cart), $340 per couple. Rates are for the period of April through October.

ARRIVAL Air: Detroit Metro Airport (15 minutes away). Car: take 1-94 to Huron Street.

SCHUSS MOUNTAIN RESORT
Schuss Mountain Road, Mancelona, MI 49659; (616) 533-8621; (800) 748-0249

The focal point of these 2,200 acres of rolling wooded hills, is the Schuss Village – composed of the Main Lodge, the Ivanhof Char Broil, gift shops, and the meeting center. Accommodations in the Village Square are fully-equipped condominiums.

A short distance away can be found the Sudendorf Condos and Schuss Mountain Chalets with various sleeping arrangements of from two to six.

Dining is provided in two restaurants. The Ivanhof is for breakfast and lunch. In the evening it transforms itself into the "Supper Club." And what a supper club it is, featuring the "Schussycats," 11 collegiate waiters and waitresses singing the hits of the 40's through the 80's.

Available during summer are an outdoor swimming pool, a six-court tennis complex, bicycling, volleyball and, on nearby Torch Lake, sailing, canoeing, snorkeling, and wind-surfing. In winter the Shanty Creek and Schuss Mountain resorts unite in offering some of the finest skiing.

Golf is played at the Schuss Mountain Golf Club, with the course stretching out a rather substantial 6,922/6,394/5,383 yards and parring at 72. An interesting affair, it presents large greens, tree-lined fairways, some strategic water holes, and traps which seem to blend with the terrain. The golf professional is Rodger Jabara.

RATES *(EP) Village room:*

$119/$139. 1-bedroom condominiums: $155/$200. Green fees: $45, including cart. Golf package: 2 nights/2 days (includes lodging, MAP, 2 rounds of golf), $432 per couple; weekends $472. There is a surcharge for play on the Legend course. Rates are for mid-June through August.

ARRIVAL *Air: Traverse City. Private aircraft: Bellaire. Car: 6 miles west of Mancelona, on Highway 88.*

SHANTY CREEK/ SCHUSS MOUNTAIN RESORT
Shanty Creek Road, Bellaire, MI 49615; (616) 533-8621; (800) 748-0249

The Inn is in the beautiful north woods of Michigan and offers the best of both worlds. It has all the traditional amenities of a fine resort, along with an outstanding meeting/conference center, yet offers a peaceful and picturesque atmosphere. While this is a difficult balance to attain, Shanty Creek has been successful.

There are guest rooms and suites in the Main Lodge, the Trapper Lodge, the Timberline Studio Apartments, as well as many one- to three-bedroom condominiums. Some accommodations are equipped with whirlpool baths and all are well appointed.

The only problem with dining here is deciding where to eat: the Main Dining Room, the pro shop Snack Bar, the Cafeteria or, located in the village, La Bodega Deli. The cozy Lounge offers top flight entertainment. (Jackets are suggested in the evening). Speaking of jackets, while it is pleasant during the day it can get nippy in the evening. I suggest you bring a jacket.

There are so many things to do, it is difficult to list them all. Fishing, tennis, golf, bicycling, bowling, horseback riding, water skiing on Torch Lake, canoeing, swimming in indoor and outdoor pools or the lake, racquetball, skeet shooting, and a one-mile exercise course are a sample. A resident tennis professional is available for lessons and setting up tournaments on the four all-weather courts.

Golf is offered on the resort's Deskin course. A Bill Diddle design, it weighs in at 6,559/ 6,197/5,285 yards, parring at 72/74. This layout has undulating fairways, 35 traps, as

well as tough greens to keep your attention. It is fairly wide open and has water on only one hole.

The Legend, an Arnold Palmer design, is the newest addition. Also parring at 72, it measures 6,764/6,269/5,801/4,953 yards. Many say this may well be Palmer's best effort. If you expect a flat country look, think again. The first hole is, in my opinion, the most beautiful opening golf hole I have ever played. A par five and tree-lined, it has a 175-foot drop from the tee area to the green. The fourth, a par-three playing 135 yards, gives you a drop of 180 feet to the green.

Tee times can also be arranged at several different courses in the area, including Schuss Mountain Resort in Mancelona (three miles away). There is a resident professional, Tom Weideman, and staff available to assist in setting up tournaments or arranging lessons.

RATES (EP) Inn: $119 / $139. 1-bedroom condo: $155 / $200. Green fees: $45, including cart; the Legend course, $75, including cart. Golf package: 2 nights / 2 days (includes lodging, MAP, 2 rounds of golf, cart extra), $432 per couple; weekends $472. Surcharge of $40 *per person to play the Legend course. Rates are for mid-June through August.*

ARRIVAL Air: Cherry Capital. Private aircraft: Antrim County Airport (5,000-foot surfaced and lighted runway, 2 miles). Car: from Mancelona take Route 88 west.

SUGAR LOAF RESORT
Route One, Cedar, MI 49621; (616) 228-5461; (800) 748-0117

Sugar Loaf Resort, nestled at the base of the mountain, is surrounded by rolling countryside, sparkling lakes, and the peaceful beauty one expects from the Leelanau Peninsula. Over 150 rooms are available in the lodge, with additional accommodations offered in the two- to four-bedroom townhouses. Business and pleasure mix well here as the resort's meeting rooms can accommodate up to 600. The Four Seasons Dining Room provides a spectacular view of the mountains and Lake Michigan beyond, while the Four Seasons Lounge offers nightly entertainment.

Their tennis complex includes five outdoor courts, along with three swimming pools (one indoor, two outdoor), a weight room and a Jacuzzi. Of course, nearby Lake Michigan makes possible many water activities.

Golf is served up on the Sugar Loaf Golf Club course which stretches out 6,813/6,124/5,134 yards. The men's par is 72, while ladies' is set at 74. Their 8th hole will make a believer out of you: a 360-yard par-four, running between two ponds, and with five traps between the ponds and the green. It calls for a fast exit to the 19th hole.

RATES (EP) Lodge rooms: $89. Townhouse: $135/$180. Green fees: $50, including cart. Golf package: 1 night/1 day (includes lodging, MAP, 1 round of golf), $158 per couple. Rates are for July-August.

ARRIVAL Air: Traverse City. Private aircraft: 3,500-foot, lighted strip, located at the resort. Car: 18 miles northwest of Traverse City on Route 651.

TREETOP/SYLVAN RESORT
3962 Wilkinson Road, Gaylord, MI 49735; (517) 732-6711; (800) 444-6711

This year-round resort is centrally located in the upper part of the lower peninsula of Michigan. Accommodations range from 172 hotel rooms and suites to individual chalets with kitchenettes. Dining as well as nightly entertainment are offered up in the Ale House Dining Room and Lounge. The resort also has excellent meeting and conference facilities with rooms designed for small groups of from 25 to 90 and others set up to handle as many as 200 people.

There are indoor and outdoor swimming pools, an indoor and an outdoor whirlpool-spa, two saunas, exercise rooms, tennis courts, hiking trails, volleyball, putting greens and, of course, golf.

During the winter months you can add cross-country skiing, ice skating, night cross-country as well as downhill skiing (225-foot vertical drop, 11 slopes, a triple and double chair lift, and rope tows).

The Treetop Links is a Robert Trent Jones, Sr. layout. It is, in fact, considered by many, including Mr. Jones, to be a masterpiece. After having played this course I would have to agree. With a par of 71, it reaches out 7,060/6,399/5,817/4,972 yards. It was built on undulating terrain with tree-lined fairways and some of the most interesting water hazards we have seen. While the wet stuff comes into play on only five holes, the eighth green with its water will get your attention. It is a beautiful layout and, while not a back breaker, will require your attention and patience. There is an excellent pro shop and a staff directed by Head Professional, Rick Smith.

A new course has been added. It is a layout by Tom Fazio, designer of many of the more prestigious courses in the United States. As a matter of fact it is the first Fazio course to be built in the state of Michigan. A bit over three miles from the resort, and parring at 72, it plays 6,871/6,280/5,821/5,045 yards. While generally open, it shows you a variety of settings ranging from spectacular views to park-like surroundings. It is also well bunkered. Mr. Fazio felt that, because of the general topography, there was no need to introduce a great deal of water. While most certainly challenging, the course is "user friendly" and playable.

RATES (EP) Lodge rooms: $89/$139. 2-room suite: $184. Green fees: $56/$65 including cart. Golf package: 2 nights/2 days (includes lodgings, MAP, two rounds of golf), $508 per couple.

ARRIVAL Air: Mackinaw City (55 miles). Private aircraft: Otesego County Airport (Gaylord). Car: from Lansing, travel State 27 intersecting I-75 approximately 170 miles north.

WATERFRONT INN
2061 U.S. 31 North, Traverse City, MI 49685; (616) 938-1100; (800) 551-9283

The Inn is set along a 750-foot stretch of beach on east Grand Traverse Bay. There are 128 guest rooms, including suites. Eight of the rooms have a two-person whirlpool tub along with a living room, and a wet bar. All have remote-controlled cable TV. On the fourth floor, the Reflections Restaurant specializes in seafood. The atmosphere is informal, as is the Shore Station Lounge with its live entertainment. The Inn is equipped to handle meeting groups of up to 320 banquet- and 350 theater-style.

There is an indoor heated swimming pool, whirlpools, a spa, a tanning booth, an exercise room, along with the beach. Rentals at the beach include wave runners, paddle boats, wind surfers, hobie cats, and there is a boat launch ramp.

Golf can be played on the High Point Golf Course located a bit over two miles away. A Tom Doales design, it offers rolling terrain, trees, and water on only two holes. Parring at 71/72, the course weighs in at 6,819/6,140/5,258 yards.

RATES (EP) Rooms: $115/$125. 1- or 2-bedroom suites: $210/$325. Green fees: $55, including cart. Golf package: 2 nights/2 days (includes lodging), $260/$280 per couple. Rates DO NOT include green fees. There are so many courses to play, setting up package rates, including green fees, is not practical.

ARRIVAL Air: Traverse City Airport. Car: resort is on U.S. Highway North at Four Mile road, two miles east of Traverse City.

Minnesota

1. Ruttger's Birchmont Lodge
2. Quadna Four Seasons Resort
3. Breezy Point Resort
4. Madden's On Gull Lake
5. Radisson Resort Arrowwood

BREEZY POINT RESORT

HCR 2 Box 70, Breezy Point, MN 56472; (218) 562-7811 MN; (800) 432-3777 NAT; (800) 328-2284

Breezy Point, not far from the Mississippi River, is only 140 miles north of the Minneapolis-St. Paul Airport. The 250-plus guest accommodations range from Lodge Apartments on Pelican Lake, Pinewood Cabanas, and Executive Beach Houses, to Beachside Apartments. Recently added to this mix are 32 Point Place condominiums ranging from one- to two-bedrooms. All units have fully-equipped kitchen, dishwasher, micro oven, and a washer/dryer. The resort can also arrange baby sitting service.

The Breezy Point Center, with 18,000 square feet of space, including 14 breakout rooms, is capable of hosting meeting groups of 750 banquet-style.

For dining there is the Marina Restaurant, overlooking Breezy Bay, the Captain's Cove at the Breezy Center, and Charlie's, located a few minutes outside the main gate, with live entertainment, steaks, and barbecued ribs.

Tennis on four Laykold courts, with a professional to assist, swimming in indoor and outdoor pools, horseback riding from stables nearby, and bicycling are some of the activities at your disposal. If you walk down to their marina you can add: fishing, canoeing, powerboating, and sailing.

Golf is played on the Breezy Point course. Called "Traditional," it plays 5,192/5,127 with a par of 68/72. The second course "Excellence," has a yardage of 6,601/6,602/5,718 with a par of 72/76. The resort also provides a golf shop and a driving range.

RATES (EP) 1-bedroom unit: $48 / $119.   Apartments: $109 / $129. VIP Accommodations: $235 / $245. MAP also available. Green fees: $25, carts $23. Rates are for the summer season. There are many different package plans available.

ARRIVAL Air: Minneapolis-St. Paul. Private aircraft and some commercial at Brainerd Airport. Car: I-94 north to Monticello; take a right to Highway 371. Turn left (north) on 371 going beyond Brainerd to Pequot Lakes. At this point take a right (east) and continue on to resort.

MADDEN'S ON GULL LAKE
8001 Pine Beach Peninsula, Brainerd, MN 56401; (218) 829-2811; (800) 233-2934

There are really three resorts: Madden Lodge, where it all began; Madden Inn & Golf Club, with its view of Gull Lake along with 45 holes of golf; and Madden Pine Portage, perched on a pine-clad ridge near the waters of Wilson Bay.

Restaurants include the main dining room of Madden Inn and Golf Club, the Coffee Shop, and the O'Madden Pub – with dancing offered each evening in the pub (except Sunday). In 1986 the resort completed a new conference center allowing them to handle meeting groups of 800 theater- or 450 classroom-style.

For tennis players, there are six Laykold courts under the supervision of a recreational director. The resort also has badminton courts, a tennis shop, and official U.S.A. croquet facilities. These activities are directed from the new Tennis and Croquet Club completed in 1991.

A few of the attractions include: indoor and outdoor swimming pools (six in total), saunas, whirlpools, game rooms and, in season, a children's program. The lake provides the opportunity to enjoy sailing, water skiing, and fishing or just relaxing on one of the three beaches.

Golf is played on two 18-hole courses, as well as a par-three nine-hole affair. Recently having undergone extensive renovation, the Pine Beach East layout plays 5,920/5,498 yards and pars at 72. The Pine Beach West measures 5,086/4,725 with a par of 67/69.

RATES (EP) Inn room: $83/$120. Inn cottage: (EP) $95/$150. Villas: $110/$164. MAP plan is also available. Package plans including lodging, MAP, golf, tennis and children's supervised programs. Green fees: $17, carts $22. Rates are for July-August.

ARRIVAL Air: Brainerd. Private aircraft: East Gull Lake. Car: from Brainerd, 4 1/2 miles on 371, left on 77 for 7 1/2 miles.

QUADNA FOUR SEASONS RESORT
100 Quadna Road, Hill City, MN 55748; (218) 697-8444; (800) 422-6649

Quadna is a Chippewa word meaning "Lake at the foot of the Mountains." The name only begins to describe the beauty and solitude of this northwoods resort, with its rustic atmosphere. Accommodations vary from a full-service campground, an economical roadside inn, a massive, rustic Main Lodge, to townhouses and villas fully-equipped for

housekeeping with dishwasher and fireplaces. They have excellent meeting facilities and can handle groups of from 10 to 500.

You can dine in the Harvester Restaurant overlooking Hill Lake with nightly dancing and entertainment available. Then there is the bar named the "Loose Moose Saloon" (I didn't name it, they did.)

Starting in November, snowmaking equipment assures outstanding conditions on the 15 varied slopes. There are also four-person chair lifts and 500 miles of groomed snowmobile trails. An indoor swimming pool and saunas complete the list. During summer, the four outdoor tennis courts, three outdoor swimming pools, hunting, fishing, canoeing, paddleboating, water skiing, and lawn games add to the fun. There is a recreational director in charge of golf and tennis. The golf course is actually a nine-hole layout with a total (if played twice) of 6,130 yards and a par of 70.

RATES (EP) Lodge: $75/$81. Motel: $50. Villas: $100/$150. Townhouses: (1 bedroom) $90. Green fees: $25 (18 holes), carts $23.

ARRIVAL *Air: Duluth (60 miles). Car: U.S. 169 north, turn in at Quadna Motel.*

RADISSON RESORT ARROWWOOD

P.O. Box 639, Alexandria, MN 56308; (612) 762-1124; (800) 333-3333

Some 130 miles northwest of the twin cities, the Arrowwood Resort has a setting of rolling grassland and gentle forests. The lodgings are in 170 rooms, some with lake views, others overlooking the golf course. They also have two floors of meeting rooms and can accommodate groups of 15 to 500.

The dining room, which overlooks the lake, specializes in fish delicacies and steaks.

While we are concerned with golf and summer activities, they also have a winter program. Due to the proximity of Lake Darling, they are able to provide sailing, motor boats, canoes, and swimming. Tennis is played on four courts, with horseback riding, and a variety of indoor amenities such as a heated pool, whirlpools, and saunas also available.

Golf is on an executive layout. Located next to the lake, it plays 5,350 yards with a par of 68.

RATES *(EP) Rooms: $115/$155. Green fees: $26, carts $24. Rates are for July-September.*

ARRIVAL *Air: Alexandria Airport (5 miles). Car: from Minneapolis, off I-94 (130 miles).*

RUTTGER'S BIRCHMONT LODGE

530 Birchmont Beach Road, Bemidji, MN 56601; (218) 751-1630; (800) 726-3866

This family-style resort is on the northern shore of Lake Bemidji. Accommodations are rooms and suites in the main lodge, or one- to four-bedroom cottages with living room and fireplace. The resort can accommodate meeting groups of from 20 to 250. They have two separate dining rooms and cocktail lounges to handle such gatherings. The Lakefront dining room prepares its own pastries daily. (I defy you to pass on these.)

There are 1,600 feet of sandy beach, two heated pools, the playground, recreation rooms, paddle boats, kayaks, canoes, sailboats, water skiing, four tennis courts, and a supervised recreational program for the younger set.

Golf can be played on two 18-hole courses: the Bemidji Town & Country Club, site of the annual Birchmont International Golf Tournament; or the Castle Highlands. The Bemidji course measures 6,385/6,198/5,489 and pars at 72/74. The Castle Highlands, also an 18-hole layout, is seven miles away.

RATES (EP) 1-bedroom housekeeping cottages: $108/$138 per couple. Green fees: $24, carts $25. MAP plan is also available.

ARRIVAL Air: Bemidji. Car: 5 miles north of Bemidji on old U.S. 71.

Missouri

1. The Lake of the Ozarks
   Dogwood Hills G C & Resort
   The Lodge of the Four Seasons
   Marriott's Tan-Tar-A Resort
2. Loma Linda Country Club

THE LAKE OF THE OZARKS

The lure of The Lake of the Ozarks with hundreds of coves and inlets, together with its proximity to both Kansas City and St. Louis, has made this a favorite year-round recreational destination. Developed with the construction of Bagnell Dam on the Osage River in 1933, the 140-mile-long lake has 1,400 miles of shoreline. With its tree-studded rolling terrain bordering the lake, it provides a full spectrum of water activity. While already offering a perfect location for resorts, the setting was further enhanced by the construction of seven golf courses.

Three resorts in this area, Dogwood Hills, the Lodge of the Four Seasons, and Marriott's Tan-Tar-A, are described on the following pages.

DOGWOOD HILLS GOLF CLUB & RESORT INN
Route 4, Box 1300, State Road KK, Osage Beach, MO 65065; (314) 348-1735; (800) 528-1234

Accommodations are in 45 rooms overlooking the golf course. There are also Fairway Villas with from one to four bedrooms, featuring fully-equipped kitchens, fireplaces, living and dining rooms.

Set as they are by the lake, there is fishing, boating, swimming in the lake or in their own heated pool. Mitch & Duffs Restaurant & Bar is in the clubhouse.

The Dogwood Hills Golf Course shows a yardage of 6,105/5,893/5,262, parring at 71/73. They have not only a driving range but a practice sand trap – something not found on many courses. Something worth checking into: the resort offers the Lake if the Ozarks School of Golf. Also new is their golf package, allowing play on four different excellent courses. Some require a surcharge.

RATES (EP) Rooms: $73 / $79. Fairway villas (2 bedrooms) $168 / $184. Green fees: $13 / $17, carts $24. Golf package: 2 nights / 3 days (includes lodging, 3 days green fees, cart for 2 rounds, one night dinner), weekdays $274; weekends $298 per couple.

ARRIVAL Air: Lee C. Fine Airport (25 minutes). Car: the resort is just off Highway 54 on State Route KK.

THE LODGE OF THE FOUR SEASONS
Lake Road HH
Lake Ozark, MO 65049
(314) 365-3000; (800) 843-5253

The Lodge of the Four Seasons is tucked away in a unique showcase of Japanese gardens and cascading waterfalls – truly a beautiful setting. The resort offers a selection of accommodations ranging from lakeside rooms and suites, to waters-edge condominiums and villas. They are equipped to handle meeting groups of from 10 to 1,500.

Dining at the Four Seasons is a treat. The Toledo Room presents French cuisine, while HK's, overlooking the golf course, has a relaxed country-club atmosphere. If that is not enough, there is the Sea Chase or Roseberry's Restaurant. Together they can destroy your will to stay trim. I almost forgot – there is another restaurant at the Racquet Club.

You may want to take advantage of the complete health spa program or try swimming in the five indoor and outdoor pools. Perhaps water skiing, horseback riding, fishing, trap shooting, or bowling will get you back in shape – it's all available.

The Racquet Club, a bit over a mile away, offers 13 outdoor and four indoor tennis courts as well as two racquetball courts. It is the home of the Dennis Van der Meer Tennis University and is rated one of the top 50 resort tennis clubs in the United States. There is also a lap swim pool and a health assessment program.

Robert Trent Jones, Sr, who designed the Four Seasons

USA Driftwood Golf Course, made it a thing of beauty and challenge. With a par of 71, it plays 6,346/5,772/5,198 yards. Shortly after its opening in 1974, the 13th hole was recognized as the apex of the course. It is bisected by an inlet of the lake, and you will need all the cunning (or skill) you possess to avoid the water and the five hungry traps guarding the green. Now a new course has come into play. The Seasons Ridge Golf Club designed by Ken Kavanaugh reaches out 6,416/6,020/5,461/4,657 yards with a par of 72. You will find, among other things, elevation changes of some 180 feet.

When we played it in the spring of the year, the dogwoods were in bloom – combining views of the lake, trees, and streams. We had not only a most enjoyable round but a difficult time keeping our minds on the game. PGA professional and Director of Golf, Chris Clark and staff, are on hand if needed.

RATES   (EP)   Rooms: $94/$144. Condominiums: $140. Green fees: $42/$47, carts $26. Golf package: 2 nights/3 days (includes standard room, green fees, cart, club storage), weekdays $365, weekends $384 per couple. Rates are

for June-August.

ARRIVAL Air: Jefferson City. Car: U.S. 54 to Bagnell Dam, exit to Lake Road HH, follow to resort.

LOMA LINDA COUNTRY CLUB
Route 5, Box 1000, Joplin, MO 64804; (417) 623-2901; (800) 633-3542

At one time Loma Linda was a working cattle ranch. Consisting of some 2,350 acres, this resort/residential community has a great many things to offer. The Clubhouse is the focal point of entertainment and various other activities, including a sauna, men's and ladies' locker rooms and the men's card room. There is also a dining room, lounge, and pro shop.

There are three tennis and racquetball courts, a 25-meter lighted swimming pool, five miles of equestrian trails (located nearby and with riding instructions available) and, of course, golf. They also tell me fishing is pretty fair in the area.

The course, situated on slightly rolling terrain, comes complete with contoured, elevated greens, several natural water hazards (water in nine holes), and tree-lined fairways. The North Course plays 6,628/6,086/5,333 yards and pars at 71/73. The newer South Course reaches out a modest 6,397/5,674/4,706 yards with a par of 71. The PGA Professional is Ben Pell.

RATES (EP) Rooms: $45 / $55. 1-bedroom suite: (kitchen, living room), $65 / $75. Green fees: $20, carts $17. Golf package: 2 nights / 3 days (includes lodging, green fees, dinner each night), $210 / $230 per couple.

ARRIVAL Air: Joplin (10 miles). Car: take 43 south to U.S. 44 west. Continue to the Baxter Springs exit and follow signs.

MARRIOTT'S TAN-TAR-A RESORT
State Road KK, Osage Beach, MO 65065; (314) 348-3131; (800) 826-8272

In 1977, Marriott purchased this magnificently-sited resort and began extensive renovations. They transformed it into an outstanding 1,000-room complex. Its sophisticated yet casual atmosphere, complemented by rustic decor, blends well within the natural setting. Accommo-

dations are rooms or suites in the hotel, as well as villas or "estate"-style homes. The majority of the villas have fully-equipped kitchens and range from one to five bedrooms. The resort, with its convention center and 47 separate breakout rooms, is well qualified to handle meeting groups of 20 to 3,000. A baby sitting service is also available.

For dining, there are eight different locations from which to choose. To name a few: the Cliff Room; the Windrose at the marina (closed in the winter); the Happy House; the Grille for casual dining; and, at the golf course, the Oaks Restaurant. Market Lane, one floor above the lobby, offers various shops and boutiques. The selection ranges from cheeses and sausages to gifts, souvenirs, sports equipment, and designer clothing.

Tennis is available on six outdoor and two indoor courts under the direction of a professional staff, plus four indoor racquetball courts, five swimming pools, bowling, and a health spa.

There are several different types of boats for rent ranging from waterskiing or trolling boats, to canoes. A tip – fishing in this lake provides a shot at some feisty bass.

The Oaks golf course, a beautifully sculptured layout designed by Van Hagge and Bruce Devlin, had some severe problems to overcome: rocky terrain, little or no top soil, and poor irrigation. But all of these problems have been corrected. The Oaks 18 reaches out a respectable 6,442/6,002/5,329/3,943 yards and pars at 71/70. Accuracy rather than distance is the prime requirement on this layout. Watch the 16th hole, a par-three, from an elevated tee. Looking down, water is almost everywhere, with the green guarded by two sand traps. Water, by the way, becomes a factor on 10 holes. The resort has an extremely well run and well-stocked pro shop, complete with restaurant, lounge, and locker rooms. The Director of Golf is Tom Gray.

A third nine, Hidden Lakes, plays 3,015/2,705 yards with a par of 35 from the men's tees and 2,232 yards parring at 36 for the ladies. It is a change of pace, as water comes into play on only two holes.

The John Jacobs' Practical Golf School is available at this resort. Using personalized teaching methods, and under the direction of PGA and LPGA teaching professionals, it is well worth looking into. For details, call: (800) 472-5007.

RATES (EP) Rooms: $129 / $149. Suites: $209 / $239. Green fees: $48, including cart. Golf package: 2 nights / 3 days (includes lodging, breakfast each morning, green fees, cart and club storage), $429 per couple. Rates are for the summer season.

ARRIVAL Air: Springfield (90 minutes). Private aircraft: Grand Glaize. Car: from Kansas City, I-70 to Route 5, to Camdenton. East on Highway 54, 10 miles to Lake Road KK, then a left, and drive 2 miles.

Montana

Eureka

Helena

Anaconda

Billings

Big Sky

1. Crystal Lakes Resort
2. Grouse Mountain Lodge
3. Meadow Lakes Golf & Ski
   Resort
4. Marina Cay Resort
5. Fairmont Hot Springs Resort
6. Big Sky

BIG SKY
P.O. Box 160001, Big Sky, MT 59716; (406) 995-4211; (800) 548-4486

The drive to this area, 44 miles from Bozeman, is something you will long recall. The highway winds its way along the Gallatin River as it tumbles down from Lone Mountain (11,166 feet) and the high country. You can occasionally spot elk or moose and pools which cry to be fished. Big Sky also happens to be only 48 miles north of the entrance to West Yellowstone National Park. The entire complex is actually spread over a wide mountain valley with Meadow Village at the lower end. Seven miles further up the valley, at the base of Lone Mountain, is the Huntley Lodge.

There are 204 guest rooms in the main lodge, plus over 194 condominiums, featuring all-electric kitchens and fireplaces, many with private Jacuzzis. They have recently added a seven-story condominium complex. Each unit is fully-equipped for housekeeping. A nice extra, located at the lodge, is a small guest laundry.

While the Lodge has two restaurants and a saloon (Chet's Bar), the resort also offers other places to eat as well as music for dancing. The new convention center is capable of handling groups of up to 750 banquet-style.

Facilities include: swimming pools, saunas, Jacuzzis, a health club, live entertainment, tennis courts, hayrides, and horseback riding. There is also stream and lake fishing, as well as white water rafting. The Adventures Big Sky Company offers a choice of half- or full-day trips on the Gallatin River. There are even two- or three-day fishing and rafting trips. The less adventurous can also arrange for a scenic float trip on calmer stretches of the Gallatin – my kind of action.

There are 35 miles of ski slopes, four-passenger gondola lifts, as well as double and triple chair lifts. At the base of the ski area are seven restaurants, two ski rental and repair shops, clothing stores, a drug store and several gift shops. Big Sky offers an International Ski School staffed by highly qualified ski instructors gathered from the United States and Europe.

Golf is played on the Arnold Palmer-designed 18-hole course in the Meadow Village area. Parring at 72, this layout stretches 6,748/6,115/5,374 yards. The elevation (some 6,500 feet above sea level) creates some interesting conditions for play. While relatively flat and open it has mountain streams and ponds coming into contention on six holes.

RATES (EP) Huntley Lodge, including breakfast: $96/$110. Condominium villas: 1-3 bedrooms $99/$424. Green fees: $24, carts $20. Golf packages are available.

ARRIVAL Air: Bozeman. Car:

Route 191. South from Bozeman (44 miles), then turn right at the Conoco station.

CRYSTAL LAKES CONDOMINIUMS
P.O. Box 255, Fortine, MT 59918; (406) 882-4586

Crystal Lakes is in northern Montana. On 1,400 acres, adjacent to Crystal Lake and with the Canadian Rockies as a backdrop, it has a magnificent setting. Accommodations are in approximately 40 condominiums and townhouses. Ranging up to two bedrooms, each is fully-equipped for housekeeping and has a washer/dryer, fireplace, and dining area. Meeting groups of up to 120 can be accommodated. Restaurants include the Crystal Lakes Dining Room and lounge as well as a snack bar at the golf course.

Tennis, volleyball, hiking, lake fishing and, of course, golf are a few of the activities. The Crystal Lakes course plays 6,500/6,202/5,643 yards and pars at 71/72. Extremely well trapped and tree-lined, it takes full advantage of the general rolling terrain. There is a professional staff available as well as a golf shop.

RATES (EP) Studio: $75. Con-
dominiums: $125/$145. Green
fees: $25, carts $20.

ARRIVAL Air: Glazier International (Kalispell 48 miles).
Private aircraft: 5,200-foot
paved strip located on property.

FAIRMONT HOT SPRINGS RESORT
Anaconda, MT 59711, (406)
797-3241 MT; (800) 332-3272
NAT; (800) 443-2381

Fairmont Hot Springs is nestled at the foot of the Pintlar
range. The resort has 151
guest rooms, with saunas to
help wipe out the travel aches.
Dining takes place in either
the main dining room or in the
coffee shop. They are set up to
handle meeting groups of from
20 to 300. Fairmont is open
year-round and also has excellent winter facilities.

During summer there is a wide
choice of activities: trail riding
(with experienced guides),
fishing for some of the feistiest
brook, brown, rainbow, and native cutthroat trout found anywhere. There are two indoor
and two larger-than-Olympic-
size pools with the mineral waters maintained at a
temperature ranging from 80
to 108 degrees.

Golf is played on a 6,732-yard,
par-72 course. The women's
tees are set at a long 6,193
yards, parring at 74. They
must grow 'em healthy in this
area as that is a long reach for
ladies. There is a full-line pro
shop and snack bar. Pro shop
manager Sparky McClean is
on deck to sort things out.

RATES (EP) Rooms: $72.
Rates include use of mineral
water pools and saunas. Green
fees: $25, carts $22.

ARRIVAL Air: Butte (15
miles). Car: I-90 exit 211, then
south approximately 3 miles.

GROUSE MOUNTAIN LODGE
1205 Highway 93W, Whitefish,
MT 59937; (406) 862-3000;
(800) 321-8822

Having opened in 1984,
Grouse Mountain Lodge is just
27 miles from Glacier National
Park. On seven acres, the setting is in one of the most beautiful parts of Montana. The
resort has 145 guest rooms
plus meeting rooms with a capacity for 300. Some special
features include ten loft rooms
with kitchenettes, two guest
laundries, a card room, a video
arcade, and a gift/sundry shop.

Dining is available in the 100-seat Logan's Bar and Grill. While Whitefish is only one mile away and provides a wide selection of excellent restaurants, Logan's is, in our opinion, one of the better choices.

The Lodge has an indoor swimming pool and sauna, an indoor and two outdoor spas, with tennis available across the road. Of possible interest to fishing buffs, the Lodge can arrange a fishing package including a one-day float on the North Fork of the Flathead. White water rafting can also be arranged.

Only eight miles from the fabulous ski area of Big Mountain, and with transportation provided by the Lodge, it becomes a base for many other activities during the winter months.

Golf is played at the 27-hole Whitefish Lake Golf Club. The Woods/Mountain nines reach out for a total of 6,548/6,322/5,593 yards with a par of 72/73. The Mountain/Lake combination weighs in at 6,458/6,200/5,489 yards, also parring at 72/73, while the Woods/Lake plays 6,460/6,302/5,590 yards and pars at 72. Though the fairways are not particularly narrow or tight, these layouts are tree-lined and bring water

into play on a total of six holes.

The course and pro shop (including a small restaurant) are directly across the road from The Grouse Mountain Lodge. The PGA Head Professional is Mike Dowaliby.

RATES (EP) Rooms: $95. Loft-kitchenette units: $125. Deluxe suites: $160. Green fees: $26, carts $20. There are golf packages available. Rates are for May 30-September 7th.

ARRIVAL Air: Glacier International (20 minutes with pickup by Lodge). Car: one mile west of Whitefish on Highway 93W.

MARINA CAY RESORT
P.O. Box 663, Bigfork, MT 59911; (406) 837-5861; (800) 433-6516

As far as natural beauty is concerned, the Flathead Lake area has few equals in the United States. Marina Cay offers nicely appointed vacation mini/suites with wet bars, or condominium suites including fully-equipped kitchens. They are a far cry from the traditional "rustic" lakeside retreats. The condominium suites, ranging from one to three bedrooms, have been professionally decorated and are fully-equipped for housekeeping. There are also laundry facilities available. The resort is able to handle group functions of up to 200.

A few steps from your lodging is Quincys, offering a smorgasbord of amenities: the lounge, restaurant, swimming pool and, nearby, the marina. The "Village" (a short walk away), has a variety of shops, galleries, and restaurants. With excellent service and food, the Big Fork Inn is a must. A quaint restaurant, ensconced in an old bank building, is the Showthyme.

The resort property is on Bigfork Bay, a delightful and picturesque inlet of scenic Flathead Lake, reputedly the largest fresh water lake west of the Mississippi. I understand the fishing is something else here. During the summer months, all types of water sports are supported by the resort's full-service marina. Boating activities range from water skiing and windsurfing, to sunset cruises. In addition trips on the *Questa,* a world-class 51-foot racing sloop, can be arranged.

During the winter months

some of the best downhill skiing to be found anywhere is on nearby Big Mountain. There are also many miles of cross-country ski trails.

Less than two miles away is the Eagle Bend Golf Club. Designed by William Hull & Associates this beautifully manicured layout plays 6,758/6,237/5,398 yards and pars at 72. A well-trapped layout, with aspen, birch, and pine trees becoming an occasional nuisance, it brings water into play on eight holes.

The new clubhouse, which equals many of the more luxurious private club layouts, has an excellent restaurant, lounge, and pro shop.

RATES (EP) Mini-Suites: (bedroom and sitting room) $90. 1-bedroom condo/suite: $160. Green fees: $38, carts $25. Rates are mid-July to late August.

ARRIVAL Air: Kalispell (15 miles). Car: U. S. 93 south to the intersection of State Road 82. Turn east to Bigfork.

MEADOW LAKE GOLF & SKI RESORT
1415 Tamarack Lane, Columbia Falls, MT 59912; (406) 892-

7601; (800) 321-4653

Meadow Lake Resort, a few miles northwest of Columbia Falls, is about 50 miles south of the Canadian border. You could easily get carried away attempting to describe the magnificent beauty of this area – mountains, meadows, valleys of waving grass as far as your eyes can see, wildlife in the form of birds, elk, bear, moose, and deer. And I don't mean one or two, but rather a profusion of each species. This is one of the few places in the world where it is possible to get your golf cart bashed by a moose.

The resort is on 330 acres within Flathead Valley. There are 40 one- and two-bedroom condominiums as well as villa homes – all of which border Meadow Lake's first and 18th fairways. These accommodations are fully-equipped for housekeeping and feature such amenities as a wood burning fireplace, all-electric kitchen, dishwasher, microwave oven, and washer/dryer. A few extras include a barbecue, blender, toaster oven, a TV in both the living room and the master bedroom, along with a VCR. Should you choose not to cook for yourself, try Tracy's Restaurant and Lounge.

Open year-round, the resort offers a variety of activities: tennis, an outdoor heated swimming pool and Jacuzzi (even though it is heated 12 months a year, remember you have to get out). In addition there is excellent trout fishing on the Meadow's private lake and horseback riding five miles away. During winter you can add cross-country skiing, ice skating, and daily transportation to one of the finest downhill ski areas in the country – nearby Big Mountain.

Golf is played on the Meadow Lake Golf Course. The first nine was completed in 1974 while the second nine came into play in 1986. With four tee settings, it measures 6,574/6/321/5,890/5,488 yards with a par of 71/72. Surrounded by towering pines, well-trapped, with water coming into contention on seven holes and with gently rolling terrain, it is one beautiful layout. Early in the morning, it is not at all unusual to see elk, moose, or deer. The golf course and pro shop are under the supervision of PGA professional Kyle Long. For tee times call (406) 892-2111.

RATES (EP) 1-bedroom condo: $145. 2-bedroom, 2-bath unit: $175.   Fairway   Villas:

$175/$250. Green fees: $30, carts $22. Golf package: 3 nights/3 days (includes Fairway Condo accommodations, 3 rounds of golf – does not include cart), $501/$882 per couple. Rates quoted are for mid-June through Labor Day.

***ARRIVAL** Air: Kalispell Glacier Park Airport (7 miles). Car: travel north on Highway 2 to the intersection of Highway 40, turn east to Meadow Lake Blvd. Travel north for one mile.*

Nevada

1. Hyatt Regency Lake Tahoe
   Incline Village
   The Ridge Tahoe
2. Peppermill Resort Hotel
   & Casino
3. Desert Inn Hotel & Casino
   Dunes Hotel Casino & CC
   Showboat Hotel & CC

DESERT INN HOTEL & CASINO
3145 Las Vegas Boulevard South, Las Vegas, NV 89109; (702) 733-4444; (800) 634-6906

It is awfully tough to keep your mind on golf in Las Vegas. While you may be losing the farm on the course, your mind keeps reverting to all that action going on back in the casinos, where you could well be winning a newer and bigger farm.

The Desert Inn is a high-rise structure offering some of the finest cuisine to be found in the area: La Promenade off the lobby, the Monte Carlo Room for French gourmet dining, Portofino, featuring Northern Italian fare, and the lavish Crystal Room, presenting some of the top names in show business. A recent addition is Ho Wan, with Chinese Mandarin, Szechuan, and Cantonese cuisine. There is also the grill room at the country club.

The resort has recently undergone a multi-million-dollar renovation and some rooms are now equipped with Hydrowhirl baths and wet bars. The meeting facilities have a capacity for groups from 10 to over 900.

In addition to five lighted tennis courts there is an Olympic-size swimming pool and 10 outdoor Hydrowhirl pools. A health spa, completed in 1985, added a new dimension to the Inn. It is some 16,000 square feet, with men's and women's facilities including a gym, hydrotherapy and thermotherapy pools, herbal wraps, massage, and five additional tennis courts.

Golf is available on the resort's own course. It is, by the way, the home of the Las Vegas Panasonic and the Las Vegas Senior Classic. Stretching out a rather awesome 7,111/6,633/5,809 yards, it pars at 72. The greens, which are large (many rebuilt and improved), are well guarded by bunkers. Tree-lined fairways and water coming into play on six holes combine to produce a lush and beautiful desert layout.

The John Jacobs' Practical Golf School is available at this resort. Using personalized teaching methods, and under the direction of PGA and LPGA teaching professionals, it is worth looking into. For details (and lower scores), call: (800) 472-5007.

RATES (EP) Rooms: $90/ $145. Suites: $250/$375. Green fees: $75/$125, including cart. Due to the extreme summer heat in this area, golf is best played in the spring or fall.

ARRIVAL Air: Las Vegas (10 minutes from the airport).

DUNES HOTEL CASINO & COUNTRY CLUB

3650 Las Vegas Boulevard South, Las Vegas, NV 89109; (702) 737-4110; (800) 243-8637

I am not sure why the resorts in Las Vegas keep building multi-storied hotels when they have millions of acres of desert to work with, but they do. The Dunes is another one. It happens to be, however, one of the best we have seen, providing enough eating places to accommodate a medium-sized city. Accommodations consist of 1,200 guest rooms divided between the twin towers and the remodeled Garden Rooms.

The Top of the Dunes offers dining, entertainment, and dancing. Other restaurants include: the Dome of The Sea, for a selection of seafoods; the Chinese Kitchen, serving Cantonese dishes; the Terrace Buffet; the Sultan's Table; and the Dunes Casino Theater, presenting lavish shows nightly.

At present there are five tennis courts (two lighted), a health club and Solaria (facilities for men and women). On the 24th floor, it has a whirlpool, gym, steam, sauna, and massage facilities.

The Dunes Golf Course, parring at 72, shows a massive 7,240/6,571/5,982 yards. While flat, it does provide more than its share of surprises with water, trees and bunkers. The course is supported by a full-line pro shop and clubhouse.

RATES (EP) Rooms: $59/$79. Suites: $130/$900. Green fees: $60/$72, including cart and club storage. Due to summer heat, the best time for golf is spring and fall.

ARRIVAL Air: Las Vegas (10 minutes).

HYATT REGENCY LAKE TAHOE
Country Club Dr. & Lakeshore Rd., Incline Village, NV 89450; (702) 831-1111; (800) 233-1234

The High Sierras with their towering pines are the setting for this beautiful hotel. There are 460 guest rooms and suites. Some of the suites are equipped with fireplaces.

The resort offers many possible activities: water skiing, boating, and use of the beach (no swimming, unless you have polar bear blood, as Lake Tahoe is deep and very cold), three tennis courts (a total of 42 nearby), an indoor health

spa, an outdoor heated pool and, not far away, horseback riding.

Dining choices include Hugo's Rotisserie, the Sierra Cafe, and Ciao Mein (believe it or not Ciao's specializes in Italian cuisine). The Hyatt Lake Casino is open 24 hours – after all this is Nevada.

Golf can be played on the two Robert Trent Jones courses at Incline Village. For a more complete description of these courses, refer to "Incline Village" below.

RATES (EP) Rooms: $199/ $239. Concierge level: $279. Suites: 1 bedroom $450/$650. Green fees: $85, including cart. Executive course: $50, including cart.

ARRIVAL Air: Reno. Car: U.S. 395, south of Reno, turn off southwest on Highway 431.

INCLINE VILLAGE
c/o B.R.A.T Reality Co, P.O. Box 7107' Incline Village, NV 89450; (702) 831-3318; (800) 468-2463 Ext BRAT

Established in 1960 on the north shores of Lake Tahoe and only 39 miles from Reno, Incline Village has a number of homes, condominiums and several casino/hotel complexes. The area not only has outstanding beauty and clear mountain air, but offers a variety of activities: horseback riding, backpacking, tennis, and the full gamut of water sports on Lake Tahoe. A word of warning: this is one extremely cold lake.

There are two courses near Incline Village which are well worth playing. Surprisingly enough, one is an executive par-58, 3,513/3,002-yard course. But it is absolutely not a pushover. Negotiating rugged terrain, this Robert Trent Jones design has embarrassed some fine golfers looking for an easy conquest. It has, in fact, been referred to by more than one golfer as a "little stinker." The Championship golf course, also a Jones design, plays 6,910/6,446/5,350 yards and pars at 72. With mean fairway traps, a stream seemingly without a home, ponds, and towering pines, this is a fun but difficult layout.

Since there are so many different choices of accommodations it is not possible to quote exact rates. One-bedroom condos range from $125 to $225. Contact the above address for reservations. If using the toll-free

number you must ask for the B.R.A.T. Realty Company extension. Green fees: Incline Championship Course, $75, including cart; Executive Course, $40, including cart.

ARRIVAL Air: Reno. Car: U.S. 395, south of Reno, turn off southwest on Highway 431.

PEPPERMILL RESORT HOTEL & CASINO
P.O. Box 360, Mesquite, NV 89024; (702) 346-5232; (800) 621-0187

Some 80 miles northeast of Las Vegas, the resort is quite close to the Utah, Arizona, Nevada borders and 75 miles to Zion, without question one of the most spectacularly scenic national parks in the country.

Should you perceive this as a "backwoods" type of resort, think again. With 728 guest rooms, including suites, surrounded by lush landscaping, six swimming pools, three spas, four restaurants, and a large casino – it is obviously much more.

Dining options consist of the Peppermill Steak House, the Coffee Shop, and the Paradise Buffet. Amenities of the Arvada Ranch are also available to guests of the hotel. A special "cowboy" breakfast is available or try an evening hayride, culminating in a steak fry. There is also horseback riding and a gun club offering skeet and trap shooting.

A Health Club & Spa offers treadmills, aerobicycles, and Nautilus stations. Of course there is always the casino. Functioning 24 hours a day, this 22,000-square-foot operation has every type of gambling action you could wish for. Craps, live poker, 21, roulette, keno, and over 700 "Reel Slot" machines await your deep pockets.

When the night is over, should you have any money or energy left, you might consider golf. Located a bit over three miles from the resort, the Peppermill Golf Course was designed by William Hull. With 26 acres of lakes, several large and deep bunkers, this layout plays 7,022/6,284/5,162 yards and pars at 72. Water comes into the picture on eight holes. While the front side is open and relatively flat, the second nine is a canyon layout with some definite elevation changes coming into play. An interesting note: while the course is just a bit over 3 miles

from the resort, it is in the state of Arizona. The clubhouse and pro shop are under the supervision of Head Golf Professional Jim Hunter, PGA.

RATES (EP) Rooms: $48 / $65. Suites: $72 / $150. Green fees: $35 / $45, including cart. Golf package: 2 nights / 2 days (includes lodging, 2 rounds of golf with cart, club storage), $308 per couple. These package plans change with the season.

ARRIVAL Air: Las Vegas (80 miles). Private aircraft: Mesquite (paved runway). Car: from Las Vegas travel north on I-15 (about 1 1 / 2 hours), exit at the first Mesquite / Bunkerville exit (120). You have arrived.

THE RIDGE TAHOE
P.O. Box 5790, Stateline, NV 89449; (702) 588-3553

Accommodations at the Ridge Tahoe consist of suites set up to handle from two to six people. They have a fireplace, wet bar, stereo/television center, fully-equipped kitchen, and gas barbecue on the patio deck. The "Five Star Award" Ridge Club is the centerpiece for The Ridge Tahoe. Staffed with health and fitness professionals, it is supported by the latest in equipment. While this is basically a time-share operation, there are rentals available.

Swimming in the indoor/outdoor pool, racquetball, aerobics, steam and sauna rooms, tennis indoor or out, are some of the activities available. Sailing and fishing in Lake Tahoe during the summer as well as skiing, tobogganing, and sleigh rides in the winter, are also possible here.

If you prefer dining out, there is the Ridge Tahoe Restaurant and the piano lounge, or you can visit Stateline, six miles away, for an evening of casino action. The Ridge is also well set up to handle group meetings or conventions.

Golf can be played on the Edgewood Lake Tahoe Golf Course. This beautiful layout, with towering pines and more water than you might like, plays at 7,725 yards from the gold, masochist tees. From the tee settings used by earthlings the yardage is 7,030/6,444/5,667 with a par of 72/73. It can sometimes be a bit difficult to secure desirable tee times. There are, however, several other courses in the area.

RATES (EP) Hotel room: $125. Studio: $140. 1-bedroom suite:

$195. 2-bedroom suites: $285. Green fees: $75, including cart. Golf packages are available.

ARRIVAL Air: Reno International (65 miles) or Lake Tahoe Airport (11 miles). Car: from Stateline take Highway 50 to Kingsbury Grade. Turn right (east) and travel 3 miles to Tramway. Take Tramway heading south to Quaking Aspen Lane. Turn left onto Quaking Aspen Lane, which will take you to the entrance gates of Ridge Tahoe.

SHOWBOAT HOTEL & COUNTRY CLUB

2800 East Fremont Street, Las Vegas, NV 89104; (702) 385-9123; (800) 826-2800

The Showboat is a large hotel complex with 500 rooms, a meeting capacity from 25 to over 3,000 people and a 106-lane bowling facility (the largest of its type in the U.S.). It also has casino gambling, and professional boxing and wrestling events held in the 45,000-square-foot arena, with a seating capacity of 4,500. The various dining areas and the coffee shop offer a wide selection of dishes ranging from foreign to American cuisine.

The Desert Rose Golf course,

about two miles away, is available to guests. Playing 6,511/6,135/5,458 yards, it pars at 71. For tee times call (702) 431-4653.

RATES   (EP)   Rooms: $45/$55/$65 per couple. Suites: $110/$165.

ARRIVAL Air: Las Vegas.

New Mexico

1. Rio Rancho Inn
2. Paradise Hills Golf Club
3. Angle Fire
4. Inn of the Mountain Gods

ANGEL FIRE
P.O. Drawer B, Angel Fire, NM 87710; (505) 377-6401; (800) 633-7463

Moreno Valley, almost 35 miles long, and 8,000 feet above sea level, is the home of two magnificent lakes: Eagle Nest and Monte Verde Lake, the location of the 22,000-acre Angel Fire resort. Lodgings are available at the 157-room Legend Hotel. The older Starfire Lodge has been converted to a time-share. There are also fully-equipped condominiums (approximately 200), with living room and kitchen. The resort can host meeting groups of up to 250 people.

A word of warning: while the days are bright and warm, the evenings can get cool. Bring jackets or sweaters.

Aside from golf there is much to do here: tennis, swimming (indoor pool), sailing or paddleboating, trout fishing and horseback riding. If you have never visited Taos (26 miles away), by all means make the effort. It is enchanting.

Golf is served up on the resort's own layout of 6,624/6,349/ 5,356 yards, parring at 72. This course introduces you to water on 10 holes, hilly terrain, and trees. And then more trees. Should you be an early morning addict, you might well run across the added distraction of elk watching your swing. Keep in mind that, at 8,000 feet you have not gotten better, the ball just flies farther. If you get too excited about your game, the resident professional, Chris Stewart, will bring you back to reality.

RATES (EP) Lodge rooms: $60. Condominiums: $70.

Green fees: $35, carts $20. Golf packages are available. Rates are for summer season July-September.

ARRIVAL Air: Albuquerque (150 miles). Private aircraft: Angel Fire 8,900-foot paved runway. Car: Route 64 to New Mexico State Highway 434.

PARADISE HILLS GOLF CLUB
10035 Country Club Lane NW, Albuquerque, NM 87114; (505) 898-0960

This is a small 16-room lodge six miles northwest of Albuquerque. As a guest you are considered a "Guest Member" of the beautiful Paradise Hills Country Club. The clubhouse provides a dining room open for breakfast and lunch, as well as meeting/conference rooms.

Golf is played on the Paradise Hills Course. Parring at 72/74, it stretches out 6,895/6,629/ 6,098 yards. There is a pro shop and a professional, Sean Carcarft and staff.

RATES (EP) Lodge: $50/$56. Green fees: $22, carts $20. Golf packages are available.

ARRIVAL Air: Albuquerque.

Car: I-40 west to Route 448 (Coors Road), go north and follow signs.

INN OF THE MOUNTAIN GODS
P.O. Box 269, Mescalero, NM 88340; (505) 257-5141; (800) 545-9011

This Mescalero Indian Reservation was established in 1873 in a remote section of south-central New Mexico. The resort itself was the dream of Tribal Chief Wendell Chino, who chose the site so that it viewed the sacred Indian grounds. After many years of political and administrative maneuvering, in 1975 The Inn of The Mountain Gods became a reality. The primary objective of the Mescalero Apache Tribe was that the resort function as a training ground and job center for their people.

The original rooms and suites (134 in number) are spacious and afford sweeping views of the lakes and mountains. A five-story complex with an additional 116 rooms was opened in 1982.

In the evening, a special charm can be found in the three restaurants and four cocktail lounges, providing dancing, entertainment, and excellent food. The Inn can handle seminars and meeting groups of up to 800 in a large conference center by the golf course.

Recreational opportunities include: hunting mule deer and elk, trap and skeet shooting, fishing, archery, bicycling, and canoeing. There is also tennis available on two indoor and six outdoor courts with a resident professional. There is no better way to experience the beauty of this area than on horseback. Trail horses are provided for all ages and riding abilities.

A few years back the Tribe purchased Ski Apache Ski Area, 17 miles away. It has become one of the most popular winter sports centers in New Mexico. This ski complex lies entirely within the 460,000-acre reservation, as does the Inn of the Mountain Gods. It offers eight ski lifts, five triple chairs, a four-passenger gondola, 25 miles of ski trails, and the services of 100 certified ski instructors. Transportation is provided from the Inn to the ski area.

The Ted Robinson-designed golf course is nestled among the pines. Due to the terrain, many of the holes have elevated tees or greens and most enjoy a panoramic view of the Sierra Blanca Mountains. The 18th hole calls for a well placed shot across Lake Mescalero, while the 10th requires a shot to an island and then to the green. Parring at 72, it stretches out a substantial 6,834/6,478/5,478 yards. Playing at an elevation of 7,200 feet, it is one heck of a course. The clubhouse, under the direction of the Head Professional Daniel Nunez, includes a restaurant, a 19th watering hole, and men's and women's locker rooms.

RATES *(EP) Rooms: $115. Suites: $120/$130. Green fees: $35, carts $22. Golf package: 3 nights/3 days and available on weekdays only (includes lodging, 3 rounds of golf with cart, breakfast each day, all taxes), $586 per couple.*

ARRIVAL *Air: El Paso (124 miles); Alamagordo (45 miles). Private & commercial aircraft: Sierra Blanca Regional Airport (21 miles). Car: 3 1/2 miles out of Ruidoso.*

RIO RANCHO INN
1465 Rio Rancho Drive, Rio Ranch, NM 87124; (505) 892-1700; (800) 528-1234

Some of the 80 motel-type rooms have kitchenettes. If you prefer condominium accommodations, equipped for housekeeping, call the Country Club Villas in New Mexico at (505) 892-9200 or (800) 545-8316.

There is dining in the Aspen Room, as well as a lounge offering nightly dancing. The resort, by the way, has meeting rooms for groups from 20 to 200.

Activities open to guests include: swimming in the Inn's large pool; a visit to the nearby Sandia Mountains to fish, hunt, or picnic; or perhaps a visit to Old Albuquerque.

While there is no course at the Rancho, they do provide playing privileges for their guests at the Rio Rancho Country Club. Less than a mile away, it reaches out a healthy 7,045/6,408/5,593 yards and pars at 72. To be sure you stay awake, there are lakes on six holes, along with cottonwoods, piñon, and juniper trees bordering the fairways.

In addition to the pro shop the clubhouse has six lighted tennis courts, a pool, lounge, and dining room.

RATES *(EP) Inn: $40/$62.*

Kitchenette: $65. Green fees: $20, carts $18.

ARRIVAL *Air: Albuquerque. Car: located on New Mexico Route 528 (Rio Rancho Drive) just north of Rio Rancho City.*

Oklahoma

1. Shangri-La
2. Western Hills Guest Ranch
3. Roman Nose State Park
4. Arrowhead Resort & Hotel
   Fountainhead Resort
5. Quartz Mountain State Park
6. Lake Murray State Park
7. Lake Texoma State Park
8. Falconhead Ranch & CC

ARROWHEAD RESORT & HOTEL
HC 67 Box 5, Canadian, OK 74425; (918) 339-2711; (800) 422-2711

A few years ago this entire property was a part of the Oklahoma State Park system. The golf course and park area still are, but the resort, including the Lodge and cottages, are owned and managed by the Choctaw Indian nation. The Lodge with its 96 guest rooms and 40 cottages is set up to handle meeting groups of up to 200 people. They also have a restaurant and lounge.

The location on the shores of Lake Eufaula provides many activities. There is tennis on two courts, horseback riding, an outdoor swimming pool, ping pong, baseball, hiking, their own marina and, of course, fishing.

Golf is played on the 18-hole park course. Reaching out 6,741/6,325/5,342 yards, it pars at 72/75.

RATES (EP) Lodge rooms: $50/$55. Parlor suites: 1 bedroom $100. Treehouse (2 bedrooms, kitchen): $90. Green fees: $12, carts $14.

ARRIVAL Air: Tulsa (75 miles). Private Aircraft: paved landing strip on property. Car: 18 miles south of I-40 on U.S. 69.

FALCONHEAD RESORT & COUNTRY CLUB
P.O. Box 206, Burneyville, OK 73430; (405) 276-9411; (800) 535-8234

Falconhead, located in Red River Valley, is a large residential resort/community covering some 3,800 acres. While lodgings and a restaurant are available in the Falcon Inn, the focal point of the resort is the plush Country Club.

Tennis on four lighted courts, two swimming pools, and golf are a few of the activities possible. Beautiful Lake Falcon adds another dimension to the ranch, providing all types of water sports.

Golf is played at the Falconhead Country Club. Parring at 72/71, it measures 6,448/5,992/5,350 yards. While the front nine is flat, the back side brings trees, as well as some rolling terrain, into play. Falcon Lake also gets into the act on four holes. There is a resident professional available and a full-service pro shop, driving range, and locker rooms.

RATES (EP) Falcon Inn: $50. Green fees: $15/$20, carts $16. Golf package: 2 nights/3 days (includes 3 days golf with cart, 2 breakfasts, and 3 lunches), $259 per couple.

ARRIVAL Air: Dallas (100 miles). Oklahoma City (125 miles). Car: I-35, 18 miles south of Ardmore exit to Route 32 at Marrietta, then 13 miles west.

FOUNTAINHEAD RESORT

HC 70 Box 453, Checotah, OK 74426; (918) 689-9173; (800) 345-6343

Although the general area, including the golf course and the park, is still operated by the State Parks system the resort hotel is now privately owned. A five-story structure, it offers accommodations in 202 rooms and suites, plus 22 cottages. The Terrace Room has dining and dancing with entertainment available in the lounge. Fountainhead can accommodate meeting groups of up to 600 and has many breakout rooms capable of handling groups from 20 to 270 classroom-style.

The resort's location on the shores of Lake Eufaula, with over 600 miles of shore line, opens up the opportunity for a variety of water sports: boating, fishing, water skiing and, of course, swimming. There is also a swimming pool, tennis, horseback riding, archery, and golf.

Golf is played on the Fountainhead State Park course. With a par of 72/74, it reaches out 6,887/6,489/6,102 yards. That yardage of 6,102 is more than a fair reach for the ladies.

RATES (EP) Parkside rooms: $75. Lake/Poolside: $85. Cottages: $85. Treehouses: $100/$120. Green fees: $11, carts $15.

ARRIVAL Air: Tulsa (80 miles). Private aircraft: adjacent to the property (a 3,000-foot paved runway). Car: 7 miles south of I-40 on Highway 150 and on Lake Eufaula.

SHANGRI-LA RESORT

Route 3, Afton, OK 74331; (918) 257-4204; (800) 331-4060

Shangri-La Resort has recently undergone a complete overhaul and renovation. Accommodations are in the Main Lodge (126 rooms), the Golden Oaks (144 rooms), and the Vista Towers, with 66 two-bedroom suites. They also have a large convention and meeting capacity and can handle groups of up to 2,000. There are three dining rooms, several snack and lunch bars, entertainment and dancing nightly.

There are indoor and outdoor swimming pools, the sandy beach, four indoor and four outdoor tennis courts with a professional staff to assist, four bowling lanes, a health spa, racquetball courts, water skiing, and fishing. The Grand Lake o' the Cherokees, with its 1,300 miles of shoreline, provides an unlimited variety of water activities. As a matter of fact, the river boat *Cherokee Queen* will stop here upon request. You can arrange for a two-hour lake tour. The resort also has a supervised program for the younger set.

Golf can be played on the Blue (east course), stretching out 6,972/6,435/5,975 yards and parring at 72/73. This layout gives you rolling terrain and trees, with each green well trapped.

The Gold (west course) is a bit more modest, playing 5,932/5,431/5,109/4,517 yards and parring at 70/71. While fairly open, with few trees, it does have its share of water and is well bunkered. The golf shop, under the direction of Head Professional Rick Reed, is one of the better ones to be found.

RATES (EP) Main Lodge: $105/$120. Golden Oaks: $120/$150. Vista Towers: $120/$160. Shangri-La Estates 1-bedroom condo: $190. Green fees: $45/$65, including cart. Golf package: 2 nights/3 days (includes lodging in main lodge, 3 days green fees, cart, club storage), $450/$498 per couple. Rates quoted are for April-October.

ARRIVAL Air: Tulsa (65 miles). Car: I-44, take Afton exit to U.S. 59, southeast to Highway 125, then south 11 miles.

OKLAHOMA'S STATE PARKS

500 Will Rogers Building, Oklahoma City, OK 73105; (405) 521-2464; (800) 654-8240

Oklahoma has five resort parks spread throughout the state. They all provide about the same amenities: outstanding accommodations, archery, bicycling, boating, a golf course, horseback riding, kiddie playground, swimming pool, tennis, water skiing (not available at Roman Nose) and a private airstrip (not available at Roman Nose or Quartz Mountain).

Each resort has a dining room and offers a golf package. These state-operated resorts are not only delightful, but they represent one of the best values for a vacation buck we have seen anywhere in the country.

LAKE MURRAY STATE PARK RESORT

The Lodge, Ardmore, OK 73402; (405) 223-6600; (800) 654-8240

The resort is in a 12,500-acre state park on 5,728-acre Lake Murray. The country-style Inn has rooms and suites with either a view of the park or of the lake. In addition to the 54 rooms at the Inn there are 88 cottages with a capacity of from two to four people. These units have kitchenettes, fireplaces, and color television. There are also 240 RV camping sites and a grocery store.

For dining there is the Quilts restaurant or the Parlor for drinks and lighter fare. Murray can handle meeting groups of up to 300 banquet- or 220 classroom-style. They have five meeting rooms with a total of almost 5,500 feet of space.

Along with tennis (lighted courts) and hiking, there is an outdoor swimming pool, and a marina, opening up all manner of water activities including fishing, paddle boating, sailing, and houseboat rentals. They also have riding stables, offering hay rides and trail rides.

The golf course is now an 18-hole layout. It is supported by a golf shop and has a resident professional.

RATES *(EP) Parkside: $54. Lake/Poolside: $59. Cottages: $45/$95. Suites $100/$150. Green fees: $8, carts $14.*

ARRIVAL *Two miles east of I-35 and seven miles south of Ardmore on Lake Murray.*

LAKE TEXOMA STATE PARK RESORT

The Lodge, Durant, OK 74701; (405) 564-2311; (800) 654-8240

Texoma, comprising 2,000 acres, is on huge (93,000-acre) Lake Texoma. Accommodations are in 97 rooms including lodge, poolside, cabana suites, and terrace rooms. There are also 67 one- and two-bedroom cottages. Texoma boast some of the best meeting facilities in the state. With their large ballroom they can handle groups of up to 500 theater-style.

For entertainment there is the Waterfront Lounge along with the Gallery Restaurant and a snack bar at the swimming pool.

A fitness center, lighted tennis

courts, a marina offering all types of water sports, as well as horseback riding are some of the activities. Should you enjoy fishing this is the place, with Lake Texoma offering some of the best year-round fishing to be found anywhere.

The golf course at Texoma State Park is an 18-hole, par-71/74, playing to a yardage of 6,128/5,868/5,145.

RATES (EP) Parkside: $54. Lake/Poolside: $61. Cabana Suites: $95. Cottages: $60. Green fees: $8, carts $14.

ARRIVAL On U.S. 70, 13 miles west of Durant and on Lake Texoma

QUARTZ MOUNTAIN STATE PARK RESORT
The Lodge, Lake Altus-Lugert, OK 73522; (405) 563-2424; (800) 654-8240

Overlooking Lake Altus-Lugert, the resort has 45 rooms in the two-story lodge, plus 16 cottages. The lodge is also where the dining room and meeting facilities are located.

There are tennis courts, indoor and outdoor swimming pools, a

game room, a swimming beach, and water sports including water skiing, boating, fishing, paddle boats, canoes, and yak boards.

The golf course is now 18 holes, with par 69.

RATES   Parkside: $48. Lake/Poolside: $55. Cottages: $65. Suites $100. Green fees $8, carts $14.

ARRIVAL Car: 141 miles west of Oklahoma City, 20 miles north of Altus on Highway 44 and 44A.

ROMAN NOSE STATE PARK RESORT
The Lodge, Watonga, OK 73772; (405) 623-7281; (800) 654-8240

This area, rich in history, was once a campground for of the Cheyenne Indian Tribe. Overlooking two small lakes, the Lodge now has 47 guest rooms and 10 cottages, the latter equipped with kitchenettes. There are also three large meeting rooms plus a dining room.

Among the activities are tennis, swimming in a natural rock pool, fishing, and boating. The golf course is a nine-hole layout measuring (when played twice) 5,830/5,202 yards with a par of 70/72.

RATES *(EP) Parkside: $54/$57. Cottages: $70/$73. Suites $125/$150. Green fees: $15, carts $15.*

ARRIVAL *Air: Watonga airport. Courtesy transportation to resort can be arranged. Car: Roman Nose is 81 miles northwest of Oklahoma City, 7 miles north of Watonga on Highway 8 and 8A.*

WESTERN HILLS GUEST RANCH RESORT
Box 509, Wagoner, OK 74467; (918) 772-2545; (800) 654-8240

Western Hills is known as "The Gettysburg of the West." A battle waged here long ago ended the Confederate influence in the Indian territory. Southwest, in Muskogee, is the Five Civilized Tribes Museum, housing historical exhibits and artifacts of the Cherokee, Chickasaw, Choctaw, Creek, and Seminole Indians.

The resort has 101 rooms, 12 cabanas, 54 cottages, deluxe suites, and a western style dining room. All rooms are air-conditioned and have color TV.

The resort also has nine meeting rooms comprising over 10,000 feet of space.

There is a trained director for the planned children's programs, offering various crafts, puppet shows, and water games.

Two lighted tennis courts, an outdoor swimming pool, along with sailboats, power boats, and paddle boats are available. Although there is a rental fee for boats, they provide free ramp and docking facilities for private craft. There is also a grocery store on premises.

Golf can be played on an 18-hole course complete with pro shop and clubhouse. Measuring 5,860/5,555 yards, it pars at 70/73.

RATES *(EP) Rooms: $62/$68. Cottages: $58/$63. Suites: $100/$175. Green fees: $8/$10. Carts: $14.*

ARRIVAL *Private aircraft: in the park is a 3,400-foot paved, lighted runway. Car: on Fort Gibson Reservoir, 8 miles east of Wagoner on Highway 51.*

Oregon

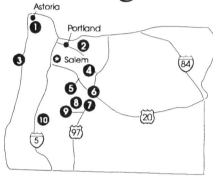

1. Gearhart-by-the-Sea
2. The Resort at the Mountain
3. Salishan Lodge
4. Kah-Nee-Ta
5. Black Butte Ranch
6. Eagle Crest Resort
7. The Riverhouse Inn
8. Inn at the Seventh Mountain
9. Sunriver Resort
10. The Village Green Resort

BLACK BUTTE RANCH
PO Box 8000, Black Butte Ranch, OR 97759; (503) 595-6211; (800) 452-7455

Black Butte has become one of our favorite retreats. It is, in every sense, a "family" resort, set on 1,800 acres of wooded, slightly undulating terrain, and surrounded by the Deschutes National Forest. From the meadow areas the

view of the many surrounding mountain peaks is spectacular.

Accommodations are provided in condominiums as well as many private homes. All are well-equipped for housekeeping. However should you elect to "pass" on the housekeeping, you will find the dining room at the lodge an excellent alternative.

The Ranch has four swimming pools, 16 miles of bicycle paths, horseback riding (Black Butte is a working ranch), tennis on 23 courts, with a separate well-stocked tennis pro shop (there is no charge for tennis), fishing, canoeing, white-water raft trips, and top movies. The fishing, by the way, is barbless fly fishing, hook and release. The kids love it and so do the fish.

Golf is offered on two of the most picturesque golf layouts to be found anywhere. Big Meadow, stretching out 6,870/6,456/5,716 yards, pars at 72. The newer of the two, Glaze Meadows, measures 6,560/6,266/5,616 yards and also pars at 72. As an added distraction (or attraction), it seems that you are looking at one of the many mountain peaks surrounding the ranch on almost every hole. These two courses have as magnificent a setting as any we have seen in this country. Each has its own driving range, putting area, and well-stocked pro shop. Both are operated under the supervision of the Director of Golf, "JD" Mowlds and a friendly staff.

RATES (EP) Rooms: $80. With fireplace: $100. 1-bedroom condo (kitchen / fireplace): $130. 2-bedroom condo: $155. 3 bedrooms: $175. There are also private homes with capacity of 6 people: $125 / $210. Green fees: $42, carts $24.

ARRIVAL Air: Redmond Airport (30 miles). Car: (135 miles from Portland). South on I-5 to Highway 20, then east on 20 (Santiam Pass) 98 miles.

EAGLE CREST RESORT
Cline Falls Road, Redmond, OR 97756; (503) 923-2453; (800) 682-4786

Overlooking two miles of the Deschutes River from a high elevation, the view from this resort is exceptional. Although Eagle Crest has been in operation for several years, it was primarily a resort community. As such, it had no accommodations for outside guests. The completion of the hotel in 1989

opened up a new dimension. In addition to the 76-room Inn, there are also some town-houses available. Along with the existing restaurant in the main clubhouse, future plans are for one in the Inn as well. The resort is capable of handling modest-size meeting groups of up to 75 theater-style.

A few of the various activities include: tennis (private and group lessons), a swimming pool, use of the Equestrian Center, and miles of hiking and jogging trails. Fishing in the Deschutes river is reputed to be excellent.

During the winter months this place really comes into its own as it sits near some of the finest skiing in Oregon. They offer ski packages including lift tickets and transportation to and from Mt. Bachelor.

The Eagle Crest Golf Club reaches out a respectable 6,673/6,292/5,395 yards and pars at 72. Your initial view of this course tells you it is open and should not be too difficult. These two assumptions are incorrect. It is neither. While the first hole will lull you, the second and third will bring you back to a fully alert status. The greens throughout the course are multi-level and difficult. All in all it is an entertaining layout but also one that requires your full attention. A nice change of pace is the fact that water comes into the picture on only four holes.

The newest addition, the Ridge Golf Course, is directly across the road from the resort entrance. Opening in mid-1993, it was designed by John Thronson. Reaching out an awesome 7,011/6,533/5,912/5,087 yards, it pars at 72. With elevated tees, undulating terrain and several large lakes, it will challenge you.

RATES Inn Rooms: $67/$80. 1-bedroom suite: $106/$133. 2-bedroom suite: up to 6 people, $163/$195. Green fees: $36, carts $24.

ARRIVAL Air: Redmond Airport (6 miles). Car: take Highway 126 west from Redmond, 5 miles, then left on Cline Falls Road.

GEARHART BY-THE-SEA
PO Box C, Gearhart, OR 97138; (503) 738-8331; (800) 547-0115

Situated on the northern Oregon coast only 15 miles south of the mouth of the Columbia River, these condominium apartments vary in size and floor plan, each having a spacious living room, fireplace, dining area, and fully-equipped kitchen.

There are two indoor swimming pools plus a therapy pool. Right in front of the resort is what may be the best razor-clamming beach in all of Oregon, with charter boat fishing available only nine miles north.

The Gearhart Golf Links is directly across the road. An 18-hole layout, it plays 6,089/5,882 yards, with a par of 72/74.

RATES (EP) Suites: 1 bedroom $98/$116; 2 bedrooms $118/$152. Green fees: $20, carts $20.

ARRIVAL Air: Astoria. Car: from Portland, west on Highway 26 (80 miles) to Highway 101. North 7 miles to Seaside, then 3 miles further.

THE INN OF THE SEVENTH MOUNTAIN
18575 Century Drive, Bend, OR 97702; (503) 382-8711; (800) 452-6810

While the resort, seven miles west of the city of Bend, has been in operation for some time, the golf course is quite new. There are several types of accommodations available: bedrooms, "Fireside studios," one-, two-, and three-bedroom condominiums, and family condos sleeping up to eight. The studios and condominiums have a fireplace and fully-equipped kitchen or kitchenette. There are washer/dryer units in every other condominium building, along with a convenience grocery store and gas station on property (functional year round). The Inn can host meeting groups of up to 225 classroom-style.

Should you choose not to cook for yourself, there are four alternatives: the Poppy Seed Cafe at the Inn, for all three meals as well as Sunday brunch; El Crab Catcher Restaurant & Lounge, specializing in seafood, prime ribs, and steak, and also the place for evening entertainment; the poolside deli; and, last but not least, the clubhouse restaurant and lounge at the golf village.

Amenities include: seven plexipaved tennis courts, two swimming pools (one with a 65-foot water slide), coed saunas and whirlpools, aerobic and aquatic exercise classes, a roller skating rink, bicycle rentals, horseback riding along with hayrides, whitewater rafting, planned and guided fishing trips, canoe tours on the more serene stretches of the Deschutes River, hiking trails and, of course, golf. They have not forsaken the younger set as you can register children of four to 11 years old in a professionally supervised day camp.

During the winter months skiing is king in this magnificent area. Featuring 54 runs, an elevation of 9,065 feet, powder snow, three Super Express Quads, and a High-speed Summit Chair along with 60 kilometers of cross-country trails, a fabulous lodge and all of the rental equipment and instructors possibly needed, Mt Bachelor (14 miles distant) has it all.

The Seventh Mountain Golf Course, designed by Robert Muir Graves, has a beautiful setting. The use of slightly undulating terrain, multi-level greens and with water on 10 holes has created a challenging course. Measuring 6,911/6,483/5,911/5,070 yards, it pars at 72. The clubhouse and the pro shop are under the supervision of PGA Professional, Walt Porterfield.

RATES (EP) Rooms: $60 / $90. Studio: $104. 1-bedroom condo: $145. Green fees: $38, carts $25.

ARRIVAL Air: Redmond Airport (16 miles north of Bend). Car: going south on Highway 97 turn right onto Division Street. Follow signs to Century Drive (Cascade Lake Highway). Drive about five miles on Century Drive to the resort.

KAH-NEE-TA
Warm Springs, OR 97761; (503) 553-1112; (800) 831-0100

The lodge, owned and operated by the Confederation of Indian Tribes, rises unexpectedly from the side of a bluff. It has a sweeping contemporary design which blends well with the rugged central Oregon landscape. A visit to this resort is like a visit to another culture. And it is delightful.

There are 140 rooms and suites, each with its own private balcony and spectacular view. Meeting space is also available. The village also offers some unique accommodations: namely tee pees! (The

children will never stop talking about the night they spent in an Indian tee pee). Neither will you if you don't bring sleeping bags or cots. The floor is concrete, **without beds.**

Dining here can be an unusual experience. You can enjoy lobster tail, rainbow trout, and salmon, or get carried away with game hen, buffalo, or venison. Kah-Nee-Ta has much to offer for those who enjoy horseback riding. There are also two tennis courts and a huge swimming pool.

The golf course plays 6,288/ 5,418 and pars at 72/73. The resort provides a small pro shop. There is also a professional on hand.

RATES (EP) Rooms: $90. Suites: $119 / $159. Chief suites: $170 / $250. Cottage: 1 bedroom $80; 2 bedrooms $100. Tee Pee: $50 for up to four persons. Green fees: $29, carts $23. Rates are for May-September.

ARRIVAL Air: Redmond (60 miles); Portland (115 miles). Private aircraft: Madras. Car: 11 miles north of Warm Springs, with turn-off signs clearly marked.

Oregon   257

THE RESORT AT THE MOUNTAIN
68010 Fairway, Welches, OR 97067; (503) 622-3101; (800) 669-7666

Accommodations include 160 guest rooms and several two- to three-bedroom condominiums. There is a restaurant (Forest Hills Dining Room) as well as a lounge. The resort has a meeting capacity of 200 classroom- or 500 banquet-style.

If your thing is golf, tennis, hiking, swimming, fishing, or white water rafting you are at the right place. Complimentary tennis can be played on six courts. They also offer a staff-supervised kid haven, with many electronic games. During the winter there is transportation provided to ski slopes nearby.

There are 27 holes to play on these gently rolling alpine meadows. Lakes, streams, and a few towering fir trees spice up the action. Using a crossover system there is the Red/Green combination reaching out 6,394/5,687 yards and parring at 72/74; the Red/Yellow nines play 5,718/5,077 yards with a par of 70/71; the Green/Yellow play 6,006/5,246 yards with a par of 70/71.

RATES   (EP)   Rooms: $85/$173. Condominiums: (kitchen, living room, fireplace), $185/$199. Green fees: $35/$45, cart $24. Golf packages are available.

ARRIVAL Air: Portland. Car: east on I-84 to Wood Village/Gresham exit. 3 miles to Burnside and turn left. Burnside will become Highway 26. Travel 25 miles.

THE RIVERHOUSE RESORT
3075 N. Highway 97, Bend, OR 97701; (503) 389-3111; (800) 547-3928

In the heart of Bend, with the Deschutes River ambling along between the dining areas and the guest rooms, this resort is uniquely situated. While the history of Bend dates back to the early 1800's, 1905 is generally accepted as the date this community of 500 was incorporated. Many things contributed to its growth but the most significant was the development of Mt. Bachelor as a major ski area. The current population estimate of the Bend urban area (an eight-mile radius) is 47,000.

The 208 accommodations range from hotel rooms to luxury suites, some with fireplace, kitchen units, and spas. Many overlook the river. In addition to the normal amenities, the resort features Showtime TV, movie video rentals and, of course, room service is available. The kitchen units have an apartment-size refrigerator, range, dishwasher, and are fully-equipped for housekeeping.

Should you prefer not to cook for yourself, there are three restaurants on property ranging from the Riverhouse Dining Room and the Poolside Cafe to Tito's Mexican Restaurant as well as a cocktail lounge. In addition Bend has a wide selection of other restaurants to choose from. With their six meeting rooms, Riverhouse can handle groups of up to 244 classroom- or 390 theater-style

There are outdoor and indoor swimming pools, two outdoor tennis courts, a sauna, an exercise room, jogging along the river, or trout fishing outside your front door. A short distance away white water rafting trips can be arranged. Trips range from a partial day to a two-day experience. During the winter months there is downhill and cross country skiing at Mt. Bachelor.

Rivers Edge Golf Course (less than 1/4 mile from the resort) was designed by the renowned Robert Muir Graves. Now an 18-hole layout, it plays 6,647/6,428/6,128/5,380 yards and pars at 72/73. Nestled among pine trees, with rock outcroppings, some substantial elevation changes from tee to green, undulating terrain, the Deschutes River making an appearance, and with a few extremely difficult greens, Rivers Edge is a "zinger."

The course is supported by a clubhouse, pro shop, and restaurant. There is also a driving range and putting green.

RATES (EP) Rooms: $49/59. Suites: $55/72. Deluxe suites: $89/$150. Green fees: $22, carts $22. Golf and skiing packages are available during appropriate times of the year.

ARRIVAL Air: Redmond Airport (16 miles). Car: the resort is located on the west side of Highway 97 in Bend, Oregon.

SALISHAN LODGE
Highway 101, Gleneden Beach, OR 97388; (503) 764-2371; (800) 452-2300

This combines the majestic Pacific Ocean and its ever changing moods on one side, and a beautiful golf course on the other.

Accommodations are in 205 guest rooms and suites, some with golf course views, others with a view of the bay. Each is well-appointed, featuring a wood-burning fireplace, private balcony, and individual covered parking. Salishan can accommodate groups of up to 250 classroom- or 300 theater-style in its 14 meeting rooms.

The Dining Room, the Cedar Tree Restaurant, the Sun Room, and the Golf Club Coffee Shop are at your disposal. They are supported by a huge wine cellar. In fact, it has become a tour attraction, offering over 21,000 bottles and some 875 different labels. For a relaxed evening of dancing and entertainment you might consider a visit to the Attic Lounge.

As good as the food is at Salishan, no one really enjoys eating at the same place each evening. For a change of pace and a delightful experience, try the Bay House. It is a couple of miles north of Salishan. Take my word for it – you will find this an eating experience long cherished and remembered. The address is 5911 SW

Highway 101, Lincoln City; phone 996-3222. Make reservations, as the local group has also discovered this place.

Salishan has three indoor lighted tennis courts, an indoor pool, a hydrotherapy pool, and men's and women's exercise rooms. In addition there are several hiking and jogging trails linking the forest and the secluded beach of Salishan Peninsula to the lodge. Inasmuch as you are fronting the Pacific, fishing also becomes an option and can be arranged from Depoe Bay approximately six miles south.

The golf course plays 6,439/ 6,246/5,693 yards with a par of 72 for men and 73 from the ladies' tees. The first nine is tree-lined and tight, while the back side is a links type and more open. Never easy, it can be difficult if the wind kicks up. They have added some potential excitement to the back nine with the addition of some pot bunkers and the planting of European Grass (similar to pampas-grass), near some of the greens. Don't snicker. If you have not had the pleasure of hitting out of this stuff you have a big surprise coming! There is a driving range as well as a practice putting green. The golf course and pro shop are under the direction of Head Professional, Grant Rogers.

RATES *(EP) Rooms: $156. Deluxe South-Golf or North-Bay view: $207. Green fees: $38, cart $26. Rates are for June-October.*

ARRIVAL *Air: Portland. Private aircraft: Siltzer Bay Airport, 3,000-foot paved runway (1/2 mile away). Car: south on I-5 to "Newberg and Ocean Beach" exit. Highway 18 to 3 miles south of Lincoln City limits.*

SUNRIVER RESORT
P.O. Box 3609, Sunriver, OR 97707; (503) 593-1221; (800) 547-3922

Accommodations range from bedrooms and suites in the Lodge to private homes and condominiums. Of course the condominiums and homes include fully-equipped kitchens. Daily maid service is not included in the rates for homes & condos but can be arranged. The resort can handle meeting groups of up to 400 people. The dining facilities include The Provision Co., with a "family" atmosphere, and The Meadows, a more formal setting.

This resort is not only large

(3,300 acres), but also an extremely busy place, with a great many people and children throughout the village and shopping areas. Baby-sitting can also be arranged.

There is a playground area for the small fry, a 28-court tennis complex, 26 miles of paved bike paths, a racquetball club, and riding stables. White water rafting on the Deschutes River, canoe trips, and fishing can also be arranged.

There are two 18-hole golf courses. The older South Course measures 6,940/6,502/6,366/5,827 yards and pars at 72. We found it flat, open, and not interesting. However the North Course, a Robert Trent Jones design, is an excellent layout. Reaching out 6,823/6,208/5,912/5,446 yards, it also pars at 72. Each course, operating under the supervision of the Director of Golf, Tim Berg, has its own golf shop with professionals available. For advance tee times call: (800) 962-1769.

RATES *(EP) Lodge: $110. Suites: $170. Homes or condominiums: $160/$205. Green fees: North Course $50, carts $25; South Course $40, carts $25. Rates are for June-September.*

ARRIVAL Air: Portland (175 miles); Redmond (33 miles). Private aircraft: Sunriver 4,500 feet, paved/lighted. Car: Highway 97 (15 miles south of Bend).

THE VILLAGE GREEN RESORT
725 Row River Drive, Cottage Grove, OR 97424; (503) 942-2491; (800) 343-7666

The setting of the Village Green is most unusual. Adjacent to I-5, approximately 25 minutes south of Eugene, the resort is surrounded by 16 park-like acres. Next to the motel is an R.V. park with a capacity of up to 42 units.

Accommodations consist of 96 rooms including 10 suites. Each features either two double beds or a king-size and is air-conditioned. Each unit also has covered parking. The resort is well-equipped to entertain meeting groups. With four conference rooms and a total of 6,000 square feet of space, they can accommodate up to 200 theater- and 160 banquet-style.

There are two restaurants on property: the Copper Rooster Coffee Shop, open daily for all three meals, and the Cascadia Dining Room for finer dining, open Wednesday through Saturday. There is live entertainment on Friday and Saturday evenings. The dress code throughout the resort is casual. The Cascadia Room also presents a delightful Sunday brunch (10 to 2 PM). As an alternative and a delightful eating experience, we suggest The Covered Bridge Restaurant, 401 Main Street; phone 942-1255.

The resort has two tennis courts, an outdoor heated swimming pool, a whirlpool, an exercise trail, a children's playground, and now a golf course.

Employing two of the finest teaching professionals in the Pacific Northwest – class A PGA Professional Al Mundle, Director of Marketing and Instruction and PGA Professional Jerry Asher (former Head Teaching Professional of the John Jacobs Golf School of Palm Desert, California) – Middlefield has become home to the Mundle/Asher Golf School. They offer a 14-acre driving range equipped with grass tees, practice bunkers, chipping/pitching greens, and a putting green. A real plus: 20 tees of the driving range are covered (rain does occur in Oregon). The school also offers electronic assistance in the form of video playback and swing analysis.

The Middlefield Village Golf Course, reaching out a modest 4,969/4,302 yards and parring at 67, is directly across the road from the Village Green. The course is supported by a golf shop and a snack bar and is under the supervision of the Director of Golf, Jerry Asher and staff. For tee times call (503) 942-8730. Tee times for weekends should be reserved on the preceding Tuesday; weekdays, 24 hours in advance.

RATES *(EP) Rooms: $79/89. Suites: $99/$125. Green fees: $20, carts $20.*

ARRIVAL *Air: Eugene Airport. Private aircraft: Cottage Grove Airport (paved runway). Car: from I-5 take exit 174.*

Texas

APRIL SOUND
Box 253 Highway 105 West, Conroe, TX 77301; (409) 588-1101

On the shores of 21,000-acre Lake Conroe, 50 miles northwest of Houstan, April Sound offers an almost endless variety of water activities.

Accommodations are in villas (hotel-type) with verandas or balconies and one- to three-bedroom townhouses, complete with living room and kitchen. The resort is equipped to handle meeting and conference groups with a banquet-style capacity of 225. The main dining room, the Fernery, overlooks the cove and part of the golf course.

Tennis is served up on 17 courts (four covered and nine lighted). It has its own tennis center, with a mini-restaurant and fully-equipped tennis shop.

The Lakeview Golf Course, parring at 71, reaches out 6,189/5,807/5,3233 yards. Although the course borders on April Sound, water only be-

comes a factor on seven holes. There is also a nine-hole par-three executive layout.

RATES (EP) Villa 1 bedroom: $89/$149. Rates are for February 15-November 15. Green fees: $25/$35, carts $20.

ARRIVAL Air: Houston. Car: from Houston (50 miles) I-45 north, then west on Highway 105 (8 miles).

BARTON CREEK RESORT & COUNTRY CLUB
8212 Barton Club Drive, Austin, TX 78735; (512) 329-4000; (800) 772-7335

The resort's location, 15 minutes from downtown Austin, opens up the opportunity to take in the city's attractions. Opening in September of 1987, the resort was built on 4,000 acres of rolling countryside just west of the capital. There are 147 guest rooms, each with a sitting area and with views of the surrounding countryside and/or the golf course. Three suites are available and five of the rooms have fireplaces.

With a total of 16,000 square feet of space, along with many separate breakout rooms and the latest electronic equipment, they can accommodate up to 200 classroom- or 320 theater-style.

The dining rooms include the Terrace Room, the Tejas Room (in the clubhouse), the Palm Court, and The Gourmet, open for dinner only. There is also The Grille, as well as the 19th Hole for lighter fare.

There is an executive fitness center (spa, steam rooms, sauna, whirlpools, loofah scrubs, herbal wraps, mas-

1. Tanglewood on Texoma
2. Four Seasons Club Resort
3. Rayburn Country
4. Mill Creek Golf & CC
5. Waterwood National
6. Horseshoe Bay CC Resort
7. The Inn on Lake Travis
8. Lakeway Resort & CC
9. Barton Creek Resort & CC
10. Waldon on Lake Conroe
    Del Largo Resort
11. April Sound
12. Woodlands Inn & CC
13. Woodcreek Resort
14. Flying L Guest Ranch
15. Tapatio Springs Resort & CC
16. South Shore Harbour
17. Columbia Lakes
18. Rancho Viejo Resort
    Valley Inn & Country Club

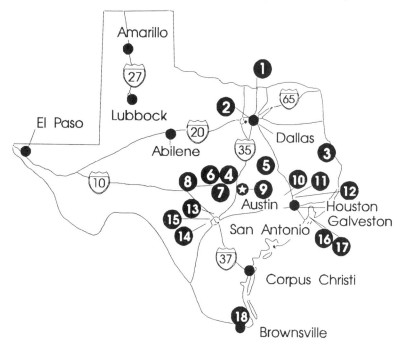

sage, an indoor running track, Lifecyles and Stairmasters). There are also eight lighted tennis courts supported by a tennis shop and professionals to assist, as well as one indoor and two outdoor swimming pools. Some 20 miles away at Lake Travis, you can enjoy water-skiing, boating, and fishing. Water sports are also available at Lake Austin four miles away.

The golf course designed by Ben Crenshaw & Bill Coore, referred to as the Crenshaw Course, reaches out a respectable 6,678/6,066/4,483 yards with a par of 71. Water is a factor on only three holes. However, on the second course, a Fazio design, someone opened the flood gates, as water comes into action on at least nine holes. Playing to a par of 72, it measures 6,956/6,513/6,231/5,875/5,905 yards. Just completed is a two-story clubhouse which includes the new pro shop, meeting facilities, a restaurant, and lounge.

A third course, designed by Arnold Palmer and located at Lake Travis (20 miles distant), is also available to resort guests. Roundtrip transportation is provided by Barton Creek Resort to the Palmer

Lakeside location.

RATES (EP) Rooms: $160. 1-bedroom suite: $285. Green fees: Crenshaw Course $70/$85, Fazio Course $100/$110, including carts. Lakeside Course: $80/$95, including cart. Golf package: 2 nights/2 days (includes lodging, MAP, green fees with cart for two rounds), $736 per couple.

ARRIVAL Air: Austin International Airport (15 miles). Car: take Bee Caves Road (RM 2244), 11 miles west of Austin.

COLUMBIA LAKES
188 Freeman Boulevard, West Columbia, TX 77486; (409) 345-5151

While Columbia Lakes has 15,000 square feet of meeting space and 38 breakout rooms for conferences, it also offers the accommodations and amenities of a luxury resort. Lodgings consist of cottages, many along the golf course, providing anything from a bedroom to an eight-plex with living room. The restaurant and lounge are in the clubhouse.

At your disposal is tennis on four lighted courts, a swimming pool, bicycles and boat rentals, a marina, and some excellent fishing.

Golf can be played on the Columbia Lakes Country Club course. Measuring 6,967/6,300/5,280 yards, it pars at 72. This layout can test you. It is well trapped, with many trees and a generous amount of water coming into play.

RATES (EP) Rooms: $79 / $99. Green fees: $40 / $55, including cart. Golf package: 2 nights / 3 days (includes lodging, green fees and cart), $306 / $390 per couple. Rates are for September-November and March-May.

ARRIVAL Air: Houston (60 minutes). Car: Highway 288 south to Highway 35, then west to Country Road 25. North to Columbia Lakes.

DEL LARGO RESORT
600 Del Largo Blvd., Montgomery, TX 77356; (409) 582-6100; (800) 833-3078

Covering over 300 acres along lovely Lake Conroe, Del Largo offers a variety of possible accommodations and activities. Lodgings are in 310 one-bedroom Tower Suites. The 22-story Tower units have kitchenettes with stoves and microwave ovens. There are also 48 golf course cottages, each with two bedrooms and baths, a wood-burning fireplace, fully-equipped kitchen, washer/dryer, and dining/living area. The lakeside villas include the same amenities as the cottages, but in addition each has a private boat slip.

The meeting and convention facilities found here are above average. Using their Tejas Ballroom and the many separate breakout rooms, the resort can handle groups of 1,000 theater- and 550 classroom-style.

Dining takes place in the Lago Vista or the less formal Cafe Verde. There is also Christy's, with an outstanding view of the lake, or the country club snack bar for lunch.

There are 13 tennis courts supported by a tennis shop and professionals, two racquetball courts, an exercise room complete with Nautilus and Universal equipment, a massage therapist, and a beauty salon. Also available: a swimming pool, bicycling, horseshoes, and all manner of fishing and boating, with a wide variety of boats available to rent. Included are water-skiing, sailing, pontoon boats, and house-boats. You are also welcome to bring your own boat. There is, in addition, a children's playground.

Designed by Dave Marr and Jay Reviere, the golf course plays 6,907/6,467/5,829 yards and pars at 71. If you really mess up you might encounter water on 11 holes. While the terrain undulates only slightly, the fairways are bordered by towering pines. The Director of Golf is Phil Dorsey.

RATES (EP) Tower suites: $102/$107. Cottages: $140/ $145. Lakeside villas: $165/ $185. Green fees: $25/$35, carts $25. Golf package: 2 nights/3 days (includes lodging, unlimited golf with cart), $332 per couple. Rates shown are for June through mid-October.

ARRIVAL Air: Houston (40 miles). Private aircraft: Montgomery Country Airport. Car: from Houston take 1-45 north. Exit to Highway 105. Turn left (west), for 13 miles. Turn right onto Walden Road for two miles. Look for signs to resort.

FLYING L GUEST RANCH
Highway 173, Bandera, TX 78003; (210) 796-3001; (800) 292-5134

The hospitality and accommodations at the resort are a blend of the old and new west. The villas, designed by Frank Lloyd Wright Associates, consist of one- to three-bedroom suites. Some feature fireplaces, some have two double beds, others king-size beds. The golf-view units are two-room suites. The resort, of course, has a dining room and lounge. The meeting rooms allow them to handle groups of up to 160 theater- and 90 classroom-style.

They offer tennis (two lighted courts), swimming, horseback riding and hay rides, along with fishing. They also can provide a few hours entertainment for the small fry while you try a round of golf.

Golf, under the direction of professional John Junker, is played on the Flying "L" Country Club course. Parring at 72, it plays a hefty 6,787/6,320/ 5,813 yards.

RATES (FAP) Rooms: $210 per couple. Green fees: $12/$15, carts $16. Golf pack-

age: 2 nights/2 days (includes lodging, breakfast, unlimited green fees, cart for each day), $236 per couple.

***ARRIVAL** Air: San Antonio. Car: from San Antonio (40 miles) west on Highway 410 to Highway 16 (Bandera Rd.). North on 16 into Bandera. Turn left onto Highway 173 for one mile.*

FOUR SEASONS RESORT & CLUB
4150 North MacArthur Blvd., Irving, TX 75038; (214) 717-0700; (800) 332-3442

The Four Seasons Inn has 315 guest rooms, including 13 suites. The 52 deluxe rooms set aside for meeting groups are unique in that each features a work area with a desk, special computer links, and a television offering closed-circuit capabilities.

There is a health spa with dry and wet saunas, whirlpools, herbal wraps, massages, weight and exercise rooms, four indoor and eight outdoor tennis courts, swimming pools, two squash courts, along with six racquetball courts.

The Cottonwood Golf Club, home of the Byron Nelson Golf Classic, was designed by Robert Trent Jones, Jr. It stretches 7,002/6,532/6,096/5,707 yards, with a par of 71. The first green is in the shape of the state of Texas, while the bunker immediately behind forms the state of Oklahoma. I am not sure how Oklahomans should react to that, but then the water hazard off the first tee is in the shape of the Gulf of Mexico. With water plus 74 sand bunkers throughout the course, it can become an interesting layout. At certain times the Cottonwood course is not available due to tournament play. A second 18, the TPC (Texas version), is also available for guest play. Parring at 70, it reaches out 6,767/6,397/5,380 yards.

***RATES** (EP) $185/$220. Suites: $350 and up. Green fees: $80, carts $28. Golf package: 1 day/1 night (includes lodging, green fees and cart), $245/$275 per couple.*

***ARRIVAL** Air: Dallas/Ft. Worth.*

HORSESHOE BAY COUNTRY CLUB RESORT
Box 7766, Horseshoe Bay, TX 78654; (210) 598-2511; (800) 531-5105

This deluxe resort is on Lake LBJ, one of the most beautiful lakes in Texas. There are guest rooms at the Inn along with some 200 condominiums of from one to three bedrooms, with fully-equipped kitchens. There are also a few private, three-bedroom homes. The resort can handle group affairs of up to 200 classroom- and 250 banquet-style.

There is a full-service marina and, with more than 22 miles of lake, you can sail, water ski, or fish. The Yacht Club Restaurant offers good food and a spectacular view of the bay.

Meanwhile, back at the Inn, they have one of the most unusual pools we have seen: an enormous black marble basin. At first glance it looks as if it had been constructed by the Romans. If you ever considered horseback riding, this is the place. The trails wind through hills and valleys, past spring-fed brooks with quail and deer in abundance. Tennis can be played on 14 lighted courts (four covered) with their own tennis shop and professionals on hand to assist.

There are now three 18-hole courses, all Robert Trent Jones designs. The Slick Rock course, parring at 72, reaches out 6,839/6,358/5,858 yards. The front nine is heavily wooded, while the back side is a little more open. You can rest assured the 72 traps, along with water coming into contention on 10 holes, will keep you occupied.

The Ram Rock course is one of the tougher layouts in Texas. Parring at 71, it plays 6,946/6,408/5,954/5,305 yards. With its 68 traps, heavily wooded fairways, and water hazards on eight holes, this gem is a stem-winder. Apple Rock golf course, the newest addition, weighs in at 6,999/6,536/6,038/5,480 yards, also with a par of 72. There are two first-class pro shops serving all three courses. Each has a grill, a lounge, and locker rooms.

RATES (EP) Inn: (minimum 2 nights) $110. Beach House: $120 / 175. Green fees: $65 / $75, cart $22. Golf package: 2 nights / 3 days available weekdays only (includes lodging, 3 rounds of golf with cart, 2 dinners, all taxes and gratuities), $672 per couple. Rates mid-March to mid-November.

ARRIVAL Air: Austin. Private aircraft: Horseshoe Bay Airport. Car: from Austin take Route 71 northwest 55 miles.

HYATT REGENCY DFW
International Parkway, DFW Airport, TX 75261; (214) 453-1234; (800) 233-1234

The location of this resort, about ten minutes from the huge DFW airport, makes it rather unusual. The hotel uses rosewood and Italian marble throughout. With 1,370 guest rooms, it is also particularly well-equipped to handle meetings. It has 32 corporate meeting rooms and all the amenities needed for groups large and small. They have a maximum capacity of 3,000. There are four restaurants offering a wide variety of cuisine and three bars.

They have a health spa, a swimming pool, three lighted indoor and four outdoor tennis courts, 10 racquetball courts, and golf.

The two golf courses, under the direction of a PGA professional, are five minutes from the hotel. The Bear Creek Club West reaches out 6,677/6,261/5,597 yards; the East Course measures 6,670/6,282/5,620 yards. Each pars at 72. Undulating terrain, many traps, and water combine to produce two fine layouts.

RATES (EP) Rooms: $165. Suites: 1 bedroom $200/$375 and up. Green fees: $35/$55, carts $24. Golf packages are available.

ARRIVAL The Dallas/Ft. Worth Airport.

THE INN ON LAKE TRAVIS
1900 American Drive, Lago Vista, TX 78645; (512) 267-1102

The Inn overlooks 65-mile-long Lake Travis, with its 300 miles of shoreline. Lodgings consist of 54 rooms, including suites. There are also some condominiums – for those, call (512) 267-7181. Dining is in the Captain's Table Restaurant, with dancing nightly in the Windjammer Lounge. The Highland Lakes Country Club's dining rooms are open to guests as well. In addition, the resort can handle conference groups of up to 300 theater-style.

A swimming and wading pool, tennis on four lighted courts, basketball, volleyball, shuffleboard, boating (boat rentals), along with excellent fishing, suggest some of the activities.

Golf can be played on the Highland Lakes course. Parring at

72/71, it is a sturdy 6,599/ 6,331/6,003/5,488 yards. The hills, traps, trees, and water will hold your interest. Guests also have playing privileges at Lago Vista Country Club. Measuring 6,579/6,193/5,851/ 5,290 yards, it pars at 72. In addition to the two regulation courses there is the Bar-K nine-hole, par-three layout.

RATES (EP) Room: $75. 1-bedroom condo: $125/$145. Golf packages are available. Green fees: $28, cart $22.

ARRIVAL Air: Austin (40 miles west). Car: take I-35 then I-183 north. 14 miles north of Austin turn off on FM # 1431. Travel 12 miles to Lohman's Crossing Road, turn left. Drive less than 3 miles to Boogy Ford. Turn right onto Boogy Ford, go 3 miles, then turn left on American Drive.

LAKEWAY RESORTS & CONFERENCE CENTER
101 Lakeway Drive, Austin, TX 78734; (512) 261-6600; (800) 525-3929

As the name indicates there is more than one resort: the Inn and The World of Tennis. They are about two miles apart. Accommodations are motel-type rooms as well as hotel suites at the Inn. There are in addition "Hillcourt Villas" (condominiums) at the World of Tennis, as well as other homes and condominiums. Both have meeting facilities along with all the needed amenities. But be warned. If you are driving, do not plan to arrive at night. This is a large complex and it is extremely difficult to find your way around.

Dining is a relaxing affair in the Inn's Travis Room. Seldom have we had better service. As an alternative there is the Trophy Room and at the Yacht Club.

Tennis can be played on 32 lighted courts (two indoor). This is a first-class tennis complex, with pro shop, locker room, saunas, steam and whirlpool baths, and a magnificent clubhouse, under the direction of a professional staff. There is also an equestrian center providing instruction and trail rides. As the resort is located on the shores of Lake Travis, a wide variety of water sports are possible.

There are two golf courses: the Live Oaks with a yardage of 6,643/6,228/5,472, parring at 72/73; and the Yaupon 18, playing 6,595/5,988/5,032 yards, also parring at 72. A third course, The Hills of Lakeway, is reserved for member play only. Each course has its own fully-equipped pro shop and snack bar.

RATES (EP) Inn: $130. Jr. suites: $140. The World of Tennis Villas: 2 bedrooms $240. Green fees: $35/$45, carts $22. Golf Packages are available. Rates are for peak golf season April to October.

ARRIVAL Air: Austin. Private aircraft: Lakeway's own airport. Car: (20 miles northwest of Austin). I-35 exit on Highway 620, continue 5 miles after you cross the Mansfield Dam.

MILL CREEK GOLF & COUNTRY CLUB
P.O. Box 67, Salado, TX 76571; (817) 947-5141; (800) 736-3441

Mill Creek Golf & Country Club, while private, allows guests use of all facilities including: swimming, tennis, golf, and attendant social activities. Accommodations are available in the Mill Creek Guest Homes or the Mill Creek Inn. These tastefully furnished units are on a bluff overlooking Mill Creek and are completely equipped for housekeeping. There are also a number of

one-, two- and three-bedroom private homes available. The Mill Creek Restaurant offers a relaxed and casual atmosphere. A must is a visit to the village of Salado, with several good restaurants and its historical points of interest.

Golf is played on the beautifully maintained Robert Trent Jones, Jr.-designed course. Measuring 6,486/6,052/5,250 yards, it pars at 71/73. Salado Creek, which wanders throughout the entire layout, not only adds to the beauty but the challenge as well.

RATES (EP) Guest House: weekdays $75, weekends $90. Green fees: $30/$40, carts $22. Golf package: 1 night/1 day (includes lodging, green fees, and cart), weekdays $127; weekends $170 per couple.

ARRIVAL Air: Austin. Car: I-35 exit on 285, travel 1/2 mile.

RANCHO VIEJO RESORT
Box 3918, Brownsville, TX 78520; (210) 350-4000; (800) 531-7400

Flowering hibiscus, oleanders, and bougainvillea welcome you to Rancho Viejo. Accommodations range from luxurious poolside suites to one- , two- or three-bedroom fairway villas. The villas all have electric kitchen and washer/dryer. The Rancho is an ideal location for business groups, with private meeting and banquet rooms.

Dining takes place in the Casa Grande Supper Club. For less formal dining, there is the Ranchero Room at the main clubhouse. Getting there is half the fun aboard the *Delta Dawn* riverboat. Relax and sip a margarita as you float down the three-mile Resaca to the clubhouse.

The huge swimming pool is unique, with a cascading waterfall and a swim-up bar. Tennis is offered on two lighted courts across from the registration center. A resident professional is available.

Golf is played on two championship courses: the El Diablo, 6,899/6,213/5,575 yards, parring at 70/72; and the El Angel. The latter is, regardless of its name, no angel, measuring 6,647/6,003/5,387 yards, again with a par of 70/72. Each of them will challenge you in its own way, with fairways that wind through citrus orchards and pines. The PGA Professional is "KC" Lauber. A nice touch: there is a half-way

house (libation stop) on each course, to hold you together for the back nine.

RATES (EP) Rooms: $103. Suites: $113. 2-bedroom villa: $206. Green fees: $30, carts $24. Golf package: 1 night/1 day (includes lodging, breakfast, green fees, cart, club storage), $160/$192 per couple. Rates are for January-March.

ARRIVAL Air: Brownsville (15 minutes). Car: 3 miles off Highway 100 and less than 1 mile off Highway 511.

RAYBURN COUNTRY RESORT
Sam Rayburn, TX 75951
(409) 698-2444; (800) 882-1442

Accommodations comprise 50 hotel rooms and 54 villa rooms, either near the Country Club or along the lush golf course.

In the evening you can dine at the Rayburn Country Club and afterwards dance to the music of the area's finest entertainers. Their meeting rooms can accommodate groups of from 10 to 200.

Tennis is served up on four lighted courts by the 25-meter pool. Additional amenities consist of locker rooms, showers, and a snack bar. There are many other activities, starting with fishing and sailing on Lake Sam Rayburn. They also offer fishing trip packages, including a professional fishing guide service.

There are now 27 holes of golf to take on. Using a crossover system you wind up with: the Green/Blue combination of nines measuring 6,754/6,266/5,524 yards; the Green/Gold, playing 6,741/6,236/5,301 yards; and the Blue/Gold Course weighing in at 6,754/6,266/5,524 yards. All three par at 72. There are more than enough water hazards, traps, dogleg holes, and trees to hold your undivided attention. They had better, as these are not easy courses.

RATES (EP) Hotel: $44/$49. Villas (1 bedroom) $55/$75. Green fees: $22/$28, carts $20. Golf package: 2 nights/3 days (includes lodging, 2 dinners, green fees, and cart) in hotel $338 weekdays, $398 weekends, per couple; in condo $378 weekdays, $418 weekends.

ARRIVAL Air: Beaumont (88 miles). Private aircraft: Pineland/Jasper Airport. Car: from Beaumont, north on U.S. 96, left on Highway 255.

SOUTH SHORE HARBOUR RESORT
2500 South Shore Boulevard, League City, TX 77573; (713) 334-1000; (800) 442-5005

The proximity (20 minutes) of Houston's Hobby Airport is one of the reasons this resort has become such a prime meeting and conference center. It is an impressive 11-story structure with a stone circular drive entrance, a jade and marble floored lobby, glass-enclosed elevators, and even a cascading lobby waterfall. There are 250 guest rooms and suites. These units are equipped with two phones, in-room movies and many have excellent views of the yacht basin fronting the hotel. The meeting center, although a part of the hotel, has its own entrance. The resort can handle groups of up to 400 classroom- or 800 theater-style.

The Paradise Reef Restaurant has a varied menu ranging from seafood to beef. The Harbour Club has a more formal setting. There is also the poolside "Hooker's Nook" for lighter fare. The name refers to a "fishing" hook (at least that's what they told me). There is also the RSVP night club, along with the Lobby Bar offering background piano music.

There are also several other restaurants in the area, ranging from an English tea room to Mexican, Italian, and German cuisine. The hotel will be happy to supply you with a list including address and phone numbers.

The resort has a large tropical pool equipped with a swim-up bar, the adjacent marina (750 boat slips), with charter fishing trips available and, a short distance away, the fitness center. The 70,000-square-foot center provides a multitude of ways to destroy yourself. Included is a 25-meter lap pool, a co-ed whirlpool, eight lighted tennis courts (two indoor), along with racquetball courts, a gymnasium, and a 5,000-square-foot fitness room with every type of exercise equipment known to exist. It also has the Last Lap Cafe.

The golf course rolling out from the clubhouse plays to a par of 71. Reaching out 6,663/6,040/5,374 yards, it brings water into play on 15 holes. The Head Professional is Greg Scott. Play can be arranged on several other golf course in the area.

RATES   (EP)   Rooms: $115/$145. Suites: $165/ $280. Green fees: $38, carts $20. Golf package: 2 nights/3 days (includes lodging, green fees for three rounds of golf), $396 per couple.

ARRIVAL Air: Houston International. Car: take Bay Area Blvd. to El Camino Egret Bay Blvd. Turn left onto Marina Bay Drive. Drive to the resort entrance.

TANGLEWOOD ON TEXOMA
P.O. Box 265, Pottsboro, TX 75076; (903) 786-2968; (800) 833-6569

Tanglewood, 80 miles north of Dallas, is a resort community nestled among wooded hills on the shore of Lake Texoma. There are 65 rooms, including five master suites in the unique nine-story "Lighthouse," as well as 120 fully-equipped condominiums. The resort is prepared to handle meeting groups of from 15 to 150 people with 13 separate meeting rooms and a full range of audio/visual equipment.

Guests can dine in the elegant Captain's Table Restaurant or The Seachest Room. The casual Yacht Club and Moonraker lounges, atop the Lighthouse, have become the focal points of most of the social activity.

Sporting action includes: a three-tiered swimming pool, two lighted tennis courts, an equestrian center, a 21-foot ski boat, and a golf course.

Golf is played on a Ralph Plummer-designed course. With three tee settings, it covers 6,997/6,354/5,572 yards and pars at 72/73. In addition to the yardage, some of the challenge is provided by the trees outlining most fairways and water hazards on six holes.

RATES (EP) Rooms: $75 / $85. Suites: $95. Lighthouse Tower: $135. Condominiums: $90 / $110. Green fees: $20 / $23, carts $20. Golf package: 2 nights (includes lodging, green fees, cart, taxes), $276 per couple. Rates are for April-October.

.ARRIVAL Air: Dallas / Ft. Worth. Private aircraft: Grayson County Airport. Car: 80 miles north of Dallas on Highway 75.

TAPATIO SPRINGS RESORT & COUNTRY CLUB
P.O. Box 550, Boerne, TX 78006; (210) 537-4611; (800) 999-3299

There are 96 rooms in the hotel, which includes a full bar and the clubhouse restaurant. The view of the golf course from the dining area is quite spectacular. The resort is well set up to handle meeting and conference groups and can accommodate up to 350 people. In addition to golf, there is swimming, tennis, a sauna, Jacuzzi, and exercise rooms.

Surrounded by stately hills and several spring-fed lakes along Frederick Creek, the 18-hole championship course is both fun and beautiful. With a par of 72, it plays 6,543/6,233/5,849/5,277 yards. A full-line golf shop and a professional staff are available.

RATES (EP) Rooms $85 / $95. Suites: $135. Condominiums: 2 bedrooms $250. Weekly rates available. Green fees: $45, including cart. Golf package: 2 nights / 2 days (includes lodging, green fees, cart, club storage), $276 per couple.

ARRIVAL Air: San Antonio (25 minutes). Car: I-10 north to Boerne, turn left (west) on John's Road to Tapatio Springs.

VALLEY INN & COUNTRY CLUB
Brownsville, TX 78521, (210) 546-5331

The Valley Inn & Country Club, in the heart of the Rio Grand Valley, is a 30-minute drive from the sandy beaches of South Padre Island on the Gulf of Mexico. There are fairway villas (two- and three-bedroom homes) equipped for housekeeping, including washer and dryer. Should you have trouble renting one of the privately-owned villas we suggest you contact one of the local real-estate brokers.

Activities include: tennis on eight lighted courts, an Olympic-size pool (a total of 15 pools throughout the complex) and, of course, golf. Matamoros, Mexico, only 10 minutes away, offers sightseeing and endless shopping.

The Valley Country Club course, with a par of 70/71, plays 6,857/6,355/5,182 yards. This layout brings lots of water into play. There is also an executive nine-hole affair to sharpen up your iron play.

RATES (EP) Fairway villas: $225/$350 per week (minimum one-week stay). Green fees: $22, carts $20. Rates are for January-April.

ARRIVAL Air: Brownsville. Car: Highway 77/83 and FM 802.

WALDEN ON LAKE CONROE
14001 Walden Road, Montgomery, TX 77356; (409) 582-6441

Walden's, situated on a 1,200-acre peninsula jutting into Lake Conroe, is an hour's drive from Houston. Accommodations include well-furnished townhouses and condominiums. There are several dining rooms: two fine restaurants, the Walden Country Club, the Commodore Room at the Yacht Club, and the 19th Hole Grill for breakfast or lunch.

This is one of the largest yacht clubs of its type, with slips for 520 boats. There are also rental boats ranging from canoes and ski-boats to a 55-foot party cruiser. Additional amenities include a tennis complex with 16 Laykold courts (10 lighted, four covered) and a professional staff.

The golf course was designed and engineered by the architectural firm of Van Hagge & Devlin. Playing 6,798/6,261/

5,122 yards, it pars at 72. It is an unusual layout in that there is no duplication of holes. Each has its own character and each seems to have water problems. Water is actually in play on at least 11 holes. It is one of the more interesting courses to navigate. And, in this case, the word navigate is appropriate.

RATES For condominium rentals call (409) 582-6995. They will quote rates for various units.

ARRIVAL Air: Houston (44 miles). Car: from Houston take Highway 45 north, off at FM 105, 12 miles west.

WATERWOOD NATIONAL RESORT
Waterwood Box One, Huntsville, TX 77340; (409) 891-5211; (800) 441-5211

Waterwood, with miles of shoreline, is on one of the most picturesque areas of Lake Livingston. Created just a few years ago, this reservoir serves up some of the finest bass fishing. Rooms are available in the lodge area, as are lodge cabanas, each equipped with refrigerator and wet bar. The clubhouse includes four lighted tennis courts, an Olympic-sized pool, and the dining room. There are also meeting rooms capable of handling groups from 12 to 200. The Marina offers boat rentals, including paddleboats, canoes, water skiing, and fishing.

Waterwood National, a Pete Dye-designed golf course, originally opened for play in October of 1975. Carved from the east Texas pine woods, its long vistas of rolling tree-lined fairways and typical Pete Dye greens will present all the challenge you will want. Stretching across half of Texas, this layout plays 6,872/6,258/5,480/5,029 yards, parring at 71/73.

RATES (EP) Lodge rooms: $70. Cabana: $90. Suites: $105/$125. Green fees: $25/$35, carts $20. Golf package: 2 nights/3 days (includes green fees, cart, club storage), lodge $356, cabana $386, per couple. Rates are for March-October.

ARRIVAL Air: Houston (98 miles). Car: I-45 from Houston north to exit 190. East at Huntsville. Continue east until you see signs.

WOODCREEK RESORT
One Woodcreek Drive, Wimber-

ley, TX 78676; (512) 847-3126; (800) 284-6505

Accommodations are lodge rooms, cabins or townhouses. The latter feature a living room and fully-equipped kitchens. The resort also has meeting facilities and can handle groups from 10 to 150. Although there is more than one place to eat, the Sam Houston Dining Room serves as good a meal as you will find. There is also the Austin room. Recently the resort obtained a liquor license and now has added a lounge.

There are a great many activities to enjoy – canoeing, paddle boating, fishing, tennis (10 courts), racquetball, handball, hot tubs, and swimming in their pool.

The Woodcreek Resort course, measuring a modest 6,470/ 5,973/5,287 yards, pars at 72. There is a pesky little creek (Cypress Creek) which runs throughout the entire 18. It creates some rather interesting golf shots. There is a particularly good golf shop with an excellent grill.

RATES (EP) Cottages: $50/$60. Townhouse suites: $75. Townhouse, 2 bedrooms: $120. Green fees: $16/$20, cart

$18. Golf package: 2 nights/3 days (includes lodging, green fees, and cart), weekdays $180, weekends $200, per couple.

ARRIVAL Air: Austin (43 miles) or San Antonio (63 miles). Car: from either I-10 or I-35 turn northwest at San Marcus to Wimberley.

THE WOODLANDS CONFERENCE CENTER & RESORT
2301 N. Millbend Drive, The Woodlands, TX 77380; (713) 367-1100; (800) 433-2624

This is a highly fashionable resort complex, with 268 rooms and suites, many with kitchenettes. Unfortunately they are not set up for housekeeping. Woodlands is well-equipped to handle meeting and convention groups. Having allocated 54,000 square feet of space to group affairs, they obviously can handle a large number of people. While there are several restaurants on the premises, the Glass Menagerie, with its view of the lake, stands out. There is also a dining room at the Country Club.

There is a health club, saunas, a steam room, herbal baths, whirlpools, Swedish massage,

the par set at 72. We were only able to play two of the courses: the West Course (home of the Houston Open) and the TPC. The introduction of water and the tree-lined fairways makes these intriguing courses. The Director of Golf is Kent Wood.

RATES (EP) Room: $145. Suites: $185/$275. Green fees: $48, including cart; TPC course $65/$80, including cart. Golf package: 2 nights/3 days (includes lodging, green fees, cart, range balls, golf clinic, bag storage, one round on the north and one round on the TPC course), $728 per couple. Rates are for mid-March through May and for October.

as well as golf and tennis. Tennis is served up on 17 outdoor and three indoor courts (12 lighted) and is supported by a separate and well-stocked tennis shop. There is a resident tennis professional and staff. If you get bored here you have a problem. In addition to the foregoing there is swimming (indoor and outdoor pools), basketball, and massage.

The touring professional associated with the Country Club is John Mahaffey. Woodlands now offers play on 54 holes. Opened in late 1982, the North Course reaches out 6,881/6,339/5,765 yards with a par of 72. The West 18, parring at 72/73, plays 6,969/6,389/5,520 yards. The TPC layout (formerly the East Course) covers 7,045/6,367/5,302 yards, with

ARRIVAL Air: Houston (25 miles). Car: I-45 north to Woodlands/Robinson Road exit. Turn west back over I-45 to Grogan's Mill Road. Take left, then go to second stoplight and turn right on N. Millbend Road.

Utah

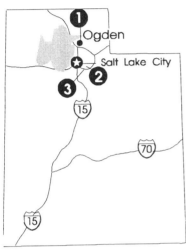

Ogden

Salt Lake City

1. Wolf Creek Lodge
2. Prospector Square Hotel
3. Homestead Resort & GC

HOMESTEAD RESORT & GOLF CLUB

700 North Homestead Drive, Midway, UT 84049; (801) 654-1102; (800) 327-7220

We were surprised to find that this resort dates back over 100 years. In fact it started, like its famous namesake (The Homestead of Hot Springs, Virginia), with hot mineral spring waters as the main attraction. Of course the entire operation, including the 92 Inn rooms, has

been updated since then. There are also a couple of two-bedroom condominiums. With their five meeting rooms, Homestead has the capacity to handle meetings up to 120 people theater-style.

Simon's is available for candle-light dining, while for lighter fare you might consider The Grill Room at the golf club. Even though you are in Utah, their dining rooms are fully licensed.

This is in every aspect a family resort. To that end there are many activities for all age groups, as suggested by their two lighted tennis courts, indoor and outdoor swimming pools, mineral baths, whirlpools, a hot tub, and sauna. Equestrian activities include horseback riding, plus hay, buggy and barnyard rides for the small fry. Nearby Deer Creek reservoir is used for boating, fishing, and water skiing. Another extra: the resort has a children's program. Designed for children three to 14 years old, it keeps them happily occupied and you free. Not a bad arrangement.

In the winter, there is snowmobiling, a sleigh ride/dinner package, and cross-country skiing. Nearby are eight downhill ski runs. The snowmobile and ski programs include instruction and supervision.

The golf course recently underwent a number of changes. Now playing 7,014/6,221/5,260 yards, it carries a par of 72. The front nine is definitely a mountain layout with elevation ranging from 5,000 to 6,000 feet. While the greens are of average size they are also multi-level affairs. The good news is that water comes into play on only three holes. The bad news – they make up for it on the back nine. While the back side is relatively flat, Snake Creek wanders all over the place making a nuisance of itself on all nine holes. The course is supported by a clubhouse including a pro shop and restaurant. Bruce Summerbays is not only the Director of Golf, but he also designed the Homestead Golf Course.

RATES   (EP)   Rooms $69/$105. Suites: $125/$140. Cottage luxury suites: $185/ $200. Condominiums: accommodations for six start at $185/$265 per night. Some of the variations are due to weekday versus weekend or holiday rates. Green fees: $18/$22, carts $22. There are various package plans as well as seasonal memberships available.

ARRIVAL Air: Salt Lake City (55 minutes). Private aircraft: Heber City Airport (paved runway 5 miles from resort). Car: take I-80 east from Salt Lake City. Continue past the Park City exit. Exit right, onto U. S. 40, and drive about 18 miles to the Homestead/Midway exit. Turn right on River Road and follow signs to resort (5 miles).

PROSPECTOR SQUARE HOTEL
P.O. Box 1698, Park City, Utah 84060; (801) 649-7100; (800) 453-3812

Located deep in the heart of Utah's ski country, the Prospector is only an hour's drive from Deer Valley, Alta, and Snowbird. Park City, a booming silver mining center in the 1860's, later becoming a ghost town, is now a rapidly growing resort community wise enough to keep its heritage alive. The movers and shakers of this city have spent much time and money preserving the area and its old structures. While you may be in an 1860s atmosphere, the resort is definitely 20th century.

There is a wide selection of accommodations: 100 hotel rooms, 180 kitchenette studios, plus many one- to three-bedroom condominiums. The condos have fully-equipped kitchen, dining room, fireplace, and washer/dryer. There are also a few private homes available. The resort has meeting and conference rooms, with a capacity of from 12 to 330 people.

While the Grub Steak Restaurant is good, there are several others, including cafes and delis along "Main Street." Despite what you may have heard about Utah, there are state liquor stores and you can purchase mini-bottles in most restaurants for consumption on premises. Kind of a "mix it yourself" arrangement.

The hotel offers a health and athletic club. Refurbished to the tune of over half a million dollars, it now has weight and aerobic rooms, an indoor pool, steamrooms, four tennis and four indoor racquetball courts, along with a resident professional.

Although our primary concern is with golf, you should be aware of their super winter activities. This is, by the way, the official home of the United States Ski Team. And little wonder, with 35 miles of groomed slopes, a lift capacity of 5,800 skiers per hour, and

much more.

While there is no golf course contiguous to the hotel, there is the Park Meadows Country Club, a Jack Nicklaus-designed layout, and the Park City Golf Course. Both are approximately one and a half miles away. In addition there is the Wasatch Mt. Golf Club (17 miles away), offering 27 holes, and the Mountain Dell, also a regulation course, 12 miles from the hotel.

RATES (EP) Rooms: $55. Studio: $65. Condos $99. Green fees: $36, including cart. Rates are May-September and include Athletic Club privileges.

ARRIVAL Air: Salt Lake City (40 minutes). Car: I-80, east-southeast of Salt Lake City.

WOLF CREEK
3615 North Wolf Creek Drive, Eden, UT 84310; (801) 745-2484; (800) 345-8824

Accommodations consist of condominiums. All have fully-equipped kitchens and wood burning fireplaces. Most border on the golf course. There are several restaurants in the area.

The Ogden Valley, due to its

climate, is a natural setting for a four-season resort. In the winter, you are on top of some of the finest skiing in the country; in summer, change over to swimming in two pools, sailing and boating in Pine View Lake, tennis, racquetball, and horseback riding. There are also weight rooms and a sauna.

The Wolf Creek Country Club Resort course reaches out a healthy 6,825/6,459/5,816 yards and pars at 72/74. Whoever designed this layout obviously liked water, as it comes into play on 13 holes.

RATES (EP) Condo: 1 bedroom (sleeps up to four) $85; 2 bedrooms (sleeps up to 6) $105. Green fees: $20/$25, carts $18.

ARRIVAL Air: Salt Lake City. Car: from Ogden, take Highway 39 east to 166, north to Highway 162. Follow 162 to resort. A total of 12 miles.

Washington

1. The Resort Semiahmoo
2. Sudden Valley Resort
3. The Resort at Port Ludlow
4. Alderbrook Inn Resort
5. Skamania Lodge

ALDERBROOK INN RESORT

E 7101 Highway 106, Union, WA 98592; (206) 898-2200; (800) 622-9370

Alderbrook is on the shores of Hood Canal, a fjord-like inlet of Puget Sound. The Inn has a total of 103 guest accommodations, 21 of which are cottages, each with two bedrooms, living room, fully-equipped kitchen and fireplace. The resort can handle meeting groups of up to 150 people.

The dining room offers the standard fare, but does a special job with seafood, oysters, clams, scallops, mahi mahi, and halibut.

Activities include: tennis on four courts, a sauna, and therapy pool. There is also a swimming pool enclosed in a year-round greenhouse.

Golf on this course is an experience you will long remember. Parring at 72/73, this little gem covers a modest yardage of 6,312/6,133/5,506. But don't allow the yardage to mislead you. The professional smiles quietly (or maybe it's a snicker) when he hears someone threaten to "tear up" this course. While the second nine is easy, the front nine is another kettle of fish. The tight fairways, towering trees, and sharp doglegs will test your nerves. I have seen a few golfers pray for a triple bogie on certain holes of the first nine.

RATES (EP) Rooms: $72 / $85. Cottages: $110. Green fees: $20, carts $18.

ARRIVAL From Seattle: the Bremerton Ferry, then Highway 101 to Highway 106, turn right on 106 and drive 15 miles.

THE RESORT AT PORT LUDLOW

9483 Oak Bay Road, Port Ludlow, WA 98365; (206) 437-2222; (800) 732-1239

This resort is set on a hillside dense with towering trees, overlooking Ludlow Bay and a 300-slip marina.

Accommodations (180 guest rooms) range from one room to suites with living room, fully-equipped kitchen, fireplace, private decks and up to four bedrooms. With its conference center now in place the resort can handle 140 classroom- , 170 banquet- , and 275 theater-style. The Harbormaster restaurant and lounge offers entertainment Tuesday through Saturday during the summer.

Activities include: tennis on seven courts, a large heated pool, clam digging, fishing, boating, hiking, beach-combing, or maybe just relaxing on the beach. A newer addition is the indoor swimming pool and whirlpool open during the winter season.

The Ludlow course was designed by one of the best golf architects on the scene today, Robert Muir Graves. Reaching out 6,787/6,262/5,598 yards and parring at 72, it is, without doubt, one of the most beautiful golf layouts we have played. Watching deer feed on the edge of the fairway and, in some cases, crossing in front of you, can make it difficult to remember why you are out here. Should you entirely lose track of what you are doing, PGA professional Lyndon Blackwell and staff will be happy to help you get your game back together. This golf course has, by the way, been rated by *Golf Digest* as one of the top 25 in the nation. I definitely agree with that evaluation. I would also suggest you use a cart, as it is extremely hilly.

A third nine is scheduled to come into play in early 1994. Also designed by Robert Muir Graves, it will play 3,233 yards (men's regular tees), and par at 36. Present plans call for the resort to use a crossover system, intermixing play with the present 18.

RATES   (EP)   Bedroom: $90/$99. Suite loft: $130 and up. Weekends $99/$115, suites $150 and up. Green fees: $50, carts $25. Golf package: 2 nights/2 days (includes lodging, green fees, cart), weekdays $372, weekends $400, per couple. Rates are for May-October.

ARRIVAL From Seattle, take the Seattle-Winslow or Edmonds-Kingston ferry, cross the Hood Canal bridge; 300 yards past the bridge, turn right and follow the signs for about 8 miles.

THE RESORT SEMIAHMOO

9665 Semiahmoo Parkway, Blaine, WA 98230; (206) 371-2000; (800) 854-2608

The Resort Semiahmoo, located in the northwest corner of the state, came into operation in mid-1987. The developers were careful to blend their structures with the historic past of this area. It was built on the tip of a sandspit, a turn-of-the-century center of the salmon canning industry, with many colorful remnants of the early cannery structure woven into the fabric of the resort itself.

Lighthouse square was planned as a historic waterfront shopping village with festive outdoor eating spots, entertainment, and local seafood markets. These activities are intermingled with those of the Inn-Athletic Club complex and the marina. As a matter of interest, of the 800 planned boat slips, over 500 are now

available and in use.

The Semiahmoo Inn is a 200-room resort hotel. Accommodations are also available in townhouse condominiums. Clusters of townhouses are built along the spit. The latter offer spectacular views of Drayton Harbor and the village complex, the San Juan Islands, and the night lights of Whiterock, Canada. The resort has 15,000 square feet of space set aside to handle meeting and conference groups.

There are three restaurants: the Stars, Packers, and the Oyster Bar & Lounge serving local seafood.

Along with two tennis courts, located at the spa, there are two indoor racquetball courts, squash courts, an exercise room, and the most unusual indoor-outdoor swimming pool we have seen. It has pull-down garage-like doors that convert it from an outdoor to an indoor pool.

Adjacent to the Inn is a dock area offering San Juan Island Cruises (Grayline water sightseeing tour). You can also arrange deep-sea fishing trips, departing from the resort on a regularly scheduled basis.

Now we come to the 18-hole championship golf course. Designed by Arnold Palmer/Ed Seay, and built on fully wooded and rolling terrain, it is about a mile from the hotel. Reaching a healthy 7,005/6,435/6,003/5,288 yards, it pars at 72.

As if the contoured hillsides and the problems introduced by densely wooded fir, hemlock, madrona, and alder trees were not enough, there are four lakes which come into play on six different holes. Even though my game was a bit shaky, I found it to be one of the better and more relaxing rounds I have played in some time. For tee times call 371-7005

The pro shop, a 23,000-square-foot structure, features stone fireplaces, a large terrace area, a bar and grill, and locker rooms. The complex also has a separate tennis center with two indoor and two outdoor courts, along with a swimming pool, saunas and a steam room. The Director of Golf is Brian Southwick

RATES   (EP)   Rooms: $135/$195. Suites: $225 and up. Green fees: $55, carts $23. Golf package: 2 days/2 nights (includes lodging, two rounds of golf, and taxes), $570 per *couple. Less on weekdays. Rates indicated are for the peak golf season mid-June through September.*

ARRIVAL From Seattle, north on I-5, then take exit 270. Continue left to Birch Bay/Linder, then on to Harbor View Road. Turn right at waterslide. Follow signs.

SKAMANIA LODGE
1131 SW Skamania Way, Stevenson, WA 98648; (509) 427-7700; (800) 221-7117

Occupying 175 acres in the heart of the magnificent Columbia River Gorge area, Skamania Lodge opened in early 1993. Using heavy timber construction along with natural stone, the four-story Lodge blends well within its setting. The lobby, a three-story "Great Room," has a massive fireplace along with slate and pine flooring.

There are 195 guest rooms, including 34 fireplace units, four parlor suites, six family rooms, and a grand suite. With some 12,000 square feet of space, including two large ballrooms and 10 break out rooms, the hotel can handle meeting groups of up to 460 classroom- and 550 banquet-style.

The 200-seat dining room and lounge has a spectacular view of the Columbia River. Room service is also available.

Activities include: two tennis courts, a full-service spa including an indoor pool, exercise rooms, a sauna and a private whirlpool, massage rooms and an outside whirlpool with a natural rock setting. There are also fabulous walking trails and several small lakes in the area. An additional attraction: you can catch a ride on the sternwheeler *Columbia Gorge* from the town of Stevenson.

The golf course is a creation of Gene C. (Bunny) Mason, designer of the spectacular Glaze Meadows course, one of two at Black Butte Ranch in central Oregon. Coming into play in the summer of 1993, it used every bit of the area's breathtaking terrain to enhance the challenge. Starting at the pro shop near the main lodge it meanders through the Gorge, providing views of the river and mountains, rolling out past water hazards and two small lakes. Built on undulating terrain, it plays to a modest 6,243/5,865/5,470/4,876 yards, parring at 70.

RATES (EP) Rooms: $95. Riv-erside rooms: $110. Fireplace Rooms: $145. Green fees: $35, carts $25. Golf packages are available.

ARRIVAL Air: Portland International Airport (45 minutes). Car: from Portland take I-84 to the Bridge of the Gods (just west of the Cascade Locks). Cross over the bridge to the Washington side. Turn right (east) on Highway 14 for one and a half miles. Turn left on Rock Creek Drive.

THE RESORT AT SUDDEN VALLEY
2145 Lake Whatcom Boulevard, Bellingham, WA 98226; (206) 734-6430

Sudden Valley is tucked away in the Chuckanut Mountains, in the-foothills of the magnificent Cascade range. Located on 1,576 acres, there are 50 condominiums, ranging from one to three bedrooms. Each unit has a living room, complete kitchen, cable TV, telephone, and superb views. The resort's meeting facilities can handle up to 150, with suites for groups as small as 10. The dining room and cocktail lounge are housed in the main building. Directly across from the entrance is a shopping mall, including a grocery and deli store – a real convenience.

With its two miles of lakeshore, Sudden Valley provides a boat launch on Lake Whatcom, along with fishing, and canoeing. There are also five tennis courts, two swimming pools, hiking. and two recreation barns set up for various children's programs.

The Sudden Valley Country Club Course is a Ted Robinson design. Weighing in at 6,553/6,143/5,627 yards and parring at 72, it ranks among the more difficult layouts in the state. With substantial elevation changes, water, and some sharp dogleg holes – it is an interesting and testing golf course. For tee times call (206) 734-6435

RATES   (EP)   Studio: $90/$110. Loft: $90/$120; 2 bedrooms: $140/$160; 3 bedrooms: $150/$175. Green fees: $25/$35, cart $23. Golf package: 1 night/1 day (includes lodging, green fees), $115/$205 per couple.

ARRIVAL North on I-5, exit #240 (north of Everett). Turn right, continue through flashing light, left at stop sign (Lake Whatcom Boulevard), continue 5 miles. Traveling south, take exit # 253, then left on Lakeway

Drive (turns into Cable Street). At bottom of hill, the road swings sharply right and you are on Lake Whatcom Boulevard. Continue on for 5 miles.

Wisconsin

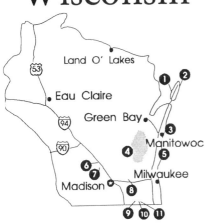

Land O' Lakes

Eau Claire

Green Bay

Manitowoc

Milwaukee

Madison

1. The Alpine Resort
2. Maxwelton Braes Resort & CC
3. Fox Hills Resort
4. Greenlake Conference Center
5. American Club
6. Dell View Resort
7. Devil's Head Lodge
8. Olympia Resort & Spa
9. Lake Lawn Lodge
10. The Abbey on Lake Geneva
    Americana Lake Geneva
    Resort
11. Nippersink Manor Resort

THE ABBEY ON LAKE GENEVA
Fontana, WI 53125; (414) 275-6811; (800) 558-2405

Accommodations range from 340 guest rooms to about 32 condominiums – with the con-dos having fully-equipped kitchens and fireplaces. The resort can also accommodate meeting groups of up to 1,000.

La Tour DeBois Restaurant serves French cuisine, while the Monaco offers less formal family dining. There is also the Waterfront Cafe. The Marina, with its 400 slips, provides boats for fishing, water skiing, or just cruising this beautiful lake.

Tennis is available on six lighted courts. Additional amenities include: an indoor and four outdoor swimming pools along with an indoor rec-reation and amusement ar-cade. Something new has been added – The Fontana Spa. I will not go into detail other than to say there are a thou-sand different ways to pamper your body: loofa scrubs, Swiss showers, Scotch hose, mas-sage, and on and on. I was afraid to ask what a Scotch hose is.

The Abbey, while having no golf course of its own, can ar-range play for guests at the Lake Lawn Lodge course a few miles away. For details on this course refer to Lake Lawn Lodge. In fact there are four additional courses, including the Abbey Springs Country

Club less than two miles away.

RATES *(EP)* *Rooms:* *$135/$175 per couple. Suites:* *$315/$425. Green fees: $70, in-cluding cart. Rates are for June-September.*

ARRIVAL *Air: Chicago (90 minutes). Airport limousine service is available. Private air-craft: paved runway capable of taking Lear jets, adjacent to the Lake Lawn Lodge (7 miles). Car: from Milwaukee, High-way 15 west to 67, south on 67 to Fontana.*

THE ALPINE RESORT
P.O. Box 200
Egg Harbor, WI 45209
(414) 868-3000

The Bertschingers, operators of Alpine since its founding, have created a delightful re-sort. The main lodge has two large screened verandas over-looking Green Bay, appropri-ate for watching the pageant of colorful boats, fishermen, and water skiers. Accommodations consist of 60 rooms in the Lodge and 40 cottages scat-tered throughout the grounds.

There is much to do here: ten-nis, riding, boating, just plain loafing, or swimming. The gen-tly sloping beach is safe for children. The resort recently added an outdoor heated pool. Social activities are informal and varied, with such things as an evening marshmallow roast, hayrides, lounge games or movies. It really is a family-oriented resort. The Alpine dining room prepares home-cooked meals and fresh pastry from their own ovens.

The challenge on this 27-hole golf course is found primarily in the rolling fairways and many trees. Using a crossover system, you play: the Red/White combination meas-uring 6,047/5,879 yards, par-ring 70/73; the Red/Blue 18 playing 5,858/5,440 yards with a par of 71/70; and the Blue/White nines parring at 71/73, with a yardage of 6,207/5,837.

RATES *(EP) Room with bath:* *$69/$89 per couple. Duplex cottage: (living room, 1 bed-room and porch), $794 per cou-ple per week. Green fees: $14, carts $16. Rates are for June 22-September 3.*

ARRIVAL *Air: Milwaukee.* *Car: from Milwaukee on I-43 to Manitowoc, then Highway 42 through Sturgeon Bay to Egg Harbor.*

THE AMERICAN CLUB

Highland Drive, Kohler, WI 53044; (414) 457-8000; (800) 344-2838

The hotel itself has an interesting history. Originally housing for immigrant workers of the Kohler Company, it was converted into a luxury hotel. The interior decor highlighted by stained class, crystal chandeliers, and oak paneling may well be one of the reasons AAA has given this hotel a Five-Diamond rating. The resort is about three miles from Lake Michigan.

Quality and attention to detail is reflected in the accommodations. Each of the 160 rooms has a private whirlpool bath. The "special" suites include four-poster beds and super baths (Kohler whirlpool baths for two). It had better be a "Kohler" or it won't be tolerated for long in this place. The Grand Hall, which can be divided into five meeting rooms, has a maximum capacity of 700 theater- , 600 banquet- , and 445 classroom-style.

With several restaurants on premises and others nearby, you most certainly should not go hungry. The Wisconsin Room, a classic hotel dining room, the Immigrant, a gourmet restaurant for more formal and intimate dining (jackets and ties are required), the Horse & Plow, a casual affair in a tavern-like setting, and The Greenhouse, offering lighter fare (pastries and ice cream), are all at your disposal. Also available is the Blackwolf Run clubhouse with its country-style restaurant. Nightly piano entertainment, along with occasional live entertainment and dancing, is served up in the Horse & Plow. There are a total of five restaurants on premises with another four in the village nearby. Transportation is provided.

Activities include: an indoor swimming pool, six indoor and six outdoor tennis courts, a whirlpool, and a two-mile jogging trail. The Sports core, located six blocks away, has a complete health spa and fitness facility. Also available within this 600-acre preserve are some of the best trout and salmon waters to be found. During winter there are 30 miles of cross-country ski trails available. There is also ice skating across from the Kohler Design Center (bring your own skates).

While the golf courses are

beautiful, there is some bad news – both are Pete Dye designs. You know you are going to be challenged (maybe punished is more accurate) by small, fast and hard greens, railroad ties all over the place, undulating terrain, and a surplus of water. The River Course, parring at 72, plays to a substantial yardage of 6,991/6,607/6,101/5,090. Its name should give you a clue – the Sheboygan River gets into the act on 14 holes. In fact Mr. Dye did a masterful job of laying the course out along the river. Thus you wind up with trees on one side, the river on the other, with rolling terrain, traps where they should not be (where your ball just stopped), and small greens. The Valley-Meadow course, while longer, is more open and brings water into play on only five holes. Reaching out a hefty 7,142/6,735/6,169/5,065 yards, it also pars at 72.

As to the Valley Meadow course, I get a bit jumpy when I find the opening hole called "Fishing Hole" and the 18th referred to as the "Salmon Trap." The River Course is not a great deal more reassuring, as the first hole is the "Snake" and number 17, the "Snapping Turtle."

The excellent golf shop and the course activities are under the supervision of Head Golf Professional Jeff Moorman.

RATES (EP) Rooms: (Category II) $180. Jr. Suite: (Category III) $225. Suites: (Category IV & V) $285/$360. Green fees: $90, including cart. Golf package: 2 nights (includes lodging, two rounds of golf, cart, bag storage), $760/$830/$940/ $1,070 per couple. Rates shown are for late-May through September.

ARRIVAL Air: Milwaukee International Airport (60 miles). Private aircraft: Sheboygan Memorial Airport (10 miles). Car: take I-43 north to exit #126. Go west on Highway 23 to exit Y. Take Y south to Kohler.

AMERICANA LAKE GENEVA RESORT
Highway 50, Lake Geneva, WI 53147; (414) 248-8811; (800) 558-3417

The Americana Lake Geneva Resort is an hour and a half from Chicago. The hotel is a complex of eight low-rise cedar, textured concrete, and glass buildings. There are 340 well appointed rooms, featuring balconies or patios, each with a view of the lush Wisconsin countryside. Dining is in The Willows and cocktails are served in the Kahoots Lounge.

The resort has two swimming pools, four indoor and eight outdoor tennis courts, six racquetball courts, horseback riding, skeet and trap shooting, boating on their 25-acre private lake, a Nautilus-equipped health and fitness center, saunas, miniature golf, and an electronic game room.

Golf is served up on two championship 18-hole courses. The Brute, a par-72/74 playing 7,258/6,855/5,974 yards, was designed by Robert Bruce Harris. This aptly-named course will confront you with some 70 bunkers, many water hazards, rolling terrain, and an abundance of trees. The greens are reputed to be among the largest in the world, at an average of 10,000 square feet.

The Briar Patch, a Dye/Nicklaus design parring at 71, plays a more modest 6,742/6,317/5,408 yards. Unlike the Brute it has little water, few trees, and small greens. There is a professional staff on hand.

RATES (EP) Rooms: $85 / $99. Green fees: $60, including cart. Golf package: 2 nights / 3 days *(includes lodging, 2 rounds of golf, cart), $360 / $425 per couple. Rates are for April-October.*

ARRIVAL Air: Milwaukee. Private aircraft: Lake Geneva 4,100-foot runway. Car: from Milwaukee take I-94 south. Exit onto Highway 50 west. Drive approximately 40 miles and the resort will be on your right side.

DELL VIEW RESORT
501 East Adams Street.
Lake Delton, WI 53940
(608) 253-1261; (800) 873-3557

Dell View is in Wisconsin's well known Dells Lake/Delton area. Accommodations are rooms in the motel. The Gryphon Room has good food showcased in a relaxed atmosphere, while the lounge offers nightly entertainment. They welcome, and are prepared to handle, modest-size meeting groups.

There are indoor and outdoor pools, tennis, riding, fishing, boating, miniature golf, steam rooms, and a whirlpool. During the winter there is cross-country skiing, snowmobiling, and ice skating.

The course, supervised by a

PGA professional, is short but can be tricky. It plays 5,750/5,497/5,363 yards with a par of 70/74. With water hazards on three holes and lateral water coming into play on another four, you need to keep alert to stay out of trouble.

RATES   *(EP)   Rooms: $75/$145. Green fees: $18, carts $22. Rates are May through Labor Day.*

ARRIVAL *Air: Madison (45 miles). Car: from I-90/94 exit 92, onto U.S. 12, then approximately 1 mile.*

DEVIL'S HEAD LODGE
Box 38, Merrimac, WI 53561; (608) 493-2251; (800) 472-6670

The lodge is just beneath the crest of Baraboo Bluff Range overlooking Lake Wisconsin. Accommodations are provided in the adjacent 238-room motel, with dining at the unique In-The-Round Chalet. There are meeting facilities for up to 300 people.

Tennis, swimming (indoor and outdoor pools), a fitness room, sauna, whirlpool, biking, sailing, and golf are available.

Golf can be played on the

Devil's Head course, measuring 6,725/6,336/5,141 yards and parring at 73. Not too much water, but dogleg holes and trees add to the tension (or fun).

RATES *(EP) Rooms: weekdays $59; weekends: $75. Condominiums: $250/$350 for 2 nights. Green fees: $25, carts $22. Golf packages are available. Rates are for June-September.*

ARRIVAL *Air: Madison (40 miles). Car: I-90/94, then southwest on 78.*

FOX HILLS RESORT & CONFERENCE CENTER
P.O. Box 129, Mishicot, WI 54228; (414) 755-2376; (800) 950-7615

There are 160 rooms, including executive suites, at Fox Hills. All have Jacuzzis and wood burning fireplaces. The resort is well-equipped to handle meeting groups. For details ask for their Meeting Planner's Kit. Special touches are the imported crystal chandeliers in the dining room, and the spacious lounge offering dancing and nightly entertainment.

There is tennis, a game room,

charter fishing on Lake Michigan, an indoor and an outdoor swimming pool, a health club, golf and, in the winter, cross country skiing.

Parring at 72, the Fox Hills National Course plays an ample 7,017/6,574/6,267/5,366 yards. It is definitely a Scottish links course. With undulating mounded terrain, water on 10 holes, and exceptionally well trapped, it has long been recognized as one of the best layouts in the area.

The Fox Hills Resort course (27 holes) plays the Front/Back nine at 6,374/6,107/5,688 yards with a par of 72/73. The combination of the Back/Blue nines measures 6,410/6,081/5,721 yards, parring at 71/73. The Front/Blue courses reach out a more modest 6,224/5,597/5,597 yards, with a par of 71/72. The resort provides a full-time resident professional as well as a newly remodeled golf shop.

RATES   (EP)   Rooms: $75/$110. Suites: $135/$150. Villas: $110/$125. Green fees: $20/$25, carts $22. There are several different golf packages available. Rates are for May 15-October 15.

ARRIVAL Air: Milwaukee or *Green Bay. Car: from Milwaukee, I-43 exit onto Highway 82 and travel east.*

GREENLAKE CONFERENCE CENTER
State Route 23, Green Lake WI 54941; (414) 294-3323; (800) 558-8898

While this resort is set up for meeting groups, with a capacity of up to 1,200 people, it also caters to those seeking a golf vacation. There are accommodations in the main lodge as well as various cottages and homes. The latter have fully-equipped kitchens, most with fireplaces. There are also camping sites.

Due to the resort's church affiliation (Greenlake is an American Baptist Assembly conference center), no alcoholic beverage can be consumed on the grounds. That means no drinks are allowed, even in your own room.

Inasmuch as it occupies 1,000 acres on the shores of Green Lake, activities include fishing, water skiing, bicycling, boating (paddleboats, rowboats, canoes, sailboards, sailboats, and pontoon boats), an indoor swimming pool, tennis, and golf. Hayrides can also be arranged.

Eighteen holes of the Lawsonia Links have been designed in the style of the famous Scottish links and have been rated by *Golf Digest* as one of the top 25 public courses in the United States. The 27 holes combine to play as follows. The South/West is 6,640/6,335/5,209 yards with a par of 72. The West/East combination is 6,754/6,469/5,077 yards, parring at 72/71. The East/South nines, 6,604/6,296/4,918 yards, also par at 72/71. With several of the holes on the South Course adjacent to the lake, and noted for its deep-faced bunkers and elevated greens, you will find it both engaging and challenging.

RATES (EP) Lodge rooms: $68. Cottages: $75 / $120. Cabins: $75 / $95. Green fees: $35, carts $23. Weekly rates as well as golf package are available.

ARRIVAL Air: Oshkosh (30 miles from airport). Private aircraft: Fond du Lac (8 miles), small sod landing strip. Car: from Oshkosh, travel State Highway 44 to intersection with Interstate 23. Go west on 23 to the resort entrance – 2 miles west of Green Lake.

THE HEIDEL HOUSE
P.O. Box 9
Green Lake, WI 54941
(414) 294-3344; (800) 444-2812

Plan to be pampered when you visit The Heidel House. It is really something special. Accommodations are varied, to say the least, ranging from rooms, semi-suites, and suites, to the Stable House (four bedrooms) and the Grey Rock Mansion (10,000 square feet, accommodating 14 people). Small groups of up to 100 find the Mansion delightful for meetings.

You have a choice of three dining areas: the main dining room, serving gourmet entrees, the Rathskeller, and the Fondue Chalet.

Green Lake, the deepest in Wisconsin, provides not only a beautiful setting but all kinds of water activities as well. From spring through fall they offer excursions and charter parties on the Heidel House yacht. They call it "yachts of fun." There is also an indoor pool, saunas, and a full-time professional in charge of their tennis program.

The Tuscumbia Golf & Country Club's course, in operation since 1896, weighs in at

6,301/5,833 yards, and pars at 71/72. Supporting the golf are a resident professional and a golf shop. There are, in addition, two other courses where play can be arranged, the Mascoutin Golf Club and the 27-hole layout at Lawsonia.

RATES (EP) Rooms: $95/$145. Lower Bungalow: $165/$175. Upper Bungalow: $175/$185. Pump House: $165/$175. Green fees: $35/$45, including cart. Golf package: 2 nights/3 days (includes lodging, 3 days green fees covering choice of 63 holes of golf and cart, plus $40 per person of Fun Money which can be applied to meals), $572/$592 per couple. Rates are for June 16-September 5.

ARRIVAL Air: Milwaukee or Madison. Car: from Milwaukee take 41, left on 23 to Green Lake.

LAKE LAWN LODGE
Box 527, Delavan, WI 53115; (414) 728-5511; (800) 338-5253

The lodge is nestled on 275 prime wooded acres fronting on Lake Delavan. There are 284 guest rooms including suites and loft rooms. Each unit has wood paneling, vaulted ceilings, and natural stone. With 28 meeting rooms, they are equipped to handle groups or banquets of up to 500 people.

Dining is available in the Frontier Room and the coffee shop, with the unique Lookout Bar for an evening cocktail. Nightly entertainment is offered in the Frontier Cocktail Lounge.

Lake Delavan provides boating, water skiing, fishing, and swimming. In addition to the lake activity, there are two indoor swimming pools, seven indoor tennis courts, horseback riding, and a health spa complete with a steam room, sauna, and hydrotherapy pools.

Golf can be played from May through October. An attractive layout, the Lake Lawn Golf Course plays 6,418/6,173/5,215 yards and pars at 70. You will, however, find it a challenge, with traps and trees in abundance. There is an excellent clubhouse and a first-rate teaching professional.

RATES (EP) Lodges: $130. Loft rooms: $160/$180. Suites, 1 bedroom: $225/$295. Green fees: $35, carts $25. Golf package: 2 nights/3 days (includes lodging, MAP, green fees, club storage, and gratuities on food), $580/$620 per couple. Rates are for July-September.

ARRIVAL Air: Chicago (75 miles). Milwaukee (50 miles). Private aircraft: The Lodge, 4,400-foot, lighted runway. Car: from Chicago, I-94 north to Highway 50, then west to Delavan.

MAXWELTON BRAES RESORT & GOLF CLUB
Bonnie Brae Road, Baileys Harbor, WI 54202; (414) 839-2321

The name Maxwelton Braes comes from the song "Annie Laurie," whose home near St. Andrew's Golf Course was called Maxwelton House. Due to the similarity in setting, the resort was given the same name. You can stay in lodge rooms or cottages, with living room, two bedrooms, and either one or two baths. They can handle modest-size groups on a seasonal basis. Dining is provided in the new Scottish Grill & Lounge. There is also dancing each evening. A less formal eatery is the Wee Inn Coffee Shop.

In addition to two lighted tennis courts, they now have a

large swimming pool. There is also boating, horseback riding, bicycling and excellent fishing.

Golf is played on the Maxwelton Braes Country Club course. This links layout with rolling fairways, unusually large bent grass greens, and dotted with bunkers, plays a modest 6,019/5,867 yards. It pars at 70/74.

RATES (MAP) Lodge: $102 per couple. Cottages: $100/$112 per couple. Green fees: $18, carts $18. Golf packages are available. Rates are for June-September.

ARRIVAL Air: Green Bay. Car: from Green Bay, north on Highway 57.

NIPPERSINK COUNTRY CLUB & LODGE
P.O. Box 130, Genoa City, WI 53128; (414) 279-5281

Lodgings here are hotel rooms, new suites, and recently renovated cottages. The Manor has convention rooms for groups of 10 to 500. There is also a baby sitting service available. The resort serves food that is not only of excellent quality but is varied as well. For example, one of the appetizers is "sweetwater gefilte fish." I was not up to this one, but I did my part on a filet mignon, and destroyed a homemade banana cream pie. Cocktail patio dancing and nightly entertainment are also provided.

Even if golf is not your thing, there is much to do here. Possibilities include swimming in their outdoor pool, boating on adjacent Lake Tombeau (including water skiing), tennis on six courts, and horseback riding nearby.

The golf course, parring at 71/76, weighs in at 6,289/5,905 yards. Although there is little water on this layout, it features small greens, many traps, and rolling terrain.

RATES *(EP) Hotel deluxe room: $85/$95 per couple. Green fees: $18/$24, carts $24. Rates are for the July-August period.*

ARRIVAL *Air: Chicago (60 miles). Car: north on U.S. 41 or I-94 to Illinois 173, west to U.S. 12, right for 1/4 mile, right on Burlington Road (Highway "P"). Follow signs for 3 miles.*

OLYMPIA RESORT & SPA
1350 Royale Mile Road, Ocono-

mowoc, WI 53006; (414) 567-0311; (800) 558-9573

The general setting here is of forested hills, rivers, and lakes, with meadows forming a backdrop. The 400 rooms and suites have a view of either the course or the lake and are nicely furnished, with the suites offering open fireplaces and wet bars. The meeting rooms can handle groups up to 1,500 banquet- and 2,000 theater-style.

For dining there is a choice of four restaurants. The Royal Cellar, a more intimate dining room supported by a large wine list, the Garden Room Coffee Shop, the Terrace Room, and the Beach House located on Silver Lake.

A tennis program is offered on four lighted indoor and seven outdoor courts. In addition to tennis and golf there are four new racquetball courts, indoor and outdoor swimming pools, and spa . The spa offers men's and women's gyms, whirlpool baths, steam rooms, saunas, Grecian showers, and massage. Should you care to venture out on Silver Lake, you can add sailing and canoeing to the mix.

If you are having "control"

problems with your golf game you might consider taking up sailing. There is enough water to accommodate you right on the course. Playing at 6,368/6,177/5,899 yards, it pars at 71/74. With water a factor on 10 holes, lots of trees and traps, you will find this a most stimulating layout. If things get too tough a staff under the supervision of the Director of Golf, Dave Hollenbeck, is on hand to help.

The Olympic, open year-round, has a winter sports package as well, including cross country skiing.

RATES (EP) Hotel: $109. Suites: $190. Villas: 1-bedroom, $99/$125; Green fees: $24, carts $23. Golf package: 2 nights/2 days (includes lodging, 1 dinner, 1 lunch, 1 breakfast, 36 holes of golf with cart), $366 per couple. Rates are for late June to mid-September.

ARRIVAL Air: Milwaukee (30 minutes). Chicago (2 hours). Car: from Milwaukee, I-94 to exit 282, continue on Route 67 for 1 1/2 miles.

Wyoming

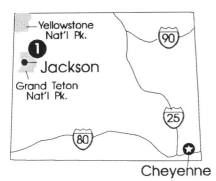

Cheyenne

1. Grand Teton—Jackson Hole Area
   Jackson Hole Racquet Club
   Teton Pines Resort

GRAND TETON-JACKSON HOLE AREA

The sheer, stark, beauty of this area is difficult to describe. It is truly "High Country." The highest point in Wyoming is 13,804 feet (Gannett Peak), but what is not generally realized is that the lowest point is still 3,100 feet above sea level (Belle Fourche River). Seven miles west of Jackson, in Teton Country, is a 40-mile-long, 8-mile-wide valley. Set within this valley is the Jackson Hole Racquet Club Resort, in operation for several years, and the newer Teton Pines Golf Course.

On the floor of the valley, surrounded by mountains on all sides, this Arnold Palmer-designed course will give you all you can handle. A few of its more challenging features include the distraction of the magnificent Teton Mountain views, 40 acres of water either threatening or coming into play on 11 holes, and three acres of sand spread over 50 bunkers. There is more than enough water to make you think you are in Florida. With its undulating fairways, the course plays 7,401/6,888/6,333/5,486 yards, parring at 72, and is without doubt one of the most beautiful layouts we have seen.

Due to the awesome scenery you may spend more time "looking up" than usual, in which case Director of Golf, John Haines, or teaching professional, Mary Carter, can help you in breaking this foolish and costly habit.

The Teton Pines clubhouse is an imposing 23,000-square-foot affair with a formal and an informal dining room, along with a bar and lounge. On the lower level are the men's and women's locker rooms, the men's card room, and the rod and gun club. On the upper level, in addition to the main lobby, there is a ladies' card room, the dining areas, conference facilities, and the pro shop.

The tennis pavilion, a separate structure, supports the seven-court complex (three indoor courts with a center stadium court). There is a tennis shop, a video instruction room, juice bar, shower rooms, and a Jacuzzi. The resident professional in charge of the "John Gardiner Tennis Center" is Dave Luebbe. Their tennis school uses all the latest state-of-the-art equipment (video replay and ball machines) to help improve your game.

There is an unusual attraction available – a fly fishing school. Headed up by nationally recognized fly fishing expert Jack Dennis, the instructions cover how to tie a fly, read a stream, cast for trout, and all the other fine points. They really get into the most advanced aspects of the sport, using videotape replay to critique and analyze your casting technique.

As for winter sports, on the property is a 10-kilometer cross-country ski course and within four miles is the Teton Village, with downhill skiing. This area represents the greatest vertical drop (4,139 feet) and is one of the largest ski areas in the United States. With 22 miles of groomed trails and spanning two mountains, its slopes are also equipped for night skiing. While the slopes and facilities for the accomplished skier are outstanding, many are also designed to accommodate the beginner and/or the intermediate ski enthusiast. Both resorts provide shuttle service during the winter.

A few additional activities within the immediate area include river rafting, horseback riding, and polo.

While it can get pretty warm during the lazy summer days, warm clothing is recommended for evening as it can turn quite cool.

In addition to the Country Club restaurants, there are two "eating experiences" awaiting you. Located in Jackson and open for lunch as well as dinner is The Blue Lion. I will not go into detail, but one of their specialties is "Jalapeno Garlic Shrimp." It is as good as it sounds. Another good restaurant, found at the Racquet Club Resort, is Stieglers, serving Austrian/continental cuisine. Listed below are the two possible places to stay. Both are on the golf course, but their accommodations are quite different.

JACKSON HOLE RAC-QUET CLUB RESORT

Star Route Box 3647, Jackson, WY 83001; (307) 733-3990; (800) 443-8616

There are 120 well-appointed condominiums ranging in size from studio and one-bedroom units to luxurious three-bedroom/loft townhouses. Each condo (including studios) has a fully-equipped kitchen, cable TV, washer/dryer, and wood burning fireplace. A nice touch – firewood is provided at no additional charge. During the evening you will be thankful for the fireplace.

Guests of the Racquet Resort have complimentary use of the private athletic club including: saunas, whirlpools, steam rooms, a Nautilus-equipped workout room, and the outdoor heated swimming pool. Although they require court fees, racquetball and tennis are also available.

A few additional amenities, located on premises, include Stiegler's Restaurant & Bar, a full-service grocery store, and a liquor store. The resort is also now capable of handling meeting groups up to 100.

RATES (EP) Studio: $139. 1-bedroom unit: $145/$159. 3 bedrooms, 2 1/2 baths: (up to 6 people) $270/$290. Rates are for July and August.

ARRIVAL Air: Jackson Hole Airport (8 miles). Car: 7 miles from Jackson on Highway 390 (also known as the Teton Village Highway), 13 miles to Grand Teton National Park, and 63 miles to the south entrance of Yellowstone National Park.

TETON PINES RESORT

Star Route Box 3669, Jackson, WY 83001; (307) 733-1005; (800) 238-2223

While Teton Pines Resort is basically a residential resort community, they have recently completed accommodations for overnight or weekly guests. Consisting of "Country Club Suites," these posh units are rented as bedrooms or as full suites. None of the units is equipped for housekeeping.

In addition to the facilities of
the clubhouse, the Teton Village (four miles away) has a
selection of restaurants, shops,
art galleries, and live stage
shows. The town of Jackson
(seven miles distant) offers
some distinctive restaurants
and shops along with the
Grand Teton Music Festival,
art exhibits, and other cultural
activities. A heated swimming
pool, adjacent to the clubhouse, is now in place.

*RATES (EP) 1 bedroom (with
deck): $250. 1 bedroom (fire-
place, deck, and living room):
$325. Green fees: $50, carts
$24.*

*ARRIVAL Air: Jackson Hole
Airport (8 miles). Car: 7 miles
west of Jackson (on Highway
390, also referred to as the Te-
ton Village Highway); 13 miles
from Grand Teton National
Park; 63 miles to Yellowstone
National Park; 82 miles to
Idaho Falls; 280 miles to Salt
Lake City.*

Canada

ALBERTA

1. Jasper Park Lodge
2. Banff Springs Hotel
3. The Lodge at Kananaskis
   The Hotel Kananaskis
   Best Western Kananaskis Inn

BANFF SPRINGS HOTEL

P.O. Box 960, Banff, Alberta, Canada T0L 0C0; (403) 762-2211; (800) 828-7447

The Banff Springs Hotel has been judged one of the top 50 resorts. The architect of the Banff Springs confronted the same breathtaking scenery as did the architect of Jasper Lodge. But he chose the opposite solution. Rather than attempting to blend the buildings in with the surroundings, he took these massive mountains head on. The result was this magnificent fortress-like structure. Although the resort dates back to the late 1800s, the current buildings opened in 1928, becoming a year-round operation in 1969. During that period a major restoration was started and is, as a matter of fact, still underway. The hotel now offers accommodations in 846 rooms and suites, including a total of 245 rooms added in 1987. With the new 107,000-square-foot conference center (opened in 1991), and including 26 breakout rooms, they can now accommodate as many as 1,600 people in various configurations. Included within the conference center (for some unknown reason) is an 18-hole miniature golf course. I guess it could keep you amused if the meeting gets too dull.

The Hotel is, in reality, a sizeable city, operating within the walls of a huge castle.

Among the dining options are: The Alberta Dining Room (breakfast, luncheon, dinner), The Alhambra Room for breakfast and dinner, The Rob Roy Room for intimate dining, and the Samurai Japanese Restaurant for a taste of the Orient. Located at the Manor Wing is the Pavilion Restaurant, serving Italian cuisine. Should you still be hungry there is the Expresso Cafe and (weather permitting) the Red Terrace for outdoor barbecues and cocktails. Added in 1991, Waldhaus Restaurant (formerly the Golf Clubhouse) has German specialties. And in case you need something to tide you over, there is also 17-hour room service. Bars include the Rundle Lounge, the Grapes Wine Bar, and King Henry's Pub.

For working off the food and drink, there is an indoor Olympic-size swimming pool, as well as a smaller outdoor pool, Jacuzzis, a sauna, an exercise area, and five tennis courts (with professional Al Robinson to assist). If water activity is your thing you may want to try your hand at fishing or sightseeing aboard *The Great Escape.*

If you can yank yourself back on dry land, a few more avenues of activity await you: horseback riding (including overnight pack trips and a morning breakfast ride), bicycling and, of course, hiking and mountain climbing. For the more adventurous, rafting tours, including a two-day trip, can be arranged. These tours supply everything – guides, rafts, tents, sleeping bags, waterproof storage for your clothing, and food. There are a variety of sightseeing tours leaving throughout the day which will allow you to see as much of this truly spectacular scenery as you wish.

Should you opt to just relax around the hotel, you will find that, between the lobby, the arcade, and the lower arcade, there must be a total of 40 different shops or services available. There is a tanning salon and masseuse, a post office, a money exchange "bank," and a beauty and barber shop. This is one busy place. I recommend that you spend the time to really explore its many delightful shops, alcoves, and levels.

One thing I did not mention: the entire area is surrounded by mile upon rolling mile of beautiful dense forests. Beautiful that is until a few trees get in front of you on the golf course. At that point they lose some of their appeal. It is not at all unusual to see elk on this course, particularly in the morning. Nor is it unusual to find huge bear paw prints in some of the sand traps early in the morning. It keeps you alert.

The Banff Golf Course now consists of three nines. Using a crossover pattern, you can play the Rundle/Sulphur combination, stretching 6,626/6,391/ 6,282/5,964 yards, with a par of 71. The Sulphur/Tunnel nines weigh in at 6,721/6,420/ 6,014 yards, also parring at 71. They must grow their ladies big and strong, as that yardage (6,014) is a bit much. The final combination is the Rundle/Tunnel course, which reaches out 6,443/6,117/5,652 yards and pars at 72. The Rundle and the Tunnel nines each bring water into play on only three holes. The Sulphur layout is, however, a different kettle of fish, as the Bow and the Spray Rivers present an interesting challenge on at least six holes.

The architects, Cornish/Robinson, went to great lengths to blend the new creation with the original Stanley Thompson design and the new nine has views even more spectacular than those on the original layout. There is also a new clubhouse. Put into operation in the fall of 1988, it has a circular design and provides an outdoor patio, a lounge and dining room, coffee shop, locker rooms, and a well-stocked golf shop. It also offers an awe-inspiring view of the entire area. Head professional Doug Wood, and staff, are on hand to assist.

RATES (EP) Twin room: $155/$325. Executive suite: $365/$395. 1-bedroom suites: $540. Green fees: $39, carts $26. Rates are for peak season May 15-October 11th.

ARRIVAL Air: Calgary (about 85 miles). Car: from the south take Highway 2 to Calgary. From Calgary go west on the four-lane Trans-Canada Highway 1.

JASPER PARK LODGE
P.O. Box 40, Jasper, Alberta, T0E 1E0 Canada; (403) 852-3301; (800) 828-7447

We were pleasantly surprised by our first view of the Jasper Park Lodge. I think we expected something more massive and imposing. Located within the heart of the Jasper National Park, this famous resort complements and blends beautifully with the surrounding countryside. The architect was indeed a wise man, recognizing that there was little

built by man that could compete with the magnificent Canadian Rockies which dominate every aspect of the area. Still, this is not a small operation. On the contrary, there are 437 guest rooms, including the deluxe Beauvert Suites. These include sitting rooms, living and dining rooms, patios, and log burning fireplaces. The Lodge, including the nearby chalets, can accommodate up to 950 guests. Should you still have a doubt as to the scope of this resort, their 13 fully-equipped conference rooms can handle groups of up to 1,000. They also provide a money exchange bank, a gift shop, fur, jewelry, clothing, and sportswear shops, and a hairdresser.

There are four dining rooms to choose from – The Beauvert, Moose's Nook, The Edith Cavell Room, and The Meadows, a new coffee shop on the promenade level. An additional source of sustenance is room service. Rather unusual is the fact that the stewards arrive at your room perched on bicycles.

The recreational possibilities seem almost endless: tennis on four hard-surfaced courts (with a professional staff), a heated outdoor swimming pool, exercise rooms, and a whirlpool for starters. There are men's and women's locker areas (with saunas and steam rooms), plus a game room with table tennis, shuffleboard, pool, and various video games. A sample of the other activities: croquet, a fully-equipped equestrian center offering trail and overnight rides, bicycling, as well as jogging and hiking on the 3.8-kilometer trail surrounding Lac Beauvert. Speaking of the lake, they also offer fishing, rowboats, canoes, sailboats, windsurfing, and pedal boats. If you really want to get serious, white water paddle rafting can be arranged on the mighty Athabasca River. There are also a number of different sightseeing excursions scheduled each day enabling you to explore as much of this magnificent area as you wish.

During the winter months you can add skating parties on Lac Beauvert, sleigh rides, snowmobiling, cross-country skiing as well as downhill skiing at Marmot Basin (12 miles from the resort – 2,300 vertical feet and 48 runs).

If you can bring yourself to part from the lodge and its activities you might consider a round of golf. The Jasper Golf Course, designed by renowned golf architect Stanley Thompson, originally came into being in 1925. It was virtually plowed under at the end of World War II, then completely rebuilt, with the present clubhouse opening in May of 1968. Parring at 71/75, it measures 6,598/6,323/6,037 yards. With gently rolling terrain, each fairway lined by trees, more than a fair number of sand bunkers coming into play, and with water becoming a nuisance on four holes, this layout will keep your undivided attention.

It is not unusual, should you be playing in the early morning, to see elk, deer, and a flock of geese, or to find a bear print in the sand traps. These prints are big. As a matter of fact they are huge. Someone suggested the professional staff attempt to teach the grizzlies a little golf etiquette and show them how to rake traps. So far there have been no volunteers.

The view of the surrounding mountains does become a definite factor. Should you keep gawking, instead of paying attention to business, you may well find yourself unable to pay your hotel bill. The operation of the course, as well as the pro shop, is under the direction of head professional, Ron

MacLeod.

RATES *(EP) Room: $236/$298. Jr. Suite: $335. Beauvert Suites: $411. Green fees: $48, carts $30.*

ARRIVAL *Air: Jasper Hinton Airport (30 minutes). Car: from Calgary take Highway 1 west to the junction of Highway 93. Take Highway 93 (Banff/Jasper Road) north to Jasper. A total of 260 miles.*

KANANASKIS VILLAGE

This beautiful 4,000-square-kilometer wildlife sanctuary has three provincial parks within its boundaries – Kananaskis, Bow Valley, and Bragg Creek. Approximately 55 miles west of Calgary, the Kananaskis Village was put together for the prime purpose of supporting the 1988 Winter Olympics. Of course, each of the facilities operates year-round. Adjacent to Nakiska at Mount Allan (location of the 1988 Winter Olympics), the area includes: a ski run with a vertical drop of 2,493 feet, one fixed-grip double chairlift, one fixed-grip triple chairlift, two detachable quad chairlifts, and one free handle tow. The total lift capacity is 8,600 people per hour.

It is aptly named a village, as it offers lodgings in the Hotel Kananaskis, the Lodge at Kananaskis, and the Best Western Kananaskis Inn. There is also a Village Center Building, providing visitors as well as overnight hotel guests some of the essential services – a post office, an information center, sports equipment rentals, showers, lockers, saunas, a lounge, two meeting rooms, and so forth. There are also various shops housed within each of the hotels. The center-piece of the village, fronting each hotel, is a most delightful outdoor ice skating rink (during the summer, a pond). The hotels surrounding the rink are within 100 yards of each other, allowing guests to walk with ease from one to the other.

While writing the above I have been avoiding a description of the surrounding area. It is not easy to do justice to this scenery. I have seen the rugged mountains in Alaska, China, Japan, and the magnificent mountains of western Colorado. While all of them are breathtakingly beautiful, none come close to these mountains. The Canadian Rockies are awesome as they stretch out from Jasper Park in the northwest, but they become even more so as you travel southeast, reaching a visual crescendo in the Kananaskis area.

Within five minutes of the village, and in the midst of this magnificent area, are two of the most interesting golf courses you will find anywhere. The Kananaskis Country Club is, in reality, two superb 18-hole layouts. The Mt. Lorette course plays to a mighty 7,102/6,643/6,155/ 5,429 yards and pars at 72. While designed by Robert Trent Jones, Sr., it must have been during a period in which he discovered that water can become a definite irritant to golfers. On the front nine, eight holes bring water into play. On the back side the Kananaskis River decides to get into the act and five holes become involved. Then, to add to the excitement which nature had provided in the form of trees, Mr. Jones scattered sand bunkers around both courses like snowflakes. As I recall there are some 136 in total.

Now we come to the Mt. Kidd layout, which operates out of the same clubhouse. It measures a masochistic 7,049/6,604/ 6,068/5,539 yards. Like the Mt.

Lorette course, it pars at 72. On the front nine, you may imagine you are playing in Florida as eight of the first nine holes introduce water into play. Our old neighbor the Kananaskis River is back and brought a friend along by the name of Evan Thomas Creek. I assume they tire of being a nuisance because on the back nine water only becomes a factor on two holes. While the Mt. Lorette course presents large, undulating and irregularly shaped greens, Mt. Kidd's are somewhat smaller. Keep in mind that you have not gotten stronger, nor are you ready for the tour. Your drives are carrying so far because of the elevation, at a bit over 4,800 feet. So tuck your ego back in and carry on.

After a round you can relax in an exceptionally fine clubhouse – offering a lounge, a dining room, two outdoor terraces, and two snack bars. There are also men's and women's locker rooms. The well-stocked pro shop, the hub of action, operates under the guidance of the Director of Golf, Brian Bygrave, and Head Professional, Wayne Bygrave.

For tee times call (403) 591-7070. The courses are public and are open to guests of all of the hotels. Green fees: $38, carts $24.

During the summer months you can add to the mix: fishing (21 stocked lakes), camping, hiking, bicycling, and horseback riding (there are four guest ranches in the area), as well as tennis on six courts.

ARRIVAL Air: Calgary (1 hour, 55 miles). Car: from Calgary travel Highway 1 west to Highway 40. Turn south to Kananaskis. The resort complex is 49 miles from Banff via Highway 1 and 40.

BEST WESTERN KANANASKIS INN
Kananaskis Village, Alberta,Canada T0L 2H0; (403) 591-7500; (800) 528-1234

The Inn, also in the village, has 96 rooms and suites. Many of the suites have fireplaces, private whirlpool baths, and balconies. Thirty-two of the suites are equipped with kitchenettes. The dining room, off the lobby, is glass-enclosed, with large windows giving a stunning view of the surrounding area. Woody's Pub on the ground floor offers an opportunity to meet friends and enjoy a cool one.

Amenities include an indoor swimming pool, hot tubs, a steam room and Jacuzzi, a patio deck for sunning, a gift shop and access to the shopping plaza of the village. There is also an underground parking garage. The Inn is capable of hosting meeting or conference groups up to 250.

For details on the golf courses refer to "Kananaskis Village."

RATES Standard: $110. Executive: $120. Loft: $140. Suites: $250/$295. Rates are for the period of June through September. Green fees: $38, carts $24.

THE HOTEL KANANASKIS
Kananaskis Village Resort, Kananaskis Country, Alberta, Canada T0L 0C0; (403) 591-7711; (800) 828-7447

In early 1988 the Hotel Kananaskis, a 69-suite VIP affair next to the lodge, came into being. It was designed as a luxurious manor-style hotel, with a lobby lounge and a dining room specializing in French cuisine. Additional attractions include a sauna, a steam room and Jacuzzi, an exercise room and, of course, access to all of the services provided by the village.

For details on the golf courses refer to "Kananaskis Village."

RATES   (EP)   Rooms: $145/$180.   Loft   suites: $225/$235. 1-bedroom suites: $255/$405. Green fees: $38, carts $24.

THE LODGE AT KANANASKIS

Kananaskis Village Resort, Kananaskis Country, Alberta, Canada T0L 0C0; (403) 591-7711; (800) 828-7447

The Lodge at Kananaskis was designed as a year-round operation. There are 255 rooms, including 64 suites with fireplaces. There is a 190-car underground heated garage beneath this three-story structure. For group functions the main ballroom can be divided into three reception or meeting rooms. Kananaskis also has a banquet capacity of 500 as well as two private dining rooms for more intimate groups.

The main guest dining room can handle 300 people. There is also a Japanese restaurant, the Sushi & Shabu Shabu bar.

Amenities include a fully-equipped health club, steam

rooms, a tanning salon, an exercise room, an indoor swimming pool, whirlpools, and a sauna.

For details on the golf courses refer to "Kananaskis Village."

RATES (EP) Rooms: $165. Executive suite: $230. 1-bedroom suite: $260/$355. Rates quoted are for the peak golf season – late June through early October. Green fees: $38, cart $24.

BRITISH COLUMBIA

BEST WESTERN 108 RESORT

R.R. #1 100 Mile House, Caribou, BC, Canada V0K 2E0; (604) 791-5211; (800) 667-5233

This resort surprised us a bit. It had more to offer than we had expected. Each room is fully carpeted, has its own private balcony, and is equipped with color television. Each has a view of the pool area, practice putting green, and the golf course. There is also a nice extra we wish all resorts offered – a coin operated laundromat.

The 108 Restaurant, with its beautiful view, offers a diverse menu. There is also cocktail service. The resort is well set up to handle meeting groups.

Within the lodge complex itself there are: saunas, whirlpools, an outdoor heated pool, barbecue pits, volleyball, horseshoes, a large playground for the younger set, and much more. There are also five plexipave tennis courts (with a professional available), bicycle rentals, horseback riding (a large stable of horses with one to match every level of expertise or lack thereof), open country riding, barbecues, and bonfire sing-a-long rides.

The beach is on a 360-acre lake just 500 yards from the resort and boat rentals are available. It is also heavily stocked with trout. Lake Watson, a bit further away, has 13 float planes as well as some conventional land aircraft used for fishing or wilderness trips. There is also a one-mile-long, lighted, fully paved, landing strip.

The resort's wildlife preserve area includes hundreds of acres of open wilderness trails stretched along some of the finest marsh breeding grounds in Canada.

The golf course, which virtually surrounds the resort, plays 6,669/6,401/6,246 yards with a par of 72/75. At first glance the Ranch Course looks easy. Do not be misled. Winding its way over slightly undulating terrain, bordered by pine and maple trees, it is no push-over. The rough is deep and you can be punished even more by straying into marshlike areas next to to some of the fairways. There is not much water on the front side (just two holes as I recall), but the back side has water in the form of a lateral ditch as well as a stream, providing a challenge on six holes. There is a large and well-stocked golf shop and a resident professional. A word of caution: be sure to bring a full supply of insect repellent.

RATES *(EP) Room: $115. Kitchenettes: $131. Executive suite: $131. Green fees: $26, carts $23. Golf packages are available. Rates are for June-September.*

ARRIVAL *Air: Vancouver or Williams Lake. Private aircraft: 1-mile-long paved runway at the resort. Car: take Highway 97 north to Mile 108 BC.*

FAIRMONT HOT SPRINGS RESORT

P.O. Box 10, Fairmont Hot Springs, BC, Canada VOB 1LO, (604) 345-6311; (800) 663-4979

We were pleasantly surprised by the excellent condition of the Canadian roads in this area. We entered Canada from northern Idaho, however, and the U.S. highways leading to the border could have been in better shape. Fairmont Hot Springs is nestled within the magnificent British Columbia Rocky Mountains.

Accommodations are in a 140-room lodge complete with a restaurant and lounge, a coffee shop, two saunas, indoor hot and cold plunge pools, and a view of the mountains which has to be seen to be believed. There is also a 265-unit trailer park (135 with full service) and about 116 time-share one- and two-bedroom villas, the latter fully-equipped for housekeeping. Something new – there are now an additional 60 condos next to the Riverside course. Should you be interested in a villa call (604) 345-6341. Some nice features include: a coin-operated laundry, two gift shops, a general convenience store, a grocery and liquor store, a gas station, and a bar-ber and beauty salon. Fairmont is also capable of handling meeting groups of up to 350.

Among the activities: swimming in four natural hot mineral outdoor pools (with temperatures ranging from 96 to 108 degrees), tennis, horseback riding, and hiking. Recently the resort has added a new "Sportsplex," offering squash, racquetball, weight rooms, an indoor swimming pool, three Jacuzzi pools, and a sauna. Two tennis courts are also at your disposal. Nearby Windermere and Columbia Lakes offer swimming, windsurfing, sailing, and water skiing. The various streams are used for white water kayaking, river raft tours, and trout fishing.

The family ski area here has a triple chair that is 4,000 feet long. There is a 1,000-foot vertical beginner's ski area, with a platter lift, a free pony tow for the younger set, night as well as cross-country and Alpine skiing nearby (3,100 vertical feet).

Golf can be played on the resort's two championship layouts. Playing from its two tee settings, the Fairmont Mountain Course measures

6,510/5,938 yards, parring at 72. It is in an area directly below the lodge, near the villas. The view from the fairways is magnificent. In fact it can be a distraction most detrimental to your game. Should you allow your attention to wander, make sure you are not playing for the family homestead.

The Riverside Course came into play in early 1989. It boasts a par-three which must carry across the mighty Columbia River. However, to be honest, it is near the headwaters and not especially mighty at this point. The Columbia River does a number throughout the course, coming into play on at least 14 holes. As a matter of fact you have to cross the river no less than four times. Parring at 71, the Riverside layout plays 6,507/6,102/5,349 yards.

The clubhouse, contains the golf shop, restaurant, and lounge. There is also a clubhouse at the new course, complete with restaurant and locker rooms.

RATES (EP) Lodge: $120. Suites: $145/$155. Villas: 1 bedroom $155, weekly $930. Green fees: $38, carts $24. There are a variety of golf package plans offered. Rates shown are for late March-September.

ARRIVAL Air: Calgary (190 miles). Private aircraft: a new 6000-foot paved runway within half a mile of the resort (equipped for commercial flights). Car: from Calgary, go west on Canada 1 to Highway 93. Turn south, continue to Radium Junction. Intersect Highway 95 south to Fairmont Hot Springs (190 miles). From Spokane, go east on I-90 to Coeur d'Alene. North on Highway 95 to the resort (260 miles).

HARRISON HOT SPRINGS HOTEL
Harrison Hot Springs, BC, Canada V0M 1K0; (604) 796-2244; (800) 663-2266

Harrison is bordered by 46-mile-long Lake Harrison on one side and the meandering Miami River on the other, with mountains surrounding the entire area. Originally put together in 1926 on 700 acres, it has undergone repeated and continuing expansion. The hotel was recently purchased by a Japanese investment group and many needed improvements have taken place. There are 81 rooms in the main hotel, 80 in the Tower, 40 in the West Wing, 14 in the Lodge, plus 15 suites and Executive Bungalows. The resort is well qualified to handle meeting groups of 15 to 600.

The Lakeside Terrace Dining Room serves breakfast, lunch, and dinner, while the Terrace Lounge is available for cocktails and live entertainment.

If you enjoy a spectacular showcase of color, then a visit to the 27-acre Minter Gardens is a must. Located 10 miles away, this theme garden will charm you. April and May are the time to be dazzled by magnolias, dogwood, and azaleas, and overwhelmed with 100,000 tulips, massive rhododendrons, and daffodils. In the summer the rose gardens, enchanting ferns, and the annuals are in their glory. In the fall add the magnificent backdrop of autumn golds and greens on 7,000-foot Mt. Cheam. Whatever else you do – bring your camera.

Meanwhile back at the resort there are seemingly endless activities: walking on the network of hiking trails, horseback riding, tennis, using the sauna and whirlpools, their famous natural hot springs, massages, croquet, jogging on special trails, bicycle riding, shuffle board, playing pickle ball or ping pong, and swimming in the outdoor heated pool. The lake offers an additional range of activity: power boating, sailing, water skiing, fishing, and two miles of sand beaches for sunbathing and swimming.

Harrison has an organized children's program with the director involving the youngsters in various games, taking them for hikes, and introducing them to creative crafts.

The golf course, while only nine holes, is a interesting layout. With more than an ample number of trees, underbrush, OB stakes, and lateral water hazards, this par-three layout will keep you busy. It plays 3,420/3,241/2,930 yards.

RATES (EP) Main hotel: $79. Tower-West Wing: $120. East Tower: $160. Suites: $185/ $385. Bungalows: $115. Green fees: (18 holes) $26, carts $22. Golf packages are available. Rates are for May-September.

ARRIVAL Air: Vancouver (80 miles). Private aircraft: seaplane landing facilities in front of the hotel. Car: take Highway 1 (Trans Canada) east. Watch for Agassiz-Harrison turn-off signs beyond Chilliwack. From Vancouver, 129 kilometers (80 miles).

KOKANEE SPRINGS GOLF RESORT

P.O. Box 49, Crawford Bay, BC, Canada V0B 1E0, (604) 227-9226

Situated along the shores of Kootenay Lake, the resort provides a magnificent vista of the Kokanee Glacier as well as the lake. The original 10 cedar A-frame chalets were installed in 1967, eight additional units were added and, finally in 1992, 26 units more were built. They have private bedrooms, bathrooms, living rooms, fully-equipped kitchens, and color TV. Ranging from one to three bedrooms, each chalet can accommodate from two to eight people. The tent and trailer park has water and electricity, fire-pits, children's playground, washrooms with showers, a coin-operated laundry, and a sani-sump. With the new lodge, Kokanee is also well set up to handle meeting groups. The clubhouse is the location of the dining room and licensed lounge as well as a golf shop.

You can swim or picnic on the sandy beach of Crawford's Bay (a five-minute walk). Fishing and a public boat launch ramp are at nearby Fishhawk Bay Marina. Fishing is, by the way, outstanding for dolly varden, kokanee salmon, and rainbow trout.

The golf course was designed by Norman R. Woods in 1967. It plays 6,537/6,193/5,747 yards with a men's par of 71, ladies' at 76. The yardage is only a sample of the challenge awaiting you. The immense rolling greens (some of the largest in Canada), coupled with 66 sand traps and 12 water hazards, backed up by mountain ash, chestnut, oak, and beech trees sprinkled throughout the course, combine to make any golfer a bit more cautious and alert than normal. At the least, I suggest you approach this layout with respect.

To illustrate the care with which the course was put together, Mr. Woods was in residence during the complete construction period and had all of the fairways hand-raked to ensure that no rocks were on the surface. For tee times call: (604) 227-9362.

RATES (EP) Chalet rooms: $102. Suites: $240. 1-bedroom chalet: $85. Tent and trailer park: $18. Green fees: $38, carts $25. Golf package: 3 nights/3 days (includes lodging, MAP, green fees, cart, and all taxes), $564/$624 per couple. Rates quoted are for late May to early September. This resort is open 6 months of the year from mid-April to mid-October.

ARRIVAL Air: a 2700-foot grass airstrip, maintained in the spring, summer, and fall. Car: 45 miles north of Creston, BC on Highway 3A. Located about 177 miles from Spokane, WA.

THE LAKESIDE RESORT
21 Lakeshore Drive, Penticton, BC, Canada V2A 7M5; (604) 493-8221; (800) 663-9400

Built along the shores of the southern tip of Okanagan Lake, this six-story hotel can offer its guests a great variety of activities. There are 204 rooms and suites – each with a balcony. A few of the amenities include: laundry and valet service, room service, color TV, and in-room movies. The Lakeside is also well set up to handle meeting groups, with a ballroom capacity of 600.

The restaurant, Peaches and Cream, is open from early morning until late evening and offers a menu ranging from full meal service to lighter fare. For more formal dining, Ripples, an elegant dining room, has an exceptional view. Then

there is the "patio," where the aroma of barbecued food may snare you. For a libation, the hotel offers the Leading Edge Lounge. With its warm, glowing fireplace this is a nice way to wind up the day.

An indoor heated swimming pool, whirlpool, two outdoor tennis courts, a Health Center complete with saunas and game room, a lakeshore jogging track, canoes, paddleboats, and a sandy beach are a sample of the activities available. A block away is a marina where you can arrange boat rentals, fishing, or a stern wheeler tour of Okanogan Lake.

Golf can be played at the Penticton Golf Club. Located in town, it measures 6,365/6,120/5,952/5,459 yards, parring at 70/72. There is a golf shop, clubhouse, and restaurant.

There are several other courses you can make arrangements to play. The Summerland Golf & Country Club is a few miles away. It has an 18-hole, par-72 course sporting a full pro shop, lounge, and dining facilities. About 40 minutes south is the Osoyoos Golf & Country Club, again a par-72, 18-hole layout. There are, in addition, several nine-hole courses in the area.

RATES *(EP) Room: $155/$170. Rates are for July-August. Green fees: $28, carts $21.*

ARRIVAL *Air: Penticton. Car: from the Okanogan Valley in Washington take Highway 97 north.*

RADIUM HOT SPRINGS GOLF RESORT
Box 310, Radium Hot Springs, BC, Canada V0A 1M0; (604) 347-9311; (800) 665-3585

Radium Hot Springs is on the western slopes of the Rocky Mountains. In the winter it is a virtual wonderland and in the summer the mountains roll on forever – the tops powdered with snow, the trees stretching out like an endless carpet. Their brochure describes the atmosphere: "We wanted a place where our guests would be removed from everyday pressures, casual, comfortable, lots to do, NO PRESSURE TO DO ANYTHING."

Accommodations at the Inn consist of studios or one- to two-bedroom suites with mini-bars. The Radium Condominiums and Villas are either one- or two-bedrooms with separate living and dining rooms, fully-equipped kitchens with dish-washers, two baths, and complete laundry facilities.

If you don't think this resort is golf-oriented, the wings bear such names as St. Andrews, Gleneagles, and Carnoustie. To carry it even further, the menu reads like a golf course map. Salads are under the heading of "Picked from the Rough," the seafood selection is "Fished from the Water Hazard and Sand Traps," and the meat entrees are "Found Grazing on the Fairway." The children's menu is called the "Pitch & Putt."

The dining room and pro shop overlook the 9th and 18th holes. The patio deck is available for lighter meals or for a cocktail. There is also the Piper Cocktail Lounge.

There is an indoor swimming pool, hot tub, whirlpool and sauna, an exercise gymnasium, massage facilities, tennis, racquetball and squash courts.

Operating first as a nine-hole layout, the Radium Hot Springs Course was enlarged to 18 holes in 1979. While not long, it is demanding. At 5,271/5,068 yards, it pars at

69/68. Although lightly trapped, with water coming into play on five holes and with tree-lined fairways, this course will demand all of your concentration.

RATES *(EP) Inn studio suite: $100/$130. Condo/Villas: 1 bedroom $150. Green fees: $26, carts $22. Golf package: 2 nights/2 days, includes lodging, green fees), $280 per couple.*

ARRIVAL *Air: Calgary (156 miles). Car: from Spokane, north on Highway 95 (278 miles).*

WHISTLER MOUNTAIN

Whistler Village, originally put together for ski buffs, is today considered one of the finest ski areas in Canada or, for that matter, in North America. The spectacular surroundings also help make it an outstanding summer golfing destination. The drive from Vancouver (75 miles) is quite picturesque. There is also train service from North Vancouver (for information call B. C. Railway 604-984-5246). Once you have arrived at the village an automobile is no longer needed.

By the way, enroute to this area you will probably pass through Vancouver. We have found a restaurant which is more than worth a stop. Located in the Park Royal Hotel, it is among the best we have ever tried. At breakfast, what they can do to a mushroom or a shrimp & crab omelette, or Eggs Park Royal (with smoked salmon and red caviar), has to be tasted to be believed. For lunch you might consider Westcoast Seafood Crepes, or thinly sliced chicken and duck. For dinner, Veal Scaloppine, Geschnetzeltes with Rosti, Roast Lamb, or Breast of Pheasant. The Park Royal is at 540 Clyde Avenue, West Vancouver, B.C., directly on your route to Whistler. Be sure to call for reservations. We find this place magnificent, but so do the locals. For reservations call the Maitre D' Hotel, Mr. Guy Easter (604) 922-2828 or 926-5511.

Whistler is, in reality, an alpine-style village, consisting of many different types of accommodations, ranging from hotels to condominiums to chalets. In fact, within the village itself there are 18 different types of lodgings, while outside the village proper (the so-called Valley Accommodations), there are another 16 ho-

tels of various kinds.

Some of the hotels provide amenities such as swimming pools, saunas, Jacuzzis, fireplaces, fully-equipped kitchens, on-premises restaurants, lounges, and tennis courts. When making reservations make clear your requirements. While a few of the inns within the village have their own restaurants, they are all grouped near a number of places to eat. The food selection is almost limitless, extending from the most sophisticated European cuisine to fast food. And they have not neglected the night life. There are 18 nightspots, ranging from neighborly pubs and rock clubs with live entertainment to romantic lounges. Their   Conference   Center

building boasts over 100,000 square feet of space and can accommodate 2,000 people.

Also within the village are a number of service and/or retail establishments: delis, bakeries, a post office and bank, a grocery, drug and liquor store, candy and ice cream shops, along with high quality stores offering brand names in knitwear, sport, and ski wear. In addition to a visiting dentist, there are two doctors on call.

A nice feature – cars are banished to convenient underground parking. The village thus becomes a "people place," with no motor vehicles to get in the way.

Activities are almost as varied as the accommodations. Whistler's five lakes and nearby rivers offer white-water canoeing, kayaking, river rafting, sailing, windsurfing and, of course, swimming and fishing. Should you tire of water action, you can wade ashore and try tennis, horseback riding, hiking, walking trails, guided mountain tours, chair lift rides, helicopter glacier skiing (that's right – glacier skiing in the summer), jogging, and cycling paths. In addition, arrangements can be made to pan for gold, tour a mine, climb a giant monolith, watch logging championships, visit hot springs, take a train ride to the desert-like Southern Cariboo, or explore the interior of British Columbia by car. Of course, you can also just relax and take it easy.

Finally, to the main focus of interest (as far as we are concerned): golf. Opened in 1983, the Whistler Golf Course, designed by Arnold Palmer, is both beautiful and a real tester. It measures 6,502/6,074/5,381 yards and pars at 72. While this layout is fun, the second nine can give you problems. At one time this was a swamp area and a great deal of water was redirected to form hazards. There is one creek which really becomes a nuisance, paralleling and then crossing one fairway no less than three times. As I recall, it was the par-five, 11th.

The first two holes are gentle and can lead you to believe it will all be smooth sailing. Not so. On the third, you will get acquainted with your first bit of water, in the form of a pond and a stream. At this point, you may begin to get the idea that you had better pay attention. If you do not, prepare yourself for a bad afternoon. A word of warning: be sure to have a supply of mosquito repellent with you – or suffer.

Should you plan to stay overnight, tee times can be reserved at the same time you make your reservations. If your visit is for golf only, you should call – not less that five days in advance – (604) 932-4544.

A new Robert Trent Jones, Jr. course opened in early 1993. To say that it is spectacular is a monumental understatement. For details on this new golf course, refer to the Chateau Whistler Resort on the following pages.

CHATEAU WHISTLER RESORT
4599 Chateau Blvd., Whistler, BC, Canada VON 1B0; (604) 938-8000; (800) 828-7447

It is more than 100 years since a grand chateau hotel has been built in Canada. One need only look at the enormous cost to understand why. In late November of 1989 the massive 12-story Chateau Whistler Resort greeted its first quests. It reflects a strange mixture – the motif is of the 1800's but it is a new structure with all of the modern amenities. The setting does little to dispel the grandeur, with beautiful towering Blackcomb Mountain forming the backdrop.

There are 343 guest rooms, including 36 suites and 14,000 square feet of space set aside for convention/meeting groups.

Restaurants are The Wildflower and La Fiesta. For cocktails try the Mallard Bar; with its piano music and warm glowing fireplace it is an excellent gathering place. As a possible alternative to dining at the Chateau I suggest a super place called Trattoria Di Umberto in the village. It serves some of the finest Italian food we have tasted, and it also has the advantage of being modestly priced. As an alternative for breakfast, try The Glacier Lodge Cafe & Deli, directly across from the hotel.

For those seeking activities, there is a health club with an indoor-outdoor swimming pool, whirlpools, an exercise room, massage, saunas, steam rooms, plus tennis, hiking, fishing, biking, canoeing, rafting, horseback riding, and mountain biking.

During the winter months the Chateau really comes into its own. The resort sits on top of some of the finest skiing in

North America. For details refer to the "Whistler Resort Association" section of this book.

The new Robert Trent Jones, Jr. golf course came into play in early 1993. Measuring 6,635/6,243/5,692/5,157 yards, it pars at 72. Literally carved out of a rugged forest setting and using abrupt elevation changes (up to 300 feet), with water a factor on 12 holes, along with ancient Douglas firs, and massive granite outcroppings, this may eventually be judged one of the finest golf courses in the country. The course manager is David Gordon, and the Head Professional is Greg McCullough, former professional at the Algonquin in New Brunswick.

There is also the Arnold Palmer-designed course, located close by. For more detail on the Palmer course, as well as the tremendous number of things to do and places to eat, refer to the "Whistler Resort Association."

RATES   (EP)   Rooms: $135 / $185. Suites: $240 / $800. Golf packages are available. Green fees: $65 / $75, including cart.

ARRIVAL Air: Vancouver (airport is 90 miles away). Private aircraft: charter flights can be arranged into Pemberton Airport (30 minutes).

Reservations can be made at the following hotels using the Whistler Resort Association telephone numbers, (604) 932-4222 or, within the U.S. & Canada, (800) 944-7853.

BLACKCOMB LODGE
72 rooms, indoor swimming pool, common-use sauna and Jacuzzi. Fireplaces in some units, kitchens in most.

CARLETON LODGE
16 rooms, a Jacuzzi, fireplace, and kitchen in most units. Satellite TV, restaurant, and lounge.

CLOCKTOWER HOTEL
15 rooms, common-use sauna, kitchen in most units, cable TV, restaurant, and lounge.

DELTA MOUNTAIN INN
290 rooms, outdoor pool, sauna, Jacuzzi, fireplace, and kitchen in some units. Satellite TV, restaurant, lounge.

FAIRWAYS HOTEL
194 rooms, an outdoor pool, sauna and Jacuzzi, restaurant, and lounge. Cable TV.

FIREPLACE INN
37 rooms, Jacuzzi, fireplace, and kitchen in most units. Restaurant, lounge, cable TV.

FITZSIMMONS CONDOS
10 units, sauna, Jacuzzi, fireplace, kitchen in most units. Cable TV. Restaurant and lounge.

HEARTHSTONE LODGE
10 units, sauna, fireplace, kitchen in most units. Satellite TV.

LISTEL WHISTLER HOTEL

97 rooms, a sauna, and Jacuzzi. Restaurant, lounge, and satellite TV.

MOUNTAINSIDE LODGE

90 units, an outdoor swimming pool. A sauna, Jacuzzi, fireplace, kitchen in most units. Restaurant, lounge, and satellite TV.

NANCY GREENE LODGE

137 units, an outdoor swimming pool, sauna, and Jacuzzi. Fireplace and kitchen available in some units. Restaurant, lounge, and satellite TV.

TANTALUS LODGE

76 units, an outdoor swimming pool, a sauna, and Jacuzzi. Fireplace and kitchen in most units. Cable TV.

TIMBERLINE LODGE

42 units, an outdoor swimming pool, sauna, and Jacuzzi. Fireplace in some units. Restaurant, lounge, and cable TV.

VILLAGE GATE HOUSE

20 units, Jacuzzi in some units. Fireplace, kitchen in most units. Cable TV.

WESTBROOK WHISTLER

49 units, Jacuzzis in some units. Fireplace, kitchen in most units. Cable TV.

WHISTLERVIEW

9 units, sauna, fireplace, kitchen in most units. Jacuzzi in some units. Restaurant, lounge, cable TV.

WHISTLER VILLAGE INN

88 units, outdoor swimming pool, sauna, and Jacuzzi. Fireplace and kitchen in most units. Restaurant, lounge, and cable TV.

WINDWHISTLE CONDOS

4 units, Jacuzzi, fireplace, kitchen, satellite TV. Restaurant and lounge.

RESORTS ON BLACKCOMB MOUNTAIN

FOXGLOVE
36 units, fireplace, kitchen, and cable TV.

GABLES
9 units, Jacuzzi, fireplace, kitchen available in most units. No TV.

GLACIER LODGE
112 units, ranging from lodge rooms to two-bedroom suites featuring fireplace and fully-equipped kitchen. An outdoor swimming pool and cable TV. Also has meeting space, laundry facilities, and a fireside lounge.

GREYSTONE LODGE
91 units, ranging from hotel rooms to two-bedroom fully-equipped suites. Indoor hot tub in the suites, use of laundry facilities, and underground parking. New hotel completed in late 1989.

LE CHAMOIS
50 studios and suites. Convenience kitchens (kitchenette) in all units, micro-wave, small refrigerator, fully-equipped for four people. There is bell service, room service, heated outdoor pool, conference and meeting facilities, two restaurants, and cocktail lounge. Virtually on top of ski facilities. Underground parking. Laundry.

THE MARQUISE
90 units, one or two bedrooms, fully-equipped kitchen, gas fireplace, cable TV, outdoor heated pool, indoor hot tub and sauna, underground parking.

STONERIDGE
Nine units, fireplace, kitchen in all units. No TV.

WILDWOOD LODGE
33 units, outdoor swimming pool. Fireplace and kitchen in all units. Cable TV.

LODGINGS OUTSIDE THE VILLAGE

FITZSIMMONS CREEK LODGE
45 units, kitchen in some units. Restaurant, lounge, and

cable TV.

GONDOLA VILLAGE
45 units. Fireplace and kitchen in most units. Cable TV.

HIGHLAND VALE
55 units, a sauna and Jacuzzi. Fireplace and kitchen in some units. Restaurant, lounge, and satellite TV.

LAKE PLACID LODGE
104 units, outdoor swimming pool, a Jacuzzi. Kitchen in most units. Cable TV.

THE SEASONS
13 units. Fireplace and kitchen in most units. Cable TV.

WHISTLER CREEK LODGE
43 units, outdoor swimming pool, a sauna, Jacuzzi, tennis courts. Fireplace, kitchen in most units. Restaurant, lounge, cable TV.

WHISTLER ON THE LAKE
24 units. Fireplace and kitchen in most units. Cable TV.

WHISTLER RESORT & CLUB
42 units, outdoor swimming pool, a sauna, Jacuzzi and tennis courts. Fireplace and kitchen in most units. Restaurant, lounge and cable TV.

WHISKI JACK RESORTS
15 units, a sauna. Jacuzzi in some units. Fireplace, kitchens in most units. Cable TV.

BED & BREAKFAST INNS

ALTA VISTA CHALET
6 units, sauna, Jacuzzi and fireplaces. Cable TV.

CHALET LUISE
6 units, sauna, Jacuzzi. Fireplace in most units. No TV.

DURLACHER HOF
7 units, sauna. Fireplace in most units. No TV.

EDELWEISS
6 units, sauna, fireplaces. No TV.

HAUS HEIDI
6 units, sauna, Jacuzzi. Fireplace in most units. No TV.

In addition to the above, there is an alternative. Should you wish to stay in some of the private homes in the area call **WHISTLER CHALETS** – from Vancouver (604) 683-7799 or toll free (800) 663-7711.

ARRIVAL Air: Vancouver, BC (75 miles from town, 95 miles from airport). Car: from Vancouver take Highway 99 northbound along Howe Sound (allow about 2 hours). Avis has a car rental office at Whistler. There is also taxi service operating year-round from Whistler Village to Vancouver International Airport (call 932-5455).

MANITOBA

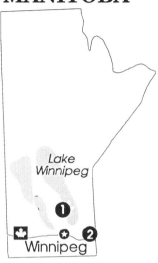

1. Gull Harbour Resort
2. Falcon Lake Resort & Club

FALCON LAKE RESORT & CLUB
Falcon Boulevard, Falcon Lake, Manitoba, Canada R0E 0N0; (204) 349-8400 Winnipeg 943-3400

The Falcon Lake Resort, a little less than two hours driving time east of Winnipeg, is at the southern end of Whiteshell Provincial Park. Accommodations vary from motel rooms to executive apartments, with kitchenette, patio, air-conditioning, color TV, VCR, and a barbecue grill. Some of the aforementioned equipment must be specifically requested at an additional charge.

The resort is well set up to handle conferences, banquets or meetings/seminars and can work with groups of from 10 to 250. There is a dining room and lounge available, as well as a games room and a children's arcade.

Situated on the shores of magnificent Falcon Lake, all kinds of water activities are possible. Within this 1,000-square-mile park setting you will find everything from wilderness to a small shopping mall. In the town (a short walk from the hotel) is a professionally maintained sports complex offering tennis, horseback riding, lawn bowling, and miniature golf. Activities located on premises include: an indoor heated swimming pool, a spa and sauna, boating, lake swimming, and fishing. During the winter months you can add downhill and cross-country skiing, snowmobiling, ice fishing, and indoor curling.

The par-72 golf course is operated by the Provincial Parks Department.

RATES (EP) Motel rooms: $57/$69. Executive apartments: $85/$95. Weekly $530.

Green fees: $18, carts $18. Rates quoted are for the peak summer season of late June through early September.

ARRIVAL Air: Winnipeg (90 miles). Car: take Trans Canada Highway 1 due east to Falcon Lake.

GULL HARBOUR RESORT
General Delivery, Riverton, Manitoba, Canada R0C 2R0; (204) 475-2354

This area has a most interesting history. In 1876 volcanic eruptions on Mount Hekla sent thousands of Icelanders fleeing to Manitoba. A few of these hardy souls, in quest of prime fishing grounds, came to Lake Winnipeg where they discovered and settled on what is now called Hecla Island. Gull Harbour Resort, some 110 miles north of Winnipeg, is on the northeastern tip of Hecla Island. Remains of the original fishing village can still be found.

There are 91 guest rooms plus two suites. Most ground floor rooms provide a patio area, while the suites have spacious living areas and fireplaces. All rooms are equipped with satellite TV. The resort can handle meeting and conference groups with a capacity from 5 to 125 people.

The dining room has a wide choice of cuisine, ranging from country fare and seafood to Icelandic baking. In addition to the lounge there also is a coffee shop. During the summer months, the resort operates an outside bar and grill for quick lunches or even an evening barbecue.

A few of the indoor activities include use of the swimming pool, sauna, whirlpool, and (in the gym) basketball, volleyball, or badminton. For the children they provide a wading pool, an arts and crafts program, and scavenger hunts. Step outside and you can try tennis, baseball, shuffleboard, windsurfing, and even horseshoes. There is always the added adventure of exploring this historic island.

Since the resort is open year-round, during winter you can add: cross-country skiing, ice fishing, tobogganing, ice skating and, should you really want to wreck yourself, snow shoeing.

The Hecla golf course is adjacent to the parking lot of the lodge and runs along the lake itself. Parring at 72, it measures 6,022/5,735/5,060 yards. There is a fair amount of water on this layout with ponds in play on #15, #16, and #17. There is also an inlet from Lake Winnipeg becoming a nuisance on numbers #10, #11, and #12. The course, owned and operated by the Manitoba Parks System, is under the supervision of golf professional Jim Mayer.

RATES (EP) Standard Rooms: $85/$95. The resort also offers golf packages. Green fees: $21, carts $23.

ARRIVAL Air: Winnipeg (110 miles). Private aircraft: Riverton (limited airstrip). Car: from Winnipeg take Highway 8 north.

Mexico

The physical dimensions of Mexico are relatively easy to describe: it is a country of some 760,000 square miles, bordered on the north by the United States, on the south by Guatemala and Belize, on the east by the Gulf of Mexico as well as the Caribbean Sea, and on the west by the majestic Pacific Ocean. But the land, the rich history, and the people are not so simple to write about. They are a people with a rich heritage, now reaching for a more modern society.

Exceptional art forms have been produced since the eighth century BC. Pyramids and temples in the mountains, jungles, and valleys, along with old churches and colonial palaces hidden away in many small villages, can provide a history buff with a lifetime of exploration.

Situated between the two Sierra Madre mountain ranges lie the flatlands of Mexico. At an elevation of 2,500 to 10,000 feet, this area enjoys a moderate climate. It also is where most of the larger cities and the bulk of Mexico's almost 70 million people can be found.

In the coastal lowland areas, where most of the major resorts are sited, the climate is definitely tropical. While extremely warm during the summer months, the temperature is pleasant during the winter.

Don't be reluctant to shop – Mexico is a bargainer's paradise. Don't be reluctant to take tours. You will often see a better selection of sights at a lower cost that way. And when the sun goes down Mexico comes alive. Take part, as there is much to see and to do. When all is said and done the best part of Mexico is the people. They are still warm and friendly. And, amazingly, they are graciously tolerant when we mutilate their beautiful language.

THINGS YOU NEED TO KNOW

For international flights, you need to arrive at the airport at least an hour and half prior to departure. For flights within Mexico, one hour is fine. Baggage limit: two checked pieces and one carry-on.

To avoid hassles, be sure to bring your passport You must

have a "tourist card" to enter Mexico. Once you have filled it out – **do not misplace it. You must present it upon departure.**

there is no need to bring converters. While most resorts will accept major credit cards, we found that none would take personal checks.

The electricity is 120 volts/60 cycle (same as U.S.). Thus

The climate is mild, in fact warm, but the nights can get

1. Los Cabos
   Palmilla Resort Hotel
2. Mazatlan
   Camino Real Mazatlan
   El Cid Resort
3. Puerto Vallarta
   Marriott Casa Magna
   Villa Quinta Real
4. Valle De Bravo
   Avandaro Golf Resort
5. Manzanillo
   Las Hadas
6. Ixtapa-Zihuatanejo

Camino Real Ixtapa
Sheraton Ixtapa
7. Acapulco
   Acapulco Princess Resort
   Las Brisas Resort
   Pierre Marques Resort
8. Cancun
   Camino Real Cancun
   Casa Maya Cancun
   Hyatt Cancun
   Krystal Cancun
   Marriott Casa Magna Resort
   Stouffer Presidente

cool. It is wise to have a jacket or sweater for the evening hours.

There are certain remote areas where travel by private vehicle is not recommended and, in fact, can be dangerous. Check with your resort management.

ACAPULCO-GUERRERO AREA

Acapulco, 150 miles south of Zihuatanejo/Ixtapa, has been referred to as one of the world's greatest playgrounds. With its magnificent bay, miles of beaches, shops galore, and many beautiful resorts, that is an apt description. But it has become crowded, so careful advance planning is necessary to assure yourself of reservations which fit your style and pocket book.

ACAPULCO PRINCESS RESORT
P.O. Box 1351, Acapulco, Guerrero, Mexico 39868; 011-52-748-4-31-00; (800) 223-1818

Set on 480 acres along Revolcadero Beach, the Princess is one of the largest resorts in Mexico. The main building is in the shape of an Aztec Pyramid with an atrium soaring 16 stories. Within this structure are 423 rooms plus junior suites and six penthouses. A short distance away, connected by a covered walkway, is the 10-story Princess Tower with additional rooms and suites. Alongside the shopping arcade is the 10-story Marquesa Tower. In total there are 1,020 rooms. All rooms have a private terrace, a bathroom with tub and shower, separate dressing area with a walk-in closet, and air-conditioning.

The eight restaurants (not including those at the golf courses) offer a wide variety of cuisine. The Veranda has authentic Chinese food. La Posadita, an open-air affair overlooking the pools and the beach area, starts with an international breakfast, has a seafood menu for lunch, then switches to a BBQ Mexican buffet during the evening. The Chula Vista offers a buffet dinner and has a marimba band performing each evening. La Princesa, the main dining room, serves continental fare, as does El Jardin. Should you prefer French cuisine there is La Gourmet. Then there is the wonderful Mexican food of La

Hacienda, one of Acapulco's most popular dining spots and a Holiday Award winner. One final point – the dress code is casual at all times. I am happy to report that this is a civilized operation – while there are eight restaurants, they have **nine** bars on the property. Included in the count are a nightclub, a dance pavilion, and two-swim up bars. This resort is well-equipped to handle meeting groups and/or banquets with a capacity ranging up to 2,000 theater- and 1,200 banquet-style.

Activities include tennis on nine outdoor and two indoor courts (there is grandstand seating for 200 and all courts are lighted), and swimming in four fresh water pools plus a salt water lagoon featuring a water slide, as well as a children's wading pool. Other activities which can be arranged are scuba diving, deep sea fishing, parasailing, waterskiing, sailing, catamaran cruises, a yacht cruise, even night club tours. Finally, all of the facilities at the nearby Pierre Marques Hotel (also a Princess Resort property) – restaurants, tennis courts, golf course – are at the disposal of guests of the Princess.

There are two golf layouts: the Acapulco Princess course and the testier Pierre Marques. The two, side by side, are directly across the street from their respective hotels. The Acapulco, playing 6,355/6,085/5,400, pars at 72. A Ted Robinson design, it presents its own challenge in the form of water on 10 holes and many trees. For detailed coverage of the more difficult Pierre Marques course, refer to the Pierre Marques Resort below. Both the Princess and the Marques courses are supported by a driving range and pro shop.

RATES During high season (mid-December through Easter) the resort per-day cost is based on MAP, while during the off-season (after Easter to mid-December) the resort is on an EP basis. (MAP) Rooms: $260 per couple. Jr. suites: $345 per couple. Executive suites: $370 per couple. Green fees: $60, including cart. Golf package: 3 nights/3 days (includes MAP, lodging, all taxes, green fees on either course, golf cart and bag storage), $1,040/$1,224/$1,426 per couple.

ARRIVAL Air: Acapulco International Airport. Government-run taxi service is available from the airport to the hotel.

LAS BRISAS RESORT
P.O. Box 281, Acapulco, Guerrero, Mexico 39868; 011-52-748-4-15-80; (800) 228-3000

I think our love affair with Las Brisas began upon arrival. Having flown from Mexico City and then driven to the hotel, our tongues were literally hanging out. Before I could even get my room confirmation forms out, some delightful person placed a tall cool tropical drink in my hand. What a great way to start a relationship. Las Brisas is more a village than a resort/hotel. As a matter of fact it seems more like a fantasy land than a real place. This magnificent resort is the essence of a posh, luxuriant life style. It also happens to be a AAA Five Diamond Award winner

Along the side and on top of Las Brisas hill the resort contains over 300 casitas. Each unit is sited in such a manner as to provide a maximum amount of privacy as well as views of Acapulco Bay. These views, outstanding during the daylight hours, are beyond description at night, as you look down on the various ships in the harbor and across the bay to brilliantly-lit Acapulco.

A few of the thoughtful amenities include: fresh flowers flown in from Mexico City each day placed on your pillows and sprinkled in your swimming pool; a continental breakfast left in a little slide-through door of your room each morning; a complimentary bowl of fresh fruit replenished daily and a fully-stocked bar. In each casita is a louvered wall which glides back to reveal a delightful pool (either private or shared). As there are 250 pools on the property this means only 96 casitas share a pool while all others have their own.

The main dining room, "Bella Vista," is a terrace patio open on three sides. It lives up to its Spanish name – Beautiful View. When evening falls you can enjoy gourmet cuisine along with music and dancing. There is also El Mexicano, located at the top of the hill, offering charcoal-broiled Mexican specialties. The dress code is casual. No ties or jackets are worn. Another nice touch, **no tipping is allowed.** The best of all, however, is having dinner served on the patio next to your private pool.

Tennis can be played on five lighted courts, or join a jeep caravan for an excursion to the bullfights (available only during the winter season). You can take a jeep safari for a visit to nearby fishing villages, plantations, or tropical lagoons; or you can arrange for your own jeep to explore the area. Las Brisas has over 300 separate casitas sprinkled over 110 acres. Jeeps decorated in the same color scheme as the buildings (pink and white) get you from one place to another. There are many of them (some 150 in total), so there is never a delay in getting where you need to go.

Descend to the beach area and another world opens up. At the foot of the bluff is the Concha Beach Club. Available only to members and guests of the resort, there is windsurfing, parasailing, waterskiing, snorkeling, sailing, and even a private scuba diving club. La Concha Restaurant is something to long remember.

Golf can be arranged for quests of Las Brisas at either the Acapulco Princess or the Pierre Marques golf courses. For detail on either of these layouts refer to the sections on these resorts.

RATES (EP) Casitas: (shared pool) $200 / $215; with (private pool) $300 / $475. 1-bedroom suites: (private pool and whirlpool) $595 and up. All rates include continental breakfast. You are charged a fee (about $20) each day of your stay to cover all tipping. This includes check-in and departure.

ARRIVAL Air: Acapulco International Airport (20 minutes). Government-operated taxi service is available from the airport to the resort.

PIERRE MARQUES RESORT
P.O. Box 474, Acapulco, Guerrero, Mexico 39868; 011-52-748-4-20-00; (800) 223-1818

The Marques offers a total of 344 rooms. The main building, has 86 rooms, as well as junior suites, and there are also accommodations in the five-story tower. All have ocean views. There is also the villa section of the hotel, with its assortment of rooms and suites offering garden views. Each room has a private bath/tub shower, radio, either a terrace or patio, and is air-conditioned.

There are several dining options: La Terraza, an outdoor restaurant, overlooks the pools and beach area; the Tabachin Room has continental cuisine; the Amigo Restaurant serves Italian cuisine. There is also a snack/bar at the golf course, offering sandwiches and bar service. The Pierre Marques is capable of handling meeting groups up to 280 school-room-style and 500 in a theater-style setting.

Tennis can be played on five lighted outdoor courts. Other amenities available include: three freshwater swimming pools plus a children's wading pool, aerobics classes, theme parties, cooking classes, and Spanish orientation classes. In addition, all of the activities offered by the Acapulco Princess Hotel are available to guests of the Pierre Marques. Additional activities which can be arranged are scuba diving, deep sea fishing, waterskiing, parasailing, catamaran or yacht cruises, and night club tours.

Originally designed by the well known golf architect Percy Clifford, the course was redone by Robert Trent Jones, Jr. in time for the 1982 World Cup Tournament. While fun to navigate (water in play on 13 holes), it places a premium on accuracy off the tee and delivers immediate chastisement for erratic shots. The yardage alone should give you some indication as to what you can face. Measuring 6,855/6,557/6,112/5,197 yards, it pars at

72/73. As a guest of the Pierre Marques Hotel, you can elect to play the Acapulco Princess layout as well. For more detailed information refer to the Acapulco Princess Resort above.

RATES   (MAP)   Rooms: $185 / $250 per couple. Jr. Suites: $270 / $290 per couple. Suites: (separate living rooms) $310 per couple. Golf package: 3 nights / 3 days (includes lodging, green fees on either the Marques or Princess courses for 3 rounds, cart, club storage, does not include meals), $890 / $990 / $1,108 per couple.

ARRIVAL Air: Acapulco International Airport. Government-operated taxi service is available from the airport to the hotel.

LOS CABOS, BAJA CALIFOR- NIA SUR

Los Cabos is at the southern tip of the Baja California peninsula. Approximately 1,000 miles (805 air miles) from San Diego, it is a two-hour flight from Los Angeles. Los Cabos encompasses two major towns: San José del Cabo and Cabo

San Lucas, with an 18-mile highway which links them. Founded in 1730, San José del Cabo is a quiet Mexican village with a population of approximately 24,000. Cabo San Lucas, on the southern tip of the peninsula, is a fast-growing community of just over 25,000. Each town offers a variety of excellent restaurants and night spots.

Los Cabos has long been recognized as one of the world's premier sport fishing areas. Although there are about 850 different species, the prize catches include marlin, sailfish, tuna, dorado, wahoo, and roosterfish. The season for golf is mid-October through mid-May. The best time for sport fishing is summer and, for whale watching, winter.

There are several developments underway which will bring to this area spectacular destination resorts, along with several golf courses.

PALMILLA RESORT HOTEL
San José del Cabo, BCS, Mexico 23400, 011 52 684 205 82; (800) 637-2226

About five km from San José del Cabo, this 900-acre development has over two miles of coastline fronting on the Sea of Cortez. Along with the hotel, plans call for custom home sites and villas offering ocean, fairway, mountain, and desert views. The Palmilla hotel has 72 guest rooms plus eight two-bedroom suites and two five-bedroom villas. Most accommodations are air-conditioned and have patios or balconies. Some include sitting rooms as well. The hotel has set aside a separate cabana to handle meeting groups of up to 200.

The dining room offers an expansive menu ranging from continental to Mexican specialties. There is also an excellent lounge. An extra not often found: upon receiving your wake-up call you will find that it is accompanied by freshly squeezed orange juice, coffee, a warm croissant, and sweet rolls.

There are two tennis courts, paddle tennis, croquet, volleyball, shuffleboard, and a swimming pool. Many additional water-related activities can be arranged: scuba diving, snorkeling, surfing, sailing, waterskiing, and some of the most fabulous sport fishing in the world. A short walk from the hotel, is a two-mile stretch of beach offering some of the area's finest swimming. During the appropriate season, whale watching also becomes popular. Excursion trips can be set up, including sunset cruises as well as an observation trip to watch sea lions basking in the sun.

When complete, Palmilla will include 27 holes of championship golf designed by Jack Nicklaus, a golf clubhouse complete with pro shop, restaurant, and lounge, a driving range, and practice putting area. The three nines – referred to as The Mountain, Ocean, and Arroyo – will be played using a "cross-over" system, allowing you to play them as three 18-hole layouts. A variety of distractions and challenges await you, such as spectacular ocean, mountain, and lake views, deep arroyos, a variety of cacti and, of course, more than a quorum of sand bunkers. The Director of Golf Operations is Johnny Pott.

Plans call for an enlarged tennis complex, featuring a stadium court and tennis shop, plus a beach club and a shopping/entertainment area.

A second resort development, Cabo del Sol, is also underway. Approximately 12 miles dis-

tant, it is destined to include 2,000 hotel rooms, at least two golf courses, and 3,000 condominiums, along with many private homes.

RATES (EP) Hotel rooms: $185/$220. 1-bedroom suite: $265/$305. Villas: $900/ $1,500. Golf packages will be available.

ARRIVAL Air: San José International Airport (25 minutes). At the time you make reservations ask for pick-up service.

CANCUN - YUCATAN PENINSULA

The Yucatan Peninsula is as deeply immersed in history as any place on earth. In fact, the mystery surrounding the Maya civilization is one of the greatest enigmas to face modern archaeologists. At a period just prior to 250 A.D. this culture began to form. From 900 to approximately 1500 it flourished and, by some estimates, reached a population of some 16 million. During this six-century period, a dynamic and sophisticated society was created, with nobles, priests, artists, scribes, craftsmen, warriors, and farmers. This structured civilization built a great many Mayan cities and temples. Their technical and architectural achievements have continued to astonish the world. The two basic questions which linger on are: how did they accomplish what they did with the limited equipment available during that period and, of course, what happened to them? True, there are some four million descendants still speaking the Maya languages, but the once proud and magnificent cities no longer rule.

On the northeastern tip of the peninsula is an area known for its fabulous beaches and mild climate – Cancun. There is much evidence, in the form of ruins, that the Mayan people also came here to play and enjoy the sand and sea. Golf is our main purpose, but to visit this area and not explore at least some of the history all about you would indeed be a travesty.

Cancun, a Mayan word, means "Pot of Gold." With an average of 240 cloudless days a year, it is little wonder the Mayan people came here for a respite from the interior rain forest. Cancun is an island connected to the mainland by two bridges and is the site of several re-

sorts, as well as a golf course.

Golf can be played on the Pok-Ta-Pok Golf Club course. Just so we stay even on the name, it comes from the Mayan language and means "game played with a stick." You can't get more basic than that. The course is a Robert Trent Jones, Jr. design. Playing to a par of 73/74, it reaches a more than respectable 6,721/6,142/5,586 yards. The clubhouse includes a pro shop and a cafeteria serving breakfast and lunch.

CAMINO REAL
P.O Box 14, Cancun, Quintana Roo, Mexico, 77500, 011-52-988-3-01-00; (800) 228-3000

The Camino literally projects out into the ocean. In fact, from a distance, it appears to be partially in the water. The hotel is a modified pyramid-style structure with 379 rooms, including suites. A recent addition, the 18-story Royal Beach Club, houses 87 of the hotel's rooms and 18 of the deluxe suites. Some of the units have a private whirlpool spa. All accommodations are air-conditioned and have color TV.

Restaurants include the Calypso, specializing in Caribbean cuisine, Azulejos and the open-air La Brisa, serving steak and the daily catch of seafood. There is also El Tucan, with regional specialties. As a matter of vital interest, the Camino has its own water purification system. The resort can handle up to 550 Banquet-style in their meeting rooms.

In addition to two outstanding beaches (water on three sides), you will find tennis available on four lighted courts and a heated fresh water pool. The pool has a swim-up bar. Snorkeling, waterskiing, sailing, deep-sea fishing, and excursions in glass-bottom boats can also be arranged. For those wishing to venture a bit further, you can set up a trimaran trip, including a five-hour excursion to the Isla Mujeres. Or you can spend a subdued, quiet day on the beach doing **nothing at all**.

Golf can be arranged on the Pok-Ta-Pok golf course. For details refer to Cancun-Yucatan Peninsula above.

RATES (EP) Rooms: $220. Beach Club: $280. Suites: $500 and up. Green fees: $50, carts $30.

ARRIVAL Air: Cancun International Airport (approximately 12 miles).

CASA MAYA CANCUN
Boulevard Kukulcan – Hotel Zone, Cancun, Quintana Roo, Mexico 77500; 011-52-988-30555; (800) 458-6888

Fronting the beach, Casa Maya, a high-rise hotel, is only five minutes from downtown Cancun and one mile from the golf course. Accommodations are in 356 rooms, including 250 suites. They have three restaurants and three bars. The hotel is equipped to handle modest-size group functions with a capacity of 150 people. There are three swimming pools, three lighted tennis courts, and a marina providing a variety of water activities, including deep sea fishing charters. Nearby are a great many places for sightseeing and entertainment: shopping centers, archaeological sites, dinner shows, excursion boat tours, and so forth.

For details on the Robert Trent Jones, Jr. golf course, refer to Cancun-Yucatan Peninsula above.

RATES (EP) Rooms: $130. Suites: $160 and up. Green fees $50, carts $30.

ARRIVAL Air: Cancun International Airport (20 minutes).

HYATT CANCUN CARIBE

P.O. Box 353, Cancun, Quintana Roo, Mexico 77500; 011-52-988-30044; (800) 233-1234

This deluxe Hyatt was built along one of the finest secluded white sand beaches on Cancun. There are 198 rooms including 21 beachfront villas. They also have meeting facilities and can handle groups of up to 125.

The restaurants are the Cocay Steak House, the Blue Bayou, La Concha, offering Mexican specialties, and the Cassis Bar.

They have a swimming pool, tennis courts, a private marina and, of course, golf. For details on the golf, located nearby, refer to Cancun-Yucatan Peninsula.

RATES   (EP)   Rooms: $180/$275. Suites & villas: $360/$450. Green fees: $50, carts $30.

ARRIVAL Air: Cancun International Airport.

KRYSTAL CANCUN

Pasea Kukulcan, Cancun, Quintana Roo, Mexico 77500; 011-52-988-311-33; (800) 231-9860

The Krystal is a high-rise directly on the beach. It is across from the 17,000-square-foot convention center. There are 330 air-conditioned rooms and suites. Some of the units have a private swimming pool, while all are equipped with mini-bars and satellite TV.

Amenities include: Bogart's Casablanca Restaurant, an outstanding disco called "Christine," a coffee shop, two large swimming pools, lighted tennis and racquetball courts, and a fully-equipped health club, including a gymnasium, a Jacuzzi and sauna, as well as a massage service. They also have meeting facilities.

Guests can play the Pok-Ta-Pok Golf Course. For details refer to Cancun-Yucatan Peninsula.

RATES   (EP)   Rooms: $170/$195. Suites: $200/$425. Green fees: $50, carts $30.

ARRIVAL Air: Cancun International Airport.

MARRIOTT CASA MAGNA RESORT

Boulevard Kukulkan, Retorno Chac Lote 41, Cancun, Quintana Roo, Mexico 77500; 011 52

988 52000; (800) 831-3131

About 10 miles from the airport, the Casa Magna is on the beach within the hotel zone. Most important, the resort's water supply is purified, including the ice supply. There are 450 guest rooms, including 38 suites. Each unit has a mini-bar, hair dryer, TV with U.S. cable service and, something not often found, an iron and ironing board. The meeting rooms are outstanding. With their Maya Ballroom, plus several breakout rooms, they can accommodate 900 theater- , 800 banquet- , or 450 classroom-style. The various outdoor areas provide an additional dimension for group activities.

There are several possible combinations for dining: La Capilla, with international cuisine, La Isla (poolside), Mikado (Japanese steak house), and the Bahia Club (seafood bar). For entertainment they offer the Sixties Club and the Lobby Bar.

The area abounds with things to do and places to see. There are tours to the ancient Maya ruins in Tulum and Chichen Itza, sailing, deep-sea fishing (some of the finest fishing to be found anywhere), reef diving at Cozumel and shopping in the many upscale boutiques.

As for activities, there is the ocean beach, an outdoor swimming pool, two lighted tennis courts, whirlpool, massage, aerobic classes, and weight lifting. Nearby you can enjoy scuba diving, snorkeling, parasailing, jet skiing, sailing and, of course, golf.

Golf is played on the Pok-Ta-Pok Robert Trent Jones, Jr. layout. For details on this course refer to Cancun-Yucatan Peninsula.

RATES *(EP)* *Rooms: $175/$195. Suites: $350/ $400. Green fees: $50, carts $30.*

ARRIVAL Air: Cancun International Airport.

STOUFFER PRESIDENTE CANCUN
Boulevard Kukulcan KM 7.5, Cancun, Quintana Roo, Mexico, 77500; 011-52-988-30200; (800) 468-3571

Accommodations here are 294 rooms, including 15 club suites (concierge level suites).

For dining there is the Mediterraneo Restaurant, El Caribeno Restaurant & Bar, and a coffee shop (Frutas y Flores). There is also the Lobby Bar for evening entertainment.

Activities include: fishing for white marlin, bluefish, tuna and sailfish, diving or snorkeling, waterskiing, sailing, parasailing, and water skiing. Aside from the magnificent white sand beach the resort has two swimming pools and five Jacuzzis. There is one tennis court and, of course, golf.

The Presidente is next to the golf course. For details on the Pok-Ta-Pok Golf Course refer to Cancun-Yucatan Peninsula.

RATES   (EP)   Rooms: $180/$215. Concierge Level suites: $240/$280. Green fees: $50, carts $30.

ARRIVAL Air: Cancun International Airport.

IXTAPA-ZIHUATANEJO

Located 150 miles north of Acapulco, the area is one of tropical tranquility. While the resorts described in Ixtapa are

modern and sophisticated, "Old Mexico" can be found six miles south in Zihuatanejo. A quiet fishing village of 40,000 people, it is a sharp contrast to Ixtapa. The literal translation of the word Zihuatanejo is "Land of Women." It seems that this area was, in ancient times, ruled by women.

CAMINO REAL IXTAPA
Playa Vista Hermosa, Ixtapa-Zihuatanejo, Guerrero, Mexico 40880, 011-52-753-3-21-21; (800) 228-3000

The Camino Ixtapa, surrounded by dense jungle, was built directly above the magnificent white sand beach of Vista Hermosa. The architectural motif of the hotel might be compared to that of an Aztec pyramid. It offers a delightful view of the beach and ocean. The beauty of the resort has been enriched by the liberal use of palm trees, bougainvillea, hibiscus, and the dramatic organ cactus. Even though this is a modern building, a traditional feeling has been introduced through the use of elegant terracotta floors, ceiling fans, and Mexican-tiled baths. The setting, the mood, the unhurried yet gentle service, all combine to turn this into an extraordinary experience.

There are 428 lanai rooms, each with an ocean view. Each room also has an intimate, partially covered terrace and is equipped with a hammock and a fully-stocked bar. What more could you desire? Although the rooms do have ceiling fans, each is air-conditioned. In addition, there are Junior, Fiesta, and Viceroy Suites, some with a private pool and whirlpool.

You can dine at El Mexicano (gourmet Mexican fare), Le Pavilion (French cuisine), or La Esfera (international menu). In addition Le Club (bar and disco) is available. Twenty-four-hour room service is also an option. One important point: Camino Real Ixtapa has its own water purification system.

The hotel meeting rooms can handle groups of from 500 banquet- to 700 theater-style.

A wide selection of activities includes: tennis on four lighted courts with pro shop, swimming in any or all of the four pools, which are connected to one another by cascading water falls. Or you can try a swim at the secluded beach. If you really want to get into it you can arrange sailing, scuba diving, snorkeling, windsurfing, parasailing, and deep-sea fishing trips. A wide variety of tours can be arranged or you can rent a jeep at the hotel to explore on your own.

About half a mile away is the Palma Real Golf Club. A Robert Trent Jones, Jr. design, playing to a par of 72, it reaches 6,898/6,408/5,801 yards. Water becomes a factor on nine of the 18 holes. While it is flat, there are enough trees and traps to keep you busy. A nice point – there is no charge for transportation to or from the golf facilities.

RATES (EP) Lanai / rooms: $170. Jr. Suites: $370. Fiesta Suites: $500. Green fees: $33, carts $28. Golf packages are available.

ARRIVAL Air: Ixtapa / Zihuatanejo International Airport (30 minutes away). Taxi service is available from the airport to the hotel.

SHERATON IXTAPA HOTEL
Pasa de Ixtapa, Ixtapa, Zihuatanejo, Guerrero, Mexico 40880, 011 52 753 318-58; (800) 325-3535

Entering the hotel you are reminded a bit of Hawaii in that everything opens to the outside. It is a multi-storied, atrium-style structure. The view from the various levels of the dining room and bar is outstanding. There are 358 guest rooms (including suites). Each has individually controlled air-conditioning, an FM radio, cable TV, a mini-bar, and a small balcony.

Dining is available in the Veranda Restaurant with a menu that is truly international. The Casa Real, a gourmet restaurant with a beautiful view of the ocean, has Mexican cuisine as well as various fish specialties. There are a number of bars, including a swim-up affair, to keep things in proper balance. Most important: the resort is equipped with a water purification plant. Another nice extra: baby sitting service can be arranged. The Sheraton meeting rooms can accommodate groups of 400 theater- and 250 classroom-style.

Activities include tennis on four lighted courts, plus pool and ocean swimming. Sailing, snorkeling, and sport-fishing can be arranged. For details on the golf course refer to the text on Camino Real Ixtapa.

RATES (EP) Rooms: $115/ $145. Suites: $205. Green fees: $33, carts $28.

ARRIVAL Air: Zihautanejo Aeropuerto. Car: from the airport take a taxi to your destination.

MANZANILLO

We were impressed with Manzanillo. The trip from the airport (30 miles) passes through beautiful countryside. The lovely tropical setting has not been spoiled by the roadside trash (bottles, newspapers) prevalent in many other parts of Mexico. About 150 miles south of Puerto Vallarta, this area was pretty well cut off until about 15 years ago. At that time a highway opened, allowing traffic into Manzanillo. The wide, uncrowded and unspoiled beaches stretch for more than 10 miles. They provide an endless array of water activity ranging from snorkeling and scuba diving to sailing and charter fishing trips.

There are a number of restaurants in Manzanillo, along with a few stores and boutiques. Accommodations include condominiums and hotels such as Maeva, Roca del Mar, or El Pueblito. The star of the show, however, is the world-class Las Hadas. A place of magic, fantasy, and complete enchantment, it truly is "the ultimate resort."

LAS HADAS
P.O. Box 158, Manzanillo, Colima, Mexico 28200; 011-52-333-3-00-00; (800) 228-3000

Las Hadas must be classified as a premier destination resort. It has, in fact, been judged one of the top 50 resorts in the western hemisphere

At the tip of the Santiago Peninsula on a hill just across the bay from Manzanillo, the white Moorish spires of Las Hadas rise dramatically. As a matter of fact you would not be to surprised to see a group, mounted on pure white horses and led by Tyrone Power, arrive on the scene.

Compared to many of the larger 1,000-room hotels, Las Hadas is an intimate affair, with its 220 guest accommodations. The deluxe rooms and suites (the word deluxe is an understatement) feature marble floors as well as tile-floored private verandas and are air-conditioned. They are also equipped with two channels of taped music and each room has a fully-stocked bar. The overall Moorish architectural motif of the resort is carried through to the guest rooms, with their graceful arched doorways and windows. The views down onto the beach and Manzanillo Bay are, to put it mildly, spectacular. All in all we would rate these accommodations among the finest we have seen.

Las Hadas can handle meeting groups of up to 200 and has all the state-of-the-art audio/visual equipment which might be required.

There are a variety of restaurants. The Legazpi Restaurant & Lounge, overlooking the upper-level swimming pool, has an elegant indoor/outdoor setting. El Terral, specializing in Mexican food, can also provide either indoor or outdoor dining from its beautiful terrace overlooking the bay. For a lighter meal El Palmer, with a view of the lagoon pool, offers a casual atmosphere for all three meals. If fresh fish intrigues you, perhaps you will enjoy Los Delfines. There is also 24-hour room service. With the beautiful view from your patio, you might well consider a private dinner for two. At poolside, should you twitch an eyebrow,

a drink is sure to appear. When the sun goes down the action starts at the lounges and the lively disco and keeps percolating until the wee hours. After a full night at the disco, if you think you can still handle it, there is tennis on 10 courts (eight hard-surface, two clay).

Between the beach and the 70-vessel private marina there are all types of water sports at your disposal, including sailfishing, scuba diving, snorkeling, water skiing, sailing, and trimaran cruises. The Puerto Las Hadas Marina & Yacht Club is the largest privately built marina in Mexico.

Then there are always the swimming pools, one with a swim-up bar, and another which is reserved for adults only. Or you might consider joining me on the beach doing nothing but soaking up some sun and watching those other fools exhaust themselves. Meanwhile the ladies may well enjoy the shopping arcade or the beauty shop.

Golf is played on the La Mantarraya course, a few minutes away. A Roy and Pete Dye design, it has been rated among the world's top 100 by *Golf Digest*. Not only challenging, it is scenic as well. If you get by the first three holes without developing the shakes you have got it made. Reaching a relatively modest 6,495/5,994/5,531/ 4,691 yards, it pars at 71. Don't let the yardage fool you as this course is tough.

RATES (EP) Santiago rooms: $185. Romantica rooms: $265. Royal Beach Club: $325. Fantasia suites: $360. Green fees: $40, carts $30. Caddies: $15. Rates quoted are for the peak season, mid-December to late April.

ARRIVAL Air: Playa De Oro International Airport. Minibus and taxi service is available to the hotel (30 miles).

MAZATLAN, SINALOA

Settled by the Spanish in the early 1600s, Mazatlan developed slowly over the years. Long known by sport fishing enthusiasts, this quiet fishing town was "discovered" and over the past 20 years has developed into one of the largest cities in Mexico (almost 600,000). There are many reasons for this growth. It's just two hours by jet from Los Angeles and 900 miles south of the Arizona border. The climate is fabulous (winter in the 70s during the day; summer in the high and humid 80s).

While Mazatlan is modern, it has kept its traditions and is definitely "Old Mexico" in flavor.

There is much to do, with beautiful beaches, water sports, shopping in many fine boutiques, back-country tours, night life activities (your hotel can direct you) and, of course, fishing and golf.

CAMINO REAL MAZATLAN
P.O. Box 538, Mazatlan, Sinaloa, Mexico 82100; 011-69-83-1111; (800) 228-3000

The Camino Real Mazatlan is on a rocky promontory of the rugged Punta del Sabalo and a short distance north of Mazatlan. A spectacular view of the entrance to the Sea of Cortez and the Pacific Ocean extends out directly below the hotel. All rooms have either a view of the ocean or of the lagoon area. Many have private balconies facing the sea and each is air-conditioned.

Dining at the Camino is a special treat. Las Terazas, available for all three meals, offers Mexican cuisine but specializes in prime ribs and is supported by one of the better wine cellars. Open from 10 AM until 2 AM, the Chiquita Banana Beach Club serves up tropical drinks and fresh seafood. Live music and dancing until midnight are found at Camino Real's posh Lobby Bar.

A few of the guest services include: purified water and ice machines, laundry and dry cleaning service, room service from 7 AM to 11 PM, and a number of interesting shops.

Mazatlan has long been recognized as one of the premier fishing areas in the world. The hotel can arrange deep sea fishing trips where record catches of black marlin or sailfish are not uncommon. For those who prefer to be in, rather than on, the water there is a freshwater swimming pool and two white sand beaches. The beaches come equipped with picturesque palapas (straw huts). Of course water skiing or snorkeling and skin diving can be arranged. Something extra – the surf here can provide big-wave surfboard excitement. In addition to all of the water action there are also two excellent tennis courts and horseback riding is nearby.

The outstanding hunting in the Mazatlan area is not well known to many people. The countryside abounds in wild fowl, deer, duck, mountain lion, and ocelot. If you have an interest, you should make all arrangements and obtain permits prior to your arrival.

Golf can be played on the El Cid Country Club course nearby. With a par of 72, this layout reaches 6,712/6,393/5,252 yards.

RATES   (EP)   Rooms: $100/$110. Jr. suites: $152. 1-bedroom suite: $284. 2-bedroom suite: $352. Green fees: $25, carts $20. Caddies are also available.

ARRIVAL Air: Mazatlan International Airport (17 miles or 35 minutes south of the city). Car: from the airport take either a mini-bus or a taxi.

EL CID RESORT
P.O. Box 813, Mazatlan, Sinaloa, Mexico 82110; 011-526-98-333-33; (800) 525-1925

Perhaps the complete title of El Cid Resort – "Hotel, Country Club and Marina" – will give you some idea of its scope. It is big and it is busy. Set on 900 acres, some of the accommodations front directly on the beach, while others reach inland to the country club area. El Moro tower, a 25-story structure on the beach, has deluxe suites, most with ocean views. El Cid tower is the location of the main lobby and reception area. There are additional accommodations across the road, connected by an overhead pedestrian walkway. In total El Cid has some 1,000 rooms and suites. Some rooms offer color satellite TV. This hotel does **not** have a water purification plant. Do not drink the tap water. Each room is supplied with bottled water. By all means use it.

The Los Tapices convention center is set up to handle group affairs ranging up to 1,500 theater-style.

Restaurants include: El Alcazar; The Prime Rib House; La Cava Supper Club; El Corral; La Concha, with its seafood specialties; and the 19th Hole. Finally, there is El Patio, a poolside bar and grill. For evening entertainment, and considered a Mazatlan must, visit El Caracol Tango Palace for dancing or listening.

There are 17 lighted tennis courts, squash and racquetball courts, and five swimming pools (one is 20,000 square feet) including waterfalls and a swim-up-bar. There are also jogging trails and bicycle paths. At the Clubhouse are a few additional amenities including a hot tub, gym, and sauna. The Aqua-Sports Center can arrange a wide variety of water sports.

At this time El Cid is the only 18-hole golf facility in the area. There are, however, plans to add an additional 18. The course, located across from the property, stretches 6,712/6,393 yards from the hombres tees. From the senoritas tees the yardage is set at 5,252. Parring at 72, this layout will give you all you want and then some.

RATES   (EP)   Rooms: $85/$115 per couple. Suites: $250/$700. Green fees: $33, carts $28. Caddy (mandatory): $12. Golf packages are available.

ARRIVAL Air: Mazatlan International Airport (17 miles, or 35 minutes south of the city). Car: from the airport take either a taxi or mini-bus to the hotel.

PUERTO VALLARTA, JALISCO

In recent years construction of

roads has made Puerto Vallarta more accessible. A few of the roads include those from Tepic (105 miles), Guadalajara (220 miles), and from Manzanillo (160 miles). With a population of over 60,000 people and some of the finest beaches in the world, spectacular fishing and related water activities, it is little wonder it has become one of the more popular vacation destinations in Mexico.

The general area is extremely photogenic. While the resorts are oceanside, their backdrop is formed by the beautiful Sierra Madre Mountains. You will be intrigued by the red tile roofs, the bougainvilleas cascading over the balconies, all to be seen in the quaint cobblestone town of Puerto Vallarta.

The Marina Vallarta Club de Golf was designed by Joe Finger, a well known American architect. Some of the more prominent features include spectacular views of the ocean as well as Bahia de Banderas and its great many beautiful yachts, sailboats and ocean cruisers. Mr. Finger brought everything but the proverbial kitchen sink into play on this layout. There are lagoons, lakes and ponds, cocoa palms and waterfalls, along with

Mexican sand cranes in great supply. Parring at 71, the course measures 6,641/6,093/5,259 yards. The club is supported by an excellent clubhouse complete with men's and ladies' locker rooms, a pro shop, and dining room.

MARRIOTT CASAMAGNA
Paseo De La Marina No. 5, Puerto Vallarta, Jalisco, Mexico, 48300, 011 52 322 10004; (800) 831-3131

The Casamagna is in the Marina Vallarta complex on the Bahia de Banderas. Lodgings are in 433 rooms, including 32 suites. All have a mini-bar, water purification system, and ceiling fan (they are also air-conditioned). Each has a balcony and TV.

Within the hotel complex there are several places to dine. Las Casitas offers oceanfront or poolside dining. Then there are La Estancia, the Mikado, a Japanese steak house, and the Sixties Club – serving up dance music from the 50's and 60's. There are, in addition, many excellent restaurants available in Puerto Vallarta. With the Vallarta Ballroom as well as four smaller breakout rooms, they can handle group affairs of up to 800 theater- or 350 classroom-style.

The 400-slip marina at the front door opens up a myriad of water activities. There are charter boats, scuba diving, sailboats, and deep-sea fishing trips. Fishing, by the way, includes the opportunity to go after small game fish (bonito, red snapper, and tuna) or big game action like dolphin, marlin, sailfish, and sea bass. As the resort is by the Pacific Ocean you can enjoy the beautiful beaches for swimming and sunning, as well as wind surfing, snorkeling, and jet skiing. In addition there are three lighted tennis courts, an outdoor swimming pool, a whirlpool, and a complete health club with sauna and massage. Tours can be arranged to many points of interest, including a visit to the flee market, shopping, or a sailing trip to nearby deserted islands.

You can walk to the new Marina Vallarta Club de Golf (the pro shop is just across the street). For details on this outstanding course refer to Puerto Vallarta, Jalisco above.

RATES   (EP)   Rooms: $125/$159. Mini suites: $275. Suites: $350 and up. Green fees: $72, including cart and

caddy.   Golf   package: 3 nights/3 days (includes lodging, 3 rounds of golf with caddy and electric cart, club storage) $789 per couple. Rates are for the peak season of January through mid-April.

ARRIVAL Air: Puerto Vallarta International Airport (5 minutes by cab). As in most resort cities in Mexico taxis are not available from the airport, so you must take an 8-passenger van (cost is about $3 per person). From the hotel take a taxi to airport (cost about $4 per taxi).

VILLAS QUINTA REAL HOTEL & GOLF RESORT
Pelicanos 311 Marina Vallarta Puerto Vallarta, Jalisco, Mexico 48300; 011 52 322-10800; (800) 227-0212

Lodgings are within the Marina Vallarta championship golf course complex. They range from junior suites, master suites with private terrace pools overlooking the 18th fairway, to 12 grand class suites, and a presidential suite with four bedrooms and a private pool. All units are air-conditioned. There are also 25 luxury villas of one, two, and three bedrooms with individual pools, Jacuzzis, and kitchenettes. In order to make reservations for the villas it is necessary to contact the hotel directly. You can do so by using the following number: (800) 362-9170.

The resort **does not** have a water purification system. We suggest you be extremely careful in the use of the ice machines. They do provide bottled water which we urge you to use.

There is a delightful restaurant, open for all three meals, highlighting international as well as regional cuisine. A few of the facilities at your disposal include: a pool with swim-up Palapa Bar, fishing, boating, snorkeling and, of course, golf. Many other activities can also be arranged: beach or city tours, boat trips, a visit to the art galleries, and shopping trips.

While you are virtually sitting on top of the golf course, for complete details refer to Puerto Vallarta, Jalisco on the foregoing pages.

RATES (EP) Jr. suite: $155. Master suite: $175. Grand Suite: $195. 1-bedroom villa: $225. Green fees: $72, including cart and caddy. Golf pack-

age: 3 nights/3 days (includes lodging, 3 rounds of golf with cart and caddy, taxes), $854 per couple. Rates are for the peak golf season of mid-December through March.

ARRIVAL Air: Puerto Vallarta International Airport (5 minutes by taxi). From the airport mini-vans are available to the hotel or villas. Taxis are available for return to the airport.

VALLE DE BRAVO, EDO DE MEXICO

Originally named by Franciscan friars "San Francisco del Valle de Tamascaltepec" (a mouth full even for the locals), the name was later changed to Valle de Bravo in honor of the renowned patriot, Nicolas Bravo. Situated deep in the Sierra Madres, the area now finds itself a popular retreat for the more affluent residents of Mexico City. These magnificent weekend homes are well worth seeing, with their huge beams, adobe brick, stone roofs, and red tile.

At an elevation of 6,000 feet, the climate is moderate, with temperatures in the 80s during the day and 40s during the night. While this is similar to western Colorado, keep in mind that here the range is pretty constant year-round. The hottest months are May through August, with the rainy season generally during July-September.

Valle de Bravo is most closely associated with the annual migration of Monarch butterflies. Starting with their arrival in November, and departure in late March, they literally take over. Hikers are cautioned to be careful, while motorists are required to slow down.

AVANDARO GOLF & SPA RESORT
Fracc. Avandaro
Valle de Bravo, Edo, Mexico
011-726-206-26; (800) 654-3732

Avandaro may well qualify as one of Mexico's best kept secrets. Approximately 80 miles west of Mexico City, nestled deep in the Sierra Madres, it has a setting much like that of the western Rockies and was once inhabited by the ancient Tarascan Indians – a mysterious people whose history is linked to the culture of Peru.

Originating in 1962 with eight rustic-style cabins, the resort has come a long way. Updated with a major renovation in 1991, Avandaro now boasts 108 rooms including 48 colonial-style bungalows and 60 adobe-style junior suites. All units feature a woodburning fireplace, satellite TV, a terrace, and views of either the mountains or the golf course. With five meeting rooms, they are capable of handling groups up to 200.

For casual dining Las Terrazas, an indoor outdoor dining room, is available. The Aquarima Restaurant, open on weekends only, presents a more elegant candlelight setting. There is also a poolside snack shop as well as two bars. The nearby 400-year-old town of Valle de Bravo offers more opportunities for dining and also has many arts and craft shops.

There are seven tennis courts, an outdoor swimming pool, hiking and nature trails, hang gliding, horseback riding and, located at Lake Avandaro, waterskiing, sailing, and fishing. As part of the massive renovation, a state-of-the-art spa was opened. It offers whirlpools, Jacuzzis and plunge pools, saunas, steam rooms, and Swiss showers, along with a variety of relaxing treatments such as facials, herbal wraps, and massages, plus exercise rooms with Lifecyles, treadmills, weights, and rowing equipment.

Club de Golf Avandaro was designed by Percy Clifford. Playing to a yardage of 6,369/5,968/5,063, it pars at 72. Enhanced by running streams, waterfalls and pine trees, heavy with bougainvilleas and wild hibiscus, this beautiful layout will enchant you. There is an additional golf course located at nearby Rancho Avandaro.

RATES (EP) Bungalow: $85/$99. Suites: $116/$150. Green fees: $45/$55, carts $29, caddies $15. There are many package plans: Golf & Spa; Monarch Butterfly Expeditions; Golf & Tennis; and group packages.

ARRIVAL Air: Mexico City International Airport (2 hours).

Index

CANADA

MEXICO

ADDITIONAL RESOURCES

Other travel books from Hunter Publishing

WHERE TO STAY IN NORTHERN CALIFORNIA

WHERE TO STAY IN SOUTHERN CALIFORNIA

The most complete sources available anywhere for every type of accommodation: B&Bs, country inns, condos and cottages for rent, hotels and motels. Over 3,500 places described in each volume, with prices, phones, special offers. 5 3/8 x 8 paperbacks/384 pp/$12.95 each/1-55650-572-8 Northern; 1-55650-573-6 Southern

THE FLORIDA WHERE TO STAY BOOK

More than 4,000 places to stay in the #1 vacation destination in the country – condos for rent, inns, motels, hotels, even beach houses for rent by the week or month. Prices, descriptions, all details. 5 3/8 x 8 paperback/448 pp/$12.95/1-55650-539-6

THE GREAT AMERICAN WILDERNESS: TOURING AMERICA'S NATIONAL PARKS

The 41 most scenic parks, from Acadia to Yosemite, and how to see them: main access routes, where to stay, where to eat, which roads are most crowded or most beautiful, how much time to allow, what you can safely skip and what you must not miss. Special sections tell how to tour each park if you have only limited time – or if time is not a factor – and 11 detailed itineraries suggest ways to combine visits to several scenic areas in a single trip. Maps of each park included, showing all surrounding access roads. 5 3/8 x 8 paperback/288 pp/$11.95/1-55650-567-1

USA BY RAIL

Details what you will encounter on the 28 long-distance trains that criss-cross North America, describing points of interest along the way and spots where the trips can be broken. Station information, sightseeing, where to stay, route maps, excursions. Over 500 destinations, including 37 major cities, are covered. 5 3/8 x 8 paperback/320 pp/$15.95/1-55650-521-3

ADVENTURE GUIDE TO THE ALASKA HIGHWAY

A complete guide to what you will find along the highway, plus all worthwhile side-trips and approaches, such as the Alaska-Marine Highway, Klondike Highway, Top-of-the-World Highway. Maps & color photos. 5 3/8 x 8 paperback/288 pp/$15.95/1-55650-457-8

ADVENTURE GUIDE TO BAJA CALIFORNIA 2nd Edition

Thorough update of this classic tourguide to the peninsula, from Tijuana and Mexicali to Cabo San Lucas at the tip. The best driving routes, fascinating history, hotels, restaurants, all practical details. 5 3/8 x 8 paperback/288 pp/$13.95/1-55650-590-6

CANADIAN ROCKIES ACCESS GUIDE

The ultimate guide to outdoor adventure, from Banff to Lake Louise to Jasper National Park. Walking and canoeing routes, climbs, cycling itineraries. Maps, photos. 6 x 9 paperback/360 pp/$15.95/0-919433 -92-8

HAWAII: A WALKER'S GUIDE

Walking the awesome Na Pali cliffs and climbing the Kilauea Volcano are just a few of the unforgettable adventures detailed here. Each hike is graded for difficulty, from multi-day excursions to scenic strolls. Detailed maps, color photos. 5 3/8 x 8 paperback/224 pp/$14.95/1-55650-215-X

THE GOLF RESORT GUIDE (Eastern Edition)

The most rewarding golf resorts in every state, plus Canada and the Caribbean. All facilities are described and rated: golf courses, pro shop, tennis, ski, lodging, special packages offered, fees, restaurants, directions for arrival. Maps. 5 3/8 x 8 paperback/416 pp/$13.95/1-55650-568-X

CALIFORNIA INSIDER'S GUIDE

Packed with stunning photographs and extensive historical & cultural background, combined with rich practical detail, the famous Insider's Guides cover the world. The California guide tells you where to stay, where to eat, what to see, how to get around, region-by-region. Large foldout map included. Hundreds of color photos. 5 5/8 x 8 3/4 paperback/256 pp/$14.95/1-55650-163-3

MEXICO INSIDER'S GUIDE
5 5/8 x 8 3/4 paperback/320 pp/$17.95/1-55650-454-3

CANADA WEST INSIDER'S GUIDE
5 5/8 x 8 3/4 paperback/256 pp/$17.95/1-55650-580-9

ADVENTURE GUIDE TO COSTA RICA

Biggest, most detailed guide on the market. Exhaustive coverage of history, people, customs, unique wildlife, restaurants, transport, where to stay. The best hiking trails, the national parks, a complete guide to San José and all other towns, with maps and photos. Offbeat, unusual adventure possibilities as well. 5 3/8 x 8 paperback/360 pp/$16.95/1-55650-456-X

ADVENTURE GUIDE TO BELIZE

Second edition. With some of the best diving in the world, 1000-foot waterfalls, virgin rainforest, 500 bird species, this is a naturalist's paradise. The latest and best color guide available. Hotels, food, maps,

color photos. 5 3/8 x 8 paperback/288 pp/$14.95/1-55650-493-4

ADVENTURE GUIDE TO THE DOMINICAN REPUBLIC

Miles of pristine beaches, jungles, soaring mountains and Old Santo Domingo, first Spanish capital of the Americas. A complete practical guide to every aspect of the island, from food to hiking, luxury hotels to budget travel bargains, shopping and transport. Maps. 5 3/8 x 8 paperback/256 pp/$13.95/1-55650-537-X

ADVENTURE GUIDE TO CANADA

The top attractions in every province. Walking through old Quebec, cruising the St. Lawrence River, driving the spectacular Cabot Trail on Cape Breton Island, touring British Columbia's super-scenic Okanagan Valley, bedding down in the baronial castle-hotels of Alberta. Maps and color photographs throughout. 5 3/8 x 8 paperback/320 pp/$15.95/1-55650-315-6

ADVENTURE GUIDE TO THE EVERGLADES & FLORIDA KEYS

Fishing, hiking, diving, or just

relaxing in southern Florida. Everything to see and do, from the wilderness canoe trails of the Everglades to the bizarre sights of Key West. Maps & color photos. 5 3/8 x 8 paperback/224 pp/$14.95/1-55650-494-2

ADVENTURE GUIDE TO JAMAICA

The definitive guide to outdoor activities in Jamaica, from hiking to white-water rafting, scuba to golf. Complete what-to-see and where-to-stay information as well. Maps and color photos. 5 3/8 x 8 paperback/288 pp/$17.95/1-55650-499-3

ADVENTURE GUIDE TO PUERTO RICO

Best-selling guide to the most popular island in the Caribbean. Aimed at all kinds of travellers from luxury to budget. History, culture, people, sightseeing all around the island, where to stay, where to dine. Color, maps. 5 3/8 x 8 paperback/224 pp/$15.95/1-55650-178-1

Write Hunter Publishing, Inc., 300 Raritan Center Parkway, Edison NJ 08818 or call (908) 225 1900 for our complete free color catalog describing these and over 1,000 other unusual travel guides and maps to all parts of the world – from Africa to South America, from Europe to Asia. Find them in the best bookstores or you can order direct by sending your check to the address above (add $2.50 to cover shipping / handling).

ɜ⍺